# IFIP Advances in Information and Communication Technology 318

T0189780

# IFIP – The International Federation for Information Processing

IFIP was founded in 1960 under the auspices of UNESCO, following the First World Computer Congress held in Paris the previous year. An umbrella organization for societies working in information processing, IFIP's aim is two-fold: to support information processing within its member countries and to encourage technology transfer to developing nations. As its mission statement clearly states,

> *IFIP's mission is to be the leading, truly international, apolitical organization which encourages and assists in the development, exploitation and application of information technology for the benefit of all people.*

IFIP is a non-profitmaking organization, run almost solely by 2500 volunteers. It operates through a number of technical committees, which organize events and publications. IFIP's events range from an international congress to local seminars, but the most important are:

- The IFIP World Computer Congress, held every second year;
- Open conferences;
- Working conferences.

The flagship event is the IFIP World Computer Congress, at which both invited and contributed papers are presented. Contributed papers are rigorously refereed and the rejection rate is high.

As with the Congress, participation in the open conferences is open to all and papers may be invited or submitted. Again, submitted papers are stringently refereed.

The working conferences are structured differently. They are usually run by a working group and attendance is small and by invitation only. Their purpose is to create an atmosphere conducive to innovation and development. Refereeing is less rigorous and papers are subjected to extensive group discussion.

Publications arising from IFIP events vary. The papers presented at the IFIP World Computer Congress and at open conferences are published as conference proceedings, while the results of the working conferences are often published as collections of selected and edited papers.

Any national society whose primary activity is in information may apply to become a full member of IFIP, although full membership is restricted to one society per country. Full members are entitled to vote at the annual General Assembly. National societies preferring a less committed involvement may apply for associate or corresponding membership. Associate members enjoy the same benefits as full members, but without voting rights. Corresponding members are not represented in IFIP bodies. Affiliated membership is open to non-national societies, and individual and honorary membership schemes are also offered.

Jan Pries-Heje    John Venable
Deborah Bunker    Nancy L. Russo
Janice I. DeGross (Eds.)

# Human Benefit through the Diffusion of Information Systems Design Science Research

IFIP WG 8.2/8.6 International Working Conference
Perth, Australia, March 30 – April 1, 2010
Proceedings

 Springer

Volume Editors

Jan Pries-Heje
Roskilde University, Department of Communication, Business and IT
4000 Roskilde, Denmark
E-mail: janph@ruc.dk

John Venable
Curtin University, School of Information Systems
Perth, WA 6845, Australia
E-mail: john.venable@cbs.curtin.edu.au

Deborah Bunker
University of Sydney, Faculty of Economics and Business
Sydney, NSW 2006, Australia
E-mail: deborah.bunker@sydney.edu.au

Nancy L. Russo
Northern Illinois University, OMIS Department
DeKalb, IL 60115, USA
E-mail: nrusso@niu.edu

Janice I. DeGross
University of Minnesota, Carlson School of Management
Minneapolis, MI 55455, USA
E-mail: jdegross@csom.umn.edu

CR Subject Classification (1998): H.2, H.3, H.5, I.2

ISSN        1868-4238
ISBN-10     3-642-42232-2 Springer Berlin Heidelberg New York
ISBN-13     978-3-642-42232-4 Springer Berlin Heidelberg New York

springer.com

© IFIP International Federation for Information Processing 2010
Softcover re-print of the Hardcover 1st edition 2010

Typesetting: Camera-ready by author, data conversion by Scientific Publishing Services, Chennai, India
Printed on acid-free paper        06/3180

# Preface

This book constitutes the proceedings of the 2010 Joint International Working Conference of the International Federation for Information Processing Working Groups 8.2 and 8.6. Both working groups are part of IFIP Technical Committee 8, the technical committee addressing the field of Information Systems. IFIP WG 8.2, the Interaction of Information Systems and Organizations, was established in 1977. IFIP WG 8.6, Diffusion, Transfer and Implementation of Information Technology, was established in 1994.

In accordance with their respective themes, both IFIP WG 8.2 and IFIP WG 8.6 have long had an interest in the human impact of information systems. In December 1998, they held a joint working conference in Helsinki, Finland, on the theme "Information Systems: Current Issues and Future Challenges." The two working groups' joint interest in and collaboration on research concerning the human side of IS is continued and extended through this joint working conference, held on the campus of Curtin University of Technology, from March 30 to April 1, 2010, in Perth, Western Australia.

This conference, "Human Benefit Through the Diffusion of Information Systems Design Science Research," combines the traditional themes of the two working groups with the growing interest within the IS research field in the area of design science research.

From the 45 submissions registered in the chosen reviewing system *EasyChair*, 17 research papers and 2 research-in-progress papers were selected for inclusion in the *Proceedings*. Of the accepted papers, 5½ are written by authors from UK universities (where ½ means co-authored with another country), 4 are from Australia, 3 are from Denmark, 2 are from Norway, nearly 2 are from the United States and Sweden (co-authoring subtracts), 1 is from Switzerland, and 1 is from New Zealand. All papers were peer reviewed by at least two reviewers (with an average of three reviews per paper); nearly all reviews were done by the 80 members of the Program Committee.

We would like to acknowledge the contributions of the Program Committee and additional reviewers, and the support of Curtin University of Technology, without whom this conference would not be possible.

January 2010

John R. Venable
Jan Pries-Heje
Deborah Bunker
Nancy L. Russo

# Organization

## Conference Chairs

### General Chairs

Deborah Bunker      University of Sydney
Nancy L. Russo      Northern Illinois University

### Program and Organizing Chairs

Jan Pries-Heje      Roskilde University
John Venable      Curtin University of Technology

## Conference Sponsor

This conference was funded with the generous support of the
Curtin University of Technology

## Program Committee

| | |
|---|---|
| Pär Ågerfalk | Uppsala University |
| Ashley Aitken | Curtin University of Technology |
| Paul Alexander | Curtin University of Technology |
| David Avison | ESSEC Business School |
| Niels Bjørn-Andersen | Copenhagen Business School |
| Gregg Boalch | Curtin University of Technology |
| Tom Butler | University College Cork |
| John Campbell | University of Canberra |
| Sven A. Carlsson | Lund University |
| Jenny Carroll | Royal Melbourne Institute of Technology |
| Dubrovka Cecez-Kecmanovic | University of New South Wales |
| Elizabeth Chang | Curtin University of Technology |
| Vanessa Chang | Curtin University of Technology |
| Kevin Crowston | Syracuse University |
| Wendy Cukier | Ryerson University |
| Jan Damsgaard | Copenhagen Business School |
| Linda Dawson | Monash University |
| Peter Dell | Curtin University of Technology |
| Brian Donnellan | National University of Ireland Galway |
| Heinz Dreher | Curtin University of Technology |

| | |
|---|---|
| Yogesh Kumar Dwivedi | Swansea University |
| Walter Fernandez | Australia National University |
| Elaine Ferneley | Salford Business School |
| Matt Germonprez | University of Wisconsin-Eau Claire |
| Anita Greenhill | Manchester Business School |
| Shirley Gregor | Australia National University |
| Helen Hasan | University of Wollongong |
| Helle Zinner Henriksen | Copenhagen Business School |
| Alan Hevner | University of South Florida |
| Dirk Hovorka | Bond University |
| Debra Howcroft | Manchester Business School |
| Sid Huff | University of Victoria Wellington |
| Juhani Iivari | Oulu University |
| Marta Indulska | Queensland University of Technology |
| Tomayess Issa | Curtin University of Technology |
| Marius Janson | University of Missouri St Louis |
| Karlheinz Kautz | Copenhagen Business School |
| Des Klass | Curtin University of Technology |
| Bill Kuechler | University of Nevada Reno |
| Tor Larsen | Norwegian School of Management |
| Nick Letch | University of Western Australia |
| Linda Levine | Carnegie-Mellon University |
| Sharman Lichtenstein | Deakin University |
| Kalle Lyytinen | Case Western Reserve University |
| Peter Marshall | University of Tasmania |
| Lars Mathiassen | Georgia State University |
| Donald McDermid | Edith Cowan University |
| Tanya McGill | Murdoch University |
| Judy McKay | Swinburne University |
| Bob McQueen | University of Waikato |
| Catherine Middleton | Ryerson University |
| Annette Mills | University of Canterbury |
| Simon Milton | University of Melbourne |
| Michael Myers | Auckland University |
| Sue Newell | Bentley University |
| Mike Newman | Manchester Business School |
| Ojelanki Ngwenyama | Ryerson University |
| Björn Niehaves | European Research Center for IS |
| Peter Axel Nielsen | Aalborg University |
| Helena Holmström Olsson | IT University Gothenburg |
| Graham Pervan | Curtin University of Technology |
| Sandeep Purao | Penn State University |
| Jan Recker | Queensland University of Technology |
| Michael Rosemann | Queensland University of Technology |
| Matti Rossi | Helsinki School of Business and Economics |

| | |
|---|---|
| Steve Sawyer | Penn State University |
| Helena Scheepers | Monash University |
| Rens Scheepers | University of Melbourne |
| Graeme Shanks | University of Melbourne |
| Carsten Sørensen | London School of Economics |
| Craig Standing | Edith Cowan University |
| Mark Toleman | University of South Queensland |
| Duane Truex | Georgia State University |
| Virpi Kristiina Tuunainen | Helskinki School of Economics |
| Tuure Tuunanen | Auckland University |
| Richard Welke | Georgia State University |
| David Wilson | University of Technology Sydney |
| Robert Winter | University of St. Gallen |
| Margot Wood | Curtin University of Technology |
| Eleanor Wynn | Intel Corporation |

# Table of Contents

Creation, Transfer, and Diffusion of Innovation in Organizations and
Society: Information Systems Design Science Research for Human
Benefit .................................................... 1
    *John R. Venable, Jan Pries-Heje, Deborah Bunker, and
Nancy L. Russo*

## Part 1: Design, Organizations, and Adoption

Incommensurability and Multi-paradigm Grounding in Design Science
Research: Implications for Creating Knowledge ...................... 13
    *Dirk S. Hovorka*

The Design and Engineering of Mobile Data Services: Developing an
Ontology Based on Business Model Thinking ....................... 28
    *Mutaz M. Al-Debei and Guy Fitzgerald*

The Role of Social Networks in Early Adoption of Mobile Devices ...... 52
    *Heidi Tscherning and Lars Mathiassen*

## Part 2: Design Exemplars

Roles in Innovative Software Teams: A Design Experiment ............ 73
    *Ivan Aaen*

A Case Study of Improving Information Technology Governance in a
University Context ...................................... 89
    *Michael Hicks, Graham Pervan, and Brian Perrin*

Extending Design Science Research Methodology for a Multicultural
World ................................................. 108
    *Carl Lawrence, Tuure Tuunanen, and Michael D. Myers*

## Part 3: Human Benefit?

The Reality of Rhetoric in Information Systems Adoption: A Case
Study Investigation of the UK National Health Service .............. 125
    *Imran Khan and Elaine Ferneley*

Social Consequences of Nomadic Working: A Case Study in an
Organization ........................................... 143
    *Ramanjit Singh and Trevor Wood-Harper*

Design Science Research for Business Process Design: Organizational
Transition at Intersport Sweden.................................... 159
   *Mikael Lind, Daniel Rudmark, and Ulf Seigerroth*

## Part 4: Designing Adoption

An Adoption Diffusion Model of RFID-Based Livestock Management
System in Australia ............................................. 179
   *Mohammad Alamgir Hossain and Mohammed Quaddus*

Developing a Broadband Adoption Model in the UK Context .......... 192
   *Yogesh K. Dwivedi, Navonil Mustafee, Michael D. Williams, and*
   *Banita Lal*

The Uneven Diffusion of Collaborative Technology in a Large
Organization ..................................................... 209
   *Gasparas Jarulaitis*

Toward an Understanding of the Evolution of IFIP WG 8.6 Research ... 225
   *Yogesh K. Dwivedi, Linda Levine, Michael D. Williams,*
   *Mohini Singh, David G. Wastell, and Deborah Bunker*

## Part 5: Design Science

Functional Service Domain Architecture Management: Building the
Foundation for Situational Method Engineering ...................... 245
   *Daniel Stock, Robert Winter, and Jörg H. Mayer*

Management Design Theories....................................... 263
   *Jan Pries-Heje and Richard L. Baskerville*

Modeling Forensic Evidence Systems Using Design Science ............ 282
   *Colin Armstrong and Helen Armstrong*

## Part 6: Participation in Design

Participatory Design Activities and Agile Software Development ....... 303
   *Karlheinz Kautz*

Participation in Living Lab: Designing Systems with Users ............ 317
   *Birgitta Bergvall-Kåreborn, Debra Howcroft, Anna Ståhlbröst, and*
   *Anita Melander Wikman*

Manufacturing Accomplices: ICT Use in Securing the Safety State at
Airports ......................................................... 327
   *Thomas Østerlie, Ole Martin Asak, Ole Georg Pettersen, and*
   *Håvard Tronhus*

# Part 7: Panels

A Brief History of IFIP WG 8.2 Research: The People, the Places, the
Methods, and the Issues ........................................... 345
    *Nancy L. Russo and Michael D. Myers*

The Role of Public Policy in Enhancing the Design and Diffusion of
Information Systems and Technology for Human Benefit .............. 346
    *John Venable, Peter Newman, Nick Letch, and Sue Ash*

Opening up the Agile Innovation Process .......................... 348
    *Kieran Conboy, Brian Donnellan, Lorraine Morgan, and
    Xiaofeng Wang*

**Author Index** ...................................................... 351

# Creation, Transfer, and Diffusion of Innovation in Organizations and Society: Information Systems Design Science Research for Human Benefit

John R. Venable[1], Jan Pries-Heje[2], Deborah Bunker[3], and Nancy L. Russo[4]

[1] Curtin University of Technology,
Perth, Western Australia
[2] Roskilde University,
Roskilde, Denmark
[3] University of Sydney,
Sydney, Australia
[4] Northern Illinois University,
DeKalb, Illinois, USA

Design science research is a way of creating and studying new technological phenomena, where the understanding comes from inventing, designing, and building new forms of solutions to problems. It has been touted as a new means for the IS field to improve its relevance as the resulting design artifact(s) can directly be used to solve relevant problems. DSR is different from other types of research in its focus on building artifacts and learning from the use and application of the artifacts. It is different in that it engages reality in a way that no descriptive or observational research method can. DSR shares the iterative process with action research but can take place in a laboratory without any involvement of users as researchers (Iivari and Venable 2009).

Herbert Simon (1996) defined the science of design as the study of the artificial and properly "the way in which that adaptation of means to environments is brought about" (p. 113). Melding science with design provides a means for designing at higher levels of abstraction, designs that are more universal and address a general class of problems rather than a single, unique design problem. In their seminal papers on DSR, Nunamaker et al. (1991), Walls et al. (1992), and March and Smith (1995) laid the foundation for DSR. The consolidation of DSR into mainstream Information Systems research came with Hevner et al.'s (2004) article in *MIS Quarterly*. In information systems, Vaishnavi and Kuechler (2004) define design science research as "the analysis of the use and performance of designed artifacts to understand, explain and very frequently to improve on the behavior of aspects of Information Systems." Central to these notions is the design of an artifact that is meant to have a presence in the real world. This artifact could be conceived as a construct, a model, a method, or a material instantiation (March and Smith 1995).

The present conference expands on DSR research approaches in IS in three key areas. First, the conference assumes that designing and developing a new technology without also considering the transfer, diffusion, and adoption of that new technology

J. Pries-Heje et al. (Eds.): IS Design Science Research, IFIP AICT 318, pp. 1–10, 2010.
© IFIP International Federation for Information Processing 2010

risks producing research that is irrelevant. Both design practice and DSR projects are conducted within an organizational and societal environment, but DSR outcomes (artifacts) must be diffused and adopted into a broad variety of organizational and societal settings. While the importance of such issues has long been the concern of both IFIP Working Groups 8.2 and 8.6, the relationship to DSR has heretofore not explicitly been considered. Bunker and Campbell (2005) have suggested that DSR has been predominantly concerned with building and evaluating artifacts aimed at achieving human-defined goals (Simon 1996), the operationalization of which is affected by contextual complexity. Adoption and diffusion are particularly important to the success of DSR in the context of information systems, due to the complex interactions of design artifacts with social and organizational contexts. Understanding of implementation context is critical to the appropriate design and use of artifacts (March and Smith 1995).

Second, the conference considers that there is a need to emphasize research in which new technologies (e.g., information systems) are designed expressly for human benefit. This theme is one that is well established in IFIP WG 8.2, for example the theme of the 1987 IFIP WG 8.1 and 8.2 Joint Working Conference addressed "Information Systems Development for Human Progress in Organizations" (Klein and Kumar 1987). As they are considered in the current conference, *technologies for human benefit* are concerned with improving the human condition, for example, by improving the quality of working life, improving health, improving the environment, reducing poverty, improving social conditions, or improving participation in and service provision by government or not-or-profit organizations. Until now, the emphasis on DSR in the IS field has been on meeting *business* needs (as in Hevner et al. 2004)—that is, on the development of new technologies that are primarily aimed at enabling increased business profit. The choices of goals and problems addressed by DSR, and who is entitled to make those choices, are seminal and should be examined critically. For example, Venable (2009) suggests that the critical systems heuristics framework (Ullrich 1981, 1987, 2002) could be used to guide proper identification of stakeholders and the selection of problem domain and system boundaries when conducting design science research. In our view, DSR cannot and should not ignore such concerns and a greater proportion of design science research, including that conducted in the IS field, should focus on human benefit (not-for-profit) rather than purely on business (for-profit). Much of the public policy debate and creation, which is so critical to resourcing of the design of IS artifacts for human benefit (i.e., IS and communications infrastructure and policy encouraging adoption practices ), is directly related to human benefit and social outcomes. Bunker and Campbell, for example, in their examination of a public consultation process in the development of a B2G online authentication framework using the DSR-based approach of perspectival punctuated action (PPA), ask how we get good policy, which leads to the more pressing question: how do we get good policy design? PPA is based on distinct decision-making configurations of intelligence, choice, and design by extending Boland's (2002) articulation of Simon's (1977) decision-making theory.

Third, design (and DSR) is informed by organizational and societal needs, is conducted in an organizational and societal environment, is diffused and adopted into organizational and societal settings, has organizational and societal consequences, and is (ideally) evaluated for how well it works and solves problems in the real (organizational and societal) world. Therefore, IS research needs to take a (more) holistic perspective, which integrates DSR and behavioral research in the creation of the IS artifact. Venable (2006) suggests that the core activity of DSR, technology invention and design, should be integrated with two other main activities in the field of applied research: *problem diagnosis* (i.e., understanding the causes and consequences of problems) and *technology evaluation* (i.e., understanding whether technologies are efficient, effective or efficacious—and why). The current emphasis in DSR is on design and evaluation (only) as the key activities (Hevner et al. 2004; March and Smith 1995). Baskerville et al. (2007, 2009) recommend the development and use of a soft design science approach to realistically address organizational and societal issues in DSR.

While software and hardware are regarded as the core "working" artifacts in information systems and technology (Orlikowski and Iacono 2001; Weber 2003), there are other artifacts that are also important components in the creation of innovative ITS. These artifacts are constructs, models, methods (Hevner et al. 2004; March and Smith 1995) and better theories (Rossi and Sein 2003). Constructs define the conceptual vocabulary of a domain, models contain an expression of how constructs are related, methods provide a description on how to perform a specific task, and better theories are derived from experiment-like proof of concept. To address these needs, the theme of this working conference incorporates issues related to the integration and cross-fertilization of DSR with the organizational and societal research areas traditionally covered by IFIP Working Groups 8.2 (Information Systems and Organizations) and 8.6 (Diffusion, Transfer, and Implementation of Information Technology).

## This Book

This book is the result of the IFIP WG 8.2/8.6 Joint International Working Conference on Human Benefit Through the Diffusion of Information Systems Design Science Research, held in Perth, Western Australia, March 30–April 1, 2010. This chapter introduces the theme of the conference and provides an overview of the research contributions that are included in the book. While not all of the issues mentioned above are explicitly addressed by the papers selected for these *Proceedings*, the breadth and variety of the research and ideas presented represent a major step forward in our understanding of the design, development, adoption, and diffusion of IT/IS artifacts that can provide human benefits.

In this book, we have grouped the papers into six areas. The first part looks at design, organization, and adoption. The second part we have called design exemplars. The third part discusses the notion of human benefit. The fourth part is about designing adoption and diffusion. The fifth part looks at the core of DSR and discusses design as science. And the sixth part focuses on participation in design. Finally, at the end of the book we have included three panels descriptions.

## Part 1: Design, Organizations, and Adoption

The first part of the book aims exactly at the area of overlapping interest between the two Working Groups that have responsibility for this conference. IFIP WG 8.2 looks at organizations and information systems and IFIP WG 8.6 looks at diffusion and adoption of information technology.

In Chapter 2, Dirk Hovorka aims at expanding DSR into the broader organizational and societal research domains. "Care must be taken," says Hovorka, to comprehend and articulate the philosophical underpinnings of theory building and evaluation in DSR, or we will end up creating incoherent design theory. The approach suggested by Hovorka is a so-called multi-paradigm grounding to ensure that the DSR approach remains a legitimate approach to knowledge creation.

Mutaz Al-Debei and Guy Fitzgerald look more specifically at design problems in mobile data services. In Chapter 3, they develop an ontology based on business model thinking. The research approach to building the ontology essentially follows the design-science paradigm but also incorporates other research methods. The developed ontology identifies four primary dimensions in designing business models for mobile data services: value proposition, value network, value architecture, and value finance. Within these dimensions, 15 key design concepts are identified along with their interrelationships and rules. The resulting ontology is of value to academics and practitioners alike, particularly those interested in strategy and telecommunication in relation to IS.

In Chapter 4, Heidi Tscherning and Lars Mathiassen present detailed insights into why and how five closely related individuals decided to adopt the iPhone before it was available through traditional supply chains. Discussing the role played by social networks, Tscherning and Mathiassen analyze how adoption threshold, opinion leaders, social contagion, and social learning shape adoption. The chapter confirms that network structures in fact have an impact, and it shows that the adoption decisions emerged as a combined result of individual adoption reflections and major influences from the social network.

## Part 2: Design Exemplars

An exemplar is a model or pattern to be copied or imitated. The second part of this book contains three very interesting exemplars of design.

In Chapter 5, Ivan Aaen asks, "How can we facilitate innovative software development in teams?" He comes up with an answer in the form of a work-in-progress design called Essence made with inspiration from role-play and improvisational theater. Based on agile principles, Essence is designed for teams of developers and an onsite customer. Essence has been applied in teaching at Aalborg University, where different roles were assigned to team members. This provided valuable insights into the design of roles in Essence. These insights were then used for redesigning the roles in Essence, thereby emphasizing the iterative nature of DSR.

In Chapter 6, Michael Hicks, Graham Pervan, and Brian Perrin explore the criteria of effective IT governance processes employed in universities and their impact on the diffusion of appropriate technology to users. A case study was conducted at a large Australian university that is currently undergoing a major restructure of its IT governance process. The case study found significant improvement in key areas of IT governance and the University realized that IT governance is an ongoing design process.

In Chapter 7, Carl Lawrence, Tuure Tuunanen, and Michael Myers propose an extension of DSR by integrating critical ethnography into the evaluation phase. Critical ethnography provides a way for IS researchers using DSR to better understand culture, and may help to ensure that IT artifacts are designed for a variety of cultural contexts. This is a very important theme to discuss, as the creation and design of artifacts lies at the heart of DSR. However, with an increasingly connected and globalized world, designing IT artifacts for a multicultural world is a challenge. This chapter offers a way to do so.

## Part 3: Human Benefit?

Is there human benefit from design? This was the key question we raised when we gave the name to this conference. In this part of the book, three chapters discuss that question from three quite different angles.

Imran Khan and Elaine Ferneley, in Chapter 8, look at the UK National Health Service, which is currently is undergoing tremendous IS led change. In the concrete, the case presented is about the design of an electronic single patient care record system. The chapter examines the extent to which persuasive discourse, or rhetoric, influences and affects the adoption of IS. Further, the chapter explores the ways in which various actors use rhetoric to advance their own agendas and the impact this has. The chapter concludes that rhetoric is an important and effective persuasive tool, employed by system trainers to coax users into not only adopting the system but also into using the system in a predefined manner.

Chapter 9 by Ramanjit Singh and Trevor Wood-Harper is a study of the challenges faced by knowledge workers in a Swedish company TeliaSonera when using wireless technology on the move. The chapter identifies five problem areas: (1) work and life balance, (2) addiction, (3) organizational involvement, (4) nomadic work and control, and (5) individual productivity. Each problem area is subsequently analyzed using socio-technical design principles. The chapter concludes that better role boundary management, self-discipline, work negotiation, and e-mail communication skills may be required for the knowledge workers to manage the demands of nomadic working.

In Chapter 10, Mikael Lind, Daniel Rudmark, and Ulf Seigerroth look at the design of business processes in another Swedish company, Intersport. The study was carried out as an action research undertaking where the purpose was to design a new process aligned with the strategic goals of Intersport. The chapter address the question of how design science research can contribute to business process design. Three heuristic guidelines for creating organizational commitment and strategic alignment in process design are presented—derived from successful actions taken. Finally these guidelines are used as a basis to reflect on the contribution of DSR in relation to business process design.

## Part 4: Designing Adoption

This part of the book contains four papers of a more classic WG 8.6 nature in that they have adoption as their primary topic. In all four chapters we can, however, find elements of design, hence the title for this part: designing adoption.

In Chapter 11, Mohammad Hossain and Mohammed Quaddus look at the adoption process and the subsequent diffusion and extended usage of RFID (radio frequency identification) for Australian livestock. A research model is designed based on Rogers' innovation-diffusion theory and Oliver's expectation-confirmation theory. The model posits that while adoption of RFID may result from legislative pressure, its further diffusion is an evaluative process, which is judged against "satisfaction" and "performance" derived from RFID systems. The implications of the designed model are then discussed and some hypotheses developed.

In Chapter 12, Yogesh Dwivedi, Navonil Mustafee, Michael Williams, and Banita Lal examine the factors affecting the consumer adoption of broadband in the UK. A conceptual model of broadband adoption is designed by selecting and justifying a number of relevant constructs from the technology adoption literature. Findings from the testing of the model suggest that relative advantage, utilitarian and hedonic outcomes, primary influence, facilitating conditions, resources, and self-efficacy all have an influence. The potential implication of this chapter is that stakeholders in broadband adoption can use the findings to encourage and promote the adoption and usage of broadband among the general population in the UK as well as in other parts of the world.

In Chapter 13, Gasparas Jarulaitis takes a closer look at the adoption of Microsoft SharePoint in a global oil company. Longitudinal data from the period 2007–2009 are analyzed focusing on two parts of the organization, R&D and oil and gas production. As a result, Jarulaitis found that the different ways in which the technology is managed and used in these contexts results in uneven diffusion.

Chapter 14 concludes this part of the book with an analysis by Yogesh Dwivedi, Linda Levine, Michael Williams, Mohini Singh, David Wastell, and Deborah Bunker of the research published in the previous 11 IFIP WG 8.6 conferences held between 1993 and 2008. Their analysis of the published material includes examining variables such as the most active authors, citation analysis, universities associated with the most publications, geographic diversity, and authors' backgrounds. The keyword analysis suggests that the work in WG 8.6 has evolved from examining basic issues such as organizational impact of technology adoption and technology transfer to contemporary issues such as open innovation.

## Part 5: Design Science

This fifth part of the book returns to design as a science. Three interesting approaches are given, spanning from situational design to designing management.

In Chapter 15, Daniel Stock, Robert Winter, and Jörg Mayer lay the foundation for the design of a situational method for functional service domain architecture management. Based on a review of current literature, a framework is proposed. In this framework, the authors find that situational method engineering for functional domains can be applied by identifying context types and goal vectors, designing fragments, and associating successfully adopted method fragments with specific situations. Finally, the validity of the proposed framework is tested by five case studies.

In Chapter 16, Jan Pries-Heje and Richard Baskerville elaborate a DSR approach for management planning anchored to the concept of a management design theory. Unlike the notions of design theories arising from information systems, management design theories can appear as a system of technological rules, much as a system of hypotheses or propositions can embody scientific theories. This chapter illustrates this form of management design theories with three grounded cases: process improvement, user involvement, and organizational change.

In Chapter 17, Colin Armstrong and Helen Armstrong present an overview of the application of DSR to the management of forensic evidence processing. The chapter begins with a discussion of DSR and socio-technical IS research in relation to the processing of forensic evidence. The discussion then presents the current problems faced by those dealing with evidence and a conceptual meta-model for a unified approach to forensic evidence is developed. Finally, Armstrong and Armstrong state that practical application of the suggested model would have to be predominantly driven by law enforcement.

## Part 6: Participation in Design

The this sixth part of the book, another theme at the core of design, namely, participation, is examined. Again we have three chapters. These span from a look at agile methods, through a living laboratory with users, to design of airport security.

In Chapter 18, Karlheinz Kautz provides a case study of a large agile development project and focuses on how customers and users participated in agile development and design activities in practice. The investigated project utilized the agile method eXtreme Programming. Planning games, user stories and story cards, working software, and acceptance tests structured the customer and user involvement. Kautz finds genuine customer and user involvement in the design activities in the form of both direct and indirect participation in the agile development project. Further, the involved customer representatives played informative, consultative, and participative roles in the project. This led to their functional empowerment: the users were enabled to carry out their work to their own satisfaction and in an effective, efficient and economical manner.

In Chapter 19, Birgitta Bergwall-Kåreborn, Debra Howcroft, Anna Ståhlbröst, and Anna Wikman employ a case study using a "living lab." The starting point is taken in the observation that while participation is established and has been reported successful in many cases, some now see it as an "old, tired concept" that is in need of revitalization in order to cater for changing IS practices. Thus the authors look at the process of participation during the design stages of a health care project for the elderly in Sweden. In this chapter, Bergwall-Kåreborn et al. reflect on how participation materializes in a context that is quite dissimilar from more traditional development settings and report on the kinds of practices that may be used to assist design with users.

In Chapter 20, Thomas Østerlie, Ole Martin Asak, Ole George Pettersen, and Håvard Tronhus describe a study of ICT use at an airport security checkpoint to explore the paradox that travelers find existing airport security measures inadequate while at the same time believing air travel to be sufficiently secure. Østerlie et al. pursue this paradox by showing that for the security checkpoint to function properly in relation to the overall function of the airport, travelers have to be enrolled in a particular program of action, one in which travelers are both ethically and morally challenged (in their own view). Nevertheless, their active participation makes it difficult for them to object to the moral and ethical issues. Thus the explanation for the paradox presented is that travelers have been made accomplices.

# References

Baskerville, R., Pries-Heje, J., Venable, J.: Soft Design Science Research: Extending the Boundaries of Evaluation in Design Science Research. In: Chatterjee, S., Rossi, M. (eds.) Proceedings of the 2nd International Conference on Design Science Research in Information Systems and Technology (DESRIST 2007), Pasadena, California, USA, May 13-15 (2007)

Baskerville, R., Pries-Heje, J., Venable, J.: Soft Design Science Methodology. In: Purao, S., Lyytinen, K., Song, I.-Y. (eds.) Proceedings of the 4th International Conference on Design Science Research in Information Systems and Technology (DESRIST 2009), Philadelphia, Pennsylvania, USA, May 7-8 (2009)

Boland, R.J.: Design in the Punctuation of Management Action. Paper presented at the Workshop on Managing as Designing, Weatherhead School of Management, Case Western Reserve University, Cleveland, Ohio, June 14-15 (2002), http://design.case.edu/2002workshop/index.html (accessed June 17, 2004)

Bunker, D., Campbell, J.: A Perspectival Punctuated Action Approach to Policy Development in Information Technology and Systems. In: Proceedings of the 16th Australasian Conference on Information System, Sydney, Australia, November 29-December 2 (2005), http://aisel.aisnet.org/ (accessed December 31, 2009)

Hevner, A.R., March, S.T., Park, J., Ram, S.: Design Science in Information Systems Research. MIS Quarterly 28(1), 75–106 (2004)

Iivari, J., Venable, J.: Action Research and Design Science Research—Seemingly Similar But Decisively Dissimilar. In: Proceedings of the 2009 European Conference on Information Systems, Verona, Italy, June 8-10, pp. 2711–2723 (2009)

Klein, H.K., Kumar, K. (eds.): Proceedings of the IFIP WG 8.2 Working Conference on Information Systems Development for Human Progress in Organizations, Atlanta, Georgia, May 29-31, 1987. North-Holland, Amsterdam (1989)

March, S., Smith, G.: Design and Natural Science Research on Information Technology. Decision Support Systems 15(4), 251–266 (1995)

Nunamaker Jr., J.F., Chen, M., Purdin, T.: Systems Development in Information Systems Research. Journal of Management Information Systems 7(3), 89–106 (2001)

Orlikowski, W.J., Iacono, C.S.: Research Commentary: Desperately Seeking the 'IT' in IT Research—A Call to Theorizing the IT Artifact. Information Systems Research 12(2), 121–143 (2001)

Rossi, M., Sein, M.: Design Research Workshop: A Proactive Research Approach. Presentation delivered at the 26th Information Systems Research Seminar in Scandinavia /(IRIS 26), August 9-12 (2003)

Simon, H.A.: The New Science of Management Decision (revised edition). Prentice Hall, Englewood Cliffs (1977)

Simon, H.A.: The Sciences of the Artificial, 3rd edn. MIT Press, Cambridge (1996)

Ulrich, W.: Critical Heuristics of Social Planning: A New Approach to Practical Philosophy. Paul Hapt, Bern (1981)

Ulrich, W.: Critical Heuristics of Social Systems Design. European Journal of Operational Research (31), 276–283 (1987)

Ulrich, W.: A Mini-Primer of Critical Systems Heuristics. In: Daellenbach, H.G., Flood, R.L. (eds.) The Informed Student Guide to Management Science, p. 72. Thomson Learning, London (2002)

Vaishnavi, V., Kuechler, W.: Design Research in Information Systems. IS World/ Association for Information Systems (2004), http://desrist.org/design-research-in-information-systems/

Venable, J.R.: The Role of Theory and Theorising in Design Science Research. In: Hevner, A., Chatterjee, S. (eds.) Proceedings of the First International Conference on Design Science Research in Information Systems and Technology, Claremont Graduate School, Claremont, CA, February 24-25 (2006)

Venable, J.R.: Identifying and Addressing Stakeholder Interests in Design Science Research: An Analysis Using Critical Systems Heuristics. In: Proceedings of the IFIP WG 8.2 Working Conference on the Tole of IS in Leveraging the Intelligence and Creativity of SME's (CreativeSME), Guimarães, Portugal, June 21-24, pp. 93–112. Springer, Berlin (2009)

Walls, J.G., Widmeyer, G.R., El Sawy, O.A.: Building an Information System Design Theory for Vigilant EIS. Information Systems Research 3(1), 36–59 (1992)

Weber, R.: Editor's Comments: Still Desperately Seeking the IT Artifact. MIS Quarterly 27(2), iii–xi (2003)

# About the Authors

**John Venable** is an associate professor and former Head of School at the School of Information Systems, Curtin University of Technology. He received a Ph.D. in Advanced Technology (Information Systems) from Binghamton University (New York) in 1994. He has taught and researched in IS at Binghamton University and Central Connecticut State University in the United States, at Aalborg University in Denmark, at the University of Waikato in New Zealand, and at Murdoch University and Curtin University of Technology in Australia. He has consulted on ICT and organizational change with large and small business organizations, government agencies, and not-for-profit organizations. His main research interests are in IS development and planning methods and practice, modeling of organizations, IS and data, problem solving methods, organizational change, group support systems, knowledge management and organizational learning, IS in the not-for-profit sector, and IS research methods, including critical research and design science research. John can be reached by e-mail at John.Venable@ cbs.curtin.edu.au.

**Jan Pries Heje** is a professor in Information Systems, Department of Communication, Business and Information Technologies, Roskilde University, and head of the User Driven IT-Innovation Research Group. His research focuses on designing and building innovative solutions to managerial and organizational IT problems. Previous and current projects explore process improvement as design, the ability for an organization to improve, and how one can design a process for making better sourcing decisions. From January 2010, Jan is the Chair of the IFIP Technical Committee 8 on Information Systems. He can be reached by e-mail at janph@ruc.dk.

**Deborah Bunker** is a senior lecturer in the discipline of Business Information Systems at the University of Sydney in Australia. She holds a Ph.D. in Information Systems Management. Her research interests are in IS management frameworks and approaches, IS innovation, adoption and diffusion, interorganizational IS and philosophical foundations of IS (phenomenology, systems thinking, system of systems) and she has published widely in these areas. Deborah is president of the Australasian Association of IS (AAIS) and is a founding member and the current Vice Chair of IFIP WG 8.6 on the adoption and diffusion of IT. She can be reached by e-mail at D.Bunker@econ.usyd.edu.au.

**Nancy L. Russo** is the Pavlović Professor of Information Systems in the Department of Operations Management & Information Systems at Northern Illinois University. She also serves as the Vice-Rector for International Cooperation at Slobomir P University in Bosnia & Herzegovina. She received her Ph.D. in Management Information Systems from Georgia State University in 1993. Her research has addressed the use and customization of system development methods, factors related to information systems success, IT innovation, and issues related to research and education in the information systems field. Her work has appeared in *Information Systems Journal, European Journal of Information Systems, Information Technology & People, Journal of Information Technology*, and other international journals and conference proceedings. Nancy is currently the Chair of IFIP WG 8.2. She can be reached by e-mail at nrusso@niu.edu.

# Part 1
# Design, Organizations, and Adoption

# Incommensurability and Multi-paradigm Grounding in Design Science Research: Implications for Creating Knowledge

Dirk S. Hovorka

Bond University,
Gold Coast, Queensland, Australia

**Abstract.** The problem identification–design–build–evaluate–theorize structure of design science research has been proposed as an approach to creating knowledge in information systems and in broader organizational and social domains. Although the approach has merit, the philosophical foundations of two specific components warrant attention. First, the grounding of design theory on potentially incommensurate kernel theories may produce incoherent design theory. In addition, design theory has no strong logical connection to kernel theories, and so cannot be used to test or validate the contributing kernel theories. Second, the philosophical grounding of evaluation may inadvertently shift from functionally based measures of utility and efficiency, to evaluation based on the pragmatic fulfillment of multidimensional human actions as people encounter information systems, resulting in evaluation errors. Although design and evaluation from a single paradigm is not desirable, sufficient, or representative of design science research, multi-paradigm grounding of design and evaluation must be realized and used consciously by the research community if the design science approach is to remain a legitimate approach to knowledge creation.

**Keywords:** Design science research, incommensurability, paradigm, pragmatism, functionalist, kernel theory.

## 1 Introduction

The emergence and influence of design science research (DSR) as a distinct research approach in information systems is gathering significant attention. IS as a discipline has always contained a significant intellectual focus on designing systems for functional goals, and the emergence of DSR lends legitimacy and credibility to the generative aspects of IS. But the suggestion that DSR has "become a new way of creating and studying phenomena where *understanding comes from building solutions to solve problems*"[1] has a number of important implications that warrant discussion.

Although the conceptualization of DSR is under discussion and is still evolving, convergence on a number of central tenets and a general structure of "problem

---

[1] "Call for Papers," IFIP 8.2 + 8.6 Joint International Working Conference (http://www.ifip.or.at/Cfp/CfP-8286%20Perth.htm, accessed November 29, 2009), emphasis added.

J. Pries-Heje et al. (Eds.): IS Design Science Research, IFIP AICT 318, pp. 13–27, 2010.
© IFIP International Federation for Information Processing 2010

identification– build–evaluate–theorize" (Winter 2008) is emerging. The primary design/build–justify/ evaluate phases suggested in Hevner et al. (2004) have been expanded by Baskerville et al. (2007) and the potential benefit of interpretive approaches (Niehaves 2007) has been suggested. In addition, the importance of extending design to the user-as-designer (Germonprez et al. 2007; Hovorka and Germonprez 2009) and expanding evaluative criteria of DSR (Baskerville et al. 2007) are gradually influencing the DSR community to incorporate a broader view. The coalescence of a community of researchers with shared problem domains, exemplars, methods, and evaluative criteria has led some to consider DSR to be achieving paradigmatic status (Hevner et al. 2004; van Aken 2004). As such, there is interest in how the DSR approach and structure can be diffused to a wider context of organizational and societal needs to create knowledge by building working solutions to problems. DSR seeks to create knowledge in the form of *technological rules* (Bunge 1967; van Aken 2004), which are composed of explicit prescriptions for building an artifact with an expected performance or outcome in a specific problem domain (Gregor and Jones 2007). Humans have long created technological rules or models intended to achieve goals including artifacts (in a broad sense), social processes, and organizational interventions and structures. Critically, technological rules must be grounded in the natural and behavioral sciences to produce coherent knowledge claims (Goldkuhl 2004a; van Aken 2004).

As DSR becomes reified into a set of guidelines (Hevner et al. 2004), and design theories are evaluated against a particular anatomical structure (Gregor and Jones 2007; March and Smith 1995), the emphasis begins to approach a dominance of method over science (Nietzsche 1968). These guidelines and structures are used to define the differences between DSR and paradigms of knowledge production such as the natural and behavioral sciences (Hevner et al. 2004) and alternative systems design paradigms (Butler and Murphy 2007; Hirschheim and Klein 1989). This paper seeks to shift the focus away from the method of DSR, to a deeper consideration of the philosophical assumptions underlying knowledge claims resulting from the DSR approach.

The goal of this research is to reinvigorate discussion of the philosophical foundations by which the DSR approach creates and evaluates knowledge. By peering underneath the guidelines and structure that are becoming dominant in DSR, in order to examine foundational concepts in the creation and refinement of scientific knowledge, researchers will be better prepared to justify their choice and use of kernel theories and the evaluation of their knowledge claims.

To focus this discussion, this research examines two aspects that have received little attention.

1. Potential incommensurability in the selection, use, and interactions of kernel theory in DSR, and subsequent implications for kernel theory validation.
2. The shift in our conceptualization of evaluation implied by a *building solutions to solve problems* approach.

The paper begins by examining issues of incommensurability and implications for the choice of kernel theories in DSR. Next, it reframes the nature of DSR as producing knowledge which mediates, rather than solves, problems. In doing so, the research specifically points to the phenomenon of secondary design to demonstrate the potential issues of incommensurate paradigms in evaluation. The paper concludes with a call for greater attentiveness to the philosophical foundations, rather than the method, by which DSR makes knowledge claims.

## 2  Kernel Theory Selection and Commensurability

Design science has long recognized that design theories are composite theories whose kernel theories (March and Smith 1995) or justificatory knowledge (Gregor and Jones 2007) are derived from reference disciplines. These kernel theories serve a dual purpose: first, they provide the often informal hypotheses that a given design principle will produce the desired phenomenon, and second, they are the target of *extension* and *refinement* rather than disconfirmation through the generate/test cycle of DSR (Kuechler and Vaishnavi 2008). The refinement and extension of kernel theory is claimed as a key contribution of the DSR approach. It has been suggested that DSR is inextricably bound to the inclusion, testing, and improvement of kernel theories (Kuechler and Vaishnavi 2008), and that artifact development relies on kernel theories that are applied, tested, modified, and extended through the creation of artifacts (Hevner et al. 2004). However, little attention has been paid to either the potential problems resulting from selection of kernel theories from paradigmatically distinct origins, or how a new design theory can be used to test a kernel theory upon which it is somehow based. Refinement of kernel theories, and evaluation of the resultant design theory, becomes problematic if the causal contributions and interactions of the kernel theories cannot be compared against a shared measurement. In raising the question of kernel theory incommensurability, it is assumed that theory incommensurability and concept incommensurability are salient (Andersen et al. 2006; Burrell and Morgan 1979; Kuhn 1977) and have not been cast aside.

The principles of design are frequently drawn from multiple disciplines. For example, Germonprez et al. (2007) grounded their research in principles from information systems, computer science, and human–computer interaction, in addition to architecture, music, and cybernetics. Each of these disciplines contributed to the proposed theory of tailorable technology. The theory of organizational memory information systems (Stein and Zwass 1995) was grounded in organizational-level effectiveness and a model of individual level memory. As a third example, the theory of learning-oriented knowledge management systems (Hall et al. 2003) was grounded in Churchman's (1971) theory of inquiring systems and Simon's (1969) intelligence–design–choice model as kernel theories (Walls et al. 2004). Interestingly, none of these design theories discussed the appropriateness of combining theories that account for phenomenon at different levels of analysis (organizational versus individual) or in distinctly different disciplines (organizational behavior versus psychology; architecture versus HCI). This raises a question of two potential types of philosophical conflict: combining incommensurate theory derived from different methodological or ontological assumptions (Kuhn 1977), and combining incommensurate concepts in which conceptual meaning varies between disciplines (Andersen et al. 2006).

## 2.1 The Problem of Incommensurability

Incommensurability is a concern in many disciplines with pluralist traditions. The term *incommensurate* refers to a relation between entities, and raises a potential problem for combining paradigms, theories, and concepts. A full discussion of the ongoing debate on incommensurability is beyond the scope of this paper, but a synopsis will provide a perspective on the problem and its relevance to theory grounding in DSR. Incommensurate theories come from epistemic or ontologically distinct paradigms, such that the theories are mutually unintelligible. Two distinct theories representing systems of orientation (e.g., methods, paradigms) are considered incommensurate if they present conflicting perspectives about possible actions or language, and an acceptable reference system from which to evaluate both theories is lacking (Scherer 1998). There exists no common measure by which to determine the appropriateness of each theory, and the result of combining these theories as justificatory knowledge for a new design theory would be incoherent. Thus, a theory based on the symbolic meaning attached to an information system by users and its subsequent use patterns is incommensurate with a theory positing the independent material variables contributing to a dependent variable measured as system performance. It is meaningless to refer to the cognitive sense-making of material variables, and unwarranted to look for a causal–mechanical explanation of human subjective understanding of systems. Suggesting that these are incommensurate as kernels for design theory does not privilege one theory over the other. Each in its own right may provide a foundation for new design theory. But we should focus a critical eye on combining paradigmatically incommensurate kernel theories in DSR, as they constitute entirely different views of the world. Furthermore, to suggest that kernel theories may be incommensurate does not contradict the value of pluralism in research (Mingers 2001), as mixed method studies are intended to discover truths about the world, not to build novel artifacts. The role of theory in discovery research is quite distinct from the role of kernel theory in DSR.

Kernel theory selection is another rarely examined area in which we are faced with the question of which theories will best serve as kernels for DSR. Kuhn (1962) suggests that the evaluation of good theory be based on accuracy, simplicity, scope, consistency, and fruitfulness, but he recognizes the inherently social and practical underpinning of these criteria. There is no objective measure by which to determine which theories would *best* serve as kernels for new designs. The approach used by Kuechler and Vaishnavi (2008) diminishes this problem by drawing kernel theory from experimental results in domains (e.g., cognitive and social psychology and education) closely associated with the problem domain of the designed artifact. But even with such an approach to reducing the potential problems of incommensurability, we are unable to claim that these kernel theories are the *best* theories upon which to base design research. For every set of selected kernel theories, there exist alternative kernel theories from which design knowledge could potentially be developed for the same problem space. This discontinuity between the subjective selection of kernel theory and the desired functionalist evaluation of design theory places a significant burden on the evaluation of all knowledge contributions made by a DSR approach.

Also salient is conceptual or linguistic incommensurability of similar terms drawn from different reference disciplines. Although there are multiple theories of concepts, some consensus suggests that conceptual incommensurability varies in degree and importance, but does occur between cognitively derived human conceptual structures (Andersen et al. 2006). Much of the debate has revolved around conceptual changes over time within a single discipline, but the problem also exists as concepts are imported across disciplinary boundaries. Two potential problems arise here. First, not recognizing differences in concepts is likely to result in an attempt to relate, in a theoretical manner, two ideas that are individually coherent and clear but are not in any way associated. Second, as the evaluation phase attempts to refine kernel theories, the researcher will have lost the ability to distinguish between the concepts and will be unable to resolve the antecedents of the artifact's success on the contributing concepts. For example, the concept of *information* may refer to the mathematical telecommunications concept, to a human psychological construct, to an object that can be stored, transmitted, and retrieved (Buckland 1991), or to a description about, for, or as reality (Borgmann 1999). The term *process* is multi-conceptual depending on context (e.g., process records; process redesign; the system development process). Thus, the seemingly simple combination of *information* and *processing* across references disciplines (*information processing* in computer science versus psychology) refers to different activities and constructs and illustrates the potential difficulties of concept incommensurability.

It should be emphasized that incommensurability does not preclude successful design. Indeed, there are examples of artifacts that *work* without researchers understanding how or why. But the distinction between DSR and design practice is the former's emphasis on the knowledge resulting from design and evaluation versus the latter's desire to simply fulfill a functional goal. An incoherent design theory from DSR is not a knowledge contribution inasmuch as it may result in functional but atheoretic instantiations.

## 2.2 Solutions or Mediations: An Evaluative Shift

A significant rhetorical issue stems from the emphasis on DSR as an inherently problem-solving process for creating solutions to problems of interest to practice (Hevner et al. 2004; Kuechler and Vaishnavi 2008). This focus raises the issue of potential epistemic incommensurability in the DSR evaluation phase. If we turn to the definition of *solution*, as "the resolution of a difficulty or the solving of a problem,"[2] we see that few technologies actually resolve or eliminate a problem at all. For example, a hammer does not solve the problem of building houses or even driving nails. Although it is a tool that allows a carpenter to more easily drive nails, the process of driving nails still needs to be accomplished. So we modify the artifact and produce different types of hammers for different contexts and even embrace the compressed-air nail-gun for greater efficiency and efficacy. But this new technological solution does not work in all circumstances. The nail-driving problem is multidimensional and the larger problem of connecting timbers to build houses still

---

[2] The definition of solution as used in this paper is from http://define.com/solution.

exists. The designed artifact creates a more *useful state of affairs* (Angell and Ilharco 2004) than previously existed, but does not resolve the root problem with a solution.

If we look at other professional disciplines to which IS is often compared, we can see that their activities do not claim to resolve or eliminate root problems. Rather, they provide a means for humans to mediate or reduce the impacts of those problems. Laws and legal procedures do not solve the problems of crime, inequality, or breeches of contract. The legal frameworks do provide mechanisms for managing problems when they arise on a case by case basis. In a similar manner, medicine does not solve the problems of disease, traumatic injury, or pain. To suggest that DSR seeks to design information technology artifacts as a *solution to a problem* implies permanent resolution of the problem that requires no future modification of the tools as designed. But laws, medicine, information technology—and even hammers—undergo large scale revision and a continuous series of localized refinements, modification, and secondary design in the context of their use.

Hard disciplines such as mathematics and physics aside, singular and permanent solutions to problems do not exist in most disciplines. In the social sciences, a solution is a model or representation of the world that works better than other models for achieving a desired outcome or mediating a problem instance within a broad problem domain. Design models are context-dependent knowledge bundles (technological rules) among a set of possible alternative contrast-classes which are expected to achieve an expected outcome relevant to a particular set of requirements derived from a specific problem domain. Models are considered better relative to other models through fulfillment of specific measurement criteria and by the context of the person formulating the problem. Thus a manager may implement a technology that selectively benefits a subset of stakeholders, while at the same time increasing problems for other actors. Design models, therefore, identify the contrast-classes of solutions, and then define the relevance relations (Hovorka et al. 2008; van Fraassen 1980) of subjectively selected criteria of the stakeholders championing the design project. As changes in context, task, or stakeholders occur, the original alternatives and requirements may expose the opportunity for secondary design or the creation of work-arounds. Therefore, the technological rule was not a solution as much as a temporarily better state of continuously changing affairs.

This argument may seem obvious as DSR, like all research, is progressive, and technological rules at the primary design phase will change over time. But the rhetorical shift from solution to mediation is a necessary part of understanding the role of pragmatism as an alternative perspective for evaluation in DSR. The ongoing process of secondary design suggests that information systems do not solve a problem, but instead provide mediation of information processes between desired states of being (goals) and current states. The designed artifact provides a *potential for human action* (Winograd and Flores 1986), which may include the creation and attachment of meaning, increased capacity for idea generation, or emancipation from organizational structures, in addition to purely rational functionalist measures of utility. But the technology itself does not provide a final solution, or even fulfill necessary or sufficient conditions of a solution. A successful design may offer a model for *change and human action* toward a more positive outcome in specific problem domains. This stance is more aligned with a pragmatist philosophy (Goldkuhl 2004b, 2005) than the DSR rational functionalist perspective. After implementation of a specific artifact, refined models, which mediate human action when faced with specific problem instances in the domain, will be offered, and each one will be modified, redesigned, or worked-around, as contexts, actors, and tasks change.

This seemingly obvious observation conceals the underlying philosophical shift from the rational functionalist perspective of DSR, in which success is evaluated in terms of utility-based goals, to a pragmatic perspective where the information systems may be evaluated as successful (or unsuccessful) due to unanticipated or intangible effects not specified in the original design, and on the ability of the system to support human action. Rational functionalism emphasizes the technology impact as measured by productivity and effectiveness of work practices, whereas pragmatism considers the rearrangement of things and people and the way in which artifacts perturb the assemblages of technologies, people, and work processes (Coyne 1995; Latour 1995). However, it is important to recognize that *pragmatic* is not the same as *utilitarian*. Pragmatism posits the researcher or the stakeholder requesting the designed artifact has values dependent on their own interpretation of the relevance and important evaluative measures associated with their purposes (Goles and Hirschheim 2000).

To examine evaluation in more detail, we must first consider whether we are evaluating the artifact based upon the criteria determined by the designers, or based upon how actors actually interact with the built artifacts.

## 3 Encountering Design

One implication of the artifact-centric conceptualization of DSR is the belief that "people will encounter technology as something that is encountered just as it was designed, to be appropriated or incorporated into practice" (Dourish 2006, p. 6). This is stated quite directly in the position that DSR does not attend to the actors using the technology, nor to the manner in which the technology or work practices are modified over time (Hevner et al. 2004). Researchers following these guidelines are likely to privilege the technical artifact over an evaluation of social processes, secondary design, or emergent benefits in their theorizing. But numerous researchers have noted the common phenomena of users redesigning technologies and the practices supported by the technologies as part of their practice (Ciborra 2002; Latour 1995; Robey and Boudreau 1999). Research in human–computer interaction has long recognized that designed systems often do not match the needs of the people using the system. MacLean et al. (1990) note that it is impossible to design systems that will fulfill the goals of all users in all situations. Dourish (2001) suggests that the designers do not share the same model of the task domain as the users. Unique functions and applications are created as systems are used in ways that the designers did not anticipate (Winograd and Flores 1986). Design theories are representations or models of the designer's view of the problem domain and the artifact that will mediate human action in that domain. If human actions are over-determined, such that the coupling of the system actions to the situated world is too rigid or incomplete, by necessity end-users will modify the information process to complete their realized, *in situ* work.     Human agency and learning play a large role in enactment of technology (Boudreau and Robey 2005). Human actors who tailor information processes are acting as secondary designers in the ongoing creation and recreation of information environments. This is fundamental human activity but currently not recognized in most design theorizing. Although guidelines for design theory fall short of creating theories that account for the end users' reflections, tinkering, and subsequent tailoring of information systems in a process of secondary design, an even larger problem is presented in the evaluation phase of DSR.

## 4  Secondary Design

The belief that artifacts are encountered just as they were designed has resulted in IS research evaluating workers' deviation from prescribed uses of information systems, and the creation of workarounds as resistance. Yet the same research calls upon designers, developers, and managers to develop adaptable and reconfigurable systems that can accommodate a wider variety of user behaviors and tasks (Ferneley and Sobreperez 2006). As an increasing number of design models are conceptualized as information environments, where actors engage in information processes through reflection and action and engage in secondary design (Germonprez et al. 2007; Hovorka and Germonprez 2009), the evaluation of the artifact solely by the initial criteria risks undervaluing innovative system modifications (Ciborra 2002).

Actors tailor systems and practices during use for many reasons. One reason for secondary design is the actors' desire that the designed artifact enable them to accomplish their own goals.  But it is unlikely that their goal coincides with the highly functionalist and rational goals upon which the artifact was designed/built and upon which evaluation will be based.  Few knowledge workers are thinking to themselves how efficient, profitable, or even how useful the artifact is.  Research from phenomenological perspectives (Boland 1985; Introna and Whittaker 2002) and from pragmatic perspectives (Goldkuhl 2005; Goles and Hirschheim 2000) reveal that technology users may be motivated by pragmatic reasons such as "this is the only information systems available," "this will work if I tailor the system to shortcut three steps," or "my modified  procedure makes more sense to me than the designed process."

A second reason for secondary design comes from the limitation of designers to fully comprehend the conditions of use. All models and evaluations are based on objects and attributes preselected by the designer. The motivation for the design model, and the rationale for how the designer arrived at that model, is absent from the actual instantiation. When the actor is incapable of achieving desired goals with the technology because the task demands placed on the artifact are different than the original model, a breakdown has occurred and there is no basis for the artifact, as designed, to operate (Winograd and Flores 1986). The only way to generate a new model or representation is from the actor's experience, which is outside the artifact's original design realm. Furthermore, many innovative processes, and the creation of new knowledge, are unexpected consequences of use. In the implementation and secondary design of technologies, many system features and user behaviors emerge that are not within the scope of the original specifications (Ciborra 2002). Evaluation of design success must include the ability to recognize beneficial outcomes that are idiosyncratic, unplanned, and emergent. It is evident that it is impossible for a primary design effort to completely specify all possible system uses *ex ante*.

Therefore, the current conceptualization of DSR brings forth a tension between our desire for a rational and emotionless logic through which information technologies are designed and evaluated, contrasted with real human actors who encounter those technologies in situated and emotion-laden practice. An examination of variable-centered IS research notes that, in most studies, the actors or managers who might benefit from the research are not represented in the study (Ramiller and Pentland 2009). In the same way, design science research neglects the actors who will be using, subjected to, and whose work processes will be evaluated through the rational lens of the technology. The actions themselves, the meaning of the actions attached by the actors for whom the system is designed, and the embodied participation of use, are expunged and not accounted for in the design or evaluation. Although researchers recognize that technology and action are inseparable in information system design (Hevner et al. 2004), the current view of evaluation is hampered by a narrow definition of design, which produces an appliance mentality of design (Lee 2001), and a rational functionalist view of evaluation, which does not account for the secondary design of the system in practice. A critical extension to design science research for both the design and evaluation phases is to incorporate the tendency of people to tinker, tweak, tailor, and otherwise modify the system to fit their particular context (Ciborra 2002; Dourish 2006; Hovorka and Germonprez 2009).

## 5 Evaluation

DSR explicitly incorporates evaluation as one of the essential guidelines, yet it is an impoverished view of evaluation based upon a narrow functionalist perspective that defines successful design only in terms of utility, quality, and efficacy of technological artifacts (Hevner et al. 2004) and thin epistemological grounding. Systematic testing is often achieved by treating the model as a black box, and by linking its use to specific outcomes (van Aken 2004). This is a very pragmatic philosophy interested in change and action (Goldkuhl 2005) and is not concerned with causality or the explanatory truth of theories (Gregor 2006; Hovorka et al. 2008). DSR recognizes that models can also be tested scientifically, whereby the functionality and use of the artifact can be explained and predicted. But phenomena such as secondary design (Germonprez et al. 2007; Hovorka and Germonprez 2009), and the separation between a user encountering an artifact and the original design specifications, makes evaluation from a solely functionalist perspective problematic. Difficulties arise in rigorous scientific testing of design theory *in situ* where pragmatic evaluation vies with rational functionalist requirements. If the DSR approach is extended to other areas of research, such as management or organizational studies (Romme 2003; van Aken 2004), for the purpose of creating knowledge, then evaluation becomes a cornerstone of its legitimacy.

To address this evaluation problem, Baskerville et al. (2007) introduce the idea of soft design science research, which includes a multistage evaluation process, but the proposed framework is fully embedded in the rational functionalist paradigm of meeting articulated requirements. The framework does suggest that the determination of success and of failures is complex, and includes multiple perspectives by multiple stakeholders, as well as the attribution of failure to externalities rather than design.

The exposition of an organizational information system case presented in Baskerville et al. (2004) illustrates the difficulties presented by incommensurate perspectives on evaluation. Although the study artifact was originally evaluated to be a success, changes in context (new managers who were not as well known or trusted by upper management) led to subversion of the information system and its eventual removal because it had become socially destructive (Baskerville and Land 2004). It is important to recognize that the philosophy underlying the evaluative criteria shifted during the time period in question. Even as the system became socially destructive, it was still capable of meeting the original functionalist goals of delivering information to senior executives. This suggests that the original requirements were instrumentalist in nature, but the later evaluation emphasized a pragmatic perspective of the ability of the system to support human actions over time. Although it is useful to classify evaluation errors in a typology of errors (Baskerville et al. 2007), it is equally important to recognize the philosophical basis upon which evaluation is based and whether it is commensurate with the design paradigms.

It comes as no surprise that shifting paradigms for evaluation will result in conflicting results, particularly if the context, task, or stakeholders have also changed. Adopting a pragmatic desire to create artifacts that *work* or that have beneficial mediation of human action (Goldkuhl 2004b) conflicts with the functionalist, radical, or critical paradigms under which the systems may have been developed (Hirschheim and Klein 1989). The risk is in not recognizing the paradigm in which the design was created and the paradigm from which we are evaluating a built artifact.

The discussion above reinforces and extends the argument that broadening of evaluation to include interpretative or critical approaches capable of capturing outcomes not included in the original utility-based performance measures necessarily requires a shift from rational functionalist paradigms to other evaluative approaches. Interpretive (Boland 1978; Niehaves 2007) or phenomenological (Introna and Whittaker 2002) approaches inform initial design and also evaluation by uncovering the ontology of the actual work (Butler and Murphy 2007; Suchman et al. 1999) and viewing the technology through the actor's eyes. Although it is recognized that organizational actors learn and modify processes or technologies to better fit their actual work (Robey and Boudreau 1999), from the functionalist perspective of the artifact this is resistance (Lapointe and Rivard 2005) and a failure of the information system. But from an interpretive or a critical perspective, respectively, it may represent an actor's creation of identity, or liberation from organizational strictures. Our understanding of the philosophical underpinnings of evaluation in DSR can be broadened to recognize and incorporate different, clearly defined criteria that will extend the domains in which DSR is a legitimate approach to knowledge creation.

## 6 Concluding Thoughts

This research has sought to clarify three implications of expanding the predominantly functionalist DSR approach to knowledge creation into broader organizational and societal research domains. Whereas the DSR approach has enormous potential for knowledge creation in a variety of domains, care must be taken to comprehend and articulate the philosophical underpinnings of theory building and evaluation to avoid grounding knowledge on unwarranted amalgamations of paradigm-bound concepts and the creation of incoherent design theory. While design theory development may be influenced by more than one paradigm, and can be evaluated from multiple perspectives, awareness of the need for clarity when grounding design theory in multiple kernel theories or potentially incommensurate concepts will strengthen the legitimacy of DSR.

First, design theories of artifacts, be they instantiations, algorithms, managerial programs, constructs, or organizational structures, are all *models* for enabling human action and change. These models are not descriptions or explanations of states of being that exist, but rather are models of "new ways of being that did not previously exist and a framework for action that would not have previously made sense" (Winograd and Flores 1986, p. 177). This aspect of DSR is a strongly pragmatic activity wherein pragmatism is concerned with goal-oriented action. Significantly, the design models exist within a spectrum of alternative models that do not have a verifiable truth-value, but rather can each satisfy a variety of predefined or emergent goals. We can only say that this design is *better* than the alternative models against a background of the particular interpretation of conditions declared as *better* by an individual or community.

Second, by focusing attention of the composite nature of design theories, this research identifies the risk of grounding design theory on disparate explanatory kernel theories which themselves may be based upon distinct philosophical stances. The risk is not that the built artifact would not work. Rather, the risk lies in confounding our understanding of why the design works, as we look to the kernel theories from which the new theory was derived. Ontologically incommensurate assumptions or conceptual conflicts in kernel theories will result in a design that may be pragmatically beneficial but atheoretic. We cannot assume that incommensurate kernel theories are operating in conjunction or in opposition. In fact, we cannot assume anything about the interactions of such theories! By concatenating theories with disparate ontological or epistemological assumptions, we lose coherence of the derived design theory or design principles. The epistemic distance between the new design theory and the kernel theories upon which it is grounded precludes any direct refinement, testing, or validation of kernel theory. In addition, the pragmatist emphasis on change and action, rather than the rationalist emphasis on truth and explanation, requires considerable discrimination to advance design knowledge while evaluating the *in situ* use of a new artifact. Whereas knowledge is often perceived as an increasingly accurate reflection of reality, pragmatism recognizes that to achieve goals, humans must perceive what features can be afforded practical action, while often neglecting to invoke basic science (Bunge 1996; Goldkuhl 2005).

Third, the tension between rational functionalist evaluation, based upon utility and efficiency, and the pragmatist emphasis on human action and change contribute to confounding evaluations of artifacts and design theories. The evaluation phase of DSR must be firmly grounded and should not meander between pragmatic, functionalist, critical, and interpretative paradigms. Evaluation may flow from any of these positions, and will result in quite different evaluative outcomes depending on the contrast-class between models of reality and the relevant criteria of the evaluator.

The conditions of satisfactory performance or fit are not necessarily determinate in advance, but may emerge during the development of the human–artifact interaction. Secondary design in the context of use and changes in the environment of use itself may further complicate evaluation. But the multiple goals of DSR during the design/build–justify/evaluate process are often at odds and may lead to inconsistent results. Greater rhetorical precision is required to insure that the paradigmatic grounding of design and evaluation phases are clearly articulated.

This research does not attempt to settle the long-standing discussion between those who would isolate paradigms and pluralists who recommend a diversity of paradigms and research methods. Most social sciences have accepted that there is a diversity of opinions about what is knowable and how we can know something exists (Mingers 2001; Scherer 1998; Tadajewski 2008). Nor does this research privilege particular research paradigms. Rather, it suggests that as DSR is expanded across IS and into other organizational and social domains as an approach to knowledge creation and evaluation, researchers must recognize and surface their paradigmatic assumptions, boundaries, and limitations. To assume away or to simply ignore the significant debate surrounding the production and validation of knowledge would be a disservice to design science research and reduce its validity as a process of knowledge creation.

# References

Andersen, H., Barker, P., Chen, X.: The Cognitive Structure of Scientific Revolutions. Cambridge University Press, Cambridge (2006)

Angell, I.O., Ilharco, F.M.: Solution Is the Problem: A Story of Transitions and Opportunities. In: Avgerou, C., Ciborra, C., Land, F. (eds.) The Social Study of Information and Communication Technology, pp. 38–61. Oxford University Press, New York (2004)

Baskerville, R., Land, F.: Socially Self-Destructive Systems. In: Avgerou, C., Ciborra, C., Land, F. (eds.) The Social Study of Information and Communication, pp. 263–285. Oxford University Press, New York (2004)

Baskerville, R., Pries-Heje, J., Venable, J.: Soft Design Science Research: Extending the Boundaries of Evaluation in Design Science Research. In: Proceedings of the Second International Conference on Design Science Research in Information Systems and Technology, Pasadena, CA, May 13-15, pp. 19–38 (2007)

Boland, R.: The Process and Product of System Design. Management Science 28(9), 887–898 (1978)

Boland, R.: Phenomenology: A Preferred Approach to Research in Information Systems. In: Mumford, E., Hirschheim, R., Fitzgerald, G., Wood-Harper, T. (eds.) Research Methods in Information Systems: Proceedings of the IFIP WG 8.2 Colloquium, pp. 181–190. North Holland, Amsterdam (1985)

Borgmann, A.: Holding on to Reality: The Nature of Information at the Turn of the Century. University of Chicago Press, Chicago (1999)

Boudreau, M.-C., Robey, D.: Enacting Integrated Information Technology: A Human Agency Perspective. Organization Science 16(1), 3–18 (2005)

Buckland, M.K.: Information as Thing. Journal of the American Society for Information Science 42(5), 351–360 (1991)

Bunge, M.: Scientific Research II: The Search for Truth. Springer, Berlin (1967)

Bunge, M.: Finding Philosophy in Social Science. Yale University Press, New Haven (1996)

Burrell, G., Morgan, G.: Sociological Paradigms and Organizational Analysis. Heinemann, London (1979)

Butler, T., Murphy, C.: Understanding the Design of Information Technologies for Knowledge Management in Organizations: A Pragmatic Perspective. Information Systems Journal 17(2), 143–163 (2007)

Churchman, C.W.: The Design of Inquiring Systems. Basic Books, Inc., New York (1971)

Ciborra, C.: The Labyrinths of Information. Oxford University Press, Oxford (2002)

Coyne, R.: Designing Information Systems in the Postmodern Age. MIT Press, Cambridge (1995)

Dourish, P.: Where the Action Is: The Foundations of Embodied Interaction. MIT Press, Cambridge (2001)

Dourish, P.: Implications for Design. In: Proceedings ACM Conference on Human Factors in Computing Systems, Montreal, Quebec, Canada, April 22-27, pp. 541–550. ACM, New York (2006)

Ferneley, E., Sobreperez, P.: Resist, Comply or Workaround? An Examination of Different Facets of User Engagement with Information Systems. European Journal of Information Systems 15(4), 345–356 (2006)

Germonprez, M., Hovorka, D., Callopy, F.: A Theory of Tailorable Technology Design. Journal of the Association of Information Systems 8(6), 351–367 (2007)

Goldkuhl, G.: Design Theories in Information Systems: A Need for Multi-Grounding. Journal of Information Technology Theory and Application 6(2), 59–72 (2004a)

Goldkuhl, G.: Meanings of Pragmatism: Ways to Conduct Information Systems Research. In: Proceedings of the Second International Conference on Action in Language, Organizations and Information Systems, Linköping University, Sweden (2004b)

Goldkuhl, G.: Socio-Instrumental Pragmatism: A Theoretical Synthesis for Pragmatic Conceptualisation in Information Systems. In: Proceedings of the Third International Conference on Action in Language, Organizations and Information Systems, Limerick, Ireland (2005)

Goles, T., Hirschheim, R.: The Paradigm is Dead, the Paradigm is Dead...Long Live the Paradigm: The Legacy of Burrell and Morgan. Omega (28), 249–268 (2000)

Gregor, S.: The Nature of Theory in Information Systems. MIS Quarterly 30(3), 611–642 (2006)

Gregor, S., Jones, D.: The Anatomy of a Design Theory. Journal of the Association of Information Systems 8(5), 312–335 (2007)

Hall, D., Paradice, D., Courtney, J.: Building a Theoretical Foundation for a Learning-Oriented Management System. Journal of Information Technology Theory and Application 5(2), 63–85 (2003)

Hevner, A.R., March, S.T., Park, J., Ram, S.: Design Science in IS Research. MIS Quarterly 28(1), 75–106 (2004)

Hirschheim, R., Klein, H.K.: Four Paradigms for Information Systems Development. Communication of the Association for Information Systems 32(10), 1199–1216 (1989)

Hovorka, D.S., Germonprez, M.: Tinkering, Tailoring, and Bricolage: Implications for Theories of Design. In: Proceedings of the 15th Americas Conference on Information Systems, San Francisco, CA, August 6-9 (2009)

Hovorka, D.S., Germonprez, M., Larsen, K.R.T.: Explanation in Information Systems. Information Systems Journal 18(1), 23–43 (2008)

Introna, L.D., Whittaker, L.: The Phenomenology of Information Systems Evaluation: Overcoming the Subject Object Dualism. In: Wynn, E.H., Whitley, E.A., Myers, M.D., DeGross, J.I. (eds.) Global and Organizational Discourse About Information Technology, pp. 155–175. Kluwer Academic Publishers, Boston (2002)

Kuechler, B., Vaishnavi, V.: On Theory Development in Design Science Research: Anatomy of a Research Project. European Journal of Information Systems (17), 489–504 (2008)

Kuhn, T.S.: The Structure of Scientific Revolutions. University of Chicago Press, Chicago (1962)

Kuhn, T.S.: Second Thoughts on Paradigms. The Essential Tension, pp. 293–319. University of Chicago Press, Chicago (1977)

Lapointe, L., Rivard, S.: A Multilevel Model of Resistance to Information Technology Implementation. MIS Quarterly 29(3), 461–491 (2005)

Latour, B.: A Door Must Be Either Open or Shut: A Little philosophy of Techniques. In: Feenberg, A., Hannay, A. (eds.) Technology and the Politics of Knowledge, pp. 272–281. Indiana University Press, Bloomington (1995)

Lee, A.: Challenges to Qualitative Researchers in Information Systems. In: Trauth, E. (ed.) Qualitative Research in IS: Issues and Trends, pp. 240–270. Idea Group Publishing, Hershey (2001)

MacLean, A., Carter, K., Lovstrand, L., Moran, T.: User-Tailorable Systems: Pressing the Issues with Buttons. In: Chew, J.C., Whiteside, J. (eds.) Proceedings of the SIGCHI Conference on Human Factors in Computing Systems: Empowering People, Seattle, WA, April 1-5, pp. 175–182. ACM, New York (1990)

March, S.T., Smith, G.S.: Design and Natural Science Research on Information Technology. Decision Support Systems 15(4), 251–266 (1995)

Mingers, J.: Combining IS Research Methods: Toward a Pluralist Methodology. Information Systems Research 12(3), 240–259 (2001)

Niehaves, B.: On Epistemological Diversity in Design Science – New Vistas for a Design-Oriented IS Research? In: Proceedings of the 28th International Conference on Information Systems, Montreal, Quebec, Canada, December 10-12 (2007)

Nietzsche, F.: The Will to Power. Vintage Books, New York (1968)

Ramiller, N.C., Pentland, B.T.: Management Implications in Information Systems Research: The Untold Story. Journal of the Association of Information Systems 10(6), 474–494 (2009)

Robey, D., Boudreau, M.C.: Accounting for the Contradictory Organizational Consequences of Information Technology: Theoretical Directions and Methodological Implications. Information Systems Research 10(2), 167–185 (1999)

Romme, A.G.L.: Making a Difference: Organization as Design. Organization Science 14(5), 558–573 (2003)

Scherer, A.G.: Theory: A Problem in Search of a Solution Pluralism and Incommensurability in Strategic Management and Organization. Organization (5), 147–168 (1998)

Simon, H.A.: Sciences of the Artificial. MIT Press, Cambridge (1969)

Stein, E.W., Zwass, V.: Actualizing Organizational Memory with Information Systems. Information Systems Research 6(2), 85–117 (1995)

Suchman, L., Blomberg, J., Orr, J., Trigg, R.: Reconstructing Technologies as Social Practice. American Behavioral Scientist 43(3), 392–408 (1999)

Tadajewski, M.: Incommensurable Paradigms, Cognitive Bias and the Politics of Marketing Theory. Marketing Theory 8(3), 273–297 (2008)

van Aken, J.: Management Research Based on the Paradigm of the Design Sciences: The Quest for Field-Tested and Grounded Technological Rules. Journal of Management Studies 41(2), 219–246 (2004)

van Fraassen, B.: The Scientific Image. The Clarendon Press, Oxford (1980)

Walls, J.G., Widemeyer, G.R., El Sawy, O.A.: Assessing Information System Design Theory in Perspective: How Useful Was Our 1992 Initial Rendition? Journal of Information Technology Theory and Application 6(2), 43–58 (2004)

Winograd, T., Flores, F.: Understanding Computers and Cognition: A New Foundation for Design. Ablex Publishing Corporation, Norwood (1986)

Winter, R.: Design Science Research in Europe. European Journal of Information Systems 17(5), 470–475 (2008)

## About the Author

**Dirk S. Hovorka** is an associate professor in Information Systems in the School of Information Technology, Bond University, Queensland, Australia. He attended Williams College (in Massachusetts) for his BA, holds an MS in Geology and an MS in Interdisciplinary Telecommunications, and received his Ph.D. in Information Systems from the University of Colorado in 2006. His research includes the philosophical foundations of IS research, the development of design theory, and the evolving role of information systems in science. He has published research in *European Journal of Information Systems, Journal of the AIS, Information Systems Journal, Communications of the AIS,* and *Decision Support Systems*, and has book chapters published in *Business Agility and Information Technology Diffusion* (IFIP 8.6), *Reframing Humans in Information Systems Development* (forthcoming), and *Perspectives on Information Management: Setting the Scene*. He has presented research at the International Conference on Information Systems, the Australian Conference on Information Systems, the European Conference on Information Systems, IFIP WG 8.2 and 8.6, and the Americas Conference on Information Systems. Dirk can be reached at dhovorka@bond.edu.au.

# The Design and Engineering of Mobile Data Services: Developing an Ontology Based on Business Model Thinking

Mutaz M. Al-Debei and Guy Fitzgerald

Department of Information Systems and Computing,
Brunel University
Middlesex, Uxbridge,
London UB8 3PH, United Kingdom

**Abstract.** This paper addresses the design and engineering problem related to mobile data services. The aim of the research is to inform and advise mobile service design and engineering by looking at this issue from a rigorous and holistic perspective. To this aim, this paper develops an ontology based on business model thinking. The developed ontology identifies four primary dimensions in designing business models of mobile data services: value proposition, value network, value architecture, and value finance. Within these dimensions, 15 key design concepts are identified along with their interrelationships and rules in the telecommunication service business model domain and unambiguous semantics are produced. The developed ontology is of value to academics and practitioners alike, particularly those interested in strategic-oriented IS/IT and business developments in telecommunications. Employing the developed ontology would systemize mobile service engineering functions and make them more manageable, effective, and creative. The research approach to building the mobile service business model ontology essentially follows the design science paradigm. Within this paradigm, we incorporate a number of different research methods, so the employed methodology might be better characterized as a pluralist approach.

**Keywords:** Business model, service design and engineering, mobile data services, ontology, design science, mobile technology, telecommunications.

## 1 Introduction

The mobile telecommunications business is undergoing major changes, driven by innovative technologies, globalization, and deregulation. Recent technological advances in telecommunications are bringing enormous change to the way mobile business is conducted and the way in which we live our lives. This is apparent from the shift of the industry from mainly voice to one that is mostly about data (Dodourova 2003). At the same time, globalization and deregulation are removing many of the legacy barriers to telecommunications and providing environment more amenable to sustainable competition.

J. Pries-Heje et al. (Eds.): IS Design Science Research, IFIP AICT 318, pp. 28–51, 2010.
© IFIP International Federation for Information Processing 2010

The implications of this transformation have changed the business rules of the telecommunications industry. Nowadays, the major challenges faced by telecommunications providers (from now on shortened to *telecoms*) are the shifts from one simple service to a portfolio of mainly convergent services (e.g., integration of voice, data, and Internet), from no or few affiliations to multiple partnerships, from simple and linear links to complex relationships (Olla and Patel 2002), from homogeneous to heterogeneous customer demands, and from customers consuming modest services to customers continuously presuming advanced, high quality services (Kim et al. 2008).

In response to these challenges, telecoms have been compelled to repackage their business; that is, overhauling the traditional way in which mobile services are designed and developed. This is particularly pertinent now, with the saturation of the voice market and the credit crunch. For telecoms to get their strategies right is critical to success as inappropriate decisions can have major adverse effects on performance. However, achieving this has proven difficult. One key indicator is that revenues generated from services other than voice telephony and SMS are below expectations, although the number of mobile users worldwide is continuously increasing (ITU 2009). In our context, the problem is clearly related to the design of appropriate mobile data services. When it comes to service design and engineering (see Bullinger et al. 2003), telecoms are facing many issues that are hindering their progress, including

(1) *The absence of a coherent framework.* Telecoms services are not clearly defined; there is no unequivocal, comprehensive identification of the service related issues such as content, associated values and benefits, needed resources, target segments, financial designs, etc.
(2) *Inappropriate organizational design.* The structure, infrastructure, and/or technological architecture of telecoms are not designed to enable efficient development and launch of new services.
(3) *Weak alignment among all organizational layers.* The service model is not tightly consistent with the strategic objectives of telecoms or their operational processes, including their information systems.

Retrospectively, there is a significant need to inform and advise service design and engineering in the telecommunications sector by looking at this issue from an integrated and cohesive perspective. Services probably need to be developed or redeveloped using a comprehensive and effective approach, if they are to be successful. One element of this is the need for an innovative business model to be developed that focuses on the achievement of strategic outcomes by aligning ICT services. A business model has been described as a "logical story" (Magretta 2002), or a "blueprint" (Chesbrough and Rosenbloom 2002) that explains the "way of doing business" (Hamel 2000) so that strategic goals and objectives can be achieved.

For the purpose of achieving clarity and semantic preciseness in the design of service business models, this paper utilizes the ontology concept as it is an explicit and formal specification of key objects, relationships, and semantics of a particular domain (Chandrasekaran et al. 1999). In particular, we develop a novel ontology that rigorously identifies the service business model components, interrelationships, and their semantics in the context of mobile data services.

The remainder of this paper is structured as follows. First, a theoretical background concerning business models and their role in service engineering is provided together with a discussion of ontologies and their functions in information systems. Next the design science research method for the ontological engineering approach that was undertaken is described. Thereafter, the constructed ontology is developed, showing its concepts (dimensions and elements), properties, and semantics. Finally, we summarize and outline the contributions of this paper.

## 2 Theoretical Background

### 2.1 The Role of Business Models in Service Design and Engineering

The business model concept, although much talked about, is somewhat fuzzy (Seddon et al. 2004; Seppänen and Mäkinen 2007) and researchers have defined it from different viewpoints. For example, Linder and Cantrell (2000) portray the business model as a tool that explains how business organizations generate revenues, while Andersson et al. (2006) describe the business model as a mechanism that makes the relationship between business actors more explicit. In an attempt to clarify this situation, Al-Debei et al. (2008a) have analytically synthesized the related literature, and define a business model as an

> abstract representation of an organization, be it conceptual, textual, and/or graphical, of all core interrelated architectural, co-operational, and financial arrangements designed and developed by an organization presently and in the future, as well as all core products and/or services the organization offers, or will offer, based on these arrangements that are needed to achieve its strategic goals and objectives (pp. 8-9).

The extant literature in both business and information systems testifies to the importance of the business model concept to the success of companies, particularly those driven by ICTs. Examples of the domains where the concept has been utilized include mobile technology (e.g., Al-Debei and Avison 2010; Al-Debei et al. 2008b; Bouwman et al. 2008; Maitland 2005), eBusiness and eCommerce (e.g., Afuah and Tucci 2003; Gordjin and Akkermans 2001; Osterwalder et al. 2005), and other emerging industries where IT innovations and technologies are of importance (e.g., Ballon 2007; Hedman and Kalling 2003; MacInnes 2005).

The underlying principle behind this increasing interest is the conception that it is not the technology itself, but rather the design of the business model, that actually determines success (Yuan and Zhang 2003), and allows high-technology companies to achieve their strategic outcomes by developing relevant and desired services and applications. For example, Chesbrough and Rosenbloom (2002) argue that "a successful business model creates a heuristic logic that connects technical potential with the realization of economic value" (p. 529). In line with this, Kamoun (2008) argues that the business model "becomes the blueprint of the way a business creates and captures value from new services, products, or innovations" (p. 638).

This is equally relevant to mobile data services. For example, the success of NTT DoCoMo's i-mode is primarily credited to its well-designed business model in action

**Fig. 1.** The Business Model as a Mediating Construct

(Ratliff 2002) and the low adoption of WAP is argued to be mainly due to the absence of a feasible business model or its inappropriate configuration (Kumar et al. 2003; Sigurdson 2001).

Therefore, we consider the employment of business models, as a mediating construct between technological artifacts and the fulfilment of strategic outcomes, as highly applicable to mobile service design and engineering (see Figure 1).

### 2.2  The Role of Ontologies

Ontology is a term that has originated in philosophy and refers to the systematic explanation and study of the nature of existence. The term has been borrowed by the information systems and computing disciplines (e.g., Guarino and Welty 2002; Wand and Weber 1990) and changed somewhat, but despite its recent extensive use in these disciplines, the term has no universal definition.

Principally, the term *ontology* means one of two related things (Chandrasekaran et al. 1999). First, the term is used to refer to a body of knowledge or theory demonstrating a particular real world phenomenon. In its second, more practical sense, ontology refers to the shared and explicit specification and representation of classes of objects (i.e., concepts and vocabularies), properties (i.e., relationships), and semantics (i.e., meaning) of particular domains. One of the most cited definitions of ontology is by Gruber (1993), who defines it as an "explicit specification of a conceptualization" (p. 1). Conceptualization is what makes ontologies shareable as it refers to the meanings captured through concepts, not the terms themselves. Furthermore, conceptualization implies abstraction, which signifies that an ontology represents only knowledge regarded as core in the specific domain.

Ontology research has gained particular recognition in the area of information systems analysis and design (e.g., Wand and Weber 2002; Wyssusek 2004). Information systems that make use of explicit and formally defined ontologies have been described as ontology-driven systems (Guarino 1998). Such ontologies are referred to as IS ontologies (e.g., Smith 2003), or computational ontologies (e.g., Kishore and Sharman 2004). We hope that developing an ontology will enable the precise identification and categorization of the key concepts and relationships in the telecom services business model and produce unambiguous semantics of them.

## 3   Research Methods

The research paradigm followed here, concerned with analytically designing and developing a business model ontology for mobile data services, is that of design science (Hevner et al. 2004).

Design artifacts are classified by March and Smith (1995), and anchored by Hevner et al. (2004), into *constructs* of vocabulary and symbols, *models* representing reality with appropriate levels of abstraction, *methods* in the form of algorithms and practices, and *instantiations*, which are implemented systems and/or their prototypes developed as proof-of-concepts. The developed ontology in this paper represents a *model* artifact that includes *constructs*. This ontology is produced using an approach developed by the authors, called OntoEng; that is, a design method for ontology engineering in the field of information systems. This method (OntoEng) and its application to build and evaluate the mobile service business model ontology are outlined in this paper and fully discussed elsewhere (see Al-Debei and Fitzgerald 2009).

Essentially, within the design science paradigm, the applied approach is best portrayed as a *pluralist* methodology, as different research methods are incorporated. A multimethod approach is beneficial because, as Mingers (2001) argues, results are richer and more reliable if different research methods are combined. We agree with Mingers since different, related research methods have their own advantages and drawbacks but, when appropriately combined, they can provide enhanced value. Based on the classification provided by Palvia et al. (2006), we now briefly discuss the various methods employed in this research.

### 3.1 Qualitative Research: Interviews

The current research utilizes empirical data as its main source. We conducted 18 semi-structured interviews with key practitioners (i.e., managers) in the telecommunications sector. Interviews were recorded and on average lasted about 90 minutes. The interviews were transcribed, verified, and then analyzed. The primary themes discussed with the interviewee managers included collaboration with value network actors, resource allocation and configuration, the creation of core competencies, costing and pricing, customer relationship management and intelligence, and other related services. The background and specialities of the interviewed managers were varied, covering marketing/sales, IS/IT, engineering, management, strategy, and finance.

In addition to the interviews, the research utilized observation and documentation. Analyzed documents include annual and internal reports, presentations, and documentation on mobile service related functions. Consistent with Orlikowski (1993), we found this triangulation useful since it allows cross-checking, which strengthens data validity, provides multiple perspectives, and supplies more complementary information.

### 3.2 Library Research: Literature Analysis

The current research has drawn upon key findings from previous research on business models in general, e-business modeling, and, more essentially, on business modeling and service engineering in the telecoms sector. This research is also inspired by previous research on ontologies. We attempt to analyze and synthesize the existing relevant literature and extend it.

### 3.3  Secondary Data

This paper utilizes existing organizational and business data in the form of statistics, published reports, available case studies, and companies' websites. This kind of data is used to demonstrate some of the claims in the paper.

### 3.4  Speculation: Commentary

As the integration of the research themes (i.e., mobile technology, service design and engineering, business models, and ontology) is novel, so inferences and speculations have sometimes been employed to build arguments and support discussion pertaining to engineering functions of mobile services.

### 3.5  Frameworks and Conceptual Models

The collected data is utilized in this paper to develop logical representations of the phenomenon under investigation in the form of frameworks and conceptual models. Developing a conceptual model is a key activity in ontology engineering (Jarrar et al. 2003; Pinto and Martin 2004). According to Wand and Weber (2002), conceptual models are useful in (1) supporting communications between users and the development team; (2) helping system analysts in understanding the domain under investigation; (3) providing rich input for the design and implementation processes; and (4) documenting the original system requirements for future reference.

The developed ontology is represented using UML class diagrams. This is because there is a strong interest and call in the ontological engineering domain to use UML for ontology representation (e.g., Eriksson and Penker 2000; Guizzardi et al. 2004) as it provides models that are visually rich and easy to use and understand.

## 4  V4 Mobile Service Business Model Ontology

Designing business models of mobile data services is a complex undertaking as it entails a comprehensive examination of many aspects. Based on our analysis we suggest that when designing service business models, telecoms need to address 15 critical concepts, organized in the following four dimensions (see Figure 2): value-proposition, value-network, value-architecture, and value-finance. These dimensions represent the upper-level constructs of our ontology and we term this the $V^4$ *service business model ontology.*

These design concepts (dimensions and elements) are interdependent (see Figure 3). Hence, addressing them separately without taking into consideration their interrelation ships is neither sufficient nor effective. One action or alteration in one concept would normally trigger changes in other concepts so as to keep the service feasible and successful. This is because, for example, what is financially viable may not be viable for value proposition purposes, or may be difficult to configure and maintain, or may even be hard to acquire through the value network. Thus, a holistic alignment and a coherent trade-off amongst the service business model components are necessary.

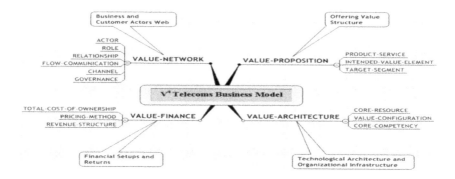

**Fig. 2.** The Taxonomic Tree of $V^4$ Service Business Model Ontology

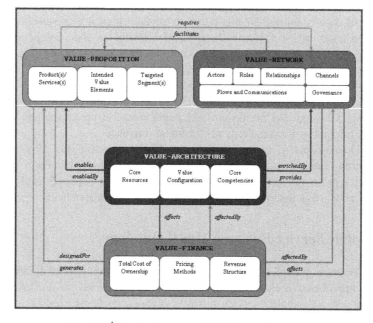

**Fig. 3.** $V^4$ Service Business Model Upper Ontology

In the next subsections, we provide more in-depth discussion for each dimension clarifying the service design concepts and their interdependencies.

### 4.1 Value-Proposition

The value-proposition dimension embraces the first three concepts of designing mobile data services: product-service, intended-value-element, and target-segment (see Figure 4). This refers to the following questions: What is the offering of a particular telecom? What sort of value is incorporated within that offering? Who are the targeted customers that are most likely to desire the proposed offering?

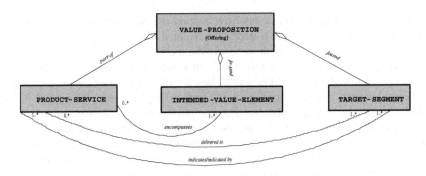

**Fig. 4.** Value-Proposition Dimension

**Product-service.** This concept describes the potential service(s) along with the information provided to target segments. New services are described by attributes such as name, type, functions, and technical/nontechnical requirements. Consider this example: Orange offers a service called *Click It*. This service is categorized as an *entertainment service* where its main functionality is to provide *information on demand*. The sort of information the service provides includes the latest in movies, sports news, general news, quotes, and weather forecasts. For customers to utilize this service, they need to be *Orange subscribers* and to have a *phase 2+ handset* device.

This sort of information is useful since (1) it gives an indication about segments seeking and willing to use such services, and (2) it helps in judging a service's feasibility through estimating the size of target segment and matching the features of the service with customer details. For example, Orange estimated that 100,000 of its youth customers are potential users of the *Click It* service. But if only 10 percent of these customers have phase 2+ handsets, the size of the target segment is significantly reduced (to 10,000), which will affect service feasibility.

At this phase, it is also of great importance to establish the strategic objective of the new service and to make sure it is consistent with the telecom's overall strategy. There are a number of reasons why services may be designed and launched. For instance, some services are launched to *build or sustain the telecom's image* in the market, thus primarily not for *revenue generation*. In some other cases, the target could be to generate *cash flow* or even to *adhere to regulations*. Moreover, some services are *disruptive* while others are ordinary *structural* services. The reason why the identification of the service objective is significant is that configurations within the design concepts differ substantially across different objectives. Proceeding with the design while objectives of services are unknown is likely to have serious negative consequences.

**Intended-value-element.** This concept mainly looks at the kinds of value with which telecoms intend to provide customers. Fundamentally, adding value depends on the ability of a telecom to provide customers with services that meet their preferences throughout their life cycle. This is vital since customer satisfaction leads to customer retention and lock-in. Value is basically created when the benefits associated with services are equivalent or exceed the offering's total price where the latter includes search, operating, and disposal costs in addition to the purchase price (Slater and

Narver 2000). But in the highly competitive market of telecoms, this is not sufficient to guarantee success. Unless delivered values are different or unique, they should surpass those delivered by competitors to win the market.

Broadly speaking, value offered to mobile customers can be categorized as *quality* or *economy*. While the design of economy-based values are somehow simple as they only depend on the cost of services in addition to the adopted pricing and billing methods, the design of quality-based values is multifaceted as the assessment criteria of mobile quality of service (QoS) are wide-ranging. Factors related to mobile QoS could be categorized as *connection* (stability and responsiveness), *content* (objectivity, believability, amount), *interaction* (structure, navigation, presentation, design and ease of use, size, color), and *contextual* (timeliness and promptness) (Chae and Kim 2001). In m-commerce applications, *security* and *privacy* are also highlighted and considered key quality factors. Furthermore, *quality of life* factors (Amanatiadis et al. 2006) in terms of *free utilities*, which depict friendliness and generosity of a telecom, *environment*, which shows the extent to which a telecom is acting in an environmentally friendly manner, *entertainment*, which depicts the sort of amusement that is communicated to users, and *public inference* related to spectrum allocation are also relevant.

From another standpoint, value can be perceived as *utilitarian* or *hedonic*. Utilitarian value is the effective achievement of a utilitarian goal, which is often suitable for customers classified as problem-solvers (Pura 2005). Location-based services is one example of mobile services providing utilitarian values such as identifying the location of a person or finding the nearest petrol station, although sometimes such services provide location-based games that deliver hedonic value. Essentially, hedonic value is delivered when mobile services successfully provide users with fun and enjoyment. Further examples include mobile music and video-clips.

The value delivered by mobile services could also be recognized as *emotional* in that it fulfils people's needs, for example in relation to status and independence. Technology also plays a role here as it has the potential to deliver what is called *epistemic value* (see Sheth et al. 1991), enticing customers looking for curiosity and novelty experience as well as new knowledge acquisition. The value of *time* is also relevant. Users may favor a particular telecom because it provides them with novel services or products faster than does its rivals, or even because the telecom responds to their queries and questions more promptly. In the telecoms sector, there are also very powerful *network effects* and *brand values* that can be communicated to customers.

Having discussed different values in the mobile telecommunication sector, the question here is what values should service designers and engineers encapsulate within the new service? Although this issue is complex and we have no straight answer, we suggest that values intended to be delivered to customers should (1) meet the terms of the service objective, (2) comply with the overall strategy and vision of the telecom, (3) be consistent with the target segment nature and behavioral patterns, (4) be able to be delivered efficiently and effectively through the infrastructure, structure, technological architecture, and value system of the telecom, and (5) be positioned successfully both internally, within the existing service portfolio, and externally, within the services offered in the market by other rivals.

**Target-segment.** This concept describes the nature of the targeted segment by a particular telecom service. Segmentation of customers implies clustering them into different groups based on shared common properties and characteristics. Segments might involve customers identified as individuals, groups, or organizations. In choosing their desired customers, telecoms could focus on a niche or a mass market. This might be considered a local, regional, or even international marketplace. Usually when customers are individuals, segmentation is done by utilizing their demographic details including income, patterns and trends, and cultural norms. If customers are enterprises, segmentation is done on the basis of one or more factors: enterprise capital, size, revenue generated from the enterprise, sector, industry, and so on.

The high level of dynamics in today's marketplace makes managing and tracking this information one of the most essential aspects to ensure services are successful in their due course. Segmentation is vital since targeting is about choosing profitable clusters. It helps in responding to changes in demand more promptly and effectively. Segmentation is also fruitful in evaluating existing groups or segments, and deciding which one to ignore, add, or cultivate.

## 4.2  Value-Network

The value-network dimension consists of six main design concepts: actor, role, relationship, flow-communication, channel, and governance (see Figure 5). This dimension represents external arrangements that revolve around the communication and collaboration telecoms conduct with others in their value systems including customers, suppliers, allies, business partners, third parties, and intermediaries.

Designing powerful value systems is critical to the success of telecoms services. In explaining why i-mode services are generating high revenues in Japan, while data services in Europe and the United States are struggling, Takeshi Natsuno, the NTT DoCoMo's managing director for i-mode services, argues that the problem is related to market arrangements and structure (Natsuno 2003). He believes that proper value systems that support the creation and delivery of mobile services are still absent in Europe and the United States.

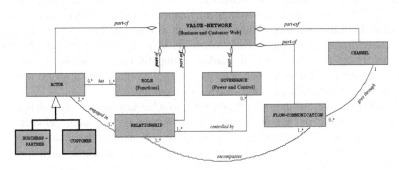

**Fig. 5.** Value-Network Dimension

Having recognized the importance of this dimension, the developed ontology suggests that telecoms need to examine the six main concepts in order to fruitfully design value networks for mobile data services.

**Actor.** This concept is about identifying the core actors with whom the telecom communicates, collaborates, and cooperates in order to launch and deliver a particular service. This not only includes business partners, but also customer actors. Examples of the business actors include engineering equipment vendors, IS/IT application vendors, cellular device manufacturers, content providers, content aggregators, telecoms retailers, and ISPs. As telecommunication regulatory commissions are playing key roles in deriving and shaping the telecoms sector, they are also considered key actors with which telecoms interact. Other actors that might provide complementary services also need to be identified. For example, in the case of provisioning m-commerce services, telecoms establish relationships with actors from the financial sector (e.g., banks) to handle and manage payments.

**Role.** This concept describes the main role(s) of each actor. While the role of different customers could be simply described as service supplicants, they could also play different, significant roles in service development (see Lacucci et al. 2000). The roles played by enterprise actors are much more varied; thus we here place more emphasis on this issue.

This research distinguishes between *functional* and *strategic* roles played by enterprise business actors in the value networks of telecoms. This distinction is based on how telecoms need to recognize the contributions of actors concerning service value creation and the overall success of the telecom. Functional roles are defined from an operational point of view. For example, the functional role of content providers may simply be defined as creating and supplying original content in the form of text, audio, graphics, and video, while the functional role of equipment vendors could be defined as providing cellular infrastructure, devices, applications, and handsets. Understanding roles from this perspective allows a telecom to identify not only its position within the network, but also the position of other actors. Moreover, it helps telecoms in understanding, managing, and controlling its different links with actors.

Other than supplying telecoms with resources, value network actors might also play contributing roles in service provisioning, and mediating roles between the telecom and its target segment in which they provide channels and conduct functions such as distribution, sales, and marketing. They might also perform after-sale functions. Banks may provide a source of finance in terms of loans and credits to establish and run the business. They can also act as payment gateways in which they manage issues related to payments and reconciliations. Regulatory bodies play major roles concerning pricing, entry to market, competition regulations, patents, and intellectual property. The role each actor is playing determines its position within the value system and hence the possible value to be captured.

The strategic roles, on the other hand, refer to what key objectives and benefits a telecom is achieving by having a particular actor within its value network. The combined strategic roles played by all involved actors signify the main motives for telecoms to create and form their own value systems. This research identifies seven main *strategic roles*.

(1) *Resource Allocation*: Principally, telecoms may not have sufficient resources to offer competitive and novel services. Thus, they establish relationships with different economic actors to get access to external resources and link them to their own assets. Sometimes, building relationships with particular actors is not

even a choice but rather a necessity. This is mostly the case when the situation includes factors as rarity of needed resources, patents, and the existence of technological fabrication secrets (Camponovo and Pigneur 2003).

(2) *Efficiency*: Consistent with transaction-cost theory (see Williamson 1985), telecoms may find it more efficient to collaborate with other business actors to acquire needed resources and specialized skills than possessing all resources on its own.

(3) *Risk Mitigation*: Especially when the cost of investment is massive and the success is not quite guaranteed, it is advantageous for telecoms to cooperate with partners to create new services rather than doing so alone. This factor has become one of the major motives, particularly after the current economic downturn.

(4) *Effectiveness*: When designing new services, telecoms may recognize that the service could be launched only by the existing resources and capabilities. If so, however, the new service would lack some important values that are essential to make the service unique and competitive. Telecoms in such cases may find it more effective to add a new actor possessing distinctive resources and capabilities so as to launch competitive, high quality services.

(5) *Time-to-Market*: The telecommunication sector is highly competitive and time-to-market has become one of the main approaches giving telecoms sustainable competitive advantage by being market leaders and pioneers. Many ideas for new services are shared among telecoms where the role of each is not only to find the most appropriate services to launch, but also importantly to launch services before other rivals do, if it is to become a winner. Retrospectively, telecoms may approach new actors if they could aid in shortening time-to-market of services.

(6) *Agility*: In the turbulent, dynamic, and fast growing telecommunications sector, a telecom may find value network formation to be the best way of achieving flexibility and providing faster response to changing needs.

(7) *Intelligence*: Telecoms, through collaboration, cooperation, and joint research and development, can create intelligence in relation to new opportunities and means of creating, delivering, and exchanging advanced value.

However, the expected benefits from participating in such value networks are not achieved easily; as actors pursue different business logic and chase different strategic goals with the collaboration (Bouwman et al. 2008). Therefore, actors need to align their strategic objectives and ensure their consistency so as to capture desired values.

**Relationship.** This concept is about identifying the sorts of links telecoms establish with their value-network actors. The relationships between telecoms and network actors could take the form of strategic alliances, affiliations, strategic partnerships, joint ventures, or any other sourcing type. The importance of the role each actor plays indicates the kind of relationship the telecom needs to build with that actor. For example, a sourcing relationship seems sensible for acquiring middleware and other software systems, while some sort of strategic partnership appears to be more rational when establishing an association with actors like content and Internet service providers as their roles are more substantial in mobile data services.

The kind of relationships telecoms develop and maintain with their customers represents another facet in this concept. Customers are the main sources of revenue;

thus creating positive relationship dynamics (Hamel 2000) with them is vital. This helps create customer intimacy and lock-in.

**Flow-communication.** This concept addresses the material communicated among various actors connected in value networks. Hence, it helps services designers in representing value exchange streams among service economic actors so as to make them more controllable, manageable, and effective.

Relationships with different actors are enriched by materials communicated between them. These materials can take the form of information, knowledge, money, products/ services, hardware, software, documents, agreements, and any other relevant objects. There are two scenarios for materials communication or flow: materials flowing between telecoms and customers, and materials flowing between telecoms and enterprise actors. In the former case, consider this example: Telecoms create intelligence by collecting information about potential customers. Consequently, they provide them with purposeful services. In response, customers allow telecoms along with other network actors to capture value through communicating money and providing other benefits such as feedback information. In the latter case, consider this example: Content flows from content provider to content aggregator. The aggregator cleans, formats, edits, customizes, and combines relevant content and communicates it to telecoms to be used by services. After revenue is generated, each participating actor receives its share from the captured value.

**Channel.** This concept describes the *communication mediums* or *ports* used to communicate materials among actors as a result of their established relationships. Channels could be physical or electronic, and can range from manual to fully automated, where the technological systems talk directly to each other. It is important for telecoms to employ varied channels since communication ports are used with different actors for different functions such as customer relationship management, service delivery, collaboration and communication, distribution and logistics, customer service, and marketing.

Furthermore, arrangements in value networks include constructing interfaces with customers. In addition to physical communication channels including intermediaries, telecoms are exploiting the Internet and other associated technologies such as portals and CRM tools to develop valuable virtual communication mechanisms with their customers. The number, type, customer reach capabilities, and the quality of communication channels telecoms build and maintain with their customers are critical to success.

This design concept is highly related to the former one as service designers and engineers need to select the most appropriate channel at each single flow of materials. For example, information concerning potential customers could be communicated virtually to telecoms using software agents as channels; while to communicate particular mobile services to customers, special handsets maybe used as the communication medium.

**Governance.** This concept examines the powers and controls of each actor within value networks. Governance tells who has which form of control and power over what kind of objects (e.g., data, relationships, channels, functions, and transactions). Typically, actors try to achieve more power and control in order to augment the value captured. Keeping track of this sort of information is important as telecoms could utilize it to identify new opportunities where they can have more power and control, evaluate risks associated with existing configuration of governance, and establish reference points for accountability purposes.

## 4.3 Value-Architecture

The value-architecture dimension adds three new, important concepts when designing new mobile data services: core-resource, value-configuration, and core-competency (see Figure 6). In this context, value-architecture can be defined as a broad plan that specifies all necessary (1) technological architecture arrangements that enable mobile communications to operate efficiently and effectively, and (2) organizational infra-structure arrangements including a telecom structure, key processes and functions, task force, management mindsets, and culture that are needed to enable telecom service provisioning as desired.

The applied analysis in this research reveals that for telecoms to tackle the afore-mentioned aspects appropriately, they need to examine the following design concepts.

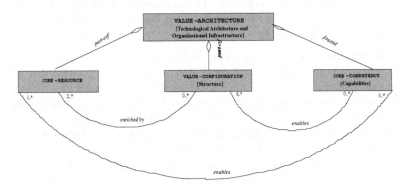

**Fig. 6.** Value-Architecture Dimension

**Core-resource.** This concept is about examining and creating useful information of the needed assets and resources to develop new services. The resource-based view (see Barney 2001; Wernerfelt 1984) is highly relevant in this context. The resource-based view assumes that each firm is a bundle of resources. Specifically, it puts emphasis on the strategic importance of *resources* coupled with their integration and *configuration* to the generation of capabilities or *core competencies* and thus sustainable competitive advantages to the firm.

In mobile services, *core resources* are viewed as cornerstones for value creation. Offering what is valued by telecom customers in the value-proposition dimension requires adequate and appropriate resources in the value-architecture dimension. To be more concise in explaining the aforementioned association we limit the following discussion by considering only cellular infrastructure.

To give just a general overview, the first generation (1G) of cellular technology can only provide voice cellular service. The second generation (2G) is a digital cellular technology that not only enhanced the cellular network capacity in general, but also introduced text messaging (SMS) as the first data service in cellular technology. This shift from a voice-centered to a data-centered cellular telecom industry has been enriched by the introduction of 2.5G cellular technology, which is an "always on" technology that adds valuable data services such as web browsing, location-based services, and audio/video downloading. The delivery of voice and advanced data services coupled with high speed has been introduced in the third generation (3G) of cellular technology. 4G is an IP-based integrated system capable of providing premium speed, quality, and security. Moreover, it is worth mentioning here that the deployed cellular technology not only affects the type and quality of services offered, but also determines the possible pricing methods. For example, GSM (2G) cellular networks support only per-minute and flat-rate charging models (Olla and Patel 2002).

At this stage of design, the main role of service engineers is to identify and classify core resources along with their characteristics. As for classifications, the developed ontology distinguishes human, organizational, informational, physical, financial, legal, and relational (Seppänen and Mäkinen 2007), in addition to technological types of resources. Also at this point of design, it is essential to connect resources with the specific services to which they contribute. This is because the value can be optimized for the customer and the firm by identifying the link between a specific resource and a specific service (Pynnönen 2008).

**Value-configuration.** This concept refers to the ability of telecoms to fruitfully integrate organizational and technological core resources in a way that allows efficient and effective roll-out of successful services. New sources of value are generated through novel deployments of resources (Moran and Ghoshal 1996). To create new or to revamp existing services, it is sometimes sufficient for telecoms to restructure and reorganize their existing resources. In other cases, however, they also need to combine and integrate new sort of resources.

The value-configuration concept is important in mobile service design. This is because unless resources are constantly superior, acquiring and possessing them would not directly allow telecoms to create unique value and gain competitive advantage. It is the manner in which resources are continuously utilized, deployed, and configured within existing structures, culture, and other organizational and technological characteristics that normally gives sustainable competitive advantage. We consider value-configuration as a key enabler of combinative capabilities (Koruna 2004) and core competencies that are important in enabling telecoms to conduct their business more effectively than do their rivals.

Given the dynamic nature of the telecom industry, this design concept has also a significant link with dynamic capabilities (Eisenhardt and Martin 2000). Dynamic capabilities refer to the ability of a firm to transform its resource base to fit the changing nature of the market including customers as well as the industry to which the firm belongs. This transformation ability is based on learning processes (Teece et al. 1997) on how and when firms should create, integrate, (re)combine, (re)configure, and release resources.

However, telecoms at this stage of design need to identify and examine the key processes by which a number of resources are linked and configured in a way that allows core competencies to emerge. This indicates that links need to be established between resources and key processes, then with core competencies, before being finally linked to new services along with their values. Equally important is the link between core business processes and the customer journey. This is essential as customers go through many phases throughout their life span that call for different supplies. Thus, telecoms must ensure the existence of effective processes guiding, supporting and leveraging each of these phases. Any misalignment here would cause huge losses to telecoms.

**Core-competency.** This concept holds information about the range of core competencies or capabilities a particular telecom possesses. Core competencies (see Prahalad and Hamel 1990) could be identified by examining what the telecom can do more efficiently and effectively than its competitors. Core competencies can also be viewed as repeatable patterns of action in the use of assets and the deployment of acquired resources to create and offer services to target segments (Osterwalder and Pigneur 2002).

Three core competency approaches (after Ballon 2007; Treacy and Wiersema 1993) have been identified to reach optimal customer value.

(1) *Operational Excellence*: The efficiency of telecoms in conducting their internal and interorganizational processes and operations. This efficiency allows cost savings which if translated into competitive prices can attract more customers.

(2) *Service Leadership*: The effectiveness that refers to the differentiation in the services offered by telecoms. It is the innovative ways in which new services are configured and packaged that give premium quality. This quality could be due to organizational infrastructure, technological architecture, or a combination of the two. Often, innovative services are the result of extensive research and development efforts, which play a key role in determining the nature of values offered to customers. This may lead to offering unique services that are difficult to imitate by rivals. Technological competency in particular may provide substantial enhancements to QoS such as reliability, availability, and performance in general.

(3) *Customer Intimacy*: The customer experience builds customers intimacy, or not. When telecoms cannot afford any of the prior strategies, customer experience becomes the main and sole competitive weapon. Telecoms need to address customer relationship management to provide customer intimacy and ensure their loyalty and retention.

When core competencies are created through the aforementioned approaches, telecoms need to guarantee the consistency between the approach undertaken and the overall strategy. By referring to Porter's (1980) classification of strategies, we argue that operational excellence fits well those operators following *cost-leadership* strategy, while product leadership fits well telecoms having *differentiation* as their principal strategy. Customer intimacy is the preferred approach for both strategy since it is very important to retain customers.

At this point of design, services designers should identify the core competencies along with their complexity levels. Thereafter, fundamental links should be established between the core competencies of the telecom and the intended value elements to be communicated to customers through the offered services.

## 4.4 Value-Finance

The value-finance dimension is composed of three main design concepts: total-cost-of-ownership, pricing-method, and revenue-structure (see Figure 7). Value-finance is a description of the core arrangements needed to ensure the economic viability of the offering which includes costing and pricing methods. It also describes the way in which a telecom seeks to generate revenue from its offerings (Timmers 1998), and how this revenue is shared among different stakeholders.

**Total-cost-of-ownership.** This concept is fundamental as it deals with financial information about the overall costs with respect to all core arrangements that are needed to create, provide, market, deliver, and maintain mobile services throughout their life spans. Total-cost-of-ownership not only includes the cost of tangible materials, but also covers the cost of development, support, and maintenance, as well as the cost of collaboration between telecoms and other value network players. Therefore, this concept represents the entire cost of any telecom service including both the fixed and the variable costs. The weight of this design concept refers to its significance in service pricing.

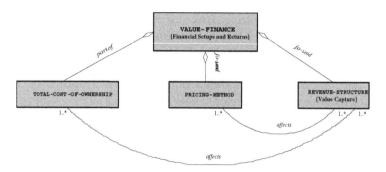

**Fig. 7.** Value-Finance Dimension

**Pricing-method.** This concept holds information about the prices of different telecom services along with the employed pricing mechanisms and billing methods. Pricing methods in the telecoms sector can be generally classified as fixed, dynamic, or a mixture of both. Fixed pricing-method implies that customers pay from time to time a certain amount of money to get a predetermined use of certain services and facilities. Typically, fixed pricing is applied in the form of contracts and packaged services. On the other hand, dynamic pricing implies that the price of a certain service differs across usage levels. This research distinguishes *time-based*, *transaction-based*, and *volume-based* as three subcategories of dynamic pricing methods. For example, surfing the Internet using your handset and being charged on the basis of the number of minutes is an example of the time-based pricing method, while charges based on the number of downloads is an example of the transaction-based method. If the charges are on the basis of the size of downloaded files, then it is the volume-based pricing method.

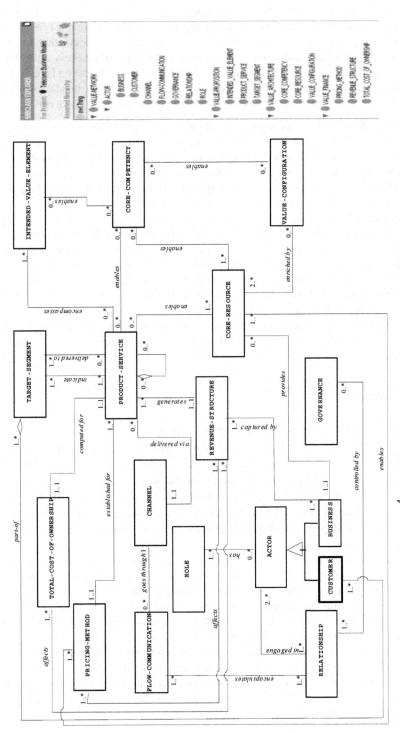

**Fig. 8.** The V$^4$ Service Business Model Ontology:  UML and OWL Representation

The role of service designers here is not only to set up fitting prices for the new services, but also to choose an appropriate pricing method. This is complex, as many factors affect the pricing of any mobile data service. Nonetheless, we argue that aspects related to the new service objective, total-cost-of-ownership, uniqueness and other features, category, perceived value by customers, affordability, competition level in the market, and whether the service is offered individually or within a bundle of other services are extremely important in guiding the design in this particular concept.

**Revenue-structure.** This concept contains information concerning generated revenue. It portrays the profitability of different service classes across customer segments. The concept of revenue-structure also shows how the generated revenue is broken down among different economic participating actors. The distributions of costs, risks, and revenues should be made explicit and the way in which revenue is divided among the economic actors should reflect the division of costs and risks.

The volume of the generated revenue is important to telecoms. It ensures the financial sustainability and competitiveness of the telecom. Furthermore, it encourages further investments and leaves greater room for research and development. The revenue generated through a service over a period of time gives an indication of the telecom's ability to translate the value underpinned by technological innovations to financial and economic values. In other words, it indicates the level of the service business model appropriateness at that point in time.

After examining the developed ontology, we now sum up our discussion by providing a cohesive representation of the design concepts and their interdependencies in Figure 8.

## 5   Conclusions

This paper examines mobile service design and engineering from an inclusive view: utilizing the business model concept as a method to structure related critical functions. In a rigorous and semantically rich approach, the $V^4$ ontology has been developed to unambiguously define dimensions, elements, properties, and semantics of service business models. The contribution comes from the novel integration of relevant research topics that provides a harmonized ontology extending current research and taking an important step toward systemizing and leveraging mobile service design and engineering functions.

This research spells out the business model concept as a coherent framework for mobile service design as it provides a holistic view of a particular business, which is not only useful in understanding the internal structure and functions, but also in realizing how telecoms are connected to their external environment and how they interact with it. This research demonstrates that designing new mobile data services requires the examination of their value proposition issues and looking closely at the service definition as well as matching the patterns and trends of the target segments with the value elements of the services. To engineer successful mobile services, it is also vital to have a strong technological architecture capable of providing high quality of service standards, as well as a suitable organizational infrastructure, including appropriate managerial mindsets.

Delineating the communication and collaboration issues telecoms have with various actors is also crucial, because the structure of the telecom industry is shifting from an autocratic state to a more democratic one, where a more complex and open system, including extensive collaboration, communication, and cooperation are prevalent. The consideration of the service financial aspects including total cost of ownership, pricing methods, and revenue models is also clearly fundamental. In addition, and in view of the fact that different aspects of service engineering are interrelated, this research reveals that it is also important to look at these aspects cohesively and to consider their interdependencies.

The developed ontology contributes to both theory and practice and provides a complete foundational framework for mobile service design and engineering. It is of value to academics and practitioners alike, particularly those interested in the strategic-oriented IS/IT and business developments of telecoms. The developed ontology not only provides a common language and terminology amongst information systems and software agents to enhance their interoperability, but also amongst people. Furthermore, the $V^4$ ontology enables capturing and reusing of application-independent knowledge and semantics (i.e., knowledge reuse rather than software reuse). From a practical perspective, this comprehensive ontology enhances the ability of telecoms to design, create, communicate, compare, analyze, evaluate, and modify their existing and future mobile data services, using a systematic and effective approach.

While this ontology has been developed specifically for mobile data services, we argue that it would be equally appropriate to the design and engineering of other technological artifacts (e.g., eServices, broadband services, telecom services and products, etc.). Indeed, the $V^4$ service business model ontology has been the preferred method of one Latin American company to design and develop not only a mobile business application, but also an eApplication for business. Due to the restrictions of space, this paper does not provide all of the details of the data collected and analyzed; it only highlights the major results and we have concentrated on defining and discussing the $V^4$ business model ontology for service design and engineering as being the main contribution.

# References

Afuah, A., Tucci, C.: Internet Business Models and Strategies, 2nd edn. McGraw-Hill, New York (2003)

Al-Debei, M.M., Avison, D.: Business Model Requirements and Challenges in the Mobile Telecommunication Sector. Journal of Organizational Transformation and Social Change (forthcoming, 2010)

Al-Debei, M.M., El-Haddadeh, R., Avison, D.: Defining the Business Model in the New World of Digital Business. In: Proceedings of the 14th Americas Conference on Information Systems, AMCIS 2008, Toronto, Canada, August 14-17 (2008a)

Al-Debei, M.M., El-Haddadeh, R., Avison, D.: Towards a Business Model for Cellular Networks and Telecommunication Operators: A Theoretical Framework. In: Proceedings of the 13th Conference of the UK Academy for Information Systems, Bournemouth, UK (2008b)

Al-Debei, M.M., Fitzgerald, G.: OntoEng: A Design Method for Ontology Engineering in Information Systems. In: ACM OOPSLA'0 – Ontology-Engineering Software Engineering Workshop, Orlando, Florida, October 25-29 (2009)

Amanatiadis, A., Drakatos, K., Tsironis, L., Moustakis, V.: Defining the Main Factors of Quality of Service in Mobile Telephony. In: Proceedings of Second International Conference on Wireless and Mobile Communications, Bucharest, Romania, July 29-31 (2006)

Andersson, B., Bergholtz, M., Edirisuriya, A., Ilayperuma, I., Johannesson, P., Grégoire, B., Schmitt, M., Dubois, E., Abels, S., Hahn, A., Gordijn, J., Weigand, H., Wangler, B.: Towards a Reference Ontology for Business Models. In: Proceedings of the 25th International Conference on Conceptual Modeling, Tucson, Arizona, November 6-9 (2006)

Ballon, P.: Business Modeling Revisited: The Configuration of Control and Value. Info–The Journal of Policy, Regulation and Strategy for Telecommunications 9(5), 6–19 (2007)

Barney, J.B.: Resource-Based Theories of Competitive Advantage: A Ten-Year Retrospective on the Resource-Based View. Journal of Management 27(6), 643–650 (2001)

Bouwman, H., De Vos, H., Haaker, T.: Mobile Service Innovation and Business Models. Springer, Berlin (2008)

Bullinger, H.J., Fahnrich, K.P., Meiren, T.: Service Engineering—Methodical Development of Service Products. International Journal of Production Economics 85(3), 275–287 (2003)

Campanovo, G., Pigneur, Y.: Business Model Analysis Applied to Mobile Business. In: Proceedings of the Fifth International Conference on Enterprise Information Systems, Angers, France, April 23-26 (2003)

Chae, M., Kim, J.: Information Quality for Mobile Internet Services: A Theoretical Model with Empirical Validation. In: Storey, V.C., Sarkar, S., DeGross, J.I. (eds.) Proceedings of 22nd International Conference on Information Systems, New Orleans, LA, December 16-19, pp. 43–53 (2001)

Chandrasekaran, B., Josephson, J.R., Benjamins, V.R.: What Are Ontologies, and Why Do We Need Them? IEEE Intelligent Systems and Their Applications 14(1), 20–26 (1999)

Chesbrough, H.W., Rosenbloom, R.S.: The Role of The Business Model in Capturing Value from Innovation: Evidence from Xerox Corporation's Technology Spin-Off Companies. Industrial and Corporate Change 11(3), 529–555 (2002)

Dodourova, M.: Industry Dynamics and Strategic Positioning in the Wireless Telecommunications Industry: The Case of Vodafone Group Plc. Management Decision 41(9), 859–870 (2003)

Eisenhardt, K.M., Martin, J.A.: Dynamic Capabilities: What Are They? Strategic Management Journal 21(10-11), 1105–1121 (2000)

Eriksson, H.E., Penker, M.: Business Modeling with UML. John Wiley, New York (2000)

Gordijn, J., Akkermanns, J.M.: Designing and Evaluating eBusiness Models. IEEE Intelligent Systems 16(4), 11–17 (2001)

Gruber, T.R.: A Translation Approach to Potable Ontology Specification. Knowledge Acquisition 5(2), 199–220 (1993)

Guarino, N.: Formal Ontology in Information Systems. IOS Press, Amsterdam (1998)

Guarino, N., Welty, C.: Evaluating Ontological Decisions with OntoClean. Communications of the ACM 45(2), 61–65 (2002)

Guizzardi, G., Wanger, G., Guarino, N., Van Sinderen, M.: An Ontologically Well-Founded Profile for UML Conceptual Models. In: Persson, A., Stirna, J. (eds.) CAiSE 2004. LNCS, vol. 3084, pp. 112–126. Springer, Heidelberg (2004)

Hamel, G.: Leading the Revolution. Harvard Business School Press, Boston (2000)

Hedman, J., Kalling, T.: The Business Model Concept: Theoretical Underpinnings and Empirical Illustrations. European Journal of Information Systems 12(1), 49–59 (2003)

Hevner, A.R., March, S.T., Park, J., Ram, S.: Design Science in Information Systems Research. MIS Quarterly 28(1), 75–105 (2004)

ITU. Measuring the Information Society, International Telecommunications Union (2009), http://www.itu.int/ITU-D/ict/publications/idi/2009/index.html (accessed June 20, 2009)

Jarrar, M., Demey, J., Meersman, R.: On Using Conceptual Data Modeling for Ontology Engineering. In: Spaccapietra, S., March, S., Aberer, K. (eds.) Journal on Data Semantics I. LNCS, vol. 2800, pp. 185–207. Springer, Heidelberg (2003)

Kamoun, F.: Rethinking the Business Model with RFID. Communications of the AIS 22(1), 635–658 (2008)

Kim, Y., Lee, Y., Kong, G., Yun, H., Chang, S.: A New Framework for Designing Business Models in Digital Ecosystem. In: Proceedings of Second IEEE International Conference on Digital Ecosystems and Technologies, Phitsanulok, Thailand, February 26-29, pp. 281–287 (2008)

Kishore, R., Sharman, R.: Computational Ontologies and Information Systems I: Foundations. Communications of the Association for Information Systems 14(8), 158–183 (2004)

Koruna, S.: Leveraging Knowledge Assets: Combinative Capabilities – Theory and Practice. R&D Management 34(5), 505–516 (2004)

Kumar, V., Parimi, S., Agarwal, D.P.: WAP: Present and Future. IEEE Pervasive Computing 2(1), 79–83 (2003)

Lacucci, G., Kuutti, K., Ranta, M.: On the Move with a Magic Thing: Role Playing in Concept Design of Mobile Services and Devices. In: Boyarski, D., Kellogg, W.A. (eds.) Proceedings of Third Conference on Designing Interactive Systems: Processes, Practices, Methods, and Techniques, New York, August 17-19, pp. 193–202 (2000)

Linder, J., Cantrell, S.: Changing Business Models: Surveying the Landscape. Working Paper, Accenture Institute for Strategic Change, Cambridge, MA (2000)

MacInnes, I.: Dynamic Business Model Framework for Emerging Technologies. International Journal of Service Technology and Management 6(1), 3–19 (2005)

Magretta, J.: Why Business Models Matter. Harvard Business Review 80(5), 86–92 (2002)

Maitland, C.F., Van De Kar, E.A.M., De Montalvo, U.W., Bouwman, H.: Mobile Information and Entertainment Services: Business Models and Service Networks. International Journal of Management and Decision Making 6(1), 47–64 (2005)

March, S.T., Smith, G.F.: Design and Natural Science Research on Information Technology. Decision Support Systems 15(4), 251–266 (1995)

Mingers, J.: Combining IS Research Methods: Towards a Pluralist Methodology. Information Systems Research 12(3), 240–259 (2001)

Moran, P., Ghoshal, S.: Value Creation by Firms. In: Academy of Management Best Paper Proceedings, pp. 41–45 (1996)

Natsuno, T.: The i-Mode Wireless Ecosystem. Wiley, Yokohama (2003)

Olla, P., Patel, N.V.: A Value Chain Model for Mobile Data Service Providers. Telecommunications Policy 26(9-10), 551–571 (2002)

Orlikowski, W.J.: CASE Tools as Organizational Change: Investigating Incremental and Radical Changes in Systems Development. MIS Quarterly 17(3), 309–340 (1993)

Osterwalder, A., Pigneur, Y.: An e-Business Model Ontology for Modeling e-Business. In: Proceedings of the 15th Bled Electronic Commerce Conference, Bled, Slovenia, June 17-19 (2002)

Osterwalder, A., Pigneur, Y., Tucci, C.L.: Clarifying Business Models: Origins, Present, and Future of the Concept. Communications of the AIS 15, 2–40 (2005)

Palvia, P., Midha, V., Pinjani, P.: Research Models in Information Systems. Communications of the AIS 17(1), 1042–1063 (2006)

Pinto, H.S., Martins, J.P.: Ontologies: How Can They Be Built? Knowledge and Information Systems 6(4), 441–464 (2004)

Porter, M.E.: Competitive Strategy. The Free Press, New York (1980)

Prahalad, C.K., Hamel, G.: The Core Competence of the Corporation. Harvard Business Review 68(3), 79–91 (1990)

Pura, M.: Linking Perceived Value and Loyalty in Location-Based Mobile Services. Managing Service Quality 15(6), 509–538 (2005)

Pynnönen, M.: Customer Lock-In in ICT Services Business: Designing and Managing Customer Driven Business Model. In: Proceedings of International Conference on Management of Engineering & Technology, Porland, Oregon, July 27-31, pp. 818–828 (2008)

Ratliff, J.M.: NTT DoCoMo and its i-Mode Success. California Management Review 44(3), 55–71 (2002)

Seddon, P.B., Lewis, G., Freeman, P., Shanks, G.: Business Models and Their Relationship to Strategy. In: Currie, E. (ed.) Value Creation from e-Business Models, pp. 11–34. Butterworth-Heinemann, Oxford (2004)

Seppänen, M., Mäkinen, S.: Assessing Business Model Concepts with Taxonomical Research Criteria. Management Research News 30(10), 735–748 (2007)

Sheth, J., Newman, B., Gross, B.: Consumption Values and Market Choices: Theory and Applications. South-Western Publishing Co., Cincinnati (1991)

Sigurdson, J.: WAP OFF: Origin, Failure, and Future, Working Paper No. 135, Stockholm School of Economics, Stockholm, Sweden (2001)

Slater, S.F., Narver, J.C.: Intelligence Generation and Superior Customer Value. Journal of the Academy of Marketing Science 28(1), 120–127 (2000)

Smith, B.: Ontology. In: Floridi, L. (ed.) The Blackwell Guide to the Philosophy of Computing and Information, pp. 155–166. Blackwell, Malden (2003)

Teece, D.J., Pisano, G., Shuen, A.: Dynamic Capabilities and Strategic Management. Strategic Management Journal 18(7), 509–533 (1997)

Timmers, P.: Business Models for Electronic Markets. Electronic Markets 8(2), 3–8 (1998)

Treacy, M., Wiersema, F.: Customer Intimacy and Other Value Disciplines. Harvard Business Review 71(1), 84–93 (1993)

Wand, Y., Weber, R.: An Ontological Model of an Information System. IEEE Transactions on Software Engineering 16(11), 1282–1292 (1990)

Wand, Y., Weber, R.: Research Commentary: Information Systems and Conceptual Modeling—A Research Agenda. Information Systems Research 13(4), 363–376 (2002)

Wernerfelt, B.: A Resource-Based View of the Firm. Strategic Management Journal 5(2), 171–180 (1984)

Williamson, O.E.: The Economic Institutions of Capitalism. Free Press, New York (1985)

Wyssusek, B.: Ontology and Ontologies in Information Systems Analysis and Design: A Critique. In: Proceedings of the 10th Americas Conference on Information Systems, New York, August 6-8, pp. 4303–4308 (2004)

Yuan, Y., Zhang, J.J.: Towards an Appropriate Business Model for m-Commerce. International Journal of Mobile Communications 1(1-2), 35–56 (2003)

## About the Authors

**Mutaz M. Al-Debei** is a Ph.D. student and teaching assistant at Brunel University's School of Information Systems and Computing. His research interests include the design and engineering of mobile (cellular) services and other technological artifacts from business model and design science perspectives. Al-Debei holds a B.Sc. in Computer Engineering and an MBA with an IS concentration. He also has more than 10 years of IT industry experience, having worked in Jordan for the Royal Scientific Society, Jordan National Bank, MasterCard, and Arab Radio and Television, as well as lecturing at the University of Jordan and Al-Ahliyya University. He is a trainer for a number of professional certificates such as OCP for Oracle Developers and DBAs, MCSE, Security+, Network+, CCNA, and Credit Card Frauds. He can be reached at Mutaz.Al-Debei@brunel.ac.uk.

**Guy Fitzgerald** is Professor of Information Systems in the Department of Information Systems and Computing (DISC) at Brunel University. Before this he was the Cable & Wireless Professor of Business Information Systems at Birkbeck College, University of London, and prior to that he was at Templeton College, Oxford. He has also worked in the computer industry with companies such as British Telecom, Mitsubishi, and CACI Inc, International. His research interests are concerned with the effective management and development of information systems and he has published widely in these areas. He has undertaken a number of cases studies in organizations that have used information systems to enable significant organizational transformation. He has also undertaken research in relation to strategy, executive information systems, outsourcing, and flexibility. He is founder and coeditor, with David Avison, of the *Information Systems Journal* from Blackwell/Wiley, is author of a well known text book on information systems development methodologies, and is currently the elected Vice-President of Publications for the Association for Information Systems. He can be reached at Guy.Fitzgerald@brunel.ac.uk.

# The Role of Social Networks in Early Adoption of Mobile Devices

Heidi Tscherning[1] and Lars Mathiassen[2]

[1] Center for Applied ICT,
Copenhagen Business School,
DK-2000 Frederiksberg, Denmark
[2] Center for Process Innovation,
J. Mack Robinson College of Business,
Georgia State University,
Atlanta, Georgia, U.S.A.

**Abstract.** As mobile devices have become the personal information-processing interface of choice, many individuals seem to swiftly follow fashion. Yet, the literature is silent on how early adopters of mobile devices overcome uncertainties related to shifts in technology. Based on purposive sampling, this paper presents detailed insights into why and how five closely related individuals made the decision to adopt the iPhone before it was available through traditional supply chains. Focusing on the role played by social networks, we analyze how adoption threshold, opinion leaders, social contagion, and social learning shaped adoption behaviors and outcomes. The analyses confirm that network structures impact the early decision to accept the iPhone; they show that when facing uncertainty, adoption decisions emerged as a combined result of individual adoption reflections and major influences from the social network as well as behaviors observed within the network, and, they reveal interesting behaviors that differed from expectations. In conclusion, we discuss implications for both theory and practice.

**Keywords:** Adoption, social networks, adopter characteristics, qualitative research.

## 1 Introduction

Advanced mobile devices, such as smart phones and personal digital assistants, have become ubiquitously available and have changed the ways people organize relationships (Haddon 1997). Mobile users carry their device everywhere, they use it around the clock, and it has become their personal information-processing interface of choice. The symbolic value of these devices has increased, and many mobile users therefore swiftly follow fashion and change brand, as new devices and features become available. As a recent example, when Apple introduced the iPhone to the U.S. market in July 2007, 270,000 devices were sold in the first 30 hours of the launch

J. Pries-Heje et al. (Eds.): IS Design Science Research, IFIP AICT 318, pp. 52–70, 2010.

weekend[1] and 8 million in total in the United States in the year 2007 (Brightman 2008). The original iPhone was subsequently made available in five other countries: the United Kingdom, Germany, and France in November 2007, and Ireland and Austria in March 2008. Early use of the iPhone was, however, not limited to these countries. Countless users around the world acquired an iPhone from the six official markets, and started to use it in their home countries. To do so, they needed to unlock the phone from the SIM-card and adapt it to network providers other than Apple's exclusive U.S. partner, AT&T. During this period, one million iPhones, equivalent to 27 percent of the 2007 U.S. sales, were adapted to other networks.[2]

While shifts in technology occur regularly, change of technology brand bears several switching costs, including initial fixed costs, uncertainty about quality of device, as well as time spent on learning how to use the new technology (Hall and Kahn 2003). For early adopters, these costs are even higher as they have no references to imitate or expert users to consult. Nevertheless, the literature is silent on why and how individuals overcome these uncertainties as they decide to adopt a new voluntary technology such as a mobile device. Early adopters have imperfect information about the benefits of a new technology and their behavior, therefore, largely depends on acquired human capital, relevant information (Wozniak 1987), and in some cases also on access to unique technical skills (Hall and Kahn 2003).

Against this backdrop, this study investigates why and how five closely related individuals made the decision to adopt the iPhone before it was made available through traditional supply chains. Contextual factors, such as one's social environment, generally have significant impact on technology adoption and usage behaviors (Lewis et al. 2003; Magni et al. 2008). The role of social networks has also been used more broadly to understand social behavior (Van den Bulte and Lilien 2001; Vidgen et al. 2004) and information systems practices (Cambell and Russo 2003). Following these insights, our assumption is that a social network perspective will help us understand the context in which the five individuals managed to adopt the iPhone despite the many uncertainties they faced.

## 2 Adoption of Mobile Devices

Our research draws upon the specific literature on adoption of mobile devices as well as the general literature on individual adoption of communication technologies within information systems research. Adoption is the result of a decision-making process where an individual, group, or organization engages in activities that lead to a decision to use an innovation (Rogers 2003). Today's advanced devices combine communication and computing into a multipurpose gadget that provides users with various types of services (Bergman 2000). They furthermore have a one-to-one binding with the user, offer ubiquitous access, and provide a set of utilitarian and

---

[1]   Press Release, "iPhone Premieres This Friday Night at Apple Retail Stores," June 28, 2007, Apple, Inc. (http://www.apple.com/pr/library/2007/06/28iphone.html).

[2]   "Quarter of US iPhones 'Unlocked'," BBC News, January 29, 2008 (http://news.bbc.co.uk/1/hi/ business/7214873.stm).

hedonic functions (Hong and Tam 2006). With this definition, we consider mobile services and applications as part of advanced mobile devices.

Since the early 1990s, research on mobile devices has gained increased attention as these devices were expected to "revolutionize many aspects of everyday life in the Western world" (Green et al. 2001, pp. 146). Adoption research has typically been centered on studies of either the artifact being adopted or the user setting. While adoption research in general has been criticized for a lack of attention to the attributes of the adopted devices and services (Orlikowski and Iacono 2001), few studies have considered the mobile artifact as an object of expression (Chuang et al. 2001) or as the related device design issues (Lee and Benbazat 2003; Tarasewitch 2003).

Historically, the majority of mobile users acquired their device through work, although this did not prevent private and leisure usage (Fisher 1994). Early studies have, therefore, in general studied mobile adoption in organizations, for example changes in organizational structure (Meehan 1998) and effects on the divide between work and leisure (Nippert-Eng 1996). Later work has also studied the blurring of work- and leisure-related functions of the mobile device (Palen et al. 2001) and the possibilities of business-to-business e-commerce (Wang and Cheung 2004). More recently, the focus has increasingly shifted toward individual adoption, as the mobile device has become the personal information-processing interface of choice. Studies are now concerned with the commercial possibilities: how mobile commerce exposure influences adoption (Khalifa and Cheng 2002); how users create value when adopting mobile banking services (Laukkanen and Lauronen 2005); which factors induce users to accept mobile devices to communicate promotional content (Bauer et al. 2005).

Pedersen and Ling (2002) suggest that adoption research in general "seeks explanations of why a particular adoption behavior may be observed at the individual level" (p. 9). They found rationalistic or utilitarian explanations, explanations based on social influence, and explanations focused on personal characteristics. Utilitarian studies use constructs such as usefulness and ease of use to measure individuals' willingness to adopt, exemplified by Carlsson et al.'s (2000) application of the UTAUT (unified theory of acceptance and use of technology) model to explain acceptance of mobile devices and services. Social influence explanations add elements of how social mechanisms influence individuals' adoption of a particular mobile device or service. One illustration is Lu et al.'s (2005) investigation of the relationships between personal innovativeness and social influences on one side and intention to adopt wireless Internet services via mobile technology on the other. Lu et al. also developed and validated measures for personal innovativeness, which is perceived as being a personal trait of adopters (Agarwal and Prasad 1999). There have also been efforts to describe different categories of adopters. Pedersen (2005) studied the adoption of mobile commerce of early adopters by extending the theory of planned behavior (TPB) with the technology acceptance model (TAM) constructs to explain early adoption of mobile commerce. Finally, Constantiou et al. (2007) developed a grouping that divides mobile users into distinct consecutive categories: talkers, writers, photographers, and surfers.

However, recent studies (Lyytinen and Yoo 2002; Sarker and Wells 2003) have called for research to further examine factors that explain the adoption of mobile devices. Against this backdrop, we are not aware of research that focuses on how early adopters of mobile devices leverage their social networks to overcome uncertainties related to shifts in technology. This gap in the literature limits our understanding of how early adoption decisions are shaped by an individual's peers and network.

# 3 Social Network Influence

A social network is a structure of individuals or organizations that are connected by some type of interdependency (Wasserman and Faust 1994). The relationship between the actors in the network depends on the context, as well as the research question being studied. Social influence is more meticulously defined as the "change in an individual's thoughts, feelings, attitudes, or behaviors that results from interaction with another individual or a group" (Rashotte 2007, p. 562). Earlier definitions included norms and roles (French and Raven 1959); however, the current notion is that individuals make genuine changes to their feelings and behaviors as a result of interaction with others, who are perceived to be similar, desirable, or experts (Rashotte 2007).

Many studies use the social network analysis technique to investigate complex sets of relationships between members ranging from interpersonal, to interorganizational, to international. Barnes (1954) was one of the first to use the term systematically when he discovered that although a community shared cultural values, most individuals made decisions with reference to personal contacts. Social network analysis has since been developed (Burt and Minor 1983; Friedkin 1980; Krackhardt 1987, 1990; Wasserman and Faust 1994) to include technological networks and derived effects; e.g. the long tail (Anderson 2006, Oestreicher-Singer and Sundararajan 2008) and user-generated content in online social networks (Oh et al. 2006). Another stream of research investigates central constructs in analysis of social network structure and interdependency between actors. These constructs describe partly overlapping forms of social network influence and they represent increasing levels of sophistication from quantitative-oriented measures toward comprehensive frameworks for understanding.

Thresholds are the proportion of adopters in a social system needed for an individual to adopt an innovation (Granovetter 1978). The threshold model (Valente 1996) follows Rogers' division of adopters and demonstrates that very low threshold individuals have thresholds two standard deviations lower than the average threshold for the network or community, and very high threshold individuals have thresholds two standard deviations higher than the average. Adoption thresholds can, therefore, be viewed as a characteristic of adopters.

Opinion leaders (Burt 1999; Oh et al. 2006; Valente and Davis 1999; Watts and Dodds 2007) are another construct when discussing social network influence. The definition of opinion leaders is more precisely "opinion brokers who carry information across the social boundaries between groups" (Burt 1999, p. 37). They are located at the edge of networks and act as brokers between groups and may induce two mechanisms: contagion by cohesion as opinion leaders diffuse information across groups, and contagion by equivalence as opinion leaders stimulate adoption within a group.

Social contagion refers to an actor's decision to adopt an innovation depending on other actors' attitudes, knowledge, or behaviors concerning an innovation. Van den Bulte and Lilien (2001) identify a number of theoretical accounts of social contagion, from the literature, that describe different causal mechanisms of social contagion. These are information transfer (Katz and Lazarzfeld 1955), which may occur from both traditional and electronic media, normative pressures (Coleman et al. 1966), which occurs when an adopter feels discomfort, when peers, whose approval they value, have adopted an innovation but they have not. Also competitive concerns (Burt 1995), which can be viewed as opposed to normative pressures, and performance network effects (Katz and Shapiro 1986), which refers to the benefits of use that increase with the number of prior adopters of the innovation, are part of the social contagion construct.

Social learning is a related factor that affects an individual's choices when faced with substantial uncertainty in sampling of new innovations. It occurs through the observation of the individual's neighbors' choices (Tarde et al. 2008). A common explanation for such changes in behavior is that innovations create uncertainty about expected consequences, and to overcome uncertainty, individuals tend to interact with their social network to consult on others' adoption decisions through informational and normative social influences (Burkhardt and Brass 1990; Katz 1980; Katz and Tushman 1979). While learning occurs as a conscious process of interactions between related individuals, contagion may be the mere result of brief encounters with individuals who share information about the iPhone. Oh et al. (2006) built on Ellison and Fudenberg's (1993) prior research and found evidence for a number of mechanisms by which social influence is transmitted, such as preference for conformity and social learning.

Exploring how five closely related individuals made the decision to adopt the iPhone before it was made available through traditional supply chains, our focus is on understanding how early adopters of mobile devices overcome uncertainties related to shifts in technology. Hence, drawing on the adoption threshold, opinion leaders, social contagion, and social learning constructs our research question is

*How and why does the social network of early adopters of the iPhone impact their decision to adopt?*

## 4   Research Method

We chose the case study method to investigate the research question for a number of reasons: the case study method is preferred when *how* or *why* questions are being posed, when the extent of control of the investigator is little, when the focus is on a contemporary phenomenon and not historical events (Yin 2008), and when the focus is on understanding the dynamics within a single setting (Eisenhardt 1989). We conducted an exploratory study, as opposed to a descriptive or experimental study (Yin 2008), with the goal of investigating and reflecting upon how and why five closely related individuals made the decision to adopt an iPhone before it was made available through traditional supply chains.

Inspired by Eisenhardt's (1989) process of building theory from case study research, we adopted a similar conceptual framing throughout our investigation, although our goal was not theory building in particular, but rather exploration and presentation of empirical insights. We first identified the research question and adopted four social network concepts as *a priori* framing constructs. We then selected specific early adopters of the iPhone as our case material to help answer the research question. After generating an interview guide, based on the identified theoretical constructs, and while collecting data, we initiated the analysis phase. In this phase, we analyzed and reflected upon the data to present new insights. As Eisenhardt emphasizes, this was a highly iterative process.

## 4.1  The Research Context

The case focuses on five individual mobile users who adopted the iPhone prior to its official release in Denmark. Denmark is among the leading countries in the use of mobile devices and communication services (Economist Intelligence Unit 2008) and is, therefore, an appropriate venue for studying adoption of the iPhone at this specific time. The way in which early adopters surmount the uncertainties related to adoption of new mobile devices is particular interesting since they experience high switching costs because of lack of references to imitate or expert users to consult. Purposive sampling provided direct access to rich data about these individuals, their mutual relationships, and their interactions with other people and information sources. Purposive sampling techniques are primarily used in qualitative studies, when the aim is to select individuals based on a specific purpose associated with answering the research question (Teddlie and Yu 2007) and extending emergent theory (Eisenhardt 1989). The aim was to gain access to a group of closely related individuals to determine how their mutual relationship as well as their wider social network influenced their decision to adopt the iPhone at this time and why.

People with similar characteristics, tastes, and beliefs may associate in the same social networks (Manski 2000) and our sampling criteria were, therefore, that the group of individuals should be homogenous with similar characteristics and interests, and they should be part of the same social network. Homogenous sampling was chosen, as the aim is to understand and describe the decision to adopt an iPhone in a particular group of early adopters. The participants were, therefore, similar with respect to several variables, such as demographics and experience with mobile phones. To recruit the five individuals, one author had access to one individual who then contacted other individuals in his network who had adopted the iPhone. Our investigation is hence based on multilevel analysis. We observed and analyzed the behavior of the five individuals as a group while at the same time focusing on each individual, his social network, and decision making.

## 4.2  Data Collection and Analysis

The study employed qualitative methods to understand the affluent nature of mobile users' thought processes when overcoming uncertainties and adopting a new mobile device. The data collection took place from April 2008 to July 2008. It involved techniques such as semi-structured interviews, archival records, and data collected from a specific discussion forum on the Internet. The triangulation of data collection methods provides stronger support in the exploration of the research question

(Eisenhardt 1989). The semi-structured interviews lasted from 60 to 80 minutes. The interview guide consisted of five main parts: demographics, the user's mobile device history, the user's iPhone history, the closed social network consisting of the five individuals, as well as each individual's extended network, and finally the adoption decision. Table 1 shows a description of the five main themes upon which the interview guide was based.

**Table 1.** The Interview Guide

| Theme | Description |
|---|---|
| *Demographics* | Demographic data |
| *Mobile device history* | Experience with mobile devices<br>Purpose of the device<br>Experience with related products |
| *iPhone history* | Experience with the iPhone prior to adoption and after adoption<br>Thoughts on future technological acquisitions |
| *Social network* | The network of the five individuals<br>The extended network of each individual |
| *Adoption decision* | Information gathering.<br>Thoughts prior to adoption of device<br>The actual decision<br>After receiving the device |

The analysis phase was broken down into three phases (Eisenhardt 1989). The first phase focused entirely on both the individual level and involved a detailed description of each of the five early adopters based on the main themes from the interview guide (Table 1). The second phase focused on the individual level as well as the group as a whole and it consisted of analyses that built on the descriptions from the first phase to explore how the four constructs—social contagion, social learning, opinion leaders, and adoption threshold—could explain the decision to adopt the iPhone before it was commercially available in Denmark. The third phase focused on explicating contributions to the literature by systematically identifying and reflecting on the empirical insights in relation to the existing literature.

# 5   Results

## 5.1   Characterizing the Group of Adopters

Several methods for categorizing adopters exist; the most well known are those by Rogers (2003) and Ryan and Gross (1943, 1950). These methods are, however, not predictive and do not provide insights into how the iPhone is received before it has gone through its adoption curve. Constantiou et al.'s (2007) categorization of mobile adopters is developed for the purpose of dividing mobile users into distinct groups based on their usage behavior. Users can be categorized as talkers, writers, photographers, and surfers. Each level is consecutive and, therefore, writers are also talkers, photographers are also talkers and writers, and surfers are also talkers, writers, and photographers.

Table 2 provides a description of the observed five mobile users.[3] They are all male, in their early to mid thirties, and they have extensive experience with mobile phones, which is apparent in years of experience with mobile devices, number of mobile devices, and service experience. The demographic data shows a homogenous group of individuals consisting of adopters of the surfer category. According to Constantiou et al.'s 2007 study, the typical surfer is male, between 20 and 40 years of age, has a higher education, and works in the private sector. Surfers seek information about new mobile phones regularly and are usually among the first to try out new mobile technologies and services. They like to experiment and find it fairly easy to make their mobile device perform as they wish.

**Table 2.** Description of Mobile Users Participating in the Study

|  | Adam | Ben | Chris | David | Eric |
|---|---|---|---|---|---|
| Gender | Male | Male | Male | Male | Male |
| Age | 36 | 33 | 33 | 34 | 33 |
| Occupation | Private sector | Private sector | Private sector | Public sector | Private sector |
| First mobile device – year | 1995 | 2000 | 1994 | 2000 | 1994 |
| Number of mobile devices | ~ 7 | ~ 5 | ~ 14 | ~ 8 | ~ 20 |
| Bought iPhone | Dec 2007 | Mar 2008 | Mar 2008 | Jan 2008 | Sep 2007 |
| Previous mobile device | Sony Ericsson W950i | Sony Ericsson K800i | Nokia N73 | Sony Ericsson K810i | Nokia N95 |
| Use of services | Talk, SMS, e-mail, calendar, Internet, MMS, Camera, Mp3, Games, 3rd party software (e.g., maps) | Talk, SMS, e-mail, calendar, Internet, MMS, Camera, Mp3, Games, 3rd party software (e.g., maps) | Talk, SMS, e-mail, calendar, Internet, Mp3, 3rd party software (e.g., maps) | Talk, SMS, e-mail, calendar, Internet, MMS, Camera, Mp3, 3rd party software (e.g., maps) | Talk, SMS, e-mail, calendar, Internet, MMS, Camera, Mp3, Games, 3rd party software (e.g., maps) |
| Service experience | Surfer | Surfer | Surfer | Surfer | Surfer |

---

[3] The identity of the five adopters is disguised.

**Table 3.** Facebook Friends, April 2008 and April 2009

|       | **April 2008** | **April 2009** |
|-------|----------------|----------------|
| Adam  | 890            | 1531           |
| Ben   | 124            | 143            |
| Chris | 635            | 1089           |
| David | 194            | 373            |
| Eric  | 672            | 2000           |

The five adopters have more characteristics in common. They display a positive attitude toward change and science, which is apparent in their interest in obtaining the iPhone even before its release in the United States. They already used most functions on their previous mobile devices—all smartphones. The users seem good in coping with risk and uncertainty, as they bought the iPhone from the United States and were forced to unlock and jailbreak the phone before being able to use it. They are highly interconnected in their social networks measured in number of Facebook "friends" (Table 3), which increases the flow of information. They furthermore benefit from vast exposure to media that delivers information about topics of interest (both mass media and interpersonal media channels, such as a discussion forum in which they participated). They are active information seekers and they display a considerable amount of knowledge of technological innovations.

The five adopters are furthermore highly interconnected as suggested by Table 4, showing the number of Facebook friends the five adopters have in common. This pattern of Facebook friends relates to Dunbar (1995), who initially used cross-cultural studies to predict that humans socialize in groups of approximately 150 individuals—also referred to as the Dunbar number. Later Hill and Dunbar (2002) raised the question of whether social networks in modern, postindustrial societies exhibit a comparable pattern, and they found that social networks are still constrained to 150 due to possible limits in the capacity of the human communication channel.

## 5.2 Evidence for Individual Adoption Decisions

The five adopters decided to adopt the iPhone at different points in time ranging from September 2007 to March 2008. In the following, we present each individual adopter and his reflections leading to the actual adoption decision.

**Table 4.** Number of Friends in Common, Facebook, April 2008

|       | Adam | Ben | Chris | David | Eric |
|-------|------|-----|-------|-------|------|
| Adam  | **890** | 115 | 254 | 115 | 165 |
| Ben   | 115  | **124** | 96  | 27  | 105 |
| Chris | 254  | 96  | **635** | 96  | 155 |
| David | 115  | 27  | 96  | **194** | 194 |
| Eric  | 165  | 105 | 155 | 105 | **672** |

Adam, 36 years of age, holds a leading position in a private company within the music industry. He obtained his first mobile device in 1994 and acquires a new device approximately every second year. He acquired the iPhone in December 2007, five months after its release in the United States. He waited five months to buy the iPhone even though he always knew he *had* to attain it, as he was concerned with the lack of 3G. Adam had possessed iPods for years; however, he is not particularly into Apple's products. He monitored the exposure of the iPhone in the media and noticed an explosion in the development of techniques on how to jailbreak the firmware on the iPhone. He is, furthermore, a member of the discussion group, HF, on the Internet where he and others discussed the recent development in releasing the iPhone and how to unlock and jailbreak the device. He decided to buy the device when a friend let him try out the iPhone.

Ben is 33 years old. He holds an analyst position in a private company and creates music in his leisure time. He obtained his first mobile device in 2000 and acquires a new device roughly every second year. He obtained his iPhone in March 2008 when he travelled to the United States, and he acquired several copies and brought them to Denmark to his friends. Ben has possessed Mac computers for approximately five years, mostly for music production purposes, and iPods for four years. He is an Apple enthusiast and was initially exposed to the iPhone through the media. He watched the MacWorld Expo presentation of the iPhone on the Internet. He also discussed the device with friends and acquaintances and was convinced early on that he would obtain the iPhone. Ben decided to adopt based on two considerations. First, the instructions on the Internet on how to unlock and jailbreak the phone had advanced and it was now rather easy to do. Second, he was traveling to the United States and could therefore easily get access. He says, "When I held it the first time, I just knew I had to get it now. I didn't want to wait any longer."

Chris is 33 years old and works as a consultant in a private company. He obtained his first mobile device in 1994 and acquires a new device approximately every year. He bought his iPhone March 2008. Chris went to the United States in December 2007 and seriously thought of acquiring the device at that time, but decided to wait. His mobile device at the time suddenly got slower and he decided to obtain the iPhone when traveling to the United States again in March 2008. Chris has been in possession of PowerBooks and iPods since 1999 and can be labeled an Apple-onsumer. He followed the presentation and release of the iPhone through the media and participated in the discussion forum HF. He had made a decision to acquire the phone even before the release. When it was released in the United States, he did not have an excessive need and thought that the device would come to Denmark quickly in a 3G version. However, as the Danish release was extended and his mobile device at the time became slow, he decided he couldn't wait any longer. He added, "I will definitely buy the phone when it comes to Denmark in a 3G version."

David is 34 years old and holds a project management position in a public institution. He obtained his first mobile device in 2000, acquires a new device approximately every year, and he bought his iPhone in January 2008. David has been using his household's Mac hardware and software although he states that since 2001 the only Apple product he has owned himself is the iPod. David has been aware of the iPhone since before Apple's presentation and he always knew he would acquire one. When asked why, he stated, "It's partly a question of practicality; gathering all gadgets into one, so that you don't have to carry all these devices in your pockets. And it's partly a question of being able to use the services that the network operators have tried to push for so long. We now have a device that shows applications as if you were sitting in front of your computer. Now mobility is for real." He was concerned that the device wasn't made for the Danish market; however, he finally decided to obtain the iPhone not waiting for the Danish release: "The iPhone was too cool and I don't want to wait for some decelerated network operator to get their stuff together... it is an unheard situation, that it's not just there, and agreements have to be made."

Eric, 33 years of age, holds a project coordinator position in a private company and performs music in his leisure time. He obtained his first mobile device in 1994 and acquires a new device approximately two times a year. He acquired his iPhone in September 2007. Eric has extensive knowledge about Apple's computers, as he has been using both iMac and MacBook for several years. However, he never had an iPod before he acquired the iPhone. Eric has been aware of the iPhone since before it was presented at the MacWorld Expo conference: "That was the first time pictures were revealed. Here it is. But even before that, in 2006, there was a lot of speculation on what the phone would look like. I remember a lot of photos of white phones that matched the look of the white MacBooks." He noticed that whenever Apple releases a new product they create a plethora of hype and he believes they succeeded in building up excitement about the iPhone. It became prestigious to possess an iPhone.

### 5.3 Analyzing Social Network Influences

**Adoption thresholds** of collective behavior are the proportion of adopters in a social system needed for an individual to adopt an innovation (Granovetter 1978).

We asked the iPhone adopters how many people in their network that they knew had adopted the iPhone prior to them, Adam replied five and the rest replied one. Given that they had between 124 and 890 Facebook friends at the time, the proportion of iPhone adopters in their networks was relatively small; between 0.0015 percent (Chris and Eric) and 0.08 percent (Ben). At the time of the interviews[4] the five adopters believed that between 10 and 60 people in their extended network had adopted the iPhone. This indicates that all five adopters have a low network threshold in regard to their extended network. Eric was the first to adopt the iPhone (September 2007) and is also the person with the lowest network threshold in regard to his close network. Adam was also aware of a benefit of adopting early: "It is still a bit nerdy. You can't go down in the local store and buy one yet." Hence, the five early iPhone adopters all have a low network threshold both in regard to their close network and their extended network.

**Opinion leaders** are "opinion brokers who carry information across the social boundaries between groups" (Burt 1999, p. 37) to stimulate contagion by cohesion or contagion by structural equivalence.

---

[4] The interviews were conducted in April 2008; eight months after the first adopters in the study acquired their iPhone, one month after the latest adopters in the study adopted the iPhone, and three months before the iPhone was released on the Danish market.

When investigating the influence of opinion leaders in the network, we asked the five adopters how many contacts they had in common (Table 4) and how many contacts they had in their extended network (Table 3). The number of Facebook friends is the most precise measure of the adopters' networks we could obtain. Adam, who had the highest number of Facebook friends at the time of the interview, reflected that the high number is a consequence of him working in the music industry, and he does not have frequent contact with most contacts. Chris' and Eric's high number of Facebook friends are also the result of their time spent socializing with individuals through the music scene. The five adopters have between 27 (Ben and David) and 254 (Adam and Chris) friends in common. According to all of them, there was no single person who brought information about the iPhone into their extended networks. Although they all had decided to obtain the iPhone at some point, it was the testing of the device from one friend that stimulated the actual acquisition. All adopters claim they actively sought information about the iPhone as soon as they became aware of it. There is hence no evidence that opinion leaders played a significant role in the adoption decision made by the five adopters.

**Social contagion** refers to an individual's decision to adopt an innovation depending on other individuals' attitudes, knowledge, or behaviors concerning the innovation (Van den Bulte and Lilien 2001). Mobile adopters with higher numbers of direct ties have greater opportunities to disseminate and receive information about the iPhone because they have more choices (Burt 1999; Granovetter 1973). Thus the number of direct ties captures the power and the opportunities to receive information about the iPhone. According to statistics on Facebook, the average user on Facebook has 120 friends,[5] which is also supported by a small-scale investigation conducted by *The Economist* (Kluth 2009). All five iPhone adopters in this study have a number of Facebook friends higher than the average, which increases the likelihood of getting contaminated with attitudes, knowledge, and behaviors toward the iPhone from their Facebook network.

As identified by Van den Bulte and Lilien (2001), four mechanisms may cause social contagion. *Information transfer* occurs both from traditional media, such as newspapers, television, and Internet-based media, such as podcasts, to the individual mobile users as well as between the individuals. The five adopters all received information and news about the iPhone from various types of media and all except Ben were part of a particular discussion forum on the Internet that, aside from the main topic of the forum (electronic music), discussed various topics including the latest news on the release of the iPhone. As the five adopters are part of the same social setting and met regularly, they also exchanged information directly. Adam even claims that he decided to buy the iPhone at the exact moment a friend in his extended network let him try out his iPhone. He says, "It is my clear belief that this is where something snaps. One thing is what you read...everybody's skeptic but that is only until you get a demonstration." Hence, information transfer and demonstrations from both different media and the social network had significant influence on each individual's decision to adopt the iPhone.

---

[5] Facebook Press Room (http://www.facebook.com/press/info.php?statistics; accessed August 16, 2009).

Normative pressure occurs when the mobile user experiences discomfort, when peers, whose approval they value, have adopted an innovation but they have not. When asked, how many people in their social network they believed owned an iPhone before they bought theirs, Adam answered five, and the four other adopters answered one. There is, therefore, no evidence that normative pressures influenced the iPhone adopters.

*Competitive concerns* can be viewed as being opposed to normative pressures and it appears that it influenced the individual's decision to adopt the iPhone. As Eric stated, "The iPhone has a high prestige factor that will probably descend when it is released in Denmark." He further argued that the iPhone attracts a lot of attention from peers who do not own an iPhone. Adam and Ben have a similar view. David, on the other hand, does not feel that competition had any influence on his adoption decision. He believes that the iPhone is simply the best phone on the market, a position with which Chris agrees.

*Performance network effects* refer to the benefits of use that increase with the number of prior adopters of the innovation. These effects are apparent for mobile devices in general, as the benefits of communication via such a device increases with the number of prior users. As all iPhone adopters studied had advanced mobile devices prior to the iPhone, they did not exhibit network effects from adopting the iPhone.

**Social learning** is related to social contagion. As mobile users are faced with uncertainty in the decision to adopt the iPhone, they may observe their neighbor's choices and interact with their social network to consult on their adoption decision through informational and normative social influences (Burkhardt and Brass 1990; Katz 19890; Katz and Tushman 1979).

When collecting data on social learning, we asked the adopters if they would be able to make the iPhone work when they received it and if they depended on other people in their network to help them. All five adopters replied they had at least one friend they relied on to help in case they weren't able to make it work by themselves; however, they all initially depended on themselves to be able to unlock and jailbreak the phone based on instructions from a website. David made the purchasing decision when he found that "the instructions became easy to comprehend and I could see myself fix everything; installation of new applications, jailbreaking, unlocking, update firmware—everything that had to do with the iPhone, I could do it myself without being dependent on others." Adam found that "it became a competition for Mac nerds to determine who could break the latest firmware. So, the information and software on the web is quite good." There is, therefore, evidence that social learning played an important part in the individual's decision to adopt the iPhone.

# 6  Discussion

We have presented a case study investigating the behaviors and decisions of early adopters of the iPhone. We analyzed both individual adoption decisions as well as social network influences. In contrast to existing studies on early adoption (Kauffman and Techatassanasoontorn 2009; Wozniak 1987), our study was based on a qualitative approach in which we used four complementary social network influence constructs:

adoption threshold, opinion leaders, social contagion, and social learning. Interestingly, these analyses confirmed some previously identified insights, but also questioned earlier findings.

The study confirms that contemporary mobile devices still revolutionize many aspects of everyday life (Green et al. 2001) as they combine many gadgets into one stylish device. The study also shows that when facing uncertainty, adoption decisions emerged as a combined result of individual adoption reflections and major influences from the social network and the behaviors observed within the network. In fact, the analyses confirmed that network structures impact the decision to accept a mobile device (Katz 1961; Rogers 2003; Vidgen et al. 2007) while also revealing new details on social network influences on early adoption decisions.

Drawing from existing utilitarian research on mobile adoption studies (Carlsson et al. 2000; Pedersen and Ling 2002) as well as studies that have established correlation between an individual's social network and the decision to adopt (Dickinger et al. 2008; Lu et al. 2005), our study provides a detailed description of adopters that faces high uncertainties when adopting the iPhone before it was readily available. We thereby offer new insights into how early adopters of mobile devices overcome uncertainties related to shifts in technology. Explaining these behaviors can be challenging, and relying on too simplistic models might not suffice. Therefore, we relied on multiple perspectives and multiple levels of analyses and were open to question insights from traditional adoption theory. Such an explorative, multiconstruct and multilevel perspective has previously been left unexamined.

Our study supports several insights from previous work on mobile adoption. Lu et al. (2005) found that perceived ease of use of wireless Internet services on mobile devices had a direct effect on the intention to adopt the service. Our study supports this finding as the early adopters of the iPhone relied on easy to use instructions on how to unlock and jailbreak their iPhone as well as their network to provide the help they needed. Similarly, Dickinger et al. (2008) found that attitude towards "push-to-talk" services had a positive effect on the intention to use the service. Our study shows that early adopters of the iPhone had a positive attitude toward the device long before it was released, contributing to their intention to adopt.

Our study also supports previous research on categorization of adopters. Lu et al. found that personal innovativeness had an impact on intention to adopt wireless Internet services via mobile technology. Constantiou et al. (2007) divided mobile users into categories that describe several traits of each category. The personal innovativeness construct, and Constantiou et al.'s description of the surfer user, fits well with our early adopters, who all belong to the surfer category. Wozniak (1987) studied early adoption of new technology in organizations and found that adoption behavior is a "human capital intensive activity" that depends on acquired human capital and investment into receiving adoption information. Our study confirms that the social influence construct *information transfer*, which is part of social contagion, had significant impact on early adoption decisions.

More explorative studies of social influences are needed to develop and validate these findings and other influences than the ones we considered may also have had an impact. The artifact itself possesses some unique characteristics that were emphasized by the adopters: design characteristics as well as utilitarian characteristics. As Orlikowski and Iacono (2001) argue, the IT artifact itself tends to be taken for granted in research. We acknowledge the importance of the artifact, and recognize that it had significant impact on our adopters' decision making beyond the focus of our analyses. It is also of interest to look at Apple's marketing effort. Van den Bulte and Lilien (2001) found that when they control for marketing efforts in the diffusion of the drug Tetracycline, contagion effects disappear. It could, therefore, be that the heavy promotion of the iPhone by Apple, the hype that was created by the media and the public, and the limited supply of iPhones (Lynn 1991; Verhallen 1982, Verhallen and Robben 1994) were important influences on the five adopters. This observation is furthermore related to Leibenstein's (1950) "snob effect." Although the five adopters did not see themselves as snobs, they agreed that owning the iPhone at the time was prestigious.

# References

Anderson, C.: The Long Tail: Why the Future of Business is Selling Less of More. Harvard Business School Press, Boston (2006)

Agarwal, R., Prasad, J.: Are Individual Differences Germane to the Acceptance of Information Technologies? Decision Sciences 30(2), 361–391 (1999)

Barnes, J.A.: Class and Committees in a Norwegian Island Parish. Human Relations (7), 39–58 (1954)

Bauer, H.H., Reichardt, T., Barnes, S.J., Neumann, M.M.: Driving Consumer Acceptance of Mobile Marketing: A Theoretical Framework and Empirical Study. Journal of Electronic Commerce Research 6(3), 181–192 (2005)

Bergman, E.: Information Appliances and Beyond. Morgan Kauffman, San Francisco (2000)

Brightman, J.: PC Game Sales Bring U.S. Industry to $18.85 Billion in 2007, GameDaily (2008), http://www.gamedaily.com/articles/news/pc-game-sales-bring-us-industry-to-1885-billion-in-07 (accessed July 17, 2008)

Burkhardt, M.E., Brass, D.J.: Changing Patterns or Patterns of Change: The Effects of a Change in Technology on Social Network Structure and Power. Administrative Science Quarterly (35), 104–127 (1990)

Burt, R.S.: Structural Holes: The Social Structure of Competition. Harvard University Press, Cambridge (1995)

Burt, R.S.: The Social Capital of Opinion Leaders. Annals (566), 37–54 (1999)

Burt, R.S., Minor, M.J.: Applied Network Analysis. Sage, Newbury Park (1983)

Campbell, S.W., Russo, T.C.: The Social Construction of Mobile Telephony: An Application of the Social Influence Model to Perceptions and Uses of Mobile Phones Within Personal Communication Networks. Communication Monographs 70(4), 317–334 (2003)

Carlsson, C., Carlsson, J., Hyvönen, K., Puhakainen, J., Walden, P.: Adoption of Mobile Devices/Services: Searching for Answers with the UTAUT. In: Proceedings of the 39th Hawaii International Conference on System Sciences, pp. 132–142. IEEE Computer Society Press, Los Alamitos (2000)

Chuang, M.C., Chang, C.C., Hsu, S.H.: Perceptual Factors Underlying User Preferences Toward Product Form of Mobile Phones. International Journal of Industrial Ergonomics 27(4), 247–258 (2001)

Coleman, J.S., Katz, E., Menzel, H.: Medical Innovation: A Diffusion Study. Bobbs-Merrill, Indianapolis (1966)

Constantiou, I.D., Damsgaard, J., Knutsen, L.: The Four Incremental Steps Toward Advanced Mobile Service Adoption. Communications of the ACM 50(6), 51–55 (2007)

Dickinger, A., Arami, M., Meyer, D.: The Role of Perceived Enjoyment and Social Norm in the Adoption of Technology with Network Externalities. European Journal of Information Systems (17), 4–11 (2008)

Dunbar, R.I.M.: Neocortex Size and Group Size in Primates: A Test of the Hypothesis. Journal of Human Evolution 28(3), 287–296 (1995)

Economist Intelligence Unit. E-Readiness Rankings 2008: Maintaining Momentum, The Economist (2008),
`http://a330.g.akamai.net//330/5828/0080331202303/`
`graphics.eiu.com/upload/ibm_ereadiness_2008.pdf`

Eisenhardt, K.M.: Building Theories from Case Study Research. Academy of Management Review 14(4), 532–550 (1989)

Ellison, G., Fudenberg, D.: Rules of Thumb for Social Learning. Journal of Political Economy 101(4), 612–643 (1993)

Fischer, C.S.: America Calling: A Social History of the Telephone to 1940. University of California Press, Berkeley (1994)

French, J., Raven, B.: The Bases of Social Power. In: Cartwright, D. (ed.) Studies in Social Power, pp. 159–167. Institute for Social Research, Ann Arbor (1959)

Friedkin, N.: A Test of Structural Features of Granovetter's Strength of Weak Ties. Social Networks (2), 411–422 (1980)

Granovetter, M.: The Strength of Weak Ties. America Journal of Sociology 78(6), 1360–1381 (1973)

Granovetter, M.: Threshold Models of Collective Behavior. American Journal of Sociology 83(6), 1420–1443 (1978)

Green, N., Harper, R.H.R., Murtagh, G., Cooper, G.: Configuring the Mobile User: Sociological and Industry Views. Personal and Ubiquitous Computing (5), 146–156 (2001)

Haddon, L. (ed.): Communications on the Move: The Experience of Mobile Telephony in the 1990s, COST 268 Report, Talia, Farsta, Sweden (1997)

Hall, B.H., Khan, B.: Adoption of New Technology. NBER Working Paper No. W9730, National Bureau of Economic Research (2003)

Hill, R., Dunbar, R.: Social Network Size in Humans. Human Nature 14(1), 53–72 (2002)

Hong, S.-J., Tam, K.Y.: Understanding the Adoption of Multipurpose Information Appliances. Information Systems Research 17(2), 162–179 (2006)

Katz, R.: The Social Itinerary of Technical Change: Two Studies on the Diffusion of Innovation. Human Organization 20(2), 70–82 (1961)

Katz, R.: A Theory of Parties and Electorial Systems. The Johns Hopkins University Press, Baltimore (1980)

Katz, R., Lazarsfeld, P.F.: Personal Influence. The Free Press, Glencoe (1955)

Katz, R., Shapiro, C.: Technology Adoption in the Presence of Network Externalities. Journal of Political Economy 94(4), 822–843 (1986)

Katz, R., Tushman, M.L.: Communication Patterns, Project Performance, and Task Characteristics: an Empirical Evaluation and Integration in an R&D Setting. Organizational Behavior and Human Performance 23(2), 139–162 (1979)

Kaufmann, R.J., Techatassanasoontorn, A.A.: Understanding Early Diffusion of Digital Wireless Phones. Telecommunications Policy (33), 432–450 (2009)

Khalifa, M., Cheng, S.K.N.: Adoption of Mobile Commerce: Role of Exposure. In: Proceedings of the 35th Hawaii International Conference on System Sciences, pp. 1–7. IEEE Computer Society Press, Los Alamitos (2002)

Kluth, A.: The Size of Social Networks. The Economist (2009),
    `http://www.economist.com/sciencetechnology/`
    `displayStory.cfm?story_id=13176775` (accessed August 23, 2009)
Krackhardt, D.: Cognitive Social Structures. Social Networks (9), 109–134 (1987)
Krackhardt, D.: Assessing the Political Landscape Culture, Cognition and Power in
    Organizations. Administrative Science Quarterly (35), 342–369 (1990)
Laukkanen, T., Lauronen, J.: Consumer Value Creation in Mobile Banking Services.
    International Journal of Mobile Communications 3(4), 325–338 (2005)
Lee, Y.E., Benbasat, I.: Interface Design for Mobile Commerce. Communications of the
    ACM 46(12), 48–52 (2003)
Leibenstein, H.: Bandwagon, Snob, and Veblen Effects in the Theory of Consumers' Demand.
    Quarterly Journal of Economics (64), 183–207 (1950)
Lewis, W., Agarwal, R., Sambamurthy, V.: Spheres of Influence on Beliefs about Information
    Technology Use: An Empirical Study of Knowledge Workers. MIS Quarterly 27(4), 657–
    678 (2003)
Lu, J., Yao, J.E., Chun-Sheng, Y.: Personal Innovativeness, Social Influences and Adoption of
    Wireless Internet Services via Mobile Technology. Journal of Strategic Information
    Systems (14), 245–268 (2005)
Lynn, M.: Scarcity Effects on Value: A Quantitative Review of the Commodity Theory
    Literature. Psychology and Marketing 8(1), 45–57 (1991)
Lyytinen, K., Yoo, Y.: Research Commentary: The Next Wave of Nomadic Computing.
    Information Systems Research 13(4), 377–388 (2002)
Magni, M., Angst, C., Argarwal, R.: A Multilevel Investigation of Normative and
    Informational Influences on Extensiveness of Individual Technology Use. In: Proceedings
    of the 28th International Conference on Information Systems, Montreal, Quebec, Canada,
    December 9-12 (2007)
Manski, C.F.: Economic Analysis of Social Interactions. Journal of Economic Perspectives
    (14), 115–136 (2000)
Meehan, A.: The Impact of Mobile Data Terminal (MDT) Information Technology on
    Communication and Recordkeeping in Patrol Work. Qualitative Sociology (21), 225–254
    (1998)
Moore, G.C., Benbasat, I.: Development of an Instrument to Develop Perceptions of Adopting
    an Information Technology Innovation. Information Systems Research 2(3), 192–222
    (2001)
Nippert-Eng, C.: Home and Work: Negotiating Boundaries Through Everyday Life. University
    of Chicago Press, Chicago (1996)
Oestreicher-Singer, G., Sundararajan, A.: Recommendation Networks and the Long Tail of
    Electronic Commerce. Mimeo, Stern School of Business, New York University (2006)
Oh, H., Labianca, G., Chung, M.: A Multilevel Model of Group Social Capital. Academy of
    Management Review 31(3), 569–582 (2006)
Orlikowski, W.J., Iacono, C.S.: Research Commentary: Desperately Seeking the 'IT' in IT
    Research – A Call to Theorizing the IT Artifact. Information Systems Research 12(2),
    121–134 (2001)
Palen, L., Salzman, M., Young, E.: Discovery and Integration of Mobile Communications in
    Everyday Life. Personal and Ubiquitous Computing 5(2), 109–122 (2001)
Patton, M.: Qualitative Research and Evaluation Methods. Sage Publications, Thousand Oaks
    (2001)

Pedersen, P.E.: Adoption of Mobile Internet Services: An Exploratory Study of Mobile Commerce Early Adopters. Journal of Organizational Computing and Electronic Commerce 15(2), 203–222 (2005)

Pedersen, P.E., Ling, R.: Modifying Adoption Research for Mobile Internet Service Adoption: Cross-Disciplinary Interactions. In: Proceedings of the 37th Hawaii International Conference on System Sciences. IEEE Computer Society Press, Los Alamitos (2003)

Rashotte, L.: Social Influence. In: Manstead, A.S.R., Hewston, M. (eds.) The Blackwell Encyclopedia of Social Psychology, pp. 562–563. Blackwell Publishing, Malden (2007)

Rogers, M.E.: Diffusion of Innovations. The Free Press, New York (2003)

Ryan, B., Gross, N.C.: The Diffusion of Hybrid Seed Corn in Two Iowa Communities. Rural Sociology 8(1), 15–24 (1943)

Ryan, B., Gross, N.C.: Acceptance and Diffusion of Hybrid Corn in Two Iowa Communities. Iowa Agricultural Experiment Station. Research Bulletin No 372 (1950)

Sarker, S., Wells, J.D.: Understanding Mobile Handheld Device Use and Adoption. Communications of the ACM 46(12), 35–40 (2003)

Tarasewitch, P.: Designing Mobile Commerce Applications. Communications of the ACM 46(12), 57–60 (2003)

Tarde, G., Warren, H., Baldwin, J.M.: Social Laws: An Outline of Sociology (1899). Kessinger Publishing, Whitefish (2008)

Teddlie, C., Yu, F.: Mixed Methods Sampling: A Typology with Examples. Journal of Mixed Methods Research 1(1), 77–100 (2007)

Tscherning, H., Damsgaard, J.: Understanding the Diffusion and Adoption of Telecommunication Innovations: What We Know and What We Don't Know. In: León, G., Bernardos, A., Casar, J., Kautz, K., DeGross, J. (eds.) Open IT-Based Innovation: Moving Towards Cooperative IT Transfer and Knowledge Diffusion, pp. 41–62. Springer, Boston (2008)

Valente, T.W.: Social Network Thresholds in the Diffusion of Innovations. Social Networks 18(1), 69–89 (1996)

Valente, T.W., Davis, R.L.: Accelerating the Diffusion of Innovations Using Opinion Leaders. Annals of the American Academy of Political and Social Science (566), 55–67 (1999)

Van den Bulte, C., Lilien, G.: Medical Innovation Revisited: Social Contagion Versus Marketing Effort. American Journal of Sociology 106(5), 1409–1435 (2001)

Vidgen, R., Madsen, S., Kautz, K.: Mapping the Information Systems Development Process. In: Proceedings of IFIP WG8.6 Working Conference on IT Innovation, IFIP, Dublin, Ireland (2004)

Verhallen, T.M.: Scarcity and Consumer Choice Behavior. Journal of Economic Psychology 2(2), 299–321 (1982)

Verhallen, T.M., Robben, H.S.: Scarcity and Preference: An Experiment on Unavailability and Product Evaluation. Journal of Economic Psychology (15), 315–331 (1994)

Wang, S., Cheung, W.: E-Business Adoption by Travel Agencies: Prime Candidates for Mobile e-Business. International Journal of Electronic Commerce 8(3), 43–63 (2004)

Wasserman, S., Faust, K.: Social Network Analysis: Methods and Applications. Cambridge University Press, New York (1994)

Watts, D.J., Dodds, P.S.: Influentials, Networks, and Public Opinion Formation. Journal of Consumer Research 34(4), 441–459 (2007)

Wozniak, G.D.: Human Capital, Information, and the Early Adoption of New Technology. Journal of Human Resources 22(1), 101–112 (1987)

Yin, R.K.: Case Study Research: Design and Methods, 4th edn. Sage Publications, Thousand Oaks (2008)

## About the Authors

**Heidi Tscherning** received her Master's in Business Administration and Economics in 2000 from Copenhagen Business School, Denmark. She is currently a doctoral student at the Center for Applied ICT at Copenhagen Business School. Prior to joining the doctoral program, she worked as a project manager and IT management consultant in companies such as IBM, Novo Nordisk, and Systematic Software Engineering. Her research interests include adoption of technologies, with a particular interest in mobile devices and services and social networks. She recently visited the Polytechnic Institute of New York University (January 2009 to February 2010). Heidi can be reached by e-mail at htj.caict@cbs.dk.

**Lars Mathiassen** received his Master's degree in computer science from Aarhus University, Denmark, in 1975, his Ph.D. in informatics from Oslo University, Norway, in 1981, and his Dr. Techn. degree in software engineering from Aalborg University in 1998. He is currently GRA Eminent Scholar and professor in the Department of Computer Information Systems and co-founder of the Center for Process Innovation at Georgia State University. His research interests are in the areas of information systems and software engineering with a particular emphasis on process innovation. He is a coauthor of *Computers in Context* (Blackwell 1993), *Object Oriented Analysis & Design* (Marko Publishing, 2000), and *Improving Software Organizations* (Addison-Wesley, 2002). He has served as a senior editor for *MIS Quarterly* and his research has been published in journals including *Information Systems Research, MIS Quarterly, IEEE Transactions on Engineering Management, Communications of the ACM, Journal of the AIS, Information Systems Journal,* and *IEEE Software.* Lars can be reached at Lars.Mathiassen@ eci.gsu.edu.

# Part 2
# Design Exemplars

# Roles in Innovative Software Teams:
# A Design Experiment

Ivan Aaen

Department of Computer Science,
Aalborg University,
DK-9220 Aalborg East, Denmark

**Abstract.** With inspiration from role-play and improvisational theater, we are developing a framework for innovation in software teams called Essence. Based on agile principles, Essence is designed for teams of developers and an onsite customer. This paper reports from teaching experiments inspired by design science, where we tried to assign differentiated roles to team members. The experiments provided valuable insights into the design of roles in Essence. These insights are used for redesigning how roles are described and conveyed in Essence.

**Keywords:** Software innovation, roles, innovation in teams, design science.

## 1 Introduction

This paper takes its point of departure in two observations: (1) in a global economy, software development in high-cost countries will increasingly depend on the ability to create high-value products in close collaboration with sophisticated customers; and (2) agile development opens up new opportunities for software innovation by allowing for changes and adaptations late in development projects (de la Barra and Crawford 2007; Highsmith 2004; Highsmith and Cockburn 2001; Judy and Krumins-Beens 2007; Nerur and Balijepally 2007).

Based on these premises and the assumption that software innovation may lead to high-value software products, this paper focuses on software innovation and innovative software teams using agile development principles. More precisely, the paper is about facilitating innovation in agile software teams by assigning particular roles to team members. We wish to know how roles can be defined to support creative interaction in the team.

The paper reports from two teaching experiments. The experiments revealed some problems in the design of Essence roles and how they are related to team members.

## 2 Creativity in Teams

In recent years, an increasing amount of research focuses on creativity in development teams: Leenders et al. (2007) discuss the relation between method and creativity in team-based product development in general. They conclude that methods and

J. Pries-Heje et al. (Eds.): IS Design Science Research, IFIP AICT 318, pp. 73–88, 2010.
© IFIP International Federation for Information Processing 2010

creativity are supportive of each other. As an alternative to using methods, Fortino (2008) proposes the use of pattern languages for innovation management.

A number of authors investigate the method/creativity relation specifically with software development in mind. Some advocate creative and innovative software development based on agile principles (Highsmith 2004; Highsmith and Cockburn 2001). Chang (2008) advocates sequential techniques that are collaborative, heuristic, and normatively guided. Tiwana and McLean (2005) investigate how expertise and creativity integrates in teams. Finally, a number of authors have investigated how infrastructures support creative work. Some address general work environments for any kind of development (Adamides and Karacapilidis 2006; Deshpande et al. 2004; Do and Gross 2007; Greene 2002; Johansson et al. 2002; Kristensen 2004; Lewis and Moultrie 2005; Satzinger et al. 1999; Terrenghi et al. 2006; Thomas et al. 2002), while others address software development more specifically (Shneiderman 1999, 2002, 2007). Some research focuses on physical infrastructures (Deshpande et al. 2004; Do and Gross 2007; Greene 2002; Johansson et al. 2002; Kristensen 2004; Lewis and Moultrie 2005; Terrenghi et al. 2006), whereas others focus on virtual environments (Adamides and Karacapilidis 2006; Satzinger et al. 1999, Schneiderman 1999, 2002, 2007; Thomas et al. 2002).

Within software requirements engineering, researchers such as Maiden and Mich have made contributions on creativity. Maiden and colleagues have experimented with innovative techniques to encourage creative thinking about requirements (Maiden, Manning, Robertson, and Greenwood 2004; Maiden and Robertson 2005; Maiden, Robertson and Gizikis 2004; Maiden, Robertson, and Robertson 2006), and pointed to improvisational theater as a possible source of new methods for requirements engineering (Mahaux and Maiden 2008). Mich et al. (2004) propose the use of a pragmatic communication model in a 16-step process applying a different user's viewpoint in each step.

Essence seeks to base software innovation on agile principles such as incremental development, low ceremony, and heterogeneous teams of customers and developers. The ambition is to widen the creative phase in a project to more than just the requirements part. Some of the ideas in Essence were presented in one conference and one journal paper in 2008 (Aaen 2008a, 2008b). Essence is very much a work-in-progress and a comprehensive description of Essence has not been published.

## 3  Design Science and Essence

Our research is concerned with the design of Essence: How can we facilitate innovative software development in teams? Being an experimental design effort, *design research* (Hevner et al. 2004; Vaishnavi and Kuechler 2004) is a suitable framework. According to Vaishnavi and Kuechler design research projects proceed through a series of sequential steps with feedback loops between the steps. The steps are (1) awareness of problem, (2) suggestion, (3) development, and (4) evaluation.

Designing a development method is a *wicked problem* (Rittel and Webber 1973) in the sense that the goals are fuzzy, there are no criteria to define a correct solution, there is no way to test if a solution meets its goals, and there is no way to control and repeat experiments. The use of the four steps, therefore, requires adaptation and common sense.

A development method such as Essence is too complicated to design and test all at once, but breaking up the design process in smaller parts introduces problems related to interdependencies between the parts. To reduce this dilemma, our experiments on design elements attempt to employ the full Essence framework.

We have covered all four steps in previous papers (Aaen 2008a, 2008b) primarily investigating the use of physical space and logical views in Essence. The present experiments cover two variations of team roles mainly covering the development and evaluation steps and how they feed back into the suggestion step (Figure 1).

In our research we combine four command variables (Simon 1996) to attain our design goals (Aaen 2008b):

1.  Extending the window of opportunity.
2.  Innovation management.
3.  Innovation process support.
4.  Mental model change.

The team role variations touch on combinations of the last two command variables. *Innovation process support* focuses on support for creativity, and on team learning. *Mental model change* focuses on the contrasting of views to spark off change in mental models, and on team integration. Essentially, we can vary these two command variables in our design of team roles: We can define the mindsets of roles in various ways, and similarly we can vary how the roles are employed. The lessons learned will result in changing team roles and/or other elements in Essence.

**Fig. 1.** The Design Cycle Used (Adapted from Vaishnavi and Kuechler 2004)

## 4 Essence: A Method Concept for Software Innovation

Since August 2006, we have experimented with infrastructures and methods to facilitate creativity and innovation in software development. We aim to build creative settings for team-based software development using modern development principles. These principles allow for flexible and incremental development and thus for incorporating new ideas even late in a project. We expect these principles to widen the window of opportunity for creativity and innovation by allowing learning experiences and discoveries from an ongoing project to feed ideas back into the project itself.

The main thrust in our research is the design of Essence. Among the ideas are:

- supporting creativity and innovation through all phases in the development project
- integrating into and extending existing development methods
- melding creative sessions with agile development to increase development speed and maintain flexibility in the project
- entrusting the development team—rather than external specialists—to be creative
- collective idea-generation in self-organizing teams
- using multiple perspectives to support divide-and-conquer strategies
- maintaining holistic overview via systematic separation
- kinesthetic thinking—using physical location and movement to support simulation and idea generation (Larssen et al. 2007)

We call Essence a *method concept*, not a method per se, to stress that Essence will find its actual form as the individual teams use and adapt it through daily routines, and integrate Essence into their main development method—for example, Scrum (Schwaber and Beedle 2002).

To support multiple perspectives we find inspiration in the four generic views: *Earth, Water, Fire,* and *Air* named by Empedocles of Acragas (ca. 495- 435 BCE). In his *Tetrasomia*, or *Doctrine of the Four Elements*, Empedocles argued that all matter is comprised of these four elements. Essence is named after *Quintessence*, the cosmic fifth element added by Aristotle to complement the four earthly elements.

Essence is intended to be lightweight, easy, and fun to use. Lightweight in the sense that ceremony and project overheads are kept at a minimum, so as not to have projects leave out Essence for lack of time. Easy to use in the sense that the time needed before Essence is useful should be short, and the activities in Essence should come naturally to the participants. Finally, it should be fun to use, to raise motivation.

The strategy for making Essence lightweight, easy, and fun to use is to organize creativity sessions in Essence as games similar to role playing games and improvisational theater (Swartjes and Vromen 2007; Yardley-Matwiejczuk 1997). Games are based on *characters* (roles), *settings* (infrastructure), and *situations* (games), whereas the events and actions are largely developed via disciplined improvisations. Both characters and settings are permanent elements of the development project to make the games a natural continuation of everyday life.

Essence has three basic design elements: *views, modes,* and *roles.*

## 4.1 Views

The views form the main part of the setting. The *setting* frames the story world in improvisational theater terms—the shared world that forms the basis for expressing each character's ideals (Swartjes and Vromen 2007). The setting for the software team consists of a physical infrastructure—the room where team members work.

Views provide a conceptual division of problem spaces, and balance overview with detail. Essence maps the software engineering 4P model (Bernstein and Yuhas 2005;

Pressman 2005) onto the aforementioned four generic views. The views are used at all times and not only during Essence sessions. The views in Essence are product, project, process, and people. These views are represented on separate boards to support kinesthetic thinking.

*The product view.* Essence stimulates creative dialogue between customers and developers in order to develop ambitious technical responses to application area challenges. The product view represents the product being built—the source code, the system architecture, etc.—to make the product and propositions for changes to it more tangible in team discussions.

*The project view* supports the customer in maintaining project status and planning throughout the project. This view gives an overview of project status.

*The process view.* Essence offers a repertoire of creative methods, tools, and techniques. The process view provides an overview of and access to this repertoire.

*The people view* visualizes organizational contexts, use scenarios, and interactions via mock-ups and simulations. Discussions on system features and user interfaces will primarily take place using this view.

## 4.2  Modes

Having defined the setting, the next step is to introduce a dynamic element: The *situation* that completes the story world. The first part of this comes in the form of creativity sessions called *Essence Games,* inspired by Hohmann's (2006) innovation games and numerous methods described in Huczynski (2001). Games are based on the principle of saying yes—accepting all offers that other characters bring into the situation (Swartjes and Vromen 2007).

Essence adapts to the project via three modes: idea, planning, and growing. *Idea* is for suggesting possible courses of action, for developing concepts and visions. This mode involves explorations, experiments, brainstorming, scenario development, experiments, etc. Creativity sessions in this mode are mainly exploratory. *Planning* involves decisions regarding what to do, when, and by whom. Creativity sessions in this mode focus mainly on inventory building to identify tasks. *Growing* is where ideas find actual form via evolution, trial, selection, maturation, expansion, enlargement, and progress. Creativity sessions are mainly confirmatory, and investigate if an appropriate level of innovation is reached in the project.

Modes have not been explored to any extent yet and will not be described further in this paper. The experiments reported on in this paper addressed the Idea mode.

## 4.3  Roles

Together, views and modes form a basis for the creative activities. Essence employs roles extensively to promote the application of multiple perspectives, and particularly to strengthen synergies between customer challenges and developer ambitions.

The role concept is quite difficult to define, as pointed out by Yardley-Matwiejczuk (1997). We use the term in a simple structuralist sense to denote the rights, duties, and expectations of an individual, as he or she participates in a social context. Thus, the role follows from a combination of socialization, social position, and the organizational context of the team.

There are four roles in Essence defining four *characters*: challenger, responder, anchor, and child. Except for the child role, these roles are permanent as a team member usually has the same role throughout the project. The roles aim to introduce different personal perspectives and expertise to the team (Tiwana and McLean 2005).

Each role has a clear *raison d'être* (Swartjes and Vromen 2007). The *challenger* is the on-site customer posing project requirements in the form of challenges. The *responder* is the developer employing technical competence to deliver ambitious responses. These two roles engage in dialogues where solutions are developed by contrasting application area needs and desires with technical opportunity. The *anchor* serves to keep the team absorbed and focused on delivering exciting solutions. The last role is the *child;* this role is fleeting in the sense, that anyone can suspend his permanent role and temporarily take the child role at any time. The child is irresponsible and may raise any idea or issue he or she sees fit—even when this is contrary to decisions made earlier by the team. This role is named after the child in *The Emperor's New Clothes* who said "but he hasn't got anything on," and thereby revealed the emperor's folly. The child is a supplier of ideas and visions, but also a safety valve in heated discussions.

## 5  Designing the Roles in Essence

Up to now, Essence has been developed primarily in an educational setting involving thesis work and a new course on software innovation for graduate students. This setting allows for brief experiments with numerous students, or experiments with fewer students over longer periods of time. The drawback is that students work under circumstances different from industrial settings although all students have worked extensively on team-based software development projects as part of their study.

Our inspiration for using role playing comes from the improvisational theater tradition and theater games originally developed as a method for training actors. The aim is to make team members adopt and apply a varied set of views, values, and rationales to facilitate the exchange of unusual ideas and promote creative thinking (Amabile et al. 1996). The characterization and function of a role frames the actions of a team member, and each role is constantly negotiated as the game progresses. Team members may improvise freely in the situation.

### 5.1  Initial Role Definitions

As Essence is intended to be lightweight, the initial definitions of the roles were very brief. We tried to make the roles self-explanatory and intuitive. The role would be presented as a personal responsibility, and the team would act the roles and use the physical space and views as they saw fit. We did not see a need for more elaborate definitions of the roles and expected them to follow naturally from function, as all except the child role were merely adaptations of preexisting roles in any agile development method.

Initially the roles were articulated in terms of functionality. The challenger was just that: a customer providing challenges to the team. Likewise, responders would meet and possibly exceed expectations when faced with challenges. The anchor was a facilitator and guardian of the creative process, while the child role would serve as a safety valve to let out odd ideas or discomfort with how things were progressing. The behavior of team members was expected to follow straightforwardly from these functional requirements. How this behavior was rooted in values, rationales, and personal nature was left for the team members to fill in.

In command variable terms, the first design of roles was lax, and how they would be employed was not prescribed.

We tried this approach in a project for software engineering thesis students as reported by Aaen (2008a, 2008b). In this laboratory experiment, four students worked on a software development project over 4 months. The development part alone took 2 full months.

The students used Scrum (Schwaber and Beedle 2002) as the basis for Essence and developed an IDE plug-in over four sprints. During the experiment, the students answered a questionnaire with 16 questions for each sprint. Their answers were analyzed qualitatively using a 48-node coding tree with TAMS analyzer.

Using a role obviously requires it to be well understood, but the students felt that this was not the case from the start, and this had implications for how useful they found the roles to be. One student wrote *"The roles should have been clearer specified from the start to indicate their implications"* and another wrote *"When I finally fell into the role it worked fine, but apart from that I don't think it went very well."*

Some students reported negative experiences. One of them doubted the potential in the child role: *"The child role does not do a whole lot. It feels odd to thwart the other team members to create ideas."* Another student criticized the responder role's responsibilities: *"I am not sure the distribution of responsibilities is even. As a responder you are fairly free from responsibility."*

Altogether, the group reported more positive than negative experiences from using roles. Roles generally help distribute responsibilities in the team. This was useful seen from the individual team member's perspective: *"This way I have specific responsibilities and can concentrate on them."* Similarly, some students observed benefits for the whole team: *"The roles help distribute responsibilities meaningfully."* Roles also benefit the team by supporting interactions among team members: *"The roles were useful tools. I knew whom to ask and I could expect to be guided in certain situations."* Individual roles had specific advantages: *"Having an anchor to settle questions fast"* was a factor that was helpful. Similarly, the challenger role helped make decisions: *"Answers, decision making....Essence gave me authority."*

On the other hand, the students found it difficult to have the roles in mind at all times: *"The customer* [challenger] *had like a double role and you quickly forgot who was customer, and the same was true for the anchor. It was mostly when our discussions went silly that we reminded ourselves of the roles."*

This experiment helped evaluate our first design of the roles. We expected roles to be intuitive and easy to learn and follow, due to being functionally defined and based on preexisting roles in agile development, but the experiment dashed this expectation. In the experiment, roles were fleeting, not always intuitive, sometimes forgotten, and hard to learn.

The roles were not as useful to the team as hoped for, and we decided to change their design.

## 5.2  Revised Role Definitions: Adding Temperaments to Roles

We assume there is a need for more definition while keeping the acting out of roles open. Prescription must be kept at a minimum. We therefore developed a design that would be easy on choreography, still more suggestive. Values and temperaments were to be internalized deeper into the player to provide a basis for his actions. In command variable terms, the second design of roles was more defined, but the process for using them was kept open.

The idea in the new design is to define the temperament—psychological archetype— for each role, the outlook, values, and rationales of the archetype. Hopefully a deeper understanding of the temperaments will help internalize values and rationales into behaviors without becoming overly restrictive. The temperaments are used to ensure variation in perspectives among team members, to support the creation of more sophisticated software solutions in line with Tiwana and McLean's (2005) empirical study of expertise integration and team creativity.

The new role definitions are based on the temperaments associated with the generic views: fire, water, earth, and air. The four temperaments have been used for thousands of years to describe and characterize archetypal personalities.

The personality types are ideal types, constructs suggesting a particular set of values and rationales for a given role. Thus they will not describe the person playing a role, only the role itself. The archetypes are used to ensure variety among roles and comprehensiveness in the team in the sense that all major outlooks are represented to facilitate that challenges and candidate solutions are seen from diverse viewpoints.

The four temperaments are the choleric, the melancholic, the phlegmatic, and the sanguine, and we relate each of these temperaments to the logical views for which each of the Essence roles has primary responsibility.

*The Choleric Responder.* The choleric is associated with the fire element. Fire is energetic and associated with passion, destruction, and creation. In Essence, fire is associated with the product view. The product should bring about change by destructing what is obsolete and creating the best replacements imaginable. The product view is associated with the responder role, and consequently the responder has a choleric temperament.

The responder represents technical skills. A strong sense of ambition makes the responder strive for the best result possible, and sometimes even disregard influences they consider nuisances. The responder is enthusiastic and does not settle for the ordinary. He is not a pleaser, but plays hard to achieve success, and when faced with obstacles he musters even more energy.

*The Melancholic Challenger.* The melancholic is associated with the earth element. Earth is traditionally restrained and associated with the practical, physical, and sensual. In Essence, earth is associated with the project view. The project is the basis for the development effort, and provides the essential resources for the change to be brought about. The project view is associated with the challenger role, and consequently the challenger has a melancholic temperament.

The challenger is the customer and represents needs and resources for the project. The challenger is reflective and has far-reaching thoughts. He is kind and pensive.

*The Phlegmatic Anchor.* The phlegmatic is associated with the water element. Water is traditionally stoic and associated with calm, rationality, and reason. In Essence, water is associated with the process view. The process offers support for the work in terms of tools, techniques, and procedures for idea generation, development, and evaluation activities. The process view offers a *Swiss Army Knife* or *Junior Woodchucks Guidebook* for the team. The process view is associated with the anchor role, and consequently the anchor has a phlegmatic temperament.

The anchor is a facilitator and represents skills for moderation, negotiation, and inspiration. He is only weakly affected by impressions and rarely engages emotionally. He is a calm observer, friendly and reliable, and acts when needed.

*The Sanguine Child.* The sanguine is associated with the air element. Air is traditionally fleeting and was associated by Plato with mobility and ability to penetrate. In Essence, air is associated with the people view. The people view is used for evaluating the product against perceived or real uses, and for provoking radically new ideas or conceptions about the environment to be changed. The people view is associated with the child role, and consequently the child has a sanguine temperament.

The child is the jester in the project and represents untamed, irresponsible, and possibly revolutionary behavior. The child is fast and eager when excited—he reacts immediately, but forgets again soon. He often engages in the part more than the whole and does not always understand the depth of a matter.

## 6  Second Experiment with Roles: The Intensive Essence Course

The second experiment took place as part of a new software innovation course for Computer Science students (third year), Software Engineering students (fourth year), and International Master's students. A total of 61 students attended the course—25 from Computer Science, 17 from Software Engineering, 15 from the International Master's, and 4 other students.

The Essence part consisted of three lectures (two on Essence and one on Scrum ) followed by two full days of work on a major challenge. Our students are always organized in groups of four or five persons, and each group shares a permanent room with another group. Every student, therefore, knows the people in the room and is used to working closely with half of them. For practical reasons, we chose to form groups by merging the preexisting collocated groups into one.

The two-day challenge was to design a superior project management tool for innovative teams using Scrum. The tool should have extraordinary features and support working with idea development and idea administration. Via a number of idea development sessions, the groups would produce a product vision over the two days.

The introduction to Essence included a presentation of the roles and temperaments. Every group appointed one anchor and one challenger, while all remaining group members were responders. Every group member wore a badge at all times with the name of their role printed in corresponding colors: red for responders, green for challengers, and blue for anchors. The badges were constant reminders of each person's role and temperament.

The pedagogy of this part of the course differed markedly from conventional courses. Although the students were exhausted by the end of two intensive days, they overall worked with enthusiasm and focus in a free atmosphere, and many students demonstrated great zest in the activities. Evaluations after the course were mainly positive or constructively critical.

The two days consisted of four blocks, each with group work ending in plenum presentations of the results. Each block used several different techniques for developing and maturing ideas including variants of well-known techniques such as traditional brainstorming and six thinking hats (de Bono 2000). The first two blocks were devoted to diverging idea generation, while the latter two were used for converging and presenting the final ideas.

## 7  Evaluation of the Revised Roles

Immediately after the two-day challenge, we issued a questionnaire to the students. The questionnaire covered simple demographics: age, study, and role. All students were male. The rest of the questionnaire focused on evaluations of the following:

- The respondent's own and the other roles in the group
- The use of views
- Each of the nine techniques used in the four blocks
- Overall views on idea-generation techniques, idea-evaluation-techniques, and Essence

A total of 38 questions were asked. Most of them were yes/no or five-point Likert scale, and each group of questions on roles, views, and individual techniques ended in a free-format question calling for additional comments. The data were collected over 2 weeks, and we received 39 responses corresponding to a response rate of over 60 percent. No incentives were used, except polite requests at lectures and gentle e-mail reminders.

Approximately one month later, the students were encouraged to prepare a written report as part of their preparations for exam. They were asked to give an evaluation of their experiences during the two-day intensive part of the course. The report was to be prepared in self-chosen groups of not more than three and be three to six pages long. The reports would not be graded, but they would act as a starting point for the oral exam. Altogether 54 students used this option and wrote 27 reports. Of these, 6 were written by single students, 15 by pairs, and the remaining 6 by groups of three.

Table 1 presents the data from the questions on the three permanent roles. About 85 percent of the students understood their own role well or very well. Challengers appear to have had slightly more problems understanding their roles, probably because few had relevant experience for this role.

Around 65 percent of the students were able to apply their own role. One anchor and one challenger were unable to do this. As these two roles are unique to a team, this suggests major problems. Both students came from the same group and no one else from this group answered the questionnaire. This group may have had massive problems, but whether or not these problems were related to the roles is not known.

Around half found their role useful. One in four was neutral, and one in four was negative. There are marked differences from role to role. Responders are overall neutral or positive (around 55 percent are positive), whereas more than half of the anchors are neutral and the rest positive. Challengers are split, half are positive, while the other half are negative, indicating the difficulties students face when playing this role.

Well over half of the students found the other roles helpful, while less than a third did not. Half of the challengers found the other roles helpful, while three out of four anchors viewed them as positive.

**Table 1.** Evaluation of Roles

| | Did you understand your own role? | | | | | | Were you able to apply your own role? | | | | | |
|---|---|---|---|---|---|---|---|---|---|---|---|---|
| | (No) | | | | (Yes) | | (No) | | | | (Yes) | |
| | 1 | 2 | 3 | 4 | 5 | Σ | 1 | 2 | 3 | 4 | 5 | Σ |
| Anchor | 0 | 0 | 0 | 5 | 2 | 7 | 0 | 1 | 1 | 3 | 2 | 7 |
| Challenger | 0 | 0 | 1 | 5 | 0 | 6 | 1 | 0 | 2 | 3 | 0 | 6 |
| Responder | 0 | 1 | 3 | 14 | 8 | 26 | 1 | 4 | 3 | 15 | 3 | 26 |
| Σ | 0 | 1 | 4 | 24 | 10 | 39 | 2 | 5 | 6 | 21 | 5 | 39 |
| | Did you find your own role helpful? | | | | | | Did you find the other roles helpful? | | | | | |
| | (No) | | | | (Yes) | | (No) | | | | (Yes) | |
| | 1 | 2 | 3 | 4 | 5 | Σ | 1 | 2 | 3 | 4 | 5 | Σ |
| Anchor | 0 | 0 | 4 | 2 | 1 | 7 | 0 | 0 | 2 | 3 | 2 | 7 |
| Challenger | 1 | 2 | 0 | 3 | 0 | 6 | 1 | 1 | 1 | 3 | 0 | 6 |
| Responder | 2 | 5 | 5 | 8 | 6 | 26 | 1 | 8 | 4 | 7 | 6 | 26 |
| Σ | 3 | 7 | 9 | 13 | 7 | 39 | 2 | 9 | 7 | 13 | 8 | 39 |

Those who saw the other roles as positive also understood their own role, were able to apply it, and found it helpful. We saw some differences between the studies. Computer Science students reported less positive experiences compared to International Master's and Software Engineering students. These differences may be related to value differences between studies and nationality, as we see no major differences related to other demographic factors.

The qualitative study offers deeper insights into how students experienced the roles. We coded the 27 reports for comments on roles and temperaments using TAMS analyzer to supplement the questionnaire data. Space limitations allow for only a few comments here.

The reports were written at a time where the students had gained a deeper understanding of the intentions in Essence. This is reflected in their comments, where roles are generally accepted as a promising idea.

Some point to difficulties in using the roles ("*A sense of like-mindedness in our group made the roles seem forced*"), while others point to lack of experience("*A reason why the roles were not that useful could be due to us being novices*").

Several point to advantages in using roles to allocate responsibilities and ensure focus. Some point to advantages of different perspectives: "*We discovered that sometimes an unusual point of view can bring better solutions than a classical one. It demonstrated the advantages of having different personalities, opinions, and technical backgrounds in the same team.*"

A number of reports comment on the temperaments as a source of problems. This quote sums up most of these views: "*The team did not succeed very well in implementing the roles. It seems that the two main reasons for this are: 1) the team members did not have sufficient time to get used to the roles 2) a probably more important reason could be that we divided the roles more or less randomly or at least not in accordance with the personality/nature of the team members .Although the roles are indeed roles, we cannot expect the personality...to fit the nature of the roles perfectly.*"

## 8  Lessons and Implications

The second design of roles sought to build values deeper into the roles based on archetypal temperaments.  We wanted a clearer definition of the roles without prescribing action.

The experiment shows that the new design also has problems. Generally roles are perceived as potentially useful, offering diversity to the team. Roles are, however, still hard to learn and easy to forget. These problems might be handled via pedagogical means, but unfortunately the new design introduced new and seemingly fundamental problems: Students complained that roles sometimes felt forced, and they consistently mentioned a difference between personal temperament and role temperament as a problem.

Therefore, we conclude that we need to change the roles a third time. We still want Essence to be lightweight, fun, and easy to use, so our next combination of the command variables must keep this objective in mind.  We believe that the third design of roles should be lax, but the process for using them should be somewhat more prescriptive, although still lightweight.

Presently our ideas are to meld the temperaments into the views rather than the roles, and to define the views more clearly in terms of values and how they are used. This will strengthen the process definition in return for relaxing the role definition.

To achieve this, we will put more focus on the people view and the child role. These two will be central in most idea generation sessions. We will use a bit more choreography: Games will take form as a series of steps beginning at the people view, where scenarios are developed without constraints by all team members taking the child role. The next step will be realistic construction at the product view led by the responders, where implementation options are developed; and the last step will be a critical examination chaired by the challenger at the project view, where the dreams are evaluated and decided on. This sequence will be iterated as needed.  Temperament thus follows the view. One view (and one temperament) at a time will take the lead. All team members will have the same temperament while at the same view. No team member will be required to have a temperament different from any other, but each role will continue to have special responsibilities.

The new design introduces new dangers to Essence: The interaction between views might be weakened, although the use of each view might be strengthened. It might also make Essence more sequential and rigid, although each step will be more focused. These dangers will be addressed in coming experiments.

## 9  Conclusion

Essence is developed iteratively as we gain experience from using it. Method design involves great complexities, and evaluating the design is complicated as too many factors are involved to single each out for systematic testing.

We use command variables as learning instruments to reason about design alternatives and learn from experiments. We cannot use command variables for systematic variation and testing, but we use them to at least have an idea about what we are changing, why we do this, and to evaluate pragmatically the implications of these variations.

Every design tested here is one that we have believed in completely. When we design, we need to passionately believe the new to be an improvement, but to some extent this is in conflict with the traditional view of the experimental researcher as a neutral observer. This is one of the challenges in design science. Our use of design variables seeks to balance this conflict.

Future research will flesh out and evaluate the third design of roles in Essence. We will try to include real-life projects in our experiments to supplement the experiments involving students.

## Acknowledgments

Thanks go to Jeremy Rose, my colleague on the software innovation course, and to our students for their patience, tolerance, and generous comments. I also would like to thank the anonymous reviewers for insightful comments and suggestions.

## References

Aaen, I.: Essence: Facilitating Agile Innovation. In: Abrahamsson, P., Baskerville, R., Conboy, K., Fitzgerald, B., Morgan, L., Wang, X. (eds.) Agile Processes in Software Engineering and Extreme Programming, pp. 1–10. Springer, Berlin (2008a)

Aaen, I.: Essence: Facilitating Software Innovation. European Journal of Information Systems 17(5), 543–553 (2008b)

Adamides, E.D., Karacapilidis, N.: Information Technology Support for the Knowledge and Social Processes of Innovation Management. Technovation 26(1), 50–59 (2006)

Amabile, T.M., Conti, R., Coon, H., Lazenby, J., Herron, M.: Assessing the Work Environment for Creativity. Academy of Management Journal 39(5), 1154–1184 (1996)

Bernstein, L., Yuhas, C.M.: People, Process, Product, Project: The Big Four. In: Bernstein, L., Yuhas, C.M. (eds.) Trustworthy Systems Through Quantitative Software Engineering, pp. 39–71. John Wiley & Sons, Inc., New York (2005)

Chang, C.M.: Collaborative, Heuristic and Normatively Guided Techniques to Creativity. In: Proceedings of the Portland International Conference on Management of Engineering & Technology (PICMET 2008), July 27-31, pp. 656–663. IEEE Computer Society, Los Alamitos (2008)

de Bono, E.: Six Thinking Hats. Penguin, London (2000)

de la Barra, C., Crawford, B.: Fostering Creativity Thinking in Agile Software Development. Springer, Berlin (2007)

Deshpande, N., de Vries, B., van Leeuwen, J.P.: Collocated, Multi-Disciplinary, Collaborative Designspace: An overview. In: van Leeuwen, J.P., Timmermans, H.J.P. (eds.) Developments in Design & Decision Support Systems in Architecture and Urban Planning, pp. 253–268. Eindhoven University of Technology, Eindhoven (2004)

Do, E.Y.-L., Gross, M.D.: Environments for Creativity: A Lab for Making Things. In: Proceedings of the 6th ACM SIGCHI Conference on Creativity & Cognition, Washington, DC, June 13-15, pp. 27–36 (2007)

Fortino, A.: A Pattern Language for Innovation Management. In: Proceedings of the Portland International Conference on Management of Engineering & Technology (PICMET 2008), July 27-31, pp. 415–419. IEEE Computer Society, Los Alamitos (2008)

Greene, S.L.: Characteristics of Applications that Support Creativity. Communications of the ACM 45(10), 100–104 (2002)

Hevner, A.R., March, S.T., Park, J., Ram, S.: Design Science in Information Systems Research. MIS Quarterly 28(1), 75–105 (2004)

Highsmith, J.: Agile Project Management: Creating Innovative Products. Addison-Wesley, Boston (2004)

Highsmith, J., Cockburn, A.: Agile Software Development: The Business of Innovation. Computer 34(9), 120–127 (2001)

Hohmann, L.: Innovation Games: Creating Breakthrough Products Through Collaborative Play. Addison-Wesley Professional, Upper Saddle River (2006)

Huczynski, A.: Encyclopedia of Development Methods. Gower, Aldershot (2001)

Johansson, M., Fröst, P., Brandt, E., Binder, T., Messeter, J.: Partner Engaged Design: New Challenges for Workplace Design. In: Proceedings of the Participatory Design Conference, Malmo, Sweden, June 23-25, pp. 162–172 (2002)

Judy, K.H., Krumins-Beens, I.: Using Agile Practices to Spark Innovation in a Small to Medium Sized Business. In: Proceedings of the 40th Annual Hawaii International Conference on System Sciences. IEEE Computer Society, Los Alamitos (2007)

Kristensen, T.: The Physical Context of Creativity. Creativity and Innovation Management 13(2), 89–96 (2004)

Larssen, A.T., Robertson, T., Edwards, J.: The Feel Dimension of Technology Interaction: Exploring Tangibles Through Movement and Touch. In: Proceedings of the First International Conference on Tangible and Embedded Interaction, Baton Rouge, LA, February 15-17, pp. 271–278 (2007)

Leenders, R.T.A.J., van Engelen, J.M.L., Kratzer, J.: Systematic Design Methods and the Creative Performance of New Product Teams: Do They Contradict or Complement Each Other? Journal of Product Innovation Management 24(2), 166–179 (2007)

Lewis, M., Moultrie, J.: The Organizational Innovation Laboratory. Creativity and Innovation Management 14(1), 73–83 (2005)

Mahaux, M., Maiden, N.: Theater Improvisers Know the Requirements Game. IEEE Software 25(5), 68–69 (2008)

Maiden, N., Manning, S., Robertson, S., Greenwood, J.: Integrating Creativity Workshops into Structured Requirements Processes. In: Proceedings of the 2004 Conference on Designing Interactive Systems: Processes, Practices, Methods, and Techniques, Cambridge, MA, August 1-4, pp. 113–122 (2004)

Maiden, N., Robertson, S.: Integrating Creativity into Requirements Processes: Experiences with an Air Traffic Management System. In: Proceedings of the 13th IEEE International Conference on Requirements Engineering, Paris, August 29-September 2, pp. 105–114 (2005)

Maiden, N., Robertson, S., Gizikis, A.: Provoking Creativity: Imagine What Your Requirements Could Be Like. IEEE Software 21(5), 68–75 (2004)

Maiden, N., Robertson, S., Robertson, J.: Creative Requirements: Invention and its Role in Requirements Engineering. In: Proceeding of the 28th International Conference on Software Engineering, Shanghai, China, May 20-28, pp. 1073–1074 (2006)

Mich, L., Anesi, C., Berry, D.M.: Requirements Engineering and Creativity: An Innovative Approach Based on a Model of the Pragmatics of Communication. In: Proceedings of the Requirements Engineering: Foundation for Software Quality (REFSQ) Workshop, Riga, Latvia (2004)

Nerur, S., Balijepally, V.: Theoretical Reflections on Agile Development Methodologies. Communications of the ACM 50(3), 79–83 (2007)

Pressman, R.S.: Software Engineering: A Practitioner's Approach. McGraw-Hill Higher Education, Boston (2005)

Rittel, H.W.J., Webber, M.M.: Dilemmas in a General Theory of Planning. Policy Sciences 4(2), 155–169 (1973)

Satzinger, J.W., Garfield, M.J., Nagasundaram, M.: The Creative Process: The Effects of Group Memory on Individual Idea Generation. Journal of Management Information Systems 15(4), 143–160 (1999)

Schwaber, K., Beedle, M.: Agile Software Development with Scrum. Prentice Hall, Upper Saddle River (2002)

Shneiderman, B.: User Interfaces for Creativity Support Tools. In: Proceedings of the Third Conference on Creativity & Cognition, Loughborough, United Kingdom, October 11-13, pp. 15–22 (1999)

Shneiderman, B.: Creativity Support Tools. Communications of the ACM 45(10), 116–120 (2002)

Shneiderman, B.: Creativity Support Tools: Accelerating Discovery and Innovation. Communications of the ACM 50(12), 20–32 (2007)

Simon, H.A.: The Sciences of the Artificial. MIT Press, Cambridge (1996)

Swartjes, I.M.T., Vromen, J.A.F.: Emergent Story Generation: Lessons from Improvisational Theater. In: Proceedings of the AAAI Fall Symposium on Intelligent Narrative Technologies, Arlington, VA, November 9-11, pp. 146–149 (2007)

Terrenghi, L., Fritsche, T., Butz, A.: The EnLighTable: Design of Affordances to Support Collaborative Creativity. In: Butz, A., Fisher, B., Krüger, A., Olivier, P. (eds.) SG 2006. LNCS, vol. 4073, pp. 206–217. Springer, Heidelberg (2006)

Thomas, J.C., Lee, A., Danis, C.: Enhancing Creative Design Via Software Tools. Communications of the ACM 45(10), 112–115 (2002)

Tiwana, A., McLean, E.R.: Expertise Integration and Creativity in Information Systems Development. Journal of Management Information Systems 22(1), 13–43 (2005)

Vaishnavi, V., Kuechler, W.: Design Research in Information Systems, January 20 (2004), last updated August 16, 2009,
http://ais.affiniscape.com/displaycommon.cfm?an=1&
subarticlenbr=279 (accessed November 24, 2009)

Yardley-Matwiejczuk, K.M.: Role Play: Theory and Practice. Sage, London (1997)

## About the Author

**Ivan Aaen** is an associate professor of computer science at Aalborg University, Denmark. His interests include software innovation, agile software engineering, and information systems. He holds a Ph.D. in computer science from Aalborg University and is a member of the ACM and IEEE Computer Society. He can be reached at aaen@acm.org.

# A Case Study of Improving Information Technology Governance in a University Context

Michael Hicks, Graham Pervan, and Brian Perrin

Curtin University of Techology,
Perth, Western Australia

**Abstract.** The objective of this study is to explore the criteria of effective information technology governance processes employed in universities and their impact on the diffusion of appropriate technology to the base level users. From this analysis, we hope to develop a set of best practice guidelines for IT governance and related processes in respect of universities. This will realize significant benefits by providing a reference model or benchmark based on the key characteristics of IT governance that are most effective in achieving high levels of IT and business goal alignment, effective use of IT resources, and IT risk management.

A large Australian university that is currently undergoing a major restructure of its IT governance process was selected to be the subject of this case study involving interviews and a survey of internal stakeholders. The results indicate there are still some problematic issues, but overall there is a perception of significant improvement in key areas of IT governance. Additionally the recognition by the university that IT governance is an ongoing process seems indicative of an IT governance structure that is rapidly improving in all accepted measures of effectiveness. A healthy sign of a good governance structure in this case is the IT governance-aware attitude of key members of the executive management.

The survey results illustrate the effect IT governance constructs may have on the diffusion of technology in larger organizations where key business functions, such as research, rest substantially at the individual level. In this case a lack of lower-level consultation is perceived by staff as an impediment to the diffusion of technology appropriate to meeting user IT needs.

**Keywords:** IT governance, business alignment, IT resources, university governance, mechanisms of IT governance.

## 1 Introduction

Universities are highly dependent on the institutional processes that create and use information to support their research, administration, and teaching activities. Information technology governance within these organizations guides, at the strategic and operational levels, these institutional processes. This study investigates the process-based relationship between the key constructs and mechanisms of IT governance typically found in universities and the level of effective IT governance

J. Pries-Heje et al. (Eds.): IS Design Science Research, IFIP AICT 318, pp. 89–107, 2010.

that the university achieves. As such, it explores the manner in which systems to capture, create, and use information are developed and integrated within the organization. This contributes to the continued discussion of IT governance in various organizations in keeping with prior International Federation of Information Processing (IFIP) conferences. Examples include papers presented on IT governance practices in small and medium-sized enterprises (Devos et al. 2009; Huang et al. 2009). This study expands this discussion to larger-scale organizations. The degree of success in IT and business goal alignment, effective use of IT resources, and IT risk management are considered essential outcomes of effective IT governance and are used as indicators of the level of effective IT governance that the university has demonstrated. IT governance from a structural and process point of view, including the typical characteristics of IT governance, is well covered in the literature. However, the approach to IT governance from the perspective of its impact on the three key outcomes of IT governance in the context of Australian universities is relatively unexplored.

## 2   IT Governance Research

### 2.1   IT Governance Importance

Business dependency on IT has been described as extreme, with IT now becoming pervasive in most organizations (Clinton 1998; International Federation of Accountants 2003; Robinson 2007). IT departments are demanding an ever-expanding amount of financial and other organizational resources to achieve their promised, but never quite realized, potential. These factors, combined with the renewed interest in corporate governance generated by the Enron, HIH, Onetel, and Parmalat corporate collapses, have led to a demand for increased governance in the area of IT (Jopson 2006, Lucy 2004). A study of 300 firms undertaken by Weill and Ross (2004a) failed to establish a "single best formula for governing IT" but concluded that effective IT governance "doesn't occur by accident." Weill and Ross (2004b) proposed that organizations with effective IT governance had IT governance patterns matched to complement the organization's strategic focus. The concept of the matching of IT governance to the organization's strategic focus is further supported by Penrod (2003), Pirani and Salaway (2008), and Council (2007) in relation to universities.

It is clear that effective IT governance has many characteristics, although it is equally clear that the omission of any particular one is not determinant of a defective or nonexistent IT governance function. This is emphasized by the many different approaches adopted in analyzing IT governance. Weill and Ross (2004b), for example, use a structured definition with the focus on the decision making rights and "accountability framework" an organization instigates in respect of IT decisions. By contrast the IT Governance Institute of ISACA (ISACA 2005) and the Standards Australia Committee on ICT Governance and Management (2005) take a process-based view of IT governance, looking at a "system established within an organization" to direct and control IT now and in the future. This approach entails a wider, more pragmatic list of IT governance determinants, such as extent and richness of communication between business and IT management (Johnson and Lederer 2003) and use of multi-constituency measures of success (Chang and King 2000) as well as many other mechanisms and processes (Clark 2005; Hardy and Guldentops 2005; Van Grembergen ND).

Both Penrod and Council discussed many of these general characteristics of IT governance as being of importance in university IT governance structures. Other studies, such as those undertaken by Bhattacharjya and Chang (2006) and Pirani and Salaway, have supported the findings of these studies in Australian universities, particularly in respect of strategic alignment.

## 2.2  IT Governance Decision Structures

IT governance decision structure refers to *who* participates in the decision making process (Weill and Ross 2004b). Penrod, and Pirani and Salaway, pointed to the importance of the interrelationships of the various university governance bodies in maintaining effective decision making.

As part of a general model for IT governance, Penrod recommended the creation of an IT policy group to make the high-level strategic IT decisions, with IT management responsible for the operational detail. Membership of the IT policy group would consist of the university's key decision makers, including the CEO, CIO, and other executives from the functional areas. Penrod foresaw that the policy group would be supported by advisory committees formed for specific issues. Policy groups would consist of representatives from both the technical IT areas and all of the functional units of the university that would be stakeholders of the issues being considered by the advisory group. Intercommunication with the policy group was considered essential and would be achieved by the advisory committees having chairs on the policy group.

## 2.3  Reporting Mechanisms and Metrics

CobiT (ISACA 2005) puts forward that IT governance is achieved through control of IT, so it delivers the information needed by the organization by managing the risks and securing IT resources, and by ensuring IT achieves objectives. This includes the support of business goals through a two step process. First, the control objectives of CobiT are used to determine the ultimate organizational goal of implementing and maintaining policy, procedures, structures, and best practices. This ensures the achievement of business objectives and prevents, detects, and corrects events of an undesirable nature. The second step is determining what should be measured and how it should be measured. This involves bench marking, determining IT goals and metrics, and establishing activity goals.

Blumenberg and Hinz (2006) argue that as IT areas emerged from being treated as cost centers to a more service-oriented approach, strongly dependent on intangible assets, the desirability of a performance measurement system based on other than tangible financial measures, such as Balanced Scorecard, became inevitable. The output of the reporting mechanism needs to be considered at an appropriate level and action taken when necessary to ensure that the strategic initiative upon which it reports continues to be strategically aligned with the overall corporate objectives (IT Governance Institute 2005; Weill and Ross 2004b).

## 2.4  IT Governance in Universities

There are a number of studies that have addressed particular aspects of IT related issues in university environments, and many that address corporate governance challenges, but there appears to be a limited amount of contemporary research of IT governance in universities. Penrod, discussed above, and Clark (2005) are examples related to IT governance in universities.    Both dealt with the building of IT governance decision structures. Other studies, such as Pirani and Salaway, have examined the relationship between the maturity of corporate governance with IT governance in universities.

These studies illustrate the increasing importance of IT governance in all organizations, including universities. There is, however, no universal model of which IT governance constructs will constitute effective IT governance in all organizations. What is clear from the literature is that there are a number of characteristics that appear to increase the likelihood that an organization will have effective IT governance. The studies that relate IT governance specifically to universities have found these general characteristics should also apply.

## 3  Research Methods

The objective of this in-depth case study was to explore the criteria of effective IT governance as used within a large Australian university. Essentially this research maps the approach to IT governance employed within the case study university and then, based on qualitative and quantitative data analysis, determines how effective this approach appears to have been.

The case study was selected on the basis that it was a large, very diverse university that had recently reviewed and restructured its IT governance structure. As such, it was expected to provide a rich source of data about IT governance effectiveness in Australian universities. As Denscombe (1998) points out, the use of case studies allows a variety of sources, data, and research methods to be employed by the researcher, which permits a flexible and thorough approach.

The research initially employed a qualitative approach, collecting data through interviewing of key personnel as shown in Table 1.

**Table 1.** List of Interviewees and Acronyms

| Interviewee | Acronym |
|---|---|
| Deputy Vice Chancellor (Academic) | DVC |
| Chief Information Officer | CIO |
| Pro-vice Chancellor | PVC |
| Director of a Corporate Service Area | DCS |
| Head of an Academic Area | HOS |
| Director Research and Development | DRD |
| Assistant Director Research | ADR |
| Dean of a Faculty | DF |

**Table 2.** Survey Response Rates

| Description | Number |
|---|---|
| Total surveys distributed | 186 |
| Survey returned as no longer employed or on extended leave | 6 |
| Total valid surveys distributed | 180 |
| Completed surveys returned | 53 |
| Percentage response rate | 29.4% |

This includes the CIO, the DVC responsible for IT, and representatives from the core business functions of the university: teaching and learning, research, and corporate applications. These were selected from a range of faculties across the university. An interview protocol for each category of interviewee was developed to ensure a standardized interview instrument that assisted in both gathering adequate data and supporting the analysis of that data in the case study. The interviews were recorded, transcribed, then checked and verified for accuracy. The data was analyzed and categorized into themes or patterns of general criteria of effective IT governance, a technique developed by Miles and Huberman (1994). The theme or pattern-based groupings were further defined or revealed through an iterative refining process as further data was gathered.

Data was also gathered through the collection of documents, policies, and memos from various university sources.

A survey of teaching, research, and administrative staff in the Faculty of Business was then undertaken to quantitatively assess how effective the IT governance structure was from a user's perspective. Table 2 outlines the details of the survey and response rates. Table 3 shows the response rates by the respondents function; the teaching and research category indicates that the respondent has significant commitments to both functions.

**Table 3.** Survey Response Rates by Main Duties

| Main Duty of Respondent | Number | Percent |
|---|---|---|
| Teaching | 5 | 9% |
| Research | 6 | 11% |
| Both Teaching & Research | 31 | 59% |
| Administration | 8 | 15% |
| Other | 3 | 6% |
| Total | 53 | 100% |

## 4 Results

This Australian university offers a wide range of courses over a number of geographically dispersed campuses. It has experienced a rapid and substantial growth in terms of student numbers, which has continued over the last two decades. It has a number of faculties, each with substantial student enrollments. Each faculty is active in research as well as teaching and learning.

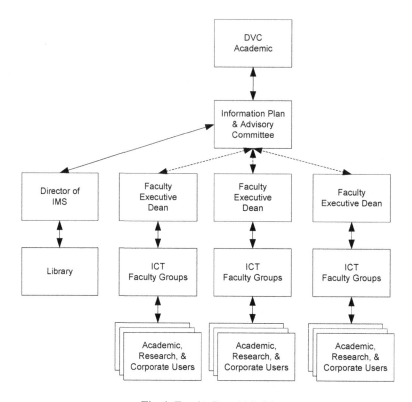

**Fig. 1.** Faculty Based Model

In 1999–2000 an initial attempt was made to move to a centralized IT structure as a result of a recommendation from an external consultant commissioned to review the university's IT governance structure. This initial attempt was not supported by the various faculties and ultimately it was decided by executive management not to proceed with the recommendation. At this point the central IT area had responsibility only for corporate applications and the central library information service.

As can be seen in Figure 1, each faculty was responsible for its own IT areas. A peak governing body, the Information Plan and Advisory Committee (IPAC), did exist to oversee the IT function. However, a second review by internal audit into ICT governance in the university in early 2005 made four key findings:

1. IPAC was not providing sufficient leadership in ICT.
2. At key points, accountability and role responsibilities were not clearly defined or designated in ICT related areas.
3. There was a lack of coordination and communication for ICT between faculties.
4. Risk assessment was incomplete and major ICT related risks had not been addressed.

Based on the audit report, the DVC responsible for ICT concluded that user needs, at all levels, were not being met. There was also widespread duplication of ICT related resources and in many areas conflicting architecture and services. As a result of this second review into ICT governance issues, the university has begun to implement major changes in its IT governance structure. The focal point for the changes has been a major restructuring and adoption of a shared services model. Central features of the new structure were the following initiatives:

1. Chief information officer (CIO) position created with responsibility for all ICT university wide.
2. Establishment of an ICT strategy and planning committee (SPC) to oversee and guide ICT across the university.
3. Membership of the SPC to include representatives from all faculties and business areas, as well as the DVC responsible for ICT and the CIO.
4. Establishment of a enterprise architecture subgroup.
5. Establishment of a ICT projects subgroup.
6. Establishment of faculty subgroups each with a representative on the SPC.

These initiatives have largely been implemented progressively over the last three years (see Figure 2).

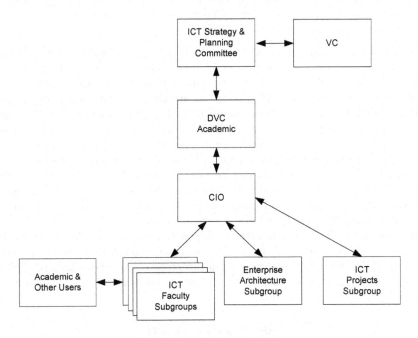

**Fig. 2.** Shared Services Model

## 4.1 Progress toward Effective IT Governance

In all of the interviews undertaken, there appeared to be a perception that the implementation of the shared services model had led to positive improvements in many areas relative to IT governance. This accompanied a general acceptance of the desirability of the change to the more centralized features of the shared services model. In some instances, it was not clear whether this perception had arisen from post implementation recognition of advantages that had occurred or was the result of continued expectation of advantages from the promotion of the original proposal. Indicative of this was the use often of "I think" rather than more definite statements of certainty when interviewees referred to improvements arising from the move to the shared services model.

This aside, there was substantial support for the restructuring of IT governance. Statements in this regard were both general and specific. Representatives from research, teaching and learning, and corporate applications were all positive about the initiative as is shown from the following comments:

> *"So in that way I think the university IT [keeping up with technology] probably has changed and probably has improved.I think from our point of view we have brought it [IT shared services] to a position where it is working for us."* (HOS)

> *"I'm very pleased [with shared services and IT support for my area]. I think what I've seen and the support provided for [my area] is very good indeed. I have no complaints, none at all."* (PVC)

Support for the changes is present but appears to diminish below the management level. The survey included management level but was distributed to a much larger number of lower-level staff. Survey respondents were asked three questions as to whether their satisfaction with IT support had increased over the last three years in respect to teaching, research, and administration. The questions solicited a response on a five-point Likert scale ranging from strongly disagree to strongly agree. Respondents had a sixth option of "does not apply to me." At the time of the survey, three years was the period since beginning implementation of the major initiatives in IT governance. Although the responses from the survey show a trend toward agreeing or strongly agreeing that there had been an improvement in all three areas, there was a significant "neither agree nor disagree" response. Table 4 gives the detail of the responses to these three questions.

In addition, respondents were asked if they were satisfied with the IT support for their area at the strategic level. In all, 54 percent of respondents agreed or strongly agreed that they were satisfied, 17 percent disagreed or strongly disagreed, and 21 percent were neutral. The other 8 percent either did not answer the question or indicated it did not apply to them.

**Table 4.** Satisfaction with IT

| Area | Not Improved | Neutral | Has Improved |
|---|---|---|---|
| Teaching | 11% | 36% | 36% |
| Research | 6% | 38% | 45% |
| Administration | 9% | 34% | 42% |
| Total | 8.8% | 38% | 41% |

The champions of the adoption and implementation of the shared services model in the university, the CIO and the DVC, both acknowledged the importance of user and management support for the changes, not only at the strategic level but also at the operational levels. In particular, evidence of this can be seen in the efforts made to gain that support before implementation began. This is typified in the following quote from the DVC: *"One of the philosophies that we took was to win the argument [to move to shared services] so that it could all move ahead."*

In addition, user support for organizational change is important to help ensure the continued operation of the change is as effective as possible and avoid any negative impact on job performance (Milton 1981). Both the CIO and DVC had also seen the effect of a negative attitude by the various faculties in the abandonment of the first attempt at centralization in 1999–2000. Much of the interview discussion relating to adopting the shared services model was centered on gaining faculty and wider user support. This is considered under the theme identified from the analysis of "User Relationship Management," discussed below.

## 4.2  Key Attributes of IT Governance

The personnel interviewed were each asked a number of questions that referred specifically to the effectiveness of IT governance as it related to their position and associated duties. The responses are discussed under the identified themes in the analysis, user relationship management, management support, IT governance mechanisms, strategic alignment, use of IT resources, IT risk management, performance measurement, and future directions.

**User Relationship Management:** The CIO and the DVC are both aware of the importance of a good relationship with the user areas, not just as clients of central IT, but also to ensure the ongoing success of the implementation of the revised IT governance structure. This is done, specifically, by avoiding dysfunctional behavior such as acquiring IT assets and resources outside the guidelines established. The university has approached this in three ways: first, through communicating IT issues and plans direct to all levels of users; second, by securing user involvement in decision making; and third, by creating a better client experience.

Richness, extent, and types of communication mechanisms established between business management and IT management is an important component of IT governance (Johnson and Lederer 2003; Jopson 2006). Not so recognized is the importance of communication to the lower levels of users, which was evident in the case study. The interviewees representative of users below management level largely believe they are well informed and the effectiveness of the dissemination of IT related plans and information is clear from comments such as: *"It came from the various IT people at the Center that we're doing this [adopting one staff email system] and this is why we're doing it. That information was transmitted and received successfully [by the area]"* (DF).

The CIO is cognizant of the importance of user consultation in ongoing IT operations as is evidenced by his plans to expand and formalize further user consultation, as suggested in the following quote: *"I've created a director of client services and that directorate is responsible for beginning to develop a client service mechanism of feedback across all areas and to identify and adopt best practices in any one faculty."*

The degree of knowledge sharing between management, user groups, and the IT area within the university was another theme that evolved from the analysis relative to IT governance (Broadbent and Kitzis 2005; Penrod 2003). Representatives from the corporate services and research and development areas, however, were critical of the reluctance of some central areas to share knowledge and data that the user areas required to service their ongoing business needs. These central areas were not under the ambit of central IT, but controlled data sources that were proprietary to their particular area of responsibility. This included the student services and finance areas. A typical example of this is the comment by the director of a corporate services area in relation to information held by the student services area: *"The university is quite arrogant with its view of who can access that information and who can't and why you would need it"* (DCS).

There was also some dissatisfaction with the lack of consultation before designing and implementing corporate applications. An instance of this was a corporate system implemented by the finance area which drew derisive comments such as: *"There was no regard to how schools operate or consultation with the main users. A lot of changes had to be made to the system because most schools could not work with the system that they brought in that they thought would be good for the area"* (DCS).

The dissatisfaction in the area of user consultation is supported by the survey responses to the following two statements included in the survey:

(1) The effectiveness of IT in teaching would be improved by increased consultation with academic staff before decisions are made.
(2) The effectiveness of IT in research would be improved by increased consultation with academic staff before decisions are made.

Responses show that 57 percent agreed or strongly agreed in relation to teaching and 63 percent agreed or strongly agreed in relation to research. Although the interviews indicated lower-level support for the changes, it is clear from the survey results that the base level users are not participating to any large extent in the IT related decisions that directly affect their key responsibilities of research and teaching. This would appear to support the major concerns of the faculties about the increased centralization that was a major feature of the proposed restructuring of IT within the university; namely, that there would a substantial loss of responsiveness and flexibility that would directly impact faculties and individual users.

The CIO is realistic in his assessment of the relationship with users and acknowledges this approach still needs further maturing, as illustrated in the following comment: *"Do we look at user expectations? Not yet. We're probably not that mature."*

This indicates that decision making has not diffused to the lower levels of the organization. Given that research within the university largely rests with individuals, this is an impediment to meeting the technology needs of researchers. Such an obstacle to the diffusion and adoption of technology to meet researchers IT needs is also an impediment to the alignment of IT with the organization's key objectives related to research and teaching and learning.

**Management Support:** The VC (vice chancellor) accepted the necessity to review the IT governance structure in 2005 due to a widely publicized systems failure that had occurred a few years prior. As a response to the system failure, the current DVC responsible for IT was assigned the IT responsibility with a clear mandate to find out what was wrong and fix it.

The degree of support given to IT governance by the VC and other executive management was considered important to effective IT governance (Broadbent and Kitzis 2005; Institute of Internal Auditors 2005; Penrod 2003). The support has been ongoing and the IT area has established a high level of credibility with both the university executive and the individual faculty executive. The support from the executive has continued and the CIO is confident that whatever resources are required they will be allocated. For example, *"When I went to the P&MC [Planning and Management Committee], I had six papers up. The VC called me in and said we are not going to overrule you on anything. That sent the right message. If you put up a paper they would say fine. If I went in and said I need three million for this and our recommendation is to do this, I think we would get it."*

The increase in IT spending transparency has also assisted in getting executive level support for IT changes. The CIO attributes the increase in credibility and ongoing executive support, at least in part, to the visibility of where IT funding is going and, conversely, being able to identify where savings are able to be made.

**Governance Mechanisms:** Since the adoption of the shared services model, a number of mechanisms to enact good IT governance have been implemented. One of the first steps under the new structure was to appoint a CIO with university-wide responsibility for IT resources and services. The only major exception to his ambit is the library information service and this is subject to review in the next stage of the restructure. The CIO is a senior level position answerable directly to the DVC academic services, although this will also be changed shortly to make the CIO, as well as the CFO and Executive Director Properties, answerable to the Vice President Corporate Services. The Vice President Corporate Services is the same level as a DVC.

Broadbent and Kitzis (2005) and Penrod (2003) both supported the need for a senior level CIO position to not only champion good IT governance, but to help enact ongoing alignment of IT with business objectives. This has also ensured the formation of formally assigned decision levels for strategic and indeed operational IT decisions as discussed by Weill and Ross (2004a), Broadbent and Kitzis, and Penrod.

An IT steering committee was also established, consisting of representatives from all user areas, as well as from the IT area, and chaired by a representative from the university executive, being the DVC responsible for IT services. As also discussed by Weill and Ross, Broadbent and Kitzis, and Penrod, this contributes greatly to stronger alignment of IT with business objectives. The membership of the body also helps to ensure efficient allocation of resources and provides an avenue for feedback to the user areas.

**Strategic Alignment:** The alignment of IT and business goals was a key issue raised in the study which has a strong link to IT governance as illustrated by Weill and Ross (2004b). The recognition of the importance of alignment is illustrated by a comment from the DVC responsible for ICT: *"The university works on three year plans. We're about to go to five. Once the strategic plan goes to five, so will the ICT plan. The ICT plan is completely aligned with the strategic plan. That's essential."*

As a result of the IT governance review, several mechanisms have been developed to assist in the alignment of IT and business goals. These have occurred at the strategic level to ensure university-wide alignment, and at the faculty level to ensure that faculties retain a voice in the IT planning process, as well as to assist in the alignment of IT with the goals and strategies of the individual faculties. The principal mechanism is the inclusion of the faculty ICT representatives on the ICT steering committee as well as a student representative. Both the CIO and the DVC responsible for ICT are also on the committee, the latter as the chair. The membership of the ICT steering committee is in accord with that recommended by Penrod and in itself should assist alignment.

Although aware of the ICT steering committee and its role, representatives from all areas indicated that they prefer to contact the CIO or DVC direct to raise issues. Problem resolution, even for strategic ongoing matters, was most likely to lead to circumvention of the formal reporting mechanism to the ICT steering committee. Typical of the reasons for this was the perceived time delay and chance of success of a submission to the ICT steering committee, as illustrated by the comment given by the corporate applications area: *"I'm not waiting for a committee to decide whether I need the information or not"* (DCS).

The DVC sits on the University Council, the strategic business decision-making structure for the university, and the Planning and Management Committee (PMC). The CIO has a standing invitation to sit on the PMC but has so far chosen not to attend due to his confidence in the DVC to represent IT at that forum. As suggested by Penrod and by Sheehan (2008), this cross membership of IT and business strategic planning committees helps in alignment.

The ICT enabling plan was construed as another opportunity to assist alignment of IT with the individual faculty strategies. This was done through focus groups using representatives from all areas and faculties across the university. This process has been followed since the decision to move to a shared services model. The ICT enabling plan has been reviewed several times by the ICT steering committee and progress against outcomes monitored and reported on. Its practicality and usefulness is shown by the CIO's statement: *"It's a real plan...it's quite a reasonable living document."*

The strategic business plan has key objectives related to increasing research quality and output as well as improvements to teaching and learning. In these areas, as the survey results have indicated, alignment may not have been optimized as key participants at the individual level believe that there is not sufficient consultation with them prior to IT decisions in these areas being concluded. Generally there appears to be strong alignment at the higher levels in the university but much weaker alignment at the lower, operational levels.

**Use of IT Resources:** The IT Governance Institute (2005) acknowledges the optimization of costs through adoption of standardized approaches as one of the outcomes of good IT governance. For the university represented in this case study, the move to a shared services model appears to have led to a rationalization of IT resources and their more efficient use. In many faculties, this has resulted in a reduced investment for the same level of IT resources and services. Representative from all areas acknowledged the improvement in the efficient use of IT resources. In several cases, there was an indication of some increase in bureaucracy and a reduction in flexibility in using and procuring IT assets. Overall, however, the outcome was accepted as positive, as shown in the following comment from a teaching and learning interviewee: *"It's a better utilization of services because now we've got [a] better load factor in our laboratories. We have to book it in advance and that sort of thing but provided you do the right thing you don't end up with a problem"* (HOS).

Faculties have demonstrated a cooperative attitude to centralization and better utilization of IT resources that were previously under their individual control. This is due in no small part to a consultation process that recognized the specialized needs of some faculties. For example, *"IT functions have become centralized but specialized labs specific to the department have been left under Department management. This means we can continue to offer and efficiently run our specialized courses"* (HOS).

The centralization of IT services under the shared services model has seen a rationalization of IT services across the university. Some of the more radical situations were illustrated in the following comment from the CIO: *"We had 13 e-mail systems. Now we have two, one for students and one for staff. We had two learning management systems, webCT and Blackboard, we are now moving to one. We had multiples of all sorts of things, multiple servers, multiple data centers. The staff said it was because they could never think holistically as an organization in respect of IT. I think the executive deans and the senior managers weren't prepared to deal with this and simply said we need to devolve this responsibility somewhere else."*

The unnecessary duplication of IT services and assets was used as one of the major selling points for the shared services model. The success of this campaign was illustrated in that each user interviewed reiterated the essence of the CIO's comment above. At an early stage in discussing the proposal to implement a shared services model with the faculties, cost savings was rejected as the principle driver of the changes. Money was saved due to rationalization but it was incidental to the improvement in IT governance. This attitude was seen by the DVC and CIO as a crucial point in gaining the support and cooperation of the faculties in the rationalization of IT resources through increased centralization.

**IT Risk Management:** One of the principal drivers of the review of the IT governance structure was a concern about the lack of risk management in respect of IT related threats. The concern at that point was clear from the DVC's comment: *"Everyone was holding me accountable and I realized I controlled 22 million, there was another 30 million [IT resources] out there of which I had no control and people doing what they want. Now [under shared services] all money and all people report through the CIO to me."*

Risk management is strongly supported in the literature as an essential component of IT governance (Hardy and Guldentops 2005; Hunton and Bryant 2004). Additionally, IT governance as a component of corporate governance requires the board of directors to oversee management activities, including the risk management and internal control functions (Bergmann and Croft 2005; OECD 2004). The centralization of the control of IT resources in itself provided the potential for risk management and established clear accountability for many aspects of IT resources and services. To capitalize on the potential, a regular review—often facilitated by an external risk management consultant— of IT related risks is undertaken. This process involves identification of the risks, strategies in place to mitigate the risk, and an assessment of the residual risk to ascertain if it is in line with the risk appetite of the university. The risk reviews have been undertaken annually since the acceptance of the shared services model and revised IT governance framework in 2005. Consideration is being given to conducting these reviews on a six-month cycle.

**Performance Measurement:** Appropriate monitoring mechanisms and associated metrics to monitor strategic-level IT initiatives have been associated with effective IT governance (Blumenberg and Croft 2005; Budd and Malcolm 2001; IT Governance Institute 2005). Both the CIO and DVC have access to a wide range of metrics regularly produced from established feedback mechanisms as well as performance metrics that can be produced on demand from regularly generated and retained systems data. The range of metrics collected and regularly disseminated is being expanded to include more operational level data, such as help desk response times and user satisfaction with the outcome of a call. The metrics produced for the CIO are generated directly by the central IT area. Surveys of students and staff are conducted and measured against prior surveys to gauge whether satisfaction levels are improving and to identify areas where improvements may be necessary. The intention is to make the surveys an annual undertaking, although at the moment that has not been formalized.

The DVC tends to be more concerned with strategic-level indicators such as how many minutes per year the university was visible on the web, how many minutes of downtime on student and staff systems, and how often the EFT transfer for payments was late. The metrics for the DVC are extracted independent of the central IT area by a team of three analysts that report directly to the DVC. Bench marking is used to report on systems achievements. The DVC's opinion of the performance measuring process was given in the following comment: *"These are very clever ways of knowing whether your system works or not. Metrics are produced by a team of three that work independent of the IT area and answer direct to me. Data from the system performance is compared to targets."*

Responsibility for some systems developed in-house by particular faculties have not yet been devolved to central IT. They provide a comparison of the currently emerging IT governance situation to the situation before shared services, as illustrated by the following comment by the director of a research area: *"I think he [contract programmer] has got all the stats [metrics on systems performance]; we just never get them because we're comfortable. We tend to only get them when people are complaining that the system's slow"* (DRD).

**Future Directions:** The CIO and DVC responsible for IT both see IT governance as an ongoing dynamic structure. In addition, they are aware that while they believe substantial progress has been made toward an effective IT governance structure, there is more that needs to be done to advance the shared services model. In this regard both have expressed dissatisfaction with some systems and are constantly reviewing what has been done and are considering future directions for all areas of IT governance (for example, outsourcing). They are continuing to advance other systems, such as the staff portal and the library information system. The ongoing and dynamic nature of the university's IT governance environment is summed up in the following comment from the CIO: *"We started the journey. We may never get there. I'm a realist. I think the destination is probably less important because it keeps changing and it probably will always. It does. It changes. But as I said to you I don't think there's any university in Australia that isn't going through the same issues with regard to IT governance."*

**Table 5.** Summary of Initiatives Implemented

|  | Attribute of Good Governance | Initiative |
|---|---|---|
| 1 | User relationship management | • Sharing of knowledge<br>• Communication<br>• Client service feedback<br>• Consultation with users |
| 2 | Management Support | • DVC championed<br>• VC supportive<br>• PM & C supportive |
| 3 | Governance mechanisms | • CIO responsible for all IT<br>• IT steering committee<br>• Implementing governance frameworks |
| 4 | Strategic alignment | • Alignment of planning time frames<br>• Business representatives on IT steering committee<br>• DVC for IT on strategic business committee<br>• Faculty voice on IT steering committee |
| 5 | Use of IT resources | • Centralization of IT functions |
| 6 | IT risk management | • Clear accountability for major IT areas<br>• CIO responsible for all IT<br>• Regular risk management reviews |
| 7 | Performance measurement | • Regular strategic measures to DVC<br>• Regular operational measures to others |

# 5  Conclusion

The case study university identified serious shortcomings in its IT governance structure. In response to these findings, several initiatives were implemented. These are summarized in Table 5 relative to the attributes of good IT governance.

The degree of success the case study university has achieved with each of these initiatives varies and several are still maturing. In particular, lower-level user consultation and lack of involvement before acquiring technology is perceived as a severe shortcoming by many staff. This is of particular concern in organizations, such as universities, where many of the strategic objectives are highly dependent on the individual's efforts. In particular, the importance of IT governance in designing effective systems to support research and teaching through the capture, creation, and use of information may not be operating as efficiently as possible. In addition, performance measurement and appropriate metrics still lack a comprehensive and structured implementation in many important areas.

These aside, it is clear from the survey and interviews that significant improvements in IT governance have been made. Conceptually the model the university is working toward is a dynamic one, where it is acknowledged that part of the process is constant review based on regular feedback from a wide range of performance measures. Enabling the ongoing development of this model of IT governance is the governance-aware attitude of key members of the executive management.

Contrary to expectations, although ultimately important, high-level management support for the IT governance restructure was dependent on first securing faculty and lower-level support. Lower-level user support has also been a feature considered critical by IT management to the continued successful operation of the revised IT governance structure. This finding contributes to the existing conceptual understanding of the role of user involvement in effective IT governance. The case study also confirms prior research into the effectiveness of IT governance and supports that it can be applied to universities.

The major limitation of the research is that it examined only a single university. This also means that only the shared services model, which happened to be the one the case study was implementing, was examined. Given the number and diversification of universities in Australia, this prevents any meaningful generalization of the results. It further prevents the valuable insight provided by cross-case analysis. However, the single case is still valuable (Yin 1994) and provides a rich context. In this study, the context has been established through qualitative data gathered through document searches and eight in-depth interviews of representatives from various positions in the university structure. In addition, quantitative data has been gathered through a user survey. Future research is planned by expanding the study to other cases from a wider range of universities throughout Australia and across different types as specified in the literature (Marginson and Considine 2000). Further research is also needed to ascertain whether the results of this study can be applied to other organizations, in particular those that rely on creativeness of lower-level users to drive the business, as is the case with research in universities.

# References

Bergmann, G., Croft, B.: Good Governance for All. Black 75(1), 54 (2005)
Bhattacharjya, J., Chang, V.: Adoption and Implementation of IT Governance: Cases from Australian Higher Education. In: Proceedings of the 17th Australasian Conference on Information Systems, Adelaide, Australia, December 6-8 (2006)
Blumenberg, S., Hinz, D.: Enhancing the Prognostic Power of IT Balanced Scorecards with Bayesian Belief Networks. In: Proceedings of the 39th Hawaii International Conference on System Sciences. IEEE Computer Society, Los Alamitos (2006)
Broadbent, M., Kitzis, E.: The New CIO Leader. Harvard Business School Press, Boston (2005)

Budd, M., Malcolm, C.: An Effective Metrics Program Can Ensure IT Performance Success. Healthcare Financial Management 55(11), 84–86, 88 (2001)

Chang, J., King, W.: The Development of Measures to Assess the Performance of the Information Systems Function: A Multiple Constituency Approach. In: Orlikowski, W., Ang, S., Weill, P., Krcmar, H.C., DeGross, J.I. (eds.) Proceedings of the 21st International Conference on Information Systems, Brisbane, Australia, December 10-13, pp. 640–646 (2000)

Clark, A.: IT Governance: Determining Who Decides. Research Bulletin (2005:24), EDUCAUSE Center for Applied Research (2005), http://net.educause.edu/ir/library/pdf/ERB0524.pdf

Clinton, B.: Remarks by the President at the United States Naval Academy Commencement, May 22 (1998), http://www.britannica.com/bps/additionalcontent/ 18/8868129/Remarks-by-the-President-at-the-United-States- Naval-Academy-Commencement/fulltext

Council, C.: Implications for the Future of COBIT Systems in Higher Education: Putting Critical Research and Theory into Practice. Information Systems Control Journal (1) (2007)

Devos, J., Van Landeghem, H., Deschoolmeester, D.: IT Governance in SMEs: Trust or Control? In: Dhillon, G., Stahl, B.C., Baskerville, R. (eds.) Information Systems— Creativity and Innovation in Small and Medium-Sized Enterprises, pp. 149–153. Springer, New York (2009)

Denscombe, M.: The Good Research Guide for Small Scale Social Research Projects. Open University Press, Philadelphia (1998)

Huang, R., Zmud, R., Price, R.: IT Governance in Small and Medium-Sized Enterprises: Recommendations from an Empirical Study. In: Dhillon, G., Stahl, B.C., Baskerville, R. (eds.) Information Systems—Creativity and Innovation in Small and Medium-Sized Enterprises, pp. 158–179. Springer, New York (2009)

Hardy, G., Guldentops, E.: COBIT 4.0: The New Face of COBIT. Information Systems Control Journal (6) (2005)

Hunton, J.E., Bryant, S.M., Bragranoff, N.A.: Core Concepts of Information Technology Auditing. John Wiley & Sons Inc., New York (2004)

Institute of Internal Auditors. Putting COSO's Theory into Practice, Tone at the Top (28) (2005), http://www.theiia.org/download.cfm?file=42122

International Federation of Accountants Education Committee, International Education Guideline 11: Information Technology for Professional Accountants, New York: Interna- tional Federation of Accountants (2003)

ISACA, COBIT and Related Products. Guidance Materials for IT Governance, Rolling Meadows, IL: IT Governance Institute (2005)

IT Governance Institute. Aligning COBIT, ITIL and ISO 17799 for Business Benefit, Rolling Meadows, IL: IT Governance Institute (2005), http://www.itgovernance.co.uk/files/ ITIL-COBiT-ISO17799JointFramework.pdf

Johnson, A.M., Lederer, A.L.: Two Predictors of CEO/ CIO Convergence. In: Proceedings of the 2003 SIGMIS Conference on Computer Personnel Research: Freedom in Philadel- phia—Leveraging Differences and Diversity in the IT Workforce, Philadelphia, PA, April 10-12, pp. 162–167. ACM Press, New York (2003)

Jopson, B.: Mutual Respect May Replace Convergence. Financial Times (FT International Accountancy Supplement), 1–2, March 6 (2006)

Lucy, J.: FSR, CLERP 9 and Surveillance Programs: ASIC Priorities Over the Next 12 Months. Presentation to the Institute of Chartered Accountants in Australia, Queensland 2004 CA Business Forum, March 13 (2004),
http://www.asic.gov.au/asic/pdflib.nsf/LookupByFileName/
ICAA_speech_130304.pdf/$file/ICAA_speech_130304.pdf

Marginson, S., Considine, M.: The Enterprise University: Power, Governance and Reinvention in Australia. Cambridge University Press, Oakleigh (2000)

Miles, M., Huberman, M.: Qualitative Data Analysis. Sage Publications, Thousand Oaks (1994)

Milton, C.: Human Behavior in Organizations. Prentice Hall, Englewood Cliffs (1981)

OECD, OECD Principles of Corporate Governance, Paris, France: Organisation for Economic Co-operation and Development (2004)

Penrod, J.: Organizing and Managing Information Resources on Your Campus. In: McClure, P. (ed.) Building an Effective Governance and Decision-Making Structure for Information Technology, pp. 15–28. John Wiley & Sons, New York (2003)

Pirani, J., Salaway, G.: Queensland University of Technology: Three Generations of IT Governance (and Counting). ECAR Case Study 4, EDUCAUSE Center for Applied Research (2008),
http://confluence.arizona.edu/confluence/download/
attachments/2459667/Case_Study_8.pdf

Robinson, N.: The Many Faces of IT Governance: Crafting an IT Governance Architecture. Information Systems Control Journal 2007(1), 14–16 (2007)

Sheehan, M.: Higher Education IT and Cyberinfrastructure: Integrating Technologies for Scholarship. EDUCAUSE Center for Applied Research 3 (2008),
http://net.educause.edu/ir/library/pdf/ers0803/rs/ERS0803w.pdf

Standards Australia Committee IT-030 IT Governance and Management. 2005. Corporate Governance of Information & Communication Technology, AS 8015-2005

Van Grembergen, W.: ND. The Balanced Scorecard and IT Governance, IT Governance Institute (reprinted from Information Systems Control Journal)

Weill, P., Ross, J.: IT Governance: How Top Performers Manage IT Decision Rights for Superior Results. Harvard Business School Press, Boston (2004a)

Weill, P., Ross, J.: IT Governance on One Page. CISR WP No. 349/Sloan WP No. 4516-09, Center for Information Systems Research, Sloan School of Management, Massachusetts Institute of Technology (2004b),
http://web.mit.edu/cisr/working%20papers/cisrwp349.pdf

Yin, R.: Case Study Research: Design and Methods, 2nd edn. Sage Publications Inc., Thousand Oaks (1994)

## About the Authors

**Michael Hicks** is a lecturer with the School of Accounting at Curtin University specialising in Accounting Information Systems and IS auditing. He is a CPA with over 20 years experience as an IS auditor and auditor in the government and private sectors. Michael is currently completing his Ph.D. in IT governance in Australian universities. Michael can be contacted at m.hicks@curtin.edu.au .

**Graham Pervan** has over 30 years experience in education, research, and practice in Information Systems and Information Technology (IS/IT). He has published on various issues related to IS/IT management, electronic commerce and decision support systems in journals such as *Journal of Management Information Systems, Journal of Information Technology, Decision Support Systems, Information and Management, Journal of Computer Information Systems, Journal of Group Decision and Negotiation, Journal of Research and Practice in IT*, and *Communications of the AIS*, as well as most major conferences. He is a senior editor for the *Journal of Information Technology*, and the IT Management Editor for *Australian Journal of Management*. Graham can be contacted at g.pervan@curtin.edu.au.

**Brian Perrin** is a senior lecturer in the School of Accounting at Curtin University of Technology, Western Australia. He currently lectures in and coordinates both undergraduate and postgraduate accounting information systems and computerized accounting courses both locally and overseas. His work experience in both financial and management accounting spans some 35 years in private practice, commerce, the public sector, and education. Brian's research interest is in the area of performance measurement systems and IT outsourcing and he has numerous textbook publications in computerized accounting. Brian can be contacted at b.perrin@curtin.edu.au.

# Extending Design Science Research Methodology for a Multicultural World

Carl Lawrence, Tuure Tuunanen, and Michael D. Myers

Information Systems and Operations Management,
University of Auckland,
Auckland 1142, New Zealand

**Abstract.** Design science research (DSR) is a relatively new approach in information systems research. A fundamental tenet of DSR is that understanding comes from creating information technology artifacts. However, with an increasingly connected and globalized world, designing IT artifacts for a multicultural world is a challenge. The purpose of this paper, therefore, is to propose extending the DSR methodology by integrating critical ethnography to the evaluation phase. Critical ethnography provides a way for IS researchers using DSR to better understand culture, and may help to ensure that IT artifacts are designed for a variety of cultural contexts.

**Keywords:** Design science research methodology, critical ethnography, mobile services, culture.

## 1   Introduction

Design science research (DSR) aims to improve our understanding of information systems phenomena by creating information technology artifacts. The artifacts created embody the solution for a problem previously defined (Hevner et al. 2004). In an increasingly connected and globalized world, however, IT artifacts are created for use in a variety of cultural contexts. The multicultural diversity of potential users and organizations suggests that information systems designers need a better understanding of culture and what it means for IS development (Kappos and Rivard 2008). We suggest that the task is much more complex than simply providing a product or service in a different language or creating a new format for a website. Complex social, cultural, political, and historical factors now come into play and potentially affect the way that information systems are perceived and adopted.

If creating effective IT artifacts is the goal, designing these artifacts to fit the needs of culturally diverse clients is what challenges us. We need to design better artifacts that truly enable people to work more effectively. We also want to find a method that uses local cultural traditions to their advantage, rather than impose alien, non-indigenous systems that will most likely end up being ineffective (Kumar et al. 1998; Ngwenyama and Lee 1997). Integrating valuable elements of culture into new innovations requires a culturally focused study prior to design in order to evaluate what is of value.

J. Pries-Heje et al. (Eds.): IS Design Science Research, IFIP AICT 318, pp. 108–121, 2010.
© IFIP International Federation for Information Processing 2010

At the moment the evaluation of IT artifacts is usually achieved by applying quantitative methods not informed by theory, and when theories have been applied, they have been primarily techno-centric in origin (Kumar et al. 1998). Traditional artifact evaluation also tends to favor a summative approach at an individual level and does not view the use of the artifact in social work spheres (Diaper and Lindgaard 2008). We suggest, however, that the evaluation phase of DSR can be modified in a way to tackle problems of cultural diversity (Klecun and Cornford 2005). Used formatively, we would be acknowledging a known issue—the potential mismatch between the design context and the use context—starting with trying to understand the culture that is the target of the artifact (Thimbleby et al. 2001). Of course, we should not underestimate the difficulty of designing information systems for multiple cultures. The problem is not just one of aesthetics (how the artifact appears), but may represent a deeper, underlying issue of what that technology represents and how it is (or is not) appropriated by people.

This paper, therefore, seeks to present arguments supporting the use of a critical ethnographic evaluation in a formative context. To do this, the paper builds on earlier work on ethnography in information systems (Harvey and Myers 1995; Myers 1999) and software design (Simonsen and Kensing 1997). The goal is to gain greater insight into culture before the design process even begins in order to understand, evaluate, and extract elements that the bring added value to the final artifact.

We begin by looking at some cultural challenges in IS research and how critical ethnography may be able to address these challenges. We look at DSR and the potential to integrate critical ethnography into DSR evaluation. We then attempt to apply that evaluation method to a recent study in design science. Finally, we present our findings and conclusions.

## 2  The Cultural Challenge in Is Research

Understanding culture represents both a challenge and an opportunity for information systems researchers (Kumar et al. 1998; Myers 1999), not least because there are many different definitions and conceptualizations of culture. Definitions range from the overly simplistic to complex. Many IS studies concerned with various cultural aspects have tended to rely on Hofstede's (1980, 1991) model of national culture. However, Hofstede's model has been described as rather simplistic (Myers and Tan 2002). McCoy, Galletta, and King (2007) define culture as a way of thinking exhibited by differing human groups and exhibited in the artifacts they create. Walsham (2002, p. 360) conceptualizes culture as "shared symbols, norms and values in a social collective." Culture can also be represented in visual form as artifacts. These artifacts can be physical, or they may be sets of rules, models, practices, and structured tasks (Kappos and Rivard 2008).

The increased use of IT artifacts globally has spurred the debate as to what degree culture influences usability of such artifacts. Studies on usability have acknowledged the need to study culture's impact and the importance of studying the use context (Bødker 2006; O'Brien et al. 1999). However, culture is constantly created and recreated, making it difficult to pin down (Avison and Myers 1995). If the creators of an IT artifact rely solely on generic predefined attributes of culture, this may not be sufficient for IS success. The key issue here is for IS researchers to understand the user. The challenge arises when the designer's culture history differs dramatically from that of the user. The metaphorical distance of the designer's culture from the users will pose problems to design. This is exemplified by studies of usability in eastern and western cultures (Diaper and Lindgaard 2008).

In striving to improve our understanding of culture, IS researchers have mostly drawn on theories and methods from the social sciences. Theories such as *activity theory* have been used to study the relationship between culture and IT artifacts. The artifact may embody the cultural attributes of its designers, or it may embody the cultural attributes of the intended users, or both. Another way is to focus on the meaning of an artifact within a social and cultural context (Orlikowski and Iacono 2001). Yet another way to study the relationship between culture and IT artifacts is to look at the impact of an artifact on social and culture entities. Hence, culture can influence the design of an artifact and conversely, an artifact may influence culture.

One complication, however, is that the adoption of IT artifacts often requires adoption of the creators' cultural norms, values, and practices in order to use the artifacts effectively (Lin and Silva 2005) Although the designers hope that their artifacts will make us more efficient and productive, sometimes a change in work practices can be counterproductive. Studies on the change in work practices with IS implementation have shown that users can experience "dissonance to consonance," where there are conflicts between existing work practices and the new practices introduced with IT artifacts (Vasst and Walsham 2005). This may lead to IS implementation failure.

We suggest that one possible way of trying to avoid such failure is for DSR to embrace some of the insights from qualitative and interpretive studies of culture in IS. These studies have shown that IT artifacts and systems can take on a different meaning depending upon the context. Hence it becomes important to explore the social and cultural context of IS innovations. One of the ways of doing so is to use ethnographic research, which has the potential to offer rich insights into IS phenomena (Harvey and Myers 1995). Ethnographic research differs from other research methods in the requirement for the researchers to immerse themselves to some extent in the everyday lives of the subjects. An ethnographic researcher uses interviews but relies heavily on data obtained via participant observation (Myers 2009). Of course, one potential downside is that this may extend the time taken for any DSR project, but we suggest that a judicious use of ethnographic research (perhaps along the lines of mini-ethnography) might be worthwhile. Ethnographically informed studies have been done in participatory systems design where both users and designers engage in learning activities meant to improve the understanding of the context and the user at work (Simonsen and Kensing 1997).

We suggest that a particular kind of ethnography, called critical ethnography, is particularly applicable and relevant for DSR. Just as DS researchers are oriented toward improving software or systems through the design of an IT artifact, so critical ethnographers are oriented toward improving social and cultural arrangements. Critical ethnography is participatory and seeks to do more that simply interpret the data. Critical ethnographers also have an interest in the "emancipation" of people from social, cultural, and technological constraints (Thomas 1993). A critical ethnographer thus engages with the subjects of the study in dialogue, attempting to reveal hidden agendas, oppressive power structures, and fallacies that inhibit the subject from participating or self-determination. Thus the critical ethnographer does not merely participate and observe, but suggests improvements (Myers 1999). In information systems, critical research has been used to aid the understanding of complex social situations involving power (Avgerou and McGrath 2007), and issues concerning the social construction of IT artifacts and their impact on organizations (Ngwenyama and Lee 1997).

## 3  Culture as an Opportunity for Decision Science Research

Stahl (2008) argues that design science researchers, like other researchers, have ethical and social responsibilities. In the design of artifacts, researchers must be aware of the potential impact of those artifacts on users. Organizations make decisions to adopt artifacts and those decisions have far reaching impacts beyond those that were intended. In the design process, researchers should be aware of these potential implications. Of course, this becomes much more important when dealing with the design of artifacts across cultures (Stahl 2008). In this paper, we seek to enhance design science research with formative evaluation, which integrates valuable attributes of the target culture to enhance the final artifact. This is consistent with the approach proposed by Pries-Heje, Baskerville, and Venable (2008). By using a formative approach to evaluation, we believe we can potentially reduce the risk of negative impact of the IT artifact by first addressing the issues of culture through critical ethnography. Design research has the potential to be empowering to the user if that user can fully participate and the culture in which he or she exists is not simply ignored or misunderstood. This has not traditionally been the approach employed in design science research (Stahl 2008) but one which we believe could be beneficial.

In Information Systems, we use design science to create IT artifacts that represent a solution to a preexisting problem or opportunity. The artifacts are broadly defined as constructs:  asystem, a piece of software, hardware or a model (Hevner et al. 2004) created to fulfill the main goal of problem solving. The design science research methodology (DSRM) of Peffers et al. (2008) suggests a way to conduct design science research in information systems. It is comprised of six phases: (1) identification of problem and motivation, (2) define objectives, (3) design, (4) demonstration, (5) evaluation, and (6) communication (Peffers et al. 2008). However, we see a challenge if we try to apply DSRM in various cultural contexts. We aim to enhance DSRM by modifying the evaluation phase of the Peffers at al. model such that it is enriched with the critical ethnographic approach.

The Peffers at al. DSRM starts with the identification of research problem(s) and motivation for the research (see Figure 1). Based on evidence, reasoning, and inference, the process continues toward defining objectives of a solution to solve the research problem. This should be based on prior knowledge in the given field of research. This knowledge is then used to design and develop an artifact and to create "how to" knowledge. Following that, the artifact is used to solve the pre-described problem and is thus demonstrated in a suitable context before evaluating its effectiveness or efficiency. This leads to disciplinary knowledge, which is then communicated to both academia and industry. Of course, the process can, and should be, iterative in nature.

DSRM has four possible entry points to the research process. The first entry point is the traditional problem-centered initiation, which is similar to qualitative and quantitative research methodologies. The second is the objective-centered solution approach, which enables researchers to approach the research endeavor by first setting objectives that can be quantitative or qualitative with the main idea of establishing how the new artifact is expected to support solutions to achieving the stated objectives. The third entry point is design-centered, where initiation can be a result of an interesting design or development problem. The fourth entry point is where the design starts with a research client.

As we stated earlier, however, our focus is in the evaluation phase of design science. In the current model, the evaluation component acts as a reality check ensuring that the research is on the right track to deliver the needed solution, as DSRM is meant to be an iterative process where multiple periods of evaluation may be needed throughout the research process. Evaluation can inform or force a change in other phases like design or defining objectives (Peffers et al. 2008). Most importantly, we see that evaluation is a key area that can be modified to inform the artifact's effectiveness in various cultural contexts, although critical ethnographic research could also be the starting point.

To summarize our arguments so far: IT artifacts interact with social entities, such as organizations or social networks. This creates added complexity for researchers. The focus is not just on the technological artifact, but also on the people who intend to use it and its context of use. Hence, design science research needs to use theories and methods from the social sciences to better understand the behavior of social actors as they interact with systems (Hevner et al. 2004; Walls et al. 1992). We can use these theories and methods to guide the research process and influence the creation of attributes represented in the artifacts. These theories and methods have the potential to help us in the formative stage of the research process (Markus et al. 2002), and may help us to unearth aspects and perspectives previously neglected, such as the suggested cultural aspect.

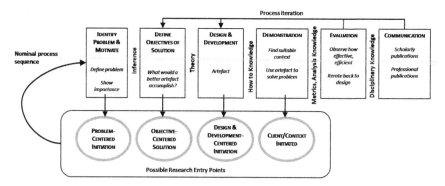

**Fig. 1.** Design Science Research Methodology (Adapted from Peffers et al. 2008)

## 4  Culture and Evaluation in DSRM

Evaluation in DSR is mainly concerned with the evaluation of DS outputs, including any theory and/or artifacts developed. Although evaluation is widely recognized as an important aspect of the DSRM methodology, it is often poorly executed (Pries-Heje et al. 2008). Choosing the appropriate evaluation strategy depends on the complexities of the context. In studies involving contexts where the researcher has control of the research, experimental methods may be appropriate. Studies in a real life context, however, will need to employ different methods of evaluation in order to capture the "naturalistic" processes of social life (Pries-Heje et al. 2008).

In IS, evaluation is usually considered to be the process of assessing quality based on predefined goals and objectives. Traditionally, the focus of such evaluations has been technically oriented, attempting to assess performance, reliability and usability using economic measures (Klecun and Cornford 2005). These evaluations have usually just checked the artifact against the requirements and objectives, and focused on evaluating individual users and their ability to learn and use the artifact. However, given the failure of many IT artifacts to fulfill their expected purpose and the long-term goals of the organization, there is a need for improvement in our evaluation methods. We suggest that using theories and methods from the social sciences may enhance the rigor of the evaluation and improve our understanding of the user's belief system and attitudes (Goodhue 1995).

Evaluation of IT artifacts using social theories is not as common as traditional evaluation, but can be effective in revealing dimensions that cannot be found using quantitative methods (Klecun and Cornford 2005). IT artifacts that have social applications warrant the use of these methods. The lack of IS evaluations has sometimes been linked to the cost associated with comprehensive evaluation, especially those involving theory. Even though there is some reluctance, theory driven evaluations have show to be effective in predicting success of IT artifacts (Goodhue 1995). It is important to note that evaluations are not simply used to assess an artifact's impact on the user community, but also to show its potential success.

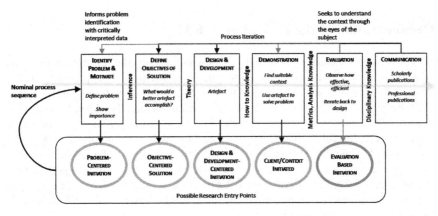

**Fig. 2.** Extending the DSRM with Critical Evaluation

The use of social theory in evaluation is predominantly to understand social behavior and culture, identifying issues that are not necessarily related to technical aspects of the systems, but may affect its use and acceptance. For example, social theory shows how users change their evaluations "post adoption" and how their evaluation continues to change over time (Kim and Malhotra 2005). Of course, as we stated earlier, culture is not static and thus users' views on IS artifacts can be expected to change over time. Simply looking at the objectives and the solution itself cannot reveal these dimensions. Research using social theories has also shown that users use existing knowledge to form their opinion of a product or service (referred to as an anchor) and develop new views as they acquire new knowledge (referred to as an adjustment) (Kim and Malhotra 2005).

We propose extending DSRM such that it integrates elements of critical ethnography to the evaluation of DSR outputs to identify any mismatch between the use context and the design context. We therefore suggest that the process of DSRM should have an entry point at evaluation. We call this *evaluation based initiation*. The extended DSRM is shown in Figure 2. Traditionally, in post-design evaluations the focus is on a the individual user's ability use the systems effectively, whereas here in the formative context we focus of the larger social group, examining real-life context and interactions (Sayago and Blat 2009). We recognize the design context and understand that that context may be vastly different from the use context resulting in inappropriate artifacts. Recognizing the danger of such a potential mismatch, we see it as logical to use formative evaluation to understand the context of use prior to commencing with problem identification. With the critical ethnographic approach, the evaluation seeks to understand the context through the eyes of the subjects. It not only interprets the users' point of view, but also has as an objective to question and reveal hidden power structures and agendas that inhibit the effectiveness of the potential artifact. This process potentially sensitizes the researcher to the cultural contexts, giving a richer perspective. This process in turn informs problem identification, giving a clearer picture of what is required. The ultimate aim, of course, is to improve the DSR process such that the resulting artifacts contribute in some way to improving the human condition.

## 5   Demonstration of the Extended DSRM

We demonstrate the extended DSRM by reviewing a study that enabled us to coin the idea of formative critical ethnography driven evaluation. The presence study, described below, was done within the DiVia (http://www.divia.fi) research project and LTT Research, Inc., a commercial research firm owned by the Helsinki School of Economics. The study was led by one of the authors of this paper and it has included 15 researchers from four continents. So far, the study has involved some 450 participants in Auckland, Helsinki, Hong Kong, and Las Vegas. The research project is still ongoing with its first iteration concluded in 2007. The study's preliminary results were reported earlier (Peffers et al. 2006; Tuunanen et al. 2006). Here, we first summarize the primary research round using the DSRM (Peffers et al. 2008), and then we focus on the on-going second iteration.

## 5.1  Problem Identification and Motivation

Presence technology allows mobile device users to share information about their current availability and status in terms of their own concepts or those of a presence-based application with subscribers to that information.  For example, a basic presence service could allow users to publish their information and share it with others in order to make mobile communication and services more sensitive and personal.  This information may include the availability of the subscriber, the preferred means of communication, the subscriber's whereabouts, as well as visual content for self expression of one's emotion, in order to guide other users' communication decisions while controlling their own information (Nokia 2005).  Examples of presence information might include "sleeping," "in a meeting—leave voice mail," "bored—call me," "at leisure and looking for fun."

First, we aimed to identify the research problem.  As presence technology was new to us and to the markets, we planned to use industry experts to provide us with a focused application scope within the domain.  Therefore, we recruited 13 marketing professionals from firms participating in DiVia to help us with this and planned a group support system (GSS) session to define the project scope. The GSS session was done in May 2004. The results included recommendations for three application problems for presence: (1) presence-enabled mobile travel services for while you are en-route; (2) presence-enabled mobile service while you are out and about in the city; and (3) presence-enabled mobile service for special interest group member/community.  We added one extra stimulus to the final list: a presence enabled mobile service "for you."  We originally set as our research problem the identification of what consumers might want to have from presence enabled mobile services.

## 5.2  Objective: Presence Enabled Mobile Marketing Applications

We were faced with a situation where we would need to discover requirements for a service that does not exist using a technology not familiar to end-users. This puts forth several objectives for a solution.  First, the number of users can be very large and they can be widely dispersed geographically. Second, the lack of control and poor incentives may result in volatile data collection. Finally, the end-users have a low level of integration to the service or it can be of a secondary nature. These characteristics are highlighted by the fact that many  end-users do not even know how to express their needs (Walz et al. 1993; Watson and Frolick 1993). In this study, we applied a specially developed method for resolving these issues: the wide audience requirements engineering (WARE) method (Tuunanen et al. 2004).

## 5.3  Design:  Using Ware to Discover Requirements

The WARE method starts with project definition and selection of participants. The second phase is data gathering.  Earlier studies have recommended interviewing approximately 30 people per research location (Griffin and Hauser 1993) as this would be a large enough sample to suffice for discovering 90 percent or more of the potential ideas about a concept from a population.  Our previous studies, which have used a similar data gathering method, have concurred with this view (Peffers et al.

2003; Peffers and Tuunanen 2005). The literature further recommends that the sample be representative of the end-user segments.

We suggest that "lead users" should be included in the sample. The sample consisted of lead users because the research literature suggests lead users can be used to forecast the needs of the majority of users of a technology (Rogers 1995; von Hippel 1986; von Hippel and Katz 2002). Therefore, we used the "snowball" method to recruit participants, a set of six questions to screen potential participants as lead users and a second set of questions to learn what kind of knowledge the participant had on the domain area of the study. This recruitment process resulted in a panel of 80 participants: 28 from Helsinki, 27 from Hong Kong, and 25 from Las Vegas.

In all locations, we interviewed each of the participants individually and in person. During the interviews, the interviewers made digital audio recordings and took notes with an electronic spreadsheet application or using pen and paper. Before conducting the interviews, the participant was shown a flash demonstration of presence technology. After the demonstration, the participants were told to try to think outside of the offered presence technology and think of something else that could use the technology. The interviews were done with the laddering interviewing technique (Browne and Ramesh 2002; Browne and Rogich 2001; Peffers et al. 2003; Peffers and Tuunanen 2005). The laddering data consisted of 597 chains of individual requirements and 3,113 specific requirements. The data was aggregated to produce a meaningful, and smaller, set of rich, unified, and aggregated models, which makes it easier for managers and designers to comprehend the data. Finally, the aggregated data was used for creating network maps by transforming the clustered chains in each theme into a network map. Further details are available in Peffers et al. (2006) and Tuunanen et al. (2006).

Based on the results of the data collection phase, we provided an analysis of the situation and described the potential needs of end users (i.e. user requirements). This was initially done in a business report delivered to project member firms and institutions. The report gave recommendations for focusing resources on developing features and develops a roadmap for presence services.

## 5.4 Demonstration: Rapid Development of Presence Services

For the demonstration phase and for building the artifact (a presence-enabled mobile marketing application), we applied the concepts of method engineering (ME). Method engineering provides means to specify, make explicit, codify, and communicate method knowledge as well as technical tools to enact such processes effectively. Tuunanen and Rossi (2004) have suggested that in order to model IS requirements we need a set of concepts during ME that can capture the content and form of any development method into a *meta-model*. Brinkkemper (1990) has said that in its simplest form, a meta-model is a conceptual model of a development method. Therefore, meta-modeling can be defined as a process, which takes place on one level of abstraction and logic higher than the primary modeling process (van Gigch 1991).

We used a domain-specific modeling method initially within MetaEdit+ (Kelly et al. 1996) and later by developing a eclipse-based meta modeling environment to rapidly produce prototypes from the requirements. There are several implementations available (e.g., Tuunanen and Rossi 2003, 2004) and we are currently working on the eclipse-based environment (Przybilski 2006) that generates running prototypes for a mobile-specific platform, like the MIDP Java or Symbian platform (Rossi and Tuunanen 2004).

## 5.5 Evaluation: Realization of the Importance of Culture

The evaluation of the artifacts was initially considered to be done with distributed conjoint analysis (Laaksonen et al. 2004). We saw that this would be necessary to ensure (1) that the potential end-users of developed services would fully understand the choices they are making about the service features, and (2) that we as researchers could better understand how we could model and discover the latent needs for such services. We ended up not doing this due the realization of the importance of culture in requirements, especially if one desires to develop a global mobile service.

In the design phase of the study and while gathering requirements data we began to understand the difficulties of global service development. Our preliminary findings on the differences of culturally based requirements (Tuunanen et al. 2006) showed that our three different data gathering locations—Helsinki, Hong Kong, and Las Vegas—had distinctly different needs for presence type mobile services. Furthermore, we concluded that even though we were able to aggregate the results of requirements discovery to several service concepts, which included features based on all three locations, we began to question if it would actually make sense to develop the requirements and later the system in this way. We would, in fact, be doing the same as mobile firms have done so far: that is, trying to stereotype the global consumer and put all the bells and whistles in the same "box." We thought that this would very likely derail us from understanding the needs of consumers of presence services in each of the three locations.

This new understanding had two major impacts on our study. First, we realized that we would have to redesign our approach of requirements analysis to include the cultural aspects of requirements. Therefore, our evaluation phase drove us to return to the design phase of the study and develop a new requirements analysis method, which would take account of cultural reasoning of requirements for systems. This led us to change the research problem to a more theory-driven approach to applying DSRM. This linkage is illustrated in the Figure 2 as a loop back to problem setting and potentially to the demonstration phase.

Second, we realized that culturally oriented DS research might be a fruitful new area where research can commence from the evaluation of the results of a research project. Peffers et al. (2008) have proposed that such an area of study might be possible. Critical ethnography in particular might be able to provide us with a better understanding of complex social situations involving culture and complex mobile services. This, in turn, might lead to new research ventures as suggested by our extended DSRM methodology.

## 6  Conclusions

Culture presents many challenges for IS design science researchers seeking to design IT artifacts for a global society. The need for theory informed evaluation to improve the final artifact is evident given the different social phenomena that influence its use, adoption, and impact. When designing for multiple cultures, we have to look beyond the surface and evaluate deeper meanings.

This paper has suggested that by applying critical ethnography to the evaluation phase of the DSRM we can extend design science research methodology (Peffers et al. 2008). This enhancement is driven by the need for greater attention to cultural issues in our global society, particularly when the artifact is being designed for different cultural contexts. The paper thus integrates critical ethnography into the evaluation phase of the DSRM, which informs the other phases of the methodology. The need for the proposed extended DSR methodology is demonstrated through a case study in global mobile service development, which drove the development of this paper.

The limitations of our paper are as follows. First, we recognize that we have only briefly summarized the vast amount of literature covering design science research, ethnography, and social theory. Our discussion of culture and critical ethnography is limited. We are first to acknowledge that our paper stops far short in its explanation of how, in a detailed practical way, critical ethnography might be applied to evaluation in DS research.

However, we believe we have sufficiently shown the need to enhance the design process when it comes to culture, and we have suggested one way in which this might be achieved. Further research involving both design science researchers and ethnographers in information systems is needed to develop a framework or model for a more precise evaluation process. It is imperative that IS designers and researchers continue to search for the best available approaches to design, so we can create more usable artifacts to enrich the users' experience.

# References

Avgerou, C., McGrath, K.: Power, Rationality, and the Art of Living Through Socio-Technical Change. MIS Quarterly 31(2), 295–315 (2007)

Avison, D.E., Myers, M.D.: Information Systems and Anthropology: An Anthropological Perspective on IT and Organizational Culture. Information Technology & People 8(3), 43–56 (1995)

Bødker, S.: When Second Wave HCI Meets Third Wave Challenges. In: Proceedings of the 4th Nordic Conference on Human-Computer Interaction, Changing Roles, Oslo, Norway (2006)

Brinkkemper, S.: Formalisation of Information Systems Modelling. Computer Science Department, University of Nijmegen (1990) (unpublished paper)

Browne, G.J., Ramesh, V.: Improving Information Requirements Determination: A Cognitive Perspective. Information & Management 39(8), 625–645 (2002)

Browne, G.J., Rogich, M.B.: An Empirical Investigation of User Requirements Elicitation: Comparing the Effectiveness of Prompting Techniques. Journal of Management Information Systems 17(4), 223–249 (2001)

Diaper, D., Lindgaard, G.: West Meets East: Adapting Activity Theory for HCI & CSCW Applications? Interacting with Computers 20(2), 240–246 (2008)

Goodhue, D.L.: Understanding User Evaluations of Information Systems. Management Science 41(12), 1827–1844 (1995)

Griffin, A., Hauser, J.R.: The Voice of the Customer. Marketing Science 12(1), 1–27 (1993)

Harvey, L., Myers, M.D.: Scholarship and Practice: The Contribution of Ethnographic Research Methods to Bridging the Gap. Information Technology & People 8(3), 13–27 (1995)

Hevner, A.R., March, S.T., Park, J., Ram, S.: Design Science in Information Systems Research. MIS Quarterly 28(1), 75–105 (2004)

Hofstede, G.: Cultural Consequences: International Differences in Work Related Values. Sage Publications, Beverly Hills (1980)

Hofstede, G.: Cultures and Organizations: Software of the Mind. McGraw-Hill, New York (1991)

Kappos, A., Rivard, S.: A Three-Perspective Model of Culture, Information Systems, and Their Development and Use. MIS Quarterly 32(3), 601–634 (2008)

Kelly, S., Lyytinen, K., Rossi, M.: MetaEdit+: A Fully Configurable Multi-User and Multi-Tool CASE and CAME Environment. In: Constantopoulos, P., Vassiliou, Y., Mylopoulos, J. (eds.) CAiSE 1996. LNCS, vol. 1080, pp. 1–21. Springer, Heidelberg (1996)

Kim, S.S., Malhotra, N.K.: A Longitudinal Model of Continued IS Use: An Integrative View of Four Mechanisms Underlying Postadoption Phenomena. Management Science 51(5), 741–755 (2005)

Klecun, E., Cornford, T.: A Critical Approach to Evaluation. European Journal of Information Systems (14), 229–243 (2005)

Kumar, K., Van Dissel, H.G., Bielli, P.: The Merchant of Prato—Revisited: Toward a Third Rationality of Information Systems. MIS Quarterly 22(2), 199–225 (1998)

Laaksonen, A., Tuunanen, T., Rossi, M.: Requirements Validation for Consumer Software by Conjoint Analysis. In: Proceedings of the 13th International Conference on Information Systems Development, Vilnius, Lithuania, August 26-28. Kluwer/ Plenum Press, Boston (2004)

Lin, A., Silva, L.: The Social and Political Construction of Technological Frames. European Journal of Information Systems 14(1), 49–59 (2005)

Markus, M.L., Majchrzak, A., Gasser, L.: A Design Theory for Systems That Support Emergent Knowledge Processes. MIS Quarterly 26(3), 179–212 (2002)

McCoy, S., Galletta, D.F., King, W.R.: Applying TAM Across Cultures: The Need for Caution. European Journal of Information Systems 16(1), 81–90 (2007)

Myers, M.D.: Investigating Information Systems with Ethnographic Research. Communications of the AIS 2(23), 1–20 (1999)

Myers, M.D.: Qualitative Research in Business & Management. Sage Publications, London (2009)

Myers, M.D., Tan, F.: Beyond Models of National Culture in Information Systems Research. Journal of Global Information Management 10(1), 24–32 (2002)

Ngwenyama, O.K., Lee, A.S.: Communication Richness in Electronic Mail: Critical Social Theory and the Contextuality of Meaning. MIS Quarterly 21(2), 145–166 (1997)

Nokia, Staying in Touch with Presence, white paper, Nokia, Inc. (2005)

O'Brien, J., Rodden, T., Rouncefield, M., Hughes, J.: At Home with the Technology. ACM Transactions on Computer-Human Interaction 6(3), 282–308 (1999)

Orlikowski, W.J., Iacono, C.S.: Research Commentary: Desperately Seeking the 'IT' in IT Research—A Call to Theorizing the IT Artifact. Information Systems Research 12(2), 121–134 (2001)

Peffers, K., Gengler, C., Tuunanen, T.: Extending Critical Success Factors Methodology to Facilitate Broadly Participative Information Systems Planning. Journal of Management Information Systems 20(1), 51–85 (2003)

Peffers, K., Tuunanen, T.: Planning for IS Applications: A Practical, Information Theoretical Method and Case Study in Mobile Financial Services. Information & Management 42(3), 483–501 (2005)

Peffers, K., Tuunanen, T., Hui, W., Gengler, C., Rossi, M., Virtanen, V., Bragge, J.: The Design Science Research Process: A Model for Producing and Presenting Information Systems Research. In: Proceedings of the First International Conference on Design Science Research, Claremont, CA, pp. 83–106 (2006)

Peffers, K., Tuunanen, T., Rothenberger, M.A., Chatterjee, S.: A Design Science Research Methodology for Information Systems Research. Journal of Management Information Systems 24(3), 45–77 (2008)

Pries-Heje, J., Baskerville, R., Venable, J.: Strategies for Design Science Research Evaluation. In: Golden, W., Acton, T., Conboy, K., van der Heijden, H., Tuunainen, V. (eds.) Proceedings of the 16th European Conference on Information Systems, Galway, Ireland, pp. 255–266 (2008)

Przybilski, M.: Requirements Elicitation in International Research Projects. In: Proceedings of the 12th Americas Conference on Information Systems, Acapulco, Mexico, August 4-6 (2006)

Rogers, R.M.: Diffusion of Innovations. The Free Press, New York (1995)

Rossi, M., Tuunanen, T.: A Method and Tool for Wide Audience Requirements Elicitation and Rapid Prototyping for Mobile Systems. In: Wang, S., Tanaka, K., Zhou, S., Ling, T.-W., Guan, J., Yang, D.-q., Grandi, F., Mangina, E.E., Song, I.-Y., Mayr, H.C. (eds.) ER Workshops 2004. LNCS, vol. 3289, pp. 629–640. Springer, Heidelberg (2004)

Sayago, S., Blat, J.: Telling the Story of Plder People e-Mailing: An Ethnographical Study. International Journal of Human-Computer Studies 10(4), 1–33 (2009)

Simonsen, J., Kensing, F.: Using Ethnography in Contextual Design. Communications of the ACM 40(7), 82–88 (1997)

Stahl, B.: Design as Reification, Commodification, and Ideology: A Critical View of IS Design Science. In: Golden, W., Acton, T., Conboy, K., van der Heijden, H., Tuunainen, V. (eds.) Proceedings of the 16th European Conference on Information Systems, Galway, Ireland, pp. 207–218 (2008)

Thimbleby, H., Cairns, P., Jones, M.: Usability Analysis with Markov Models. ACM Transactions on Computer-Human Interaction 8(2), 99–132 (2001)

Thomas, J.: Doing Critical Ethnography. Sage Publications, Newbury Park (1993)

Tuunanen, T., Peffers, K., Gengler, C.: Wide Audience Requirements Engineering (WARE): A Practical Method and Case Study, electronic working paper series, Helsinki School of Economics (2004)

Tuunanen, T., Peffers, K., Gengler, C., Hui, W., Virtanen, V.: Developing Feature Sets for Geographically Diverse External End Users: A Call for Value-Based Preference Modeling. Journal of Information Technology Theory & Application 8(2), 41–55 (2006)

Tuunanen, T., Rossi, M.: An Advanced Requirements Elicitation Method and Tool. In: Proceedings of the WITS 2003, Seattle, Washington (2003)

Tuunanen, T., Rossi, M.: Engineering a Method for Wide Audience Requirements Elicitatation and Integrating It to Software Development. In: Proceedings of the 37th Hawaii International Conference on System Sciences. IEEE Press, Los Alamitos (2004)

van Gigch, J.: System Design Modeling and Metamodeling. Plenum Press, New York (1991)

Vasst, E., Walsham, G.: Representations and Actions: The Transformation of Work Practices with IT Use. Information and Organization (15), 65–89 (2005)

von Hippel, E.: Lead Users: A Source of Novel Product Concepts. Management Science 32(7), 791–805 (1986)

von Hippel, E., Katz, R.: Shifting Innovation to Users Via Toolkits. Management Science 48(7), 821–833 (2002)

Walls, J.G., Widmeyer, G.R., El Sawy, O.A.: Building an Information System Design Theory for Vigilant EIS. Information Systems Research 3(1), 36–59 (1992)

Walsham, G.: Cross-Cultural Software Production and Use: A Structurational Analysis. MIS Quarterly 26(4), 359–380 (2002)

Walz, D., Elam, J., Curtis, B.: Inside a Software Design Team: Knowledge Acquisition, Sharing and Integration. Communications of the ACM 36(10), 62–77 (1993)

Watson, H.J., Frolick, M.N.: Determining Information Requirements for an EIS. MIS Quarterly 17(3), 255–269 (1993)

## About the Authors

**Carl Lawrence** is a Ph.D. student at the University of Auckland in the field of information systems. He has over 12 years experience in corporate IT management, project management and systems analysis. His research interests include cross-cultural innovation, information systems in developing countries, activity theory and design science. Mr. Lawrence can be reached by e-mail at claw054@aucklanduni.ac.nz.

**Tuure Tuunanen** is a senior lecturer in the Department of Information Systems and Operations Management at the University of Auckland. He is also Visiting Professor of Work Informatics at the University of Turku, an associate professor (adjunct) of MIS at the University of Nevada, Las Vegas, and Center of Service Leadership Global Faculty Member at Arizona State University. He holds a D.Sc. (Economics) from the Helsinki School of Economics. His current research interests lie in the areas of IS development methods and processes, requirements engineering, risk management, and convergence of IS and marketing disciplines, specifically in design of interactive consumer services and products. His research has been published in *Information & Management, Journal of the Association for Information Systems, Journal of Database Management, Journal of Information Technology Theory and Application, Journal of Management Information Systems,* and *Technology Analysis and Strategic Management.* Dr. Tuunanen is a member of Association of Computing Machinery, Association for Information Systems, and Institute of Electrical and Electronics Engineers. Dr. Tuunanen is a coeditor-in-chief of *Journal of Information Technology Theory and Application.* He can be reached by e-mail at tuure@tuunanen.fi.

**Michael D. Myers** is Professor of Information Systems and Head of the Department of Information Systems and Operations Management at the University of Auckland Business School, New Zealand. His research articles have been published in many journals and books. He won the Paper of the Year award (with Heinz Klein) for the most outstanding paper published in *MIS Quarterly* in 1999. This paper has been cited over 1,500 times and is third most cited paper to appear in *MIS Quarterly.* He also won the Best Paper Award (with Lynda Harvey) for the best paper published in *Information Technology & People* in 1997. He currently serves as a senior editor of *Information Systems Research* and as editor of the *ISWorld Section on Qualitative Research.* He previously served as a senior editor of *MIS Quarterly* from 2001–2005 and as an associate editor of *Information Systems Journal* from 1995–2000. He also served as President of the Association for Information Systems (AIS) in 2006–2007 and as Chair of the International Federation of Information Processing (IFIP) Working Group 8.2 from 2006–2008. Dr. Myers can be reached at m.myers@auckland.ac.nz.

# Part 3
# Human Benefit?

# The Reality of Rhetoric in Information Systems Adoption: A Case Study Investigation of the Uk National Health Service

Imran Khan and Elaine Ferneley

University of Salford,
Salford, United Kingdom

**Abstract.** The UK National Health Service is undergoing a tremendous IS -led change, the purpose of which is to create a service capable of meeting the demands of the 21st century. The aim of this paper is to examine the extent to which persuasive discourse, or rhetoric, influences and affects the adoption of information systems within the health sector. It seeks to explore the ways in which various actors use rhetoric to advance their own agendas and the impact this has on the system itself. As such, the paper seeks to contribute to diffusion research through the use of a case study analysis of the implementation of an Electronic Single Patient Care Record system within one UK Health Service Trust. The findings of the paper suggest that rhetoric is an important and effective persuasive tool, employed by system trainers to coax users into not only adopting the system but also using the system in a predefined manner.

**Keywords:** Rhetoric, NHS, healthcare systems, diffusion theory, social actors.

## 1 Introduction

The UK's National Health Service (NHS) is in the midst of a metamorphosis aimed at modernizing and transforming the organization to one that befits the 21st century. The drive for modernization is founded upon the design and implementation of new information systems into every facet of the organization, thereby homogenizing the NHS by means of harmonious systems among the various Trusts and Practices. The adoption of information systems into organizations has been examined and addressed by the diffusion of innovations theory, which has spawned significant interest within the Information Systems community and, as such, it is one wing of the IS library to which authors have made significant contributions during the field's relatively brief history (Agarwal and Prasad 1997; Moore and Benbasat 1991; Mustonen-Ollila and Lyytinen 2003).

While the various diffusion theories approach the topic of IS adoption from a number of angles, we would suggest that such models universally fail to account for an important element in human interaction and discourse: the notion of rhetoric. Rhetoric, while informing a number of studies in other fields (Hamilton 2003), has thus far been relatively neglected by IS researchers. The term *rhetoric* is generally

J. Pries-Heje et al. (Eds.): IS Design Science Research, IFIP AICT 318, pp. 125–142, 2010.

misunderstood due to the negative connotations we now associate with the word, but in its true sense it is closely linked with the notion of persuasion (Cockcroft and Cockcroft 1992, Watson 1995). It is in this context that we suggest that it can contribute to our understanding of IS diffusion and adoption, given that Rogers' original concept of diffusion identifies persuasion as an integral part of the innovation decision process (Papazafeiropoulou 2004; Rogers 1995).   In this regard, an investigation of rhetoric provides a means through which to appreciate the nuances of persuasive discourse, in that it allows one to "extract a deeper understanding of some of the intrinsically argumentative aspects of discourse" (Hamilton 1998, p. 435), while also creating reality through the construction and use of social structures (Sillince 2006).

We are in the midst of exploring the issue of rhetoric within IS diffusion through a case study exploration of the UK's NHS, which is in the midst of a politically engineered modernization program referred to as the National Programme for IT or NPfIT (NAO 2006).  Previous studies have shown that the organization as a whole has not traditionally been particularly receptive to the introduction of new information systems (Eason 2007), especially as it is a highly differentiated environment (Clegg and Sheppard 2007), consisting of a multitude of different groups and professional allegiances set within the politically sensitive, risk-averse arena of the UK public sector (Wainwright and Waring 2007).

In that light, this research seeks to present a case study informed by Lamb and Kling's (2005) concept of the social actor, used in response to the multiple "actors" who are to engage with the system (e.g.,clinicians, administrative personnel, trainers, information managers) and whose multifaceted interaction with the system and one another, we argue, cannot be fully understood by the thin label of *user*. The research will explore the role that rhetoric can make to diffusion theory and in doing so may help to negate some of the criticisms directed at diffusion theory with respect to its limited appreciation of cultural, social, and contextual issues (Vega et al. 2007). As a result, the ultimate aim of the research is to contribute constructively to the diffusion theory literature by means of enhancing diffusion theory such that it takes greater heed of the cultural, social, and contextual issues.  In this regard, our research question is as follows:

> *Can the diffusion of information systems within the health sector be better understood through an examination of the rhetorical discourses that flow between different social actors?*

The reminder of this paper is organized in such a manner as to present a review of the literature concerning both diffusion theory and rhetoric, followed by our theoretical model and research method. We then present our case study, after which we present our analysis and findings before concluding the paper.

## 2   Literature Review

As mentioned in the introduction, there are a wide range of diffusion theories that perforate the field and upon which one can found one's research. As such, in attempting to negotiate these various approaches and theoretical standpoints, there appears little in the way of consensus as to an agreed common ground. Indeed,

McMaster and Wastell (2005) note that "from an analysis of several hundred citations in the IS diffusion literature, as few as 3 percent of the total could be described as representing a common or shared knowledge in the field" (p. 387).

The literature has, if anything, clouded our understanding of adoption and diffusion (Ramdani and Kawalek 2007) and is accorded by Kautz et al. (2005) the unwanted distinction of being fragmented, unobjective, and generally weak. Vega et al. (2007) suggest that these approaches have thus far neglected or failed to appreciate the cultural assumptions ingrained within an IS or software artefact, which can at best be abrasive to the culture of the host organization, or, in the worst case, totally incompatible with the context in which it is to serve. They thus lament the lack of studies that regard the contextual influences of adoption and diffusion, while at the same calling for studies to broaden their approach to include suppliers and the government. This is of particular relevance for a study centered within the NPfIT, in which the infusion of information systems into NHS Trusts is very much at the behest of the government and enacted by various IS vendors.

Vega et al.'s criticisms were voiced at the 2007 Working Conference of the International Federation for Information Processing's (IFIP) Working Group 8.6 on the Diffusion, Transfer, and Implementation of Information Technology, an event firmly established within the Information Systems calendar since its inception over a decade ago. Casting a curious glance across the proceedings from that initial conference, the authors are immediately struck by a sense of *déjà vu*; A number of authors (Mumford, Galliers, Kautz) from that original conference raised concerns with regard diffusion theory studies similar to those voiced by Vega and his colleagues. Not only this, the first proceedings from an IFIP WG 8.6 conference gave particular consideration to incorporating socio-technical issues into the diffusion model first suggested by Rogers. Kautz (1996), for instance, anchors his research within an interpretative framework as a means of identifying factors that may sway the adoption and diffusion process one way or the other. In doing so, he suggests that "such a perspective uncovers cultural and political elements" (p. 93), an objective which on the surface appears to placate some of the objections presented by Vega et al.

An additional voice among the dissenters, and one not associated with the IFIP proceedings mentioned above, is provided by Gallivan (2001), who is critical of the traditional diffusionist theories such as Rogers' diffusion of innovations (Rogers 2003) and the technology acceptance model (Davis 1989), given that they do not sufficiently account for situations in which the use of a particular system is mandatory. In their stead, Gallivan proposes a two-pronged strategy that draws attention to both primary adoption by management and decision makers and the subsequent secondary adoption process mandated upon other groups within an organization. Such an approach removes the blinkers imposed by what McMaster and Wastell (2005) term the *standard model* of diffusion of innovations and the technology acceptance model, thereby allowing issues such as power, context, and culture to enter one's field of vision (Wainwright and Waring 2007) and going some way to appeasing the likes of Vega et al.

A recurring concern within the diffusion literature, and one which appears not to have been satisfied over the past decade judging from recent criticisms, is how to successfully address the so-called softer, fuzzier issues, such as culture and politics, and all that this implies. As such, each successive paper on the subject raises these very concerns when reviewing its predecessors while at the same time seeking to solve the very same conundrum. In this respect perhaps it would be prudent return to the source of the theory and the work of Rogers himself, which spawned the work of the authors mentioned previously. Rogers work, while simple, linear, and sequential (Robertson et al. 1996), still beats at the heart of most of the current theories, a piece of work that rests on the innovation–decision process, a five-stage process involving knowledge, persuasion, decision, implementation, and confirmation (Rogers 1983).

Rogers places particular importance on the persuasion stage, whereby "an individual forms a favorable or unfavorable attitude towards the innovation" (Rogers 1983, p. 174). As such, an individual seeks "social reinforcement from others of his or her attitude toward the innovation" and thus "the individual wants to know whether his or her thinking is on the right track in the opinion of peers" (Rogers 1983, p. 175). In this respect, the persuasion stage within Rogers' original concept of diffusion advocates a distinct link or correlation between an individual's attitude toward an innovation and that of his/her peers and associates. As such, one's own self interests form the fulcrum upon which one evaluates an innovation, with an individual seeking an answer to the question, "what are the innovation's advantages and disadvantages in my situation?"—the answer to which is sought from those around us. In light this, Rogers original theory firmly positions diffusion within a social context in which the subjective opinions of our peers, which may or may not be based upon their actual experience with the innovation, are *more accessible and convincing* and serve as a persuasive force in our formation of an opinion toward said innovation. This latter point, whereby one party, intentionally or otherwise, seeks to change the opinion of another, is the basis of persuasive discourse or rhetoric as it has come to be known and has been relatively neglected in IS research and more specifically in the diffusion and adoption literature.

While diffusion theory, as prescribed by Rogers, identifies the role of persuasive discourse within the adoption process, it is found wanting when one extends it beyond the neat arena of individual adoption. In this respect, traditional diffusion theory fails to lend itself particularly well in situations similar to those currently transpiring within the NHS, whereby adoption is a multilayered phenomenon in which the decision to embrace a new IS a taken by senior management and the end users are mandated to utilize the system. Such instances are termed *contingent authority innovation decisions* by Zaltman et al. (1973) and form the basis upon which Gallivan attempts to address a particular limitation of Rogers' theory. Gallivan seeks to address a particular limitation by identifying what he terms primary and secondary adopters, with the latter representing the actual end users of the system and upon whose behalf the primary adopters decide to adopt the system in the first place. In doing so, Gallivan provides a means by which one can begin to examine not only mandatory information system adoption but also how decision makers attempt to persuade users as to the merits of their decisions, thereby facilitating adoption.

Gallivan's work forms the basis upon which Wainwright and Waring (2007) construct their study into the NPfIT, and the template from which they develop their diffusion framework. However, both this latter study and Gallivan's framework gloss over the means by which different actor groups perpetuate their own self interests and thereby impact upon the diffusion process itself. The reader of these texts is lead effortlessly through the stages of various diagrams and frameworks addressing the diffusion process, without pausing to examine the interactions and engagements between different actors. As such, one particular critique, which can be leveraged against diffusion studies based on authority innovation decision, is that they fail to successfully address the *how*:   how diffusion takes place in mandated contexts proliferated by actor groups  keen to pursue or push their own agendas and whereby social interaction and bonds form an integral part of the opinion process.

The term *rhetoric* carries with it a negative connotation as illustrated by the Oxford English Dictionary, which acknowledges rhetoric's persuasive nature in that it is  the "art of effective or persuasive speaking or writing, especially the exploitation of figures of speech and other compositional techniques," adding that it is "language designed to have a persuasive or impressive effect but which is often regarded as lacking in sincerity or meaningful content." On the basis of this definition, the term is generally regarded with suspicion (Hamilton 2003), although in its purest sense rhetoric was regarded by the ancient Greeks as an art that required skill (Booth 2004) and dwelt upon substantially by the likes of Socrates and Cicero (Bilig 1996). Indeed, Socrates devoted significant energy into its study, culminating in his opus to the subject, *On Rhetoric* (Olmsted 2006).

Whether one subscribes to the modern day interpretation of rhetoric, as alluded to by the latter part of the OED's definition, or gravitates toward its classical interpreta- tion its link to persuasion is inescapable. As such, Black (2005) sheds some light upon this link, in that "rhetoric is the art of persuading others, therefore rhetoric and persuasion are inseparable since any definition of rhetoric necessarily includes the idea of persuasion" (p. 9).

On such a basis, rhetorical discourse is said to fall into one of three modes of persuasion, which although first identified by Aristotle still permeate rhetorical studies to date (Corbett and Connors 1999). These are *logos, ethos,* and *pathos.* Logos is persuasion through reasoning, ethos is that aspect of rhetoric centered upon persuasion through force of personality, and pathos centers upon persuasion through the arousal or manipulation of emotion (Cockcroft and Cockcroft 1992). This triumvirate of devices forms the basis upon which Aristotelian rhetoric is set yet still manifests itself in rhetorical studies conducted today. One such example is provided by Van de Ven and Schomaker (2002), who raise the specter of rhetoric in the possible adoption of evidence- based medicine within a healthcare setting. While not specifically addressing IS, their paper lends itself well to the issue of new IS adoption through its discussion of attempts to introduce an innovative practice. As such, Van de Ven and Schomaker suggest that the adoption of an innovation rests not only upon the argument provided the latter's proponents but also upon their credibility, values, and experience, not to mention the interests of the likely adopters. In this respect, Van de Ven and Schomaker state that "innovations are more likely to be adopted when a convincing argument [logos] is presented by credible proponents [ethos] who stir the interests, needs and emotions of the potential adopters [pathos]" (p. 90).

That said, the authors go on to make the point that adoption of innovations in a healthcare setting is seldom this simple, in that adoption involves communication and negotiation between divergent stakeholders, each of which seeks to further its own interests are far as possible. Van de Ven and Schomaker are not alone in casting a rhetorical net over events transpiring within healthcare given that the NHS also has served as a setting through which to examine rhetoric in use. As such, studies that focus on the use of rhetoric within the NHS have enlightened readers as to the role of rhetoric in negotiation (Hamilton 2003), management (Mueller et al. 2004), cultural change (Hughes 1996), and identity formation (Bleakley 2006). Hamilton, in particular, has regularly contributed to the study of rhetoric and has chosen the NHS to anchor his research on a number of occasions, although it must be said that none of his studies consider IS adoption in any way. Hamilton examines the notion of rhetoric as a framework through which one can examine persuasive efforts of different parties in their attempts to influence and convert others to their way of thinking, an example being Hamilton's (2000) paper highlighting a shop steward's use of a number of tropes from rhetoric's repertoire through which he tilts the negotiations in his favor.

Hamilton's work, as well as the work by Mueller et al. (2004) and Hughes (1996), demonstrates the true nature and role of rhetoric, in that there is far more substance to rhetoric than the modern day colloquial use of the word suggests. As such, pausing to examine the use of the term *rhetoric* among publications of an IS nature reveals that it is very much cast as the villain of the piece: usage suggests a lack of substance or a veneer beneath which the truth lurks (as in style versus substance) and is epitomized by titles that feature a phrase containing "rhetoric" and/or "reality" after a conjunction (Ennew and Fernandez-Young 2006; Hartley et al 2002; Moon 2002; Orlikowski and Baroudi 1989).

Returning to the issue of rhetoric as persuasive discourse, one can build upon Aristotle's rhetorical triangle by classifying the rhetoric in use by means of Booth (2004) and his trident of deliberative, forensic, and epideictic rhetoric. The first form is that concerned with attempts to construct the future and is a particular favorite of politicians and forms of policy makers. The forensic form of rhetoric is very much regarded as the domain of historians and lawyers, in that it is concerned with interpreting past events, epideictic rhetoric is firmly centered within the here and now and aims to shape one's interpretation of the present. These forms of rhetoric are not mutually exclusive and it is through exposure that our realities are questioned and formed, where one can seek to persuade or elicit agreement by creating a vision of the future (deliberative), (re)interpreting or manipulating the past (forensic), or reshape views of the present (epideictic). Booth eloquently states that "when words and images remake our past, present or future, they also remake the personae of those of us who accept the new realities" (p 17).

# 3    Theoretical Framework

When attempting to recall a diagrammatical representation of Rogers' diffusion of innovation theory, one is invariably reminded of the classic bell curve graph, which surfaces throughout the pages of his work. The graph purports to depict the frequency with which an innovation is adopted, with Rogers allocating sections of the curve to the five classifications into which all adopters can be designated. As such, Rogers refers to this model as the "adopter categorization on the basis of innovativeness" and in itself it does not represent a framework for his theory.

In order to find something a little more representative of Rogers' work, it is necessary to cast one's gaze toward his notion of the innovation decision process to which reference was made earlier. Rogers' liking for the number five is in evidence once again in his proposition as to a five stage model through which an individual traverses when engaging in the adoption process.   By his own admission, Rogers' model is sequential, and is geared toward an individual afforded the liberty of whether to except or reject a new innovation.  In this respect, Rogers supplements the framework with an additional model geared toward organizational adoption, but this too is guilty of the fallibilities leveraged against the individual model by the likes of Gallivan (2001) and Robertson et al. (1996).

According to the model, an individual (or organization) first acquires or gains knowledge as to a new innovation, after which s/he enters a persuasion stage.  In this respect, we would suggest that the Rogers' model has a flatness to it which does not take into account the way various actors shape and mold one another's opinions.  This is epitomized by Rogers' persuasion stage whereby one finds an almost one-to-one relationship between the innovation and the adopter, an exclusivity to which  third parties have limited influence.

A further issue as to the model centers on the issue of knowledge of an innovation, particularly in an organization in which adoption is mandatory.  While Rogers does indeed acknowledge the fact that this is often the case, going so far as to designate such instances as being "authority innovation-decisions" (1983, p. 29), he does not take this any further, therefore failing to integrate this into his model and thus rendering his theory nonrepresentative of the type of information systems diffusion that is currently under way within the context of this study.   As such, Roger's framework does not sufficiently address the dynamism of adoption, especially in a context proliferated with multiple social actors.  In this respect, we would suggest the answer lies in a re-reading of Rogers' identification of the main elements of diffusion. Rogers suggest that "the main elements in the diffusion of a new idea are (1) an innovation (2) that is communicated  through certain channels (3) over time (4) amongst members of a social system" (1995, p. 11) and it is to the latter part of this definition that the answer may lay.  As such, we propose that it is the notion of a social system that has been insufficiently addressed in previous conceptualizations of diffusion and an area to which rhetoric can be of use.

The mandatory diffusion of IS into the health service invariably involves and affects a range of different actors with differing agendas.   These actor groups represent and form the social system(s) espoused by Rogers (1983), (re)creating and reinforcing the opinions and understanding of those found within their ranks.  This particular sentiment, that of the social formation of individual thought, forms an integral part of the teachings of French philosopher Pierre Bourdieu and is formalized in his notion of *habitus* (Bourdieu 1992).   Allowing for, and in fact actively incorporating, habitus into one's conceptual development allows for the consideration of social constraints on the formation of knowledge and, as such, is described by Mutch (2003) as a means by which to examine how "patterns of though are unconsciously acquired and the links between social actors and their backgrounds" (p. 388).  In this respect, both habitus and Bourdieu himself have lent themselves to a number of IS studies (Mingers 2004; Mutch 2003), as well as those specifically concerned with diffusion (Kvasny and Truex 2000), and allows for a greater understanding as to the introduction of new IS, not to mention the subsequent rippling affects.  In this respect, when fixing one's gaze firmly upon diffusion, as is the case of this study, Bourdieu's habitus  facilitates the "exploration of expectations, aspirations, and attitude towards technology, in addition to how and if one engages technology" (Kvasny and Truex 2000, p. 284)

That said, the questions arises as to how habitus fits in the purpose of this study, one which seeks to determine the role of rhetoric and persuasion on the diffusion of information systems. The answer, we would suggest, lies in the fact that our understanding and interpretation of the world around us is in a state of flux, we share our understanding of the world with those around us and, therefore, habitus is both an individual and shared concept (Kvasny and Truex 2000). In light of this, habitus is durable yet not fixed and is "malleable and in constant negotiation with the world" (Kvasny and Truex 2000, p. 283). If mandatory adoption is to be imposed upon a social group, as is the case in the NHS and the NPfIT, it is the individual and collective habitus of said group which must be permeated and changed, and is it rhetoric, we suggest, which facilitates this end.

Adapting Rogers' framework to take into account persuasive discourses that flow between the social actors functioning within the NHS, we propose a *rhetorical cycle* in which actors from one group redefine their own thoughts and opinions while also trying to change the *habitus* of those around them. This cycle suggests that diffusion is not a linear process as espoused by Rogers, nor is persuasion simply a stage that must be traversed on the way to the ultimate adoption of a new technology (Figure 1). Rather, the social actors in the diffusion process are continually seeking to persuade and influence one another, utilizing their relationships, strength of argument, and emotions to do so (pathos, logos, and ethos).

## 4  Research Method

This study gravitates toward the interpretative tradition of IS research but will adopt aspects of critical hermeneutics as a means of infusing the study with rigor, enabling one to "portray the real complexity of organizations as social, cultural and political systems... allowing the researcher to look at information systems through the different perspectives of various stakeholders and real value conflicts there may be" (Myers 1997, p. 250).

Critical hermeneutics, therefore, bridges the divide between the interpretivist and critical schools of thought and has been developed from the philosophical hermeneutics of Gadamer by theorists such as Ricour (Thompson 1981), who have sought to infuse hermeneutics with elements of critical theory. It has germinated from the discussions between Habermas and Gadamer, in so far as there are commonalities between the thoughts of the two theorists and elements within their writing which are complimentary. As such, Bernstein (1984) has shown that critical theory based upon the thought of Habermas and philosophical hermeneutics espoused by Gadamer, while different and diverse in many respects, are not totally antagonistic or dichotomous. Within information systems, Myers (1994, 1997) is the main advocate of a critical hermeneutic approach, using it to examine IS failure within the health sector and issues such as the exercise of power among IS professionals.

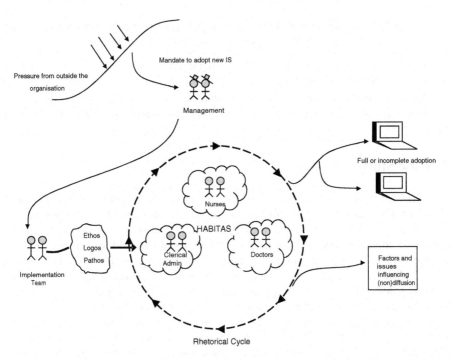

**Fig. 1.** Conceptual Model

The advantages of employing a critical hermeneutic approach, as far as this research is concerned, are expounded by Myers (2004) in his elevation of a hermeneutic approach in general, whereby the latter enables one to "portray the complexity of organizations as social, cultural and political systems" (p. 123). The application of critical hermeneutics thus affords us the means by which to examine the tide of rhetorical discourses that ebb and flow between the various social actors involved in the diffusion of IS into the research context.

The method by means of which the research will seek to explore the field of study is that of a case study. Research within the NHS is shrouded in bureaucracy and, as such, we have had to engage in a lengthy process to secure ethical approval, the result of which has allowed us to contact, recruit, and interview members of the organization. In addition, we have also obtained permission to attend team meetings. We have conducted a phased interview process whereby information elicited from the research participants was taped and transcribed at a later date. The mode of analysis was that of hermeneutics, whereby the interpretation of the transcripts was in keeping with the context of the study, complementing and supporting our desire to explore persuasive discourse.

We intend to call upon Lamb and Kling's (2005) concept of the social actor to provide greater insight and understanding as to the nature of the various research participants. In this respect, the notion of a *user* is far too narrow and it is only through an understanding as to the social actors' affiliations, identity, environment, and interactions that one can truly begin to appreciate the rhetorical discourse taking place. As a result, the study identifies the following social actors:

- **Clinicians**—would be conventionally regarded as the end user and include doctors and nurses
- **Clinical Leads**—former clinicians who have been seconded into the implementation team and are responsible for ensuring the smooth transition to the new system

## 5  Case Study

The NHS has developed a history of IT-led innovation (NAO 2006), albeit one which upon scrutiny its somewhat checkered as far as success is concerned (Clegg and Shepherd 2007). Since the turn of the millennium, the development of an integrated clinical records system has been the focus of the NHS's IT agenda and has manifested itself as various initiatives within the National Programme for IT (NPfIT). These initiatives include the implementation of an electronic single patient care records system, the development of an NHS IT spine, a "choose and books" system to facilitate patient choice, and a picture archiving and communication system.

The full brunt of the NPfIT will be felt at the operational level of NHS, at the various semi-autonomous Trusts which constitute the UK's National Health Service. One such trust is HealthCo Primary Care Trust, which is responsible for the delivery of non-emergency health care to the residents in the local area and is charged with the responsibility of implementing systems such as those responsible for patient records and insuring that the various clinicians and administrative staff are of a sufficient level of competence to use the systems.

The Trust has been allocated a particular variant of electronic patient records system by virtue of the tendering process, whereby CompProvider was awarded the contract for the Trust's geographic location. As such, the system on offer is the Pegasus Community Care system which was implemented as a bare-bones system upon which various layers of functionality are to be added when available. The diffusion of this system into the organization centered on determining the various working practices of the clinicians and tailoring these in such a way as to be fully system compliant. In order to do so, process mapping exercises were held by the clinical leads and the implementation team after which the new processes were introduced by the clinical leads and system trainers.

Problems have arisen as to the performance and usage of the system, with the clinicians wary as to the requirement of the system whereby they must account for all of their time. Management, meanwhile, have voiced their dissatisfaction as to the poor quality of the data extracted from the system and the degree to which the system is actually used by the clinicians. As things stand, clinicians are not entering data into the system on a daily basis as directed, preferring to enter the details of all their patient activities in one go up to two weeks later. The clinical leads, meanwhile, are coming under pressure from management to ensure that the system is used in the correct manner and at the required times.

# 6  Case Study Analysis

This section seeks to apply our theoretical framework to the above case study, whereby we examine the rhetorical cycle taking place among  member of two of the key actor groups within the implementation of NPfIT, the clinicians, who form the primary users of the new system, and the clinical leads, whose role it is to ensure a smooth transition to the new technology.

## 6.1  Clinical Leads

**Persuasion through Pathos.** Persuasion by means of pathos was a key instrument within the rhetorical cycle taking place, whereby the clinical lead's rhetoric centered on what could be perceived as the manipulation of the clinician's emotions and sense of duty. The clinical lead, when required to justify the need for a change in systems (the clinicians had as far as they were concerned recently adopted a new system which itself has been superseded by Pegasus as a result of the dictates of the NPfIT), retorted that *"these systems and services are essential for creating the modern, safer, joined-up NHS to which **we** all aspire."* This served to draw upon the clinicians' collective sense of purpose, especially with the emphasis upon the "we," as with the clinicians, and the hand gesture which accompanied it. (As an aside, it was only later that we discovered that the clinical lead's statement was in fact the mantra of Richard Granger, the former director of the NPfIT).

The clinicians' sense of purpose was a constant target for the clinical lead's rhetoric, with statements such as *"being able to access patients' information is going to help us save lives"* as well as *"electronic care records will mean patients will have fewer forms to fill in,"* reminding the clinicians as to why they had originally entered the profession.

**Persuasion Using Ethos.** Persuasion by means of ethos or strength of personality manifests itself primarily through the clinical lead, who is keen to emphasize her camaraderie and sense of kinship with the clinicians themselves. This is most clearly illustrated by the clinical lead's own assertion that

> *It's as much about personality as anything else. You've got to have those influencing and negotiating skills to be able to change people's minds about things. Our background is obviously nursing but we have to develop an understanding how other services work and make suggestions of different ways of working. If they're [the clinicians] not for moving, its very much about nudging them to achieve our aims.*

Statements such as *"I am a nurse.  Once a nurse always a nurse"* served to soften the attitudes of the clinicians as to their refusal to, in the manager's words *"play ball"* and use the system in the designated manner.

This initial hard line was overcome by the clinical lead through her continual use of ethos (as well as the aforementioned pathos), reinforcing her understanding of the difficulties encountered by the clinicians to such an extent that the clinicians began to sympathize with the clinical lead's position.  Statements such as *"we realize you are only doing your job"* and *"we can see why you would want us to input data on a daily basis*" contrasted significantly with the initial mood of the group. The clinical lead's assertion that *"you don't necessarily have to be doing hands-on nursing care to be able to have an impact on patients care, do you know what I mean?"* coupled with her personality and character allowed her to enter the clinician's habitus in a way that was beyond any other member of the implementation team.

**Persuasion through Logos.** The adoption of Pegasus by the Trust has not produced the desired results in terms of the way in which the clinicians are using the system. The clinical leads  are particularly suited to addressing such issues in that they straddle the divide between "us and them," with their clinical background affording them certain privileges in terms of permeating the clinicians' habitus, while focusing on  their main role as system implementers.

Their unique position, drawn upon through the use of ethos, allows them to highlight logical reasons as to why clinicians should be more receptive to the new system given that *"electronic care records will mean patients will have fewer forms to fill in"* Logical arguments are particularly useful when addressing a group of clinicians who have embraced technology and use it on a daily basis for their own ends. Such groups are referred to by the clinical leads as *"our champions"* in that it is often only necessary to highlight or go through the system's proposed benefits  with such clinicians and they are *"onboard"* with any suggested changes.

The clinical leads make specific reference to a specific clinician who *"wears a utility belt of gadgets"* as one such champion. That said, the clinical leads are also highly suspicious of such groups, referring to them as *"dangerous users"* or *"uneducated educated users,"* given that their *"use of PDA's and smart-phones"* or the fact that *"[he] managed to install Windows Vista on his laptop"* gives them a *"false impression that they know a lot about technology."*  It is these clinicians who later *"bad mouth the technology to others"* if it does not meet their expectations.

### 6.2  Clinicians

**The Use of Pathos.** Rhetoric among the clinicians primarily makes use of their sense of shared purpose and the habitus to which they belong.  As such, collective identity of the clinicians was reinforced by statements such as *"a necessary evil"* when referring to the need to engage with, and produce reports for, management. When one clinician stated that such activities were an aside to the *"reason we are all here...to help and treat patients,"* the rest of the group nodded in approval and another further reinforced the perceived sense of collective purpose when, choosing to speak on behalf of the whole group, she stated that *"we feel that clinicians should be practicing nursing rather than acting as data entry clerks!"*

The use of the collective "we" serves to unite the clinicians around this one goal while also separating them from the counter-argument that clinicians ought to be more receptive to the use of the new computer system and the additional responsibilities that this brings. Those clinicians with, in the words of one nurse, *"horror stories"* as to the experience of other clinical teams, continued to draw upon the fact that *"we are not IT"* (referring to the IT department) in so much that patient care is universally within the group  regarded as the central tenet of being a clinician.

Most telling was the clinicians' use of pathos in the direction of the managers in that *"the training does not prepare us to use that system...it's impacting because Monday mornings clinicians aren't out with patients, they are out doing computer work, which is not how we all perceive the clinicians role to be."* As if to ensure that no doubt is left in the minds of those present, one senior clinicians draws a line under the whole discussion by declaring that *"fundamental change is really about power and control. **They** just want to keep an eye on us,"* to which no one in the group offers objections.

**The Use of Ethos.** The impact of the previous statements was all the more effective given that a number of the more dramatic comments emanated from more senior clinicians, both in terms of age and position. One clinician was particularly vocal as to her opposition to the new system and was keen to elicit examples from younger clinicians as to how their friends and acquaintances in other departments were also encountering difficulties in using the system. Her repeated emphasis as to the fact that *"I have been in this job for over 20 years"* appeared to grant her the right to speak on behalf of others, while also imbuing her assertions with greater credibility.

Persuasion through force of personality was evident throughout, as the afore-mentioned clinician continued to highlight her experience and also the experience of others, asserting that *"I was here when they brought in the old system, as were you Jean. All that fuss and bother but for what? So that we can go through whole process again. And again and again!"* The defiance of the clinician in the face of mandatory use of the system when she stated that *"although we've electronic records, I'm still avoiding them and feign ignorance about them all"* brought smiles all round, as did her commitment to her patients in that while *"the top floor"* (management) continue to push the new IT program, *"I will just get on with treating and looking after folk."*

**The Use of Logos.** Persuasion through logic does not feature as extensively as the pathos or ethos discussed previously. Those designated as *"dangerous users"* by the clinical leads sought to emphasize the futility in resisting or dragging one's feet, in that *"at the end of the day, the decision has been made that this system is to be used and there is nothing we can do to change that. The sooner we accept that and open our minds to this new technology, the quicker we can get to learning how to use if effectively."* These assertions as to logic in using the system were, however, overshadowed by those relying upon personality and emotion to convey and secure their message.

# 7  Discussion

Our case studies help to shed light on a neglected aspect of the adoption and diffusion process, one in which the posturing of the various social actors is examined and analyzed with respect to its impact upon other actors. As such, we argue that introducing a new system into an organization, especially one in which the system is very much seen as something that takes people away from performing their "actual" roles, involves a level of persuasive discourse as a means of not only reducing resistance but also allowing for the possible limitations to the system itself.

As such, the rhetoric used by the clinical lead to persuade clinicians to use the system, with non-use impacts not only on the service and organization but on the patient and society as well, hits at the very identity of the clinician. An identity at the core of which is the duty to help people, alleviate suffering, and ultimately improve lives (Timmons 2003).

The same can be said of the clinicians themselves, with their ability to deflect criticism from management onto the system implementers who were then instructed to redesign training methods to facilitate the clinicians' adoption of the system and address their concerns. Interestingly enough, the research cast light on how the clinical leads designated those more technologically literate clinicians as *"dangerous users,"* while at the same time seeking to have the same clinicians on their side as their *"champions."*

Both the clinical leads and the *"dangerous user"* clinicians approach the system from a certain perspective—that of expert (in the latter's case, this is their own assessment)— and have been more willing to use logic in their persuasive discourse. One possibility for this may be the notion of expert versus novice, with clinicians lacking in knowledge about the system, therefore not feeling confident or comfortable formulating an argument around the notion of logic.

We would suggest, given that the clinicians function within the same habitus, one to which the clinical lead was also privy, that the social actors were far more comfortable and accepting of ethos and pathos, while the trainers, as outsiders, had to confine their persuasion attempts to logic alone. This may also have something to do with the asymmetry of power within the organization, whereby those with a degree of power, such as managers, had the luxury of relying simply on logic to persuade others.

In light of our findings, we argue that the study of IS adoption can be further enhanced through an examination of the rhetorical discourse which takes place between the various actors in the midst of the system. In this regard, diffusion of innovation frameworks such as those espoused by Mustonen-Ollila and Lyytinen (2003) and Gallivan (2001), while embracing contextual issues to a greater extent than previous diffusion of innovation theories (Wainwright and Waring 2007), stop shy of discussing persuasion among actors as a facilitator, or otherwise, of information systems adoption. Furthermore, while persuasion is a key factor within Rogers' innovation–decision process, it is very much regarded as focused upon the adopter and his or her direct interaction with the innovation. Our case study would suggest that not only is the adoption of a system influenced through rhetoric, non-adoption, or unintended outcomes, such as the lack of reports, can all also be addressed in a similar manner, thereby altering perceptions as to what a system can and cannot do. This is of particular relevance when one considers the challenge posed by the implementation of the new system: *"The biggest thing about the whole thing isn't the IT or data migration or training. It is the change management of altering the way in which people work"* (HealthCo's informatoin manager).

The case has illustrated how rhetoric is used as a tool to increase the adoption of a system and secure support, given that the clinical leads are not only responsible for activities such as process mapping but also *"communicating the benefits of the system"* to users. In this respect, a particularly telling indicator as to the role of

**Table 1.** Intersections of the Two Dimensions of Interest Groups and Mode of Persuasion

|        | Clinical Lead | Clinician |
|--------|--------------|-----------|
| Ethos  | *I am a nurse. Once a nurse always a nurse.* | *All that fuss and bother but for what? So that we can go through whole process again. And again and again!* |
| Pathos | *Using the system will ultimately help save lives.* | *We feel that clinicians should be practicing nursing rather than acting as data entry clerks!* |
| Logos  | *The system will help improve patient care* | *The system takes too much of our time* |

rhetoric within NHS IS adoption is the clinical lead's statement whereby *"part of the job is to communicate our sales pitch to sell people on the technology. But we also take part in a lot of ego stroking, bigger egos require a lot more stroking....I sometimes feel like a used car salesman!"*

# 8 Conclusion

Healthcare organizations continue to invest resources in the development and implementation of information system with the intention of improving efficiency and service. Diffusion frameworks have thus far been found wanting with regard to studying the nature of adoption within these organizations and to this end we have proposed expanding the scope of investigation to include the rhetoric discourse that takes place between the various social actors. In this regard, our study introduces a group of social actors heavily engaged in the diffusion of an information system and whose actions significantly influence the extent to which it is adoptioned.

# References

Agarwal, R., Prasad, J.: The Role of Innovation Characteristics and Perceived Voluntariness in the Acceptance of Information Technologies. Decision Sciences 28(3), 557–582 (1997)

Bernstein, R.J.: Beyond Objectivism and Relativism: Science, Hermeneutics and Praxis. University of Pennsylvania Press, Philadelphia (1984)

Billig, M.: Arguing and Thinking: Arhetorical Approach to Social Psychology. Cambridge University Press, Cambridge (1996)

Black, J.: Politicians and Rhetoric: The Persuasive Power of Metaphor. Palgrave Macmillian, New York (2005)

Bleakley, A.: You Are Who I Say You Are: The Rhetorical Construction of Identity in the Operating Theater. Journal of Workplace Learning 18(7/8), 414–425 (2006)

Booth, W.: The Rhetoric of Rhetoric: The Quest for Effective Communication. Blackwell Publishing, Oxford (2004)

Bourdieu, P.: The Logic of Practice. Polity Press, Cambridge (1992)

Clegg, C., Shepherd, C.: The Biggest Computer Program in the World..Ever! Time for a Change in Mindset. Journal of Information Technology 22(3), 212–221 (2007)

Cockcroft, R., Cockcroft, S.: Persuading People: An Introduction to Rhetoric. Macmillan Press, Ltd., Hampshire (1992)

Corbett, E.P.J., Connors, R.J.: Classical Rhetoric for the Modern Student, 4th edn. Oxford University Press, New York (1999)

Davis, F.D.: Perceived Usefulness, Perceived Ease of Use, and User Acceptance of Information Technology. MIS Quarterly 13(3), 319–340 (1989)

Eason, K.: Local Sociotechnical System Development in the NHS National Program for Information Technology. Journal of Information Technology 22(3), 257–264 (2007)

Ennew, C., Fernandez-Young, A.: Weapons of Mass Instruction? The Rhetoric and Reality of Online Learning. Marketing Intelligence & Planning 24(2), 148–157 (2006)

Gallivan, M.: Organizational Adoption and Assimilation of Complex Technological Innovations: Development and Application of a New Framework. The DATA BASE for Advances in Information Systems 32(3), 51–85 (2001)

Hamilton, P.M.: Implementing Local Pay: Rhetorically Analyzing Irritation. Personnel Review 27(6), 433–447 (1998)

Hamilton, P.M.: Attaining Agreement: A Rhetorical Analysis of an NHS Negotiation. International Journal of Public Sector Management 13(3), 285–300 (2000)

Hamilton, P.M.: The 'Vital Connection': A Rhetoric on Equality. Personnel Review 32(6), 694–710 (2003)

Hartley, S., Shepperd, S., Bosanquet, N.: Information Flows in the New Primary Care Organizations: Rhetoric Versus Reality. The Journal of Clinical Governance 10(3), 113–119 (2002)

Hughes, M.: NHS Managers as Rhetoricians. Sociology of Health and Illness (18), 291–314 (1996)

Kautz, K.: Information Technology Transfer and Implementation: The Introduction of an Electronic Mail System in a Public Sector Organization. In: Kautz, K., Pries-Heje, J. (eds.) Diffusion and Adoption of Information Technology, pp. 83–95. Chapman & Hall, London (1996)

Kautz, K., Henriksen, H.Z., Breer-Mortensen, T., Poulson, H.H.: IT Diffusion Research: An Interim Balance. In: Baskerville, R., Mathiassen, L., Pries-Heje, J., DeGross, J.I. (eds.) Business Agility and Information Technology Diffusion, pp. 11–34. Springer, Boston (2005)

Kvasny, L., Truex, D.P.: Information Technology and the Cultural Reproduction of Social Order: A Research Paradigm. In: Baskerville, R., Stage, J., DeGross, J.I. (eds.) Organizational and Social Perspectives on Information Technology, pp. 277–294. Kluwer Academic Publishers, New York (2000)

Lamb, R., Kling, R.: Reconceptualizing Users as Social Actors in Information Systems Research. MIS Quarterly 22(2), 197–235 (2003)

McMaster, T., Wastell, D.: Diffusion – or Delusion? Challenging an IS Tradition. Information Technology & People 18(4), 383–404 (2005)

Mingers, J.: Re-establishing the Real: Critical Realism and Information Systems. In: Mingers, J., Willcocks, L. (eds.) Social Theory and Philosophy for Information Systems, pp. 372–406. John Wiley & Sons, New York (2004)

Moon, M.: The Evolution of E-Government Among Municipalities: Rhetoric or Reality? Public Administration Review 62(4), 424–433 (2002)

Moore, G.C., Benbasat, I.: Development of an Instrument to Measure the Perceptions of Adopting an Information Technology Innovation. Information Systems Research 2(3), 192–222 (1991)

Mueller, F., Sillince, J., Harvey, C., Howorth, C.: Discourse, Rhetorical Strategies and Arguments: Conversations in an NHS Hospital Board. Organizational Studies 25(1), 75–93

Mustonen-Ollila, E., Lyytinen, K.: Why Organizations Adopt Information System Process Innovations: A Longitudinal Study using Diffusion of Innovation Theory. Information Systems Journal 13(3), 275–297 (2003)

Mutch, A.: Communities of Practice and Habitus: A Critique. Organization Studies 24(3), 383–401 (2003)

Myers, M.D.: Hermeneutics in Information Systems Research. In: Mingers, J., Willcocks, L. (eds.) Social Theory and Philosophy for Information Systems, pp. 103–128. John Wiley, Chichester (1994)

Myers, M.D.: Interpretive Research in Information Systems. In: Mingers, J., Stowell, F. (eds.) Information Systems: An Emerging Discipline?, pp. 239–266. McGraw-Hill, New York (1997)

NAO. The National Programme for IT in the NHS, Session 2005/2006, National Audit Office (2006)

Olmsted, W.: Rhetoric: An Historical Introduction. Blackwell Publishing, Oxford (2006)

Orlikowski, W.J., Baroudi, J.J.: The Information Systems Professional: Myth or Reality? Office, Technology, and People 4(1), 13–30 (1989)

Papazafeiropoulou, A.: A Framework for the Investigation of the Institutional Layer of IT Diffusion. Using Stakeholder Theory to Analyze Electronic Commerce Diffusion. In: Damsgaard, J., Henriksen, H.Z. (eds.) Networked Information Technologies: Diffusion and Adoption, pp. 167–179. Kluwer Academic Publishers, Norwell (2004)

Robertson, M., Swan, J., Newell, S.: Interorganisational Networks and the Diffusion Process: The Case of Networks not Working. In: Kautz, K., Pries-Heje, J. (eds.) The Adoption and Diffusion of Information Technology, pp. 147–159. Chapman & Hall, London (1996)

Rogers, E.M.: Diffusion of Innovations, 3rd edn. The Free Press, New York (1983)

Rogers, E.M.: Diffusion of Innovations, 4th edn. The Free Press, New York (1995)

Rogers, E.M.: Diffusions of Innovations, 5th edn. The Free Press, New York (2003)

Sillince, J.A.A.: Resources and Organizational Identities: The Role of Rhetoric in the Creation of Competitive Advantage. Management Communication Quarterly (20), 186–211

Thompson, J.B.: Critical Hermeneutics: A Study in the Thought of Paul Ricoeur and Jurgen Habermas. Cambridge University Press, Cambridge (1981)

Timmons, S.A.: Failed Panopticon: Surveillance of Nursing Practice Via New Technology. New Technology, Work and Employment (18), 143–153 (2003)

Van de Ven, A.H., Schomaker, M.S.: The Rhetoric of Evidence-Based Medicine. Health Care Management Review 27(3), 88–90 (2002)

Vega, A., Chiasson, M., Brown, D.: Extending the Research Agenda on Diffusion of Innovations: The Role of Public Programs in the Diffusion of E-Business Innovations. In: McMaster, T., Wastell, D., Ferneley, E., DeGross, J.I. (eds.) Organizational Dynamics of Technology-Based Innovation: Diversifying the Research Agenda, pp. 379–392. Springer, Boston (2007)

Wainwright, D.W., Waring, T.S.: The Application and Adaptation of a Diffusion of Innovation Framework for Information Systems Research in NHS General Medical Practice. Journal of Information Technology 22(1), 44–58 (2007)

Watson, T.J.: Rhetoric, Discourse and Argument in Organizational Sense Making: A Reflective Tale. Organizational Studies 16(5), 805–821 (1995)

Zaltman, G., Duncan, R., Holbeck, J.: Innovations and Organizations. Wiley & Sons, New York (1973)

## About the Authors

**Imran Khan** is currently a doctoral candidate and graduate teaching assistant at the University of Salford. His research interests center on large-scale, collaborative information systems development, organizational discourse, and rhetoric. He can be reached by e-mail at i.m.khan@pgt.salford.ac.uk.

**Elaine Ferneley** is a professor of Information Systems at the University of Salford. She can be reached at e.ferneley@salford.ac.uk.

# Social Consequences of Nomadic Working: A Case Study in an Organization

Ramanjit Singh and Trevor Wood-Harper

Manchester Business School,
University of Manchester,
Oxford Road,
Manchester M13 9PL, United Kingdom

**Abstract.** This research study identified social challenges that knowledge workers in the Swedish organization TeliaSonera (Telia) face when utilizing wireless technologies to conduct work on the move. Upon collecting the relevant research data, five problem areas were identified: work and life balance, addiction, organizational involvement, nomadic work and control, and individual productivity. Each problem area was examined with the philosophical underpinning of socio-technical design principles. The results confirm that better role boundary management, self-discipline, work negotiation, and e-mail communication skills may be required for the knowledge workers to manage the demands of nomadic working. Similarly, rewarding nomadic work performance, building employee-supervisor trust relations, and designing jobs that enhance work and life balance can be imperative.

**Keywords:** Nomadic work, wireless technology, socio-technical, work–life balance, career development, productivity.

## 1 Introduction

There is a major restructuring going on in various industries. Organizations are moving away from traditional hierarchies to networks and from centralization to decen-tralization in that parts of the organization are operated as semi-autonomous work units (Malone 2004). These structural changes are not necessarily new. When Ken Olsen founded the Digital Equipment Corporation in 1957, his initial business was based on a decentralized network structure, each unit being responsible for its own production, supervision, and profits. As business grew, this was changed to a more hierarchical structure. The network structure was believed to be destructive as it resulted in replication of resources and intense competition between various business units. In Mumford's (2006) view, companies may face problems in applying these new organizational structures since they may not understand them well. For example, who ought to make major decisions in these companies and how is performance measured? It is believed that complexity can be lessened by discretion, cooperation, and knowledge sharing. Although there are few examples of the network approach in the world, Scandinavian companies have been most successful in combining efficiency with equality. Nevertheless, opponents of this approach suggest that

J. Pries-Heje et al. (Eds.): IS Design Science Research, IFIP AICT 318, pp. 143–158, 2010.

managing complexity requires flexibility and a loose organizational formation, whereas profit maximization requires command and control management. These two strands of thinking may have difficulty coming together. Also, democratic work methods may receive little attention when capitalism first and foremost requires wealth for the shareholders.

The nature of work has been changing for a long time and in the last decade there has been a shift from manufacturing to service jobs. There has also been an increase in highly skilled knowledge jobs. Knowledge work can be defined as intellectual work performed to generate valuable information and knowledge. Since an important part of knowledge work consists of nomadic computing, the positive and negative impacts on productivity are subject to the work processes of knowledge workers (Davis 2002). When compared to traditional ways of working, nomadic work provides greater flexibility while freeing the knowledge worker from time and place constraints. Knowledge work is an important part of many organizations today, hence the efficiency of knowledge workers is an important concern (Grudin 2002). Because of the need to excel, knowledge workers require greater freedom, autonomy, and diversity in their work. Hence, decentralized network structures are adopted so that individuals may work in groups and have greater responsibility over their tasks. These recent changes in organizational structure may encourage the adoption of nomadic working. There are many reasons for organizations to test this type of work formation, particularly given the rapid increase in affordable wireless technologies.

Although nomadic work arrangements enable firms to reduce costs while increasing work flexibility, there are numerous challenges and threats faced by knowledge workers (Sorensen 2004). Thus, this research study will identify social challenges that knowledge workers in the Swedish organization TeliaSonera (Telia) face when utilizing wireless technologies to conduct work on the move. More specifically, knowledge workers' management, computing, communication practices with respect to the use of laptops, pocket PCs, PDAs, and/or cell phones in nomadic working will be investigated.

## 2  Literature Review

The major departure point of this research study was the observation that within the literature on mobility, research on the use of wireless technologies in organizations was underrepresented. Aside from a small number of research initiatives that consider the social impact of wireless technology in organizations, much of the literature has been on conceptualizing mobility. There has been a focus on studying the mobile interaction of mobile workers and thereby creating models of mobility (i.e., spatial, temporal, contextual). These models have been used to understand how mobile workers define various categories of context such as work and home given the use of wireless technology in spatial mobile work. There also have been attempts to examine how mobile workers dynamically reconfigure their workspace and move between various work locations. In an attempt to gain an understanding of the potential impact of novel technological developments on organizational communication and cooperation, numerous studies on the use of the mobile phone have been conducted. But here too, the aim of these studies has been to develop a conceptual discussion of mobile work practices (Elaluf-Calderwood et al. 2005).

Although the existing literature highlights advantages of increased mobility, there is little evidence that identifies the problems that individuals face while utilizing wireless technologies in the workplace. The importance of identifying social consequences of nomadic working has been echoed by many scholars given the diminishing boundaries between work and social life. It was also found that nomadic working may reduce visibility in the organization, which in turn may lower career advancement prospects (Davis 2002; Jarvenpaa et al. 2005; Lamond et al. 2003). Finally, the inability to use wireless devices securely can slow down the adoption process (Lyytinen et al. 2004). All of these claims provide a need to study how wireless technologies are used in organizations and what are the inherent social consequences involved in nomadic working. Especially pertaining to the literary context, it is important to investigate whether nomadic working reduces work–life balance, involvement in the organization, and individual productivity, and whether nomadic working increases management control and adds to the cost of information. The conceptual framework will be discussed next.

## 3  Conceptual Framework

The nature of work has been changing for a long time and in the last decade there has been a shift from manufacturing to service jobs. There has also been an increase in highly skilled knowledge jobs. Knowledge work is an important part of many organizations today, hence the efficiency of knowledge workers is an important concern (Grudin 2002). Because of the need to excel, knowledge workers require greater freedom, autonomy, and diversity in their work. Hence, decentralized network structures are adopted so that individuals may work in groups and have greater responsibility over their tasks. These recent changes in organizational structure may encourage the adoption of nomadic working. There are many reasons for organizations to test this type of work formation, particularly given the rapid increase in affordable wireless technologies.

For organizations, the benefits of nomadic working are lower overhead costs such as office space and supplies, while individuals benefit from more flexible working hours; more time for managing home and family life; reduced need for commuting; greater autonomy over work processes; fewer interruptions while working; and the chance to remain at work even if becoming sick or taking child-care leave. Most of these direct benefits have an indirect impact on the job and life satisfaction, including physical health. The set of benefits for society as a whole includes heightened community stability; improved entrepreneurial effort; less environmental pollution; and more effective use of energy sources. Although there may be many perceived benefits, possible negative consequences of nomadic working include poor career advancement opportunities, increased conflict between work and family life, and social isolation. Negative organizational consequences may include purchase of suitable equipment, training and support overhead, along with health and safety provisions (Lamond et al. 2003).

It is believed that there will be a significant increase in nomadic working in the future (Sorensen 2004). Although the idea is not new, advances in information and communication technologies are enabling workers to access organizational data, collaborate with colleagues, and remain in touch with customers and suppliers, working effectively anytime anywhere (Lyytinen and Yoo 2002). The success of nomadic working requires that both employer and employee have mutual trust. In addition, it is important that the employer provides the employee with acceptable rewards, job satisfaction, and job security. Creating a nomadic culture in an organization will not be an easy task, but failure to do so will lead to alienation and a dissatisfied workforce (Mumford 2006). Although Fok et al. (1987) provided important guidelines for designing socio-technical jobs in the past, their use may no longer be fruitful in designing the work systems of today. Hence, Singh et al. (2008) propose the use of socio-technical principles for designing jobs for the decentralized organization of the 21$^{st}$ century.

- Assumptions about the organization:
  - It is an open system, which interacts with the environment
  - It is composed of two autonomous yet interrelated subsystems: social and technical
- Assumptions about employees:
  - From Theory Y's point of view, it is ethical to let people participate in the decision-making process
- Socio-technical work design aims:
  - Joint satisfaction of technical (work efficiency) and social(work–life) goals of the organization
- Assumptions about the socio-technical work design process:
  - Worker participation is essential
- Socio-technical work design concepts:
  - Work system, not single job, as design unit
  - Workgroup not single jobholder
  - Internal regulation of group
  - Redundancy of function, not redundancy of parts
    - ○  Members have discretion, not highly prescribed work
  - Develop flexible learning system
    - ○  Autonomous workgroup is superior form of organization
- Role changes:
  - Designer: facilitator not expert
  - Worker: designer of the system
  - Manager: boundary manager, not supervisor of workers

# 4  Research Method

Since the purpose of this study is to identify social consequences of wireless technology for nomadic working, socio-technical theory provides a powerful tool for analyzing the research findings. The socio-technical view sees organizational workers as social actors who interact with technological artifacts and institutional forces to construct a meaningful reality in the workplace (Lamb and King 2003). In addition, the socio-technical theory views ICT as a social phenomenon enmeshed within institutional structures (Orlikowski and Iacono 2001). The enmeshed nature of ICT implies that it may be difficult to classify best practices and use them in another context. Hence, since people and technology in organizations are both social entities, their countless interactions demand stronger conceptualizations. Socio-technical theory provides this feature for such interpretive analysis (Lamb 2005). Because socio-technical theory is concerned with social phenomena, it is also commensurate with interpretive epistemology.

There are many ways to investigate the social consequences the employees face while using wireless technologies for nomadic work. In order to research this area of interest, the decision was made to perform a case study at Telia. Case study research provides an in-depth analysis of complex social phenomena in its natural setting, asking why certain events occurred in the situation (Oates 2006). There are many data collection techniques that can be used to conduct a case study. Data gathered from multiple sources can provide researchers with rich and detailed facts. For the purpose of this research, structured interviews and documents were utilized for data collection. According to Benbasat et al. (1987), case study research may be important for understanding individuals' experiences and viewpoints, as well as the action context. Hence, the case study approach will be very useful for identifying the social consequences that knowledge workers face while utilizing wireless technologies for nomadic working.

## 5   Case Study at Teliasonera

TeliaSonera is the leading telecommunication organization and mobile network operator in the Nordic region and it has also a strong hold on the mobile communication market in Eurasia. In Sweden, TeliaSonera is known as Telia. Telia offers a broad range of telecommunication services to residential and business customers. The residential customers are served by Telia stores and other independent retailers in the country. In addition to the retail stores, Telia has management offices for its four divisions in major cities and towns in Sweden (TeliaSonera 2007c). In order to facilitate out-of-office work, all management employees are provided with a wireless laptop and a cell phone. By using the wireless laptop, employees can access the company intranet as well as the Internet (Telia 2007). The primary purpose of Telia's intranet is to increase workforce productivity by enabling employees to instantly locate and view information and applications appropriate to their roles and responsibilities. By the use of a web page, employees can retrieve the data held in any database anytime anywhere, increasing their ability to carry out jobs faster and with confidence that they have the correct information. Once updated, the information is easily published and stored for others to see and use (Kuu and Lundberg 2007).

Employee health and safety is very important to Telia (TeliaSonera 2007b). This involves not only safe working conditions but also psychological well-being and social welfare. Thus, Telia recognizes the need for a balance between work and life, and the organization offers flexible working hours and provides for telework (TeliaSonera 2007a). Hence, employees can work at home, while traveling, or from a telecenter, while rights and duties remain the same as in the fixed workplace (office).

Telework is a voluntary work option and it can be changed at any time; financial rewards are based on work performance rather than employee visibility in the organization. Before the employee can start working, he/she needs to agree with their supervisor on the hours that they can spend working out-of-office.

For the purpose of data collection at Telia, two trips to Sweden were made between November 2007 and January 2008. During the first trip, seven interviews were conducted with knowledge workers (management employees) from the Broadband Services and Mobility and the Integrated Enterprise Service divisions in Stockholm. The participants selected performed a significant amount of their work out-of-office using wireless technologies such as laptop and cell phone. During the second trip, 12 additional interviews were conducted with Telia's knowledge workers in Stockholm and Gavle. Although there was an attempt to conduct additional interviews, it was not possible due to Telia workers unwillingness to provide information on company's work methods and technologies. Also, many individuals were reluctant to reveal the impact of work–life imbalance on their mental and physical health. Upon collecting and transcribing the data from interviews and documents, a case study on Telia's knowledge workers' nomadic work practice was developed and five themes were identified. The five research themes are work and life balance, addiction, organizational involvement, nomadic work and control, and individual productivity.

## 5.1 Work and Life Balance

A flexible work hour scheme requires individuals to work from home, leaving little time for social activities with family and friends. When asked if work during the evenings and weekends is reducing social time with family and friends, one employee said: *"It happens; I work both during evenings and weekends. I read and reply to e-mails on Sundays because I do not get the time to read all the mails during weekdays. This happens when I have many meetings in the office. All meetings generate action points and these actions points often require immediate attention."* Another employee commented: *"I may work during weekends if I need to meet a deadline or resolve a customer complaint. For instance, we sent incorrect electronic invoices to customers once; this fault required that we had to work during the weekend to correct the invoices so that we could resend them on Monday."* Work from home leads also to social isolation as there is room for face-to-face interaction with work colleagues. One employee's remark on the matter is worth repeating: *"Yes, I was working in the Telia's retail store last year and I was spending eight to nine hours each day at work. Even though I was physically tired at the end of the week, I was able to find time for my family and friends during weekends. But now, since I have limited interaction with people at work, I am sometimes feeling isolated and depressed. Due to the depression, I do not meet-up with my friends during weekends. Also, I do not enjoy the company of my family because I am concerned if I will be able to complete the assigned work on my own and within the allocated time."*

## 5.2 Addiction

Individuals have developed an urge to log onto their laptop or cell phone and engage in work related e-mail communication during evenings and weekends. When asked, one employee said: *"A major part of my work consists of e-mail communication. So, I do read e-mails as they come in my Inbox. I need to also write reports in my work, but due to the excessive e-mail communication, I am sometimes unable to complete work on-time. I believe this is due to lack of discipline. I should not be engaging in e-mail conversations when I am writing reports. But due to the strong urge to read e-mails, I am sometimes overusing the technology."* Another employee expressed similar concerns, saying: *"I am working during evenings but I try not to work during the weekends. I switch off my cell phone and I never log onto my laptop during weekends. You need to have self-control and not overuse the technology to get this balance between work and social life. For instance, last week, I was browsing the Internet and before knowing it, I had spent 4 hours on the Internet. That is really scary to me, that's why I try not to log onto the laptop during weekends. I think it is very important for us to go out in the fresh air and meet other people."*

## 5.3   Organizational Involvement

Nomadic working leads to low information awareness for making sense of what is going on in the organization. When asked, one employee said: *"My entire work group is geographically dispersed in Sweden so I meet them once every month. I would like to meet them more because you can never know on the phone how the other person is feeling. So, this distant work relationship may impede the socialization process and the formation of social bonds among group members."* Low visibility in the organization also deteriorates interpersonal relations with key officials in the organization, which in turn may reduce promotion prospects. When asked, one employee summed the viewpoint of many: *"It is important that you have a regular face-to-face contact with your supervisor. By having a regular contact with your supervisor, you can better market yourself and 'demand' promotion when the opportunity emerges. If you are working too much from home or are based at a different city than your supervisor, then you may not receive the work guidance that you need for producing good results."* In addition, employees based in small-town offices feel that they are at a disadvantage since they do not have the opportunity to visit the head office in Stockholm regularly. When asked, one employee said: *"It is important that you are based in the same office as your supervisor. For instance, since most of the supervisors are based at the Stockholm office, it is important for your career that you work at the Stockholm office. I believe that individuals that are based at small cities such as Gavle or Lulea may have lower advancements opportunities because they do not have regular face-to-face contact with their supervisor."*

## 5.4   Nomadic Work and Control

Nomadic working is not fully trusted as the organization requires its employees to be where they can be seen. Lack of trust can lead to severe consequences for the firm. If workers believe they are not trusted, they will engage in bureaucratic activities to show their work-efficiency and protect themselves against a system they do not trust. When asked why Telia requires its employees to spend more time in the office, one employee reported: *"For the past two or three years, management has been tightly regulating nomadic work arrangements since there have been disciplinary problems in a few work groups. So supervisors nowadays advise people to come to the office on daily basis. But, on the other hand, Telia's nomadic working policy encourages you to work where you feel most productive and convenient. So, it is a contradiction from management's side. This controlling behavior may be having a negative impact on mutual trust relations between the workers and the management."*

### 5.5 Individual Productivity

Communication at Telia is primarily via cell phone and e-mail. Although cell phone communication is not disturbing, the sheer volume of e-mail communication can be overwhelming. One senior management employee summed up the viewpoint of many: *"I believe that people are sending a lot of e-mails in the organization. I receive between 70 and 80 e-mails per day. There are e-mails where I am the main recipient and there are e-mails where I am the copy recipient. I read e-mails where I am the main recipient but I do not read e-mails where I am the copy recipient. I do not have time for reading copy recipient e-mails. I forward these e-mails to a folder which I never read. So, I ask myself, what is the benefit of sending so many copies of e-mails? Why do people send them? I think we have a sickness about informing everyone in the organization and this is why we send so many e-mail copies. We need to be more serious about sending e-mail copies to each other. Information should be sent to those that really need it and not to everyone."* Although e-mail communication is an important part of work at Telia, it may reduce productivity. When asked about the impact on productivity, one employee said: *"The e-mail communication can be time consuming; it takes time to sort and read through all the relevant e-mails. If I reply to all e-mails, I will have less time to finish work. So, yes it is stressful to receive so many e-mails and I believe it is having a negative impact on my productivity."* Another employee expressed similar concerns: *"A major part of my work consists of e-mail communication. So, I do read the e-mails as they come to my in-box. I also need to write reports in my work, but due to the excessive e-mail communication, I am sometimes unable to complete work on time. I believe this is due to the lack of self-discipline. I should not be engaging in e-mail conversations when I am writing a report."*

## 6   Result Discussion

### 6.1   Work and Life Imbalance

Socio-technical theory has been based on the assumption that organizations are physical entities and their members are all physically present in one place. This, however, is not the case nowadays as organizations are loosely structured and workers have the freedom to work out-of-office using wireless technologies. Given this decentralized nature of work, some of the basic design principles are false. The increasing utilization of wireless technologies and electronic-mediated communication increases the means by which individuals can cross work and life boundaries. The increasing need to be responsive to organizational demands has made boundary crossing a requirement of nomadic working. Utilizing ICT for enabling anytime anywhere work may increase the productivity of individuals or it may disrupt either sphere (i.e., work and social life). Boundary crossing in this way may become problematic for organizations, especially when conventional management techniques are used to manage work (e.g., command and control rather than coordinate and cultivate). The emphasis on traditional management approaches can significantly reduce trust building in an organization. Moreover, there is a risk that boundary crossing may damage interpersonal relations with family and friends. As there is everywhere to go but nowhere to hide from work demands, little time may be available for engaging in social activities.

On the organizational level, it is important that companies design jobs that enhance the work and family balance. Although many organizations have restructured their work to meet $21^{st}$ century demands (e.g., adding telework and leave policies), they have not changed their organizational culture and values because this is much more difficult to achieve. According to the socio-technical view, a more flexible organization should be aligned with workers' homes in terms of purpose and culture. Not surprisingly, many companies have developed telework programs to serve their own purpose with disregard to employees and their families, which eventually results in unrealized expectations and cynicism. In addition, if it is not feasible or desirable for an organization to alter its culture, then work and family systems must be kept separate so that workers can attain balance. A call has been made by researchers to rethink cultures in order to accommodate families, but these propositions have yet to be considered seriously by most organizations. The socio-technical theory suggests balance by increasing support structures that facilitate communication between organizational members (supervisors and employees). In addition, most supervisors are given discretion to bend rules. They need to use this authority to accommodate individuals' family situations. Supervisors are very important to employees' ability to attain balance, and a handful of organizations have required supervisors to undertake training in handling situations that require support for employees' family situations. Consistent with the research findings, a final suggestion for increasing work and life balance is employee empowerment. For instance, employees who have the authority to take leave for handling their family responsibilities will undoubtedly improve the work and family balance. Similarly, the ability to say no to additional work assignments can improve the balance.

Furthermore, improved communication may be required for achieving a better balance between work and social life; for example, by regularly talking about what individuals have been doing at various times—sharing some of the stories about challenges and successes at work with family, or telling colleagues and supervisors about family events and social happenings. Individuals can also inform others of their unavailability in either system through ICT-enabled context switches (e.g., using voice mail or auto-reply e-mail). Understanding and support are more likely to come from colleagues, supervisors, family members, or friends if they are aware of other-system events and happenings. Trust will also be reinforced if others are informed of individuals' unavailability in either system. Employees can also increase their involvement at both work and home by developing strong interpersonal relations at work and home, becoming proficient at work as well as in household tasks, and making both work and home more important parts of self-identity. Increased involvement in both systems can result in increased influence over others, thereby creating better prospects for an improved work and life balance.

## 6.2  Compulsive Work Behavior

Addiction to information is another growing problem among Telia employees. Since individuals can easily access information on the intranet as well as the Internet, they may have developed an urge to engage in work-related activities, e-mail communication, or social media (e.g., Facebook, blogging, podcasts, etc.) using wireless technologies. In fact technology has become a part of knowledge workers and that they experience high levels of anxiety when set apart from their wireless devices. They have continual thoughts about their involvement with technology, and their hobbies are technology related. They are frequent users of the Internet, which often intrudes on their social life, and on vacation they bring along their laptop, pocket PC, PDA, and/or cell phone, even though they do not need to do any work.

Research on workaholism reports that technology increasingly facilitates addiction to information, which in turn gives rise to workaholic behavior. Individuals that show workaholic behavior spend a lot of time in work activities, even if it means giving up important family or recreational activities. Workaholics are also psychologically attached to their work even at times whey they are not working, while their work performance almost always exceeds the expectations of people working around them. Although it may be difficult to control the behavior of workaholism, increasing work demands provide a condition in which workaholic behaviors thrive. If workaholism is encouraged in an organization, it may give rise to a culture that requires adaptation of all employees to the workaholic behavior. Porter and Kakabadse (2006, p. 548) define this adaptation "as a process in which the person is adapting to that very behavior that for some becomes the addiction." An important factor that provides additional support to the organization's rising demands and the employee's inner desire to stay connected to work is the rise of wireless technology as it enables people to stay connected to the organization around the clock. Although not all people become addicted to a given substance, there is a possibility that some people may over-adapt and start to direct all their attention to the addiction by giving up other satisfactions in life. Just as some smokers and drinkers cannot quit even when their physical health badly deteriorates or their family and friends find life with them difficult, the same is true for people who show a constant need to be involved with their computer and work.

There are health consequences in both cases, as well as interpersonal problems with family members and friends. According to the socio-technical view, when new technologies are adopted, there are unintended consequences for the workers involved. The necessary focus on the implementation of the technology overshadows the social and personal needs of the users. The ever-increasing nomadic work environment, hence, leads not only to new commercial opportunities, but also to new social challenges (i.e., addiction to handheld devices and workaholism). It would seem that the recent technological advances and decentralized organizational structure offer an opportunity to realize the fit between human needs and managerial performance that Mumford strove to promote through her own research work. Nevertheless, the most complex barrier to break through may be the ethical one, as we continually aim to reconcile the values and viewpoints of employers with those of employees in the face of ever-increasing global competition fueled by a ubiquitous ability to access and manipulate information.

## 6.3 Lower Career Development

Telia's telework policy allows employees to work from where they feel most comfortable and effective. Employees can work from home, while travelling or from a remote location using wireless technologies, and their presence in the office has little significance as rewards are based on performance. However, interviews with Telia's management employees revealed that visibility in the office and regular face-to-face contact with supervisors has an important impact on career development. An organization serious about promoting nomadic work must base its rewards on employee work performance rather than on work location. It is also recommended that reward structures must be based on efficiency gains through alternative work methods (i.e., nomadic work). Ensuring workers that pay is comparable to that of workers in different locations is also important in cultivating decentralized work methods. Yet, Telia still values and rewards in-office work and takes for granted that time spent in the office equals higher commitment and productivity. Thus, for nomadic working to be successful, the culture in the organization must be one of trust. A culture that is based on the principles of trust requires reconsideration of what it means to be working and how the organization values and rewards performance. An organization serious about promoting a nomadic work culture must reward its employees based on their performance rather than on time spent in the office.

At the organizational level, a telework policy is necessary for establishing formal communication between the employees and supervisors. Although Telia has a telework policy that employees and supervisors can follow to establish formal nomadic working agreements, including the ways of communicating, this policy is not widely communicated and used in the organization. As nomadic working is a new phenomenon, there are still many issues that need to be resolved and communicated to employees through a formal telework policy. While formal communication is necessary for informing workers about work-related issues, informal communication is also necessary for developing social relations and for fostering community spirit in the organization. Hence, supervisors need to develop relationships with employees who may not be in the same place. A critical factor for the success of nomadic working, communication must be bilateral, flowing not only from supervisors to employees but also from employees to supervisors and colleagues. Communication is particularly important at the employee level. As this study has shown, without the social interaction of a conventional workplace, employees are more likely to feel social isolation. Lack of emotion and non-immediate response over the phone or Web can make communication superficial and formal. The socio-technical design principles suggest effective organizations must provide opportunities for team members to meet face-to-face so that they can know each other on a personal level for facilitating open exchanges of ideas and knowledge sharing in the organization. This can be attained through face-to-face team-building exercises, which combine workshops with fun social events such as go-carting or bowling.

## 6.4  Heightened Management Control

Although Telia's telework policy allows its employees to work anytime anywhere, many supervisors want the employees to come to the office on a regular basis. An organization that requires its employees to be where they can be seen may be going against the fundamental values and beliefs of nomadic working, and this behavior will undoubtedly cause the trust relations in the company to deteriorate. Lack of trust can lead to severe consequences for the firm. If workers believe they are not trusted, they will engage in bureaucratic activities to show their work efficiency and protect themselves against a system they do not trust. Sadly, there are no short cuts for cultivating mutual trust relations in the company. It is important that both workers and supervisors apply appropriate ethics and reward systems when designing telework programs. This can happen if the workers are allowed to create and share knowledge in a self-regulating group. Likewise, supervisors must lessen the control and enable the group members to handle the issue of trust internally. The duty of top management may be to nurture supportive behaviors, encourage open communication, and arrange social events in the organization. Technology-mediated communication does not express the same level of emotional response that face-to-face communication provides; thus group members may be unaware of contextual and situational cues that stimulate other team members; what is normal behavior to some may be disturbing to others. When group members are only available virtually, it is more difficult to develop the social bonds that may result in trust based on judgment.

Therefore, the challenge for supervisors is to develop trust in teams and cultivate trust throughout the team's life. This challenge is overwhelming because evidence shows that trust develops at different phases in a team's lifecycle. Also, it was found that training and reward systems have a significant impact on the development of trust in teams. First, it is important to ensure that selected team members can fulfil their respective functional roles; if the potential members do not possess the skills, training must be provided so that they can carry out the project tasks successfully. Training on "being virtual" is also critical at this phase, as team members may come from different technical and cultural backgrounds and, therefore, may be unaware of the importance of careful composition and expression of ideas and opinions. Lags in e-mail responses can also be misinterpreted as a lack of commitment or lack of functional ability, something which may result in faster dissolution of trust than would be otherwise expected.

Training can help the organization to become aware of these issues and thereby educate its employees in how to avoid them. An organization serious about developing trust in virtual teams must provide training to both employees and supervisors, with an emphasis on trust and working to agreed objectives and work outcomes. Team members need to demonstrate their integrity by not abusing the freedom they have in the nomadic work environment. Supervisors (with the support of the organization) need to determine whether employees are employed to generate outcomes or to perform activities in the office. They need to believe that employees will carry out their duties and behave even though they are not being watched; that they will have self-initiative and self-discipline.

## 6.5  Information Overload

Even though ubiquitous access to information and people may have a positive impact on productivity, it was found that many employees at Telia reported lower productivity, due to the sheer volume of unstructured and irrelevant e-mail communication that takes place in the organization. While unstructured e-mail communication may be due to self-negligence and lack of e-mail composition skills, the irrelevant e-mail communication may be due to the distribution of e-mails copied to multiple recipients. While e-mail is an important part of everyday work communication, the sheer volume generated is an increasing problem.  Everyone in the organization is facing information overload, but is unable to do anything about it since information may be coming from several communication sources.

While it is important to build a network of information exchanges in the organization, it must not lead to information overload, and to reduce it individuals should have the autonomy to determine the amount of communication in which they engage (Singh et al. 2008). One way knowledge workers can reduce the likelihood of information overload is by turning off the e-mail alert and sound.  Then, limiting the use of the "e-mail-to-all" and "reply-to-all" button is important for reducing the spread of e-mail; also, using more targeted recipient groups may be useful. Configuring the inbox to display only sender, subject area, and the initial three lines of the content is an important consideration as it will enable the recipient to quickly determine if the message is urgent and requires an urgent response.  Configuring the e-mail software to look for messages no more than every 45 minutes is also essential in training all employees in how to create e-mail priority, perform e-mail maintenance with message rules, create recipient groups and address books, and structure the subject and content of the e-mail. "Outlook" offers several message processing add-ins that can be used to analyze e-mail for errors before sending. The reviewer can suggest changes to the structure or content by adding comments to the message.  This tool can be useful for training new employees who may be unaware of corporate e-mail etiquette.

## 7  Theoretical Contribution

Although Singh et al. (2008) provide important guidelines for designing socio-technical jobs, these guidelines may need to be modified given the social challenges faced by knowledge workers in a nomadic work environment. It is important the workers are given freedom to accommodate their work preferences and life situation. For implementing effective teleworking in the organization, it is important the rewards are based on work performance rather than time spent in the office. The socio-technical work design requires worker participation in the development of various work policies and systems in the organization. Workers need around the clock support for coordinating and communicating on work tasks; they need self-regulation and autonomy to carry out work where they cannot be seen by the management; they need training in a virtual environment; when work is performed by autonomous workgroups, each group member needs ubiquitous access to informational resources.

The socio-technical principles below depict the necessary steps Telia needs to take for implementing successful nomadic working.

- Assumptions about employees:
  — From Theory Y's point of view, it is ethical to let people work where it is most convenient given their life situation and preference
- Socio-technical work design aims:
  — Design jobs that enhance the work and family life balance
  — Rewards based on employee work performance rather than on work location
- Assumptions about the socio-technical work design process:
  — Worker participation is essential
- Socio-technical work design concepts:
  — Members have discretion; work can take place anytime anywhere
  — Internal regulation of group as well as self discipline
  — Availability of shared workspace facilities
  — Information awareness support
  — Face-to-face team building exercises
  — Basic e-mail communication skills
  — Autonomous workgroup is superior form of organization
  — Role changes:
    o  Designer: facilitator not expert
    o  Worker: designer of the system
    o  Manager: boundary manager, not supervisor of workers

# 8  Conclusion

Knowledge work can be defined as intellectual work performed to generate valuable information and knowledge. Since an important part of knowledge work consists of nomadic computing, the positive and negative impacts on productivity are subject to the work processes of knowledge workers. When compared to traditional ways of working, nomadic work provides greater flexibility while freeing the knowledge worker from time and place constraints. Even though nomadic work may increase knowledge workers' productivity, it may also have unintended and undesirable consequences. Thus, the identification of social consequences of nomadic working with respect to the use of wireless technologies such as laptops, pockets PCs, PDAs, and cell phones was investigated in this research. Management workers at the Telia organization in Sweden were approached for the purpose of carrying out the research study. Upon collecting the relevant research data, five problem areas (themes) were identified: work and life balance, addiction, organizational involvement, nomadic work and control, and individual productivity. Each theme was discussed with the philosophical underpinning of socio-technical theory. On the individual level, the findings confirm that better role boundary management, self-discipline, work negotiation, and e-mail communication skills may be required for knowledge workers to manage the demands of nomadic working. On the organizational level, rewarding nomadic work performance, building employee–supervisor trust relations, and designing jobs that enhance work and life balance can be fruitful.

# References

Benbasat, I., Goldstein, D.K., Mead, M.: The Case Research Strategy in Studies of Information Systems. MIS Quarterly 11(3), 369–386 (1987)

Davis, G.B.: Anytime/Anyplace Computing and the Future of Knowledge Work. Communications of the ACM 45(12), 67–73 (2002)

Elaluf-Calderwood, S., Kietzmann, J., Scaccol, A.Z.: Methodological Approach for Mobile Studies: Empirical Research Considerations. London School of Economics, London (2005)

Fok, L.M., Kumar, K., Wood-Harper, A.T.: Methodologies for Socio-Technical Systems (STS) Development: A Comparative Review. In: DeGross, J.I., Kriebel, C.H. (eds.) Proceedings of the Eighth International Conference on Information Systems, Pittsburgh, PA, pp. 319–334 (1987)

Grudin, J.: Group Dynamics and Ubiquitous Computing. Communications of the ACM 45(12), 74–78 (2002)

Jarvenpaa, S.L., Lang, K.R., Tuunainen, V.K.: Friend or Foe? The Ambivalent Relationship between Mobile Technology and its Users. In: Sørensen, C., Yoo, Y., Lyytinen, K., DeGross, J.I. (eds.) Designing Ubiquitous Information Environments: Socio-Technical Issues and Challenges, pp. 29–42. Springer, Boston (2005)

Kuu, T., Lundberg, A.: A Role-Based Intranet: Overcoming Information Overload?, Vaxjo University, Sweden (2007) (unpublished paper)

Lamb, R.: On Extending Social Informatics from a Rich Legacy of Networks and Conceptual Resources. Information Technology & People 18(1), 9–20 (2005)

Lamb, R., Kling, R.: Reconceptualizing Users as Social Actors in Information Systems Research. MIS Quarterly 27(2), 197–235 (2003)

Lamond, D., Daniels, K., Standen, P.: Teleworking and Virtual Organizations: The Human Impact. In: David Holman, T.D.W., Clegg, C.W., Sparrow, P., Howard, A. (eds.) The New Workplace: A Guide to the Human Impact of Modern Working Practices, pp. 197–216. John Wiley & Sons, Ltd., Chichester (2003)

Lyytinen, K., Yoo, Y.: Issues and Challenges in Ubiquitous Computing. Communications of the ACM 45(12), 62–65 (2002)

Lyytinen, K., Yoo, Y., Varshney, U., Ackerman, M.S., Davis, G.B., Avital, M., Robey, D., Sawyer, S., Sorensøn, C.: Surfing the Next Wave: Design and Implementation Challenges of Ubiquitous Computing Environments. Communications of the Association for Information Systems (13), 697–716 (2004)

Malone, T.W.: The Future of Work: How the New Order of Business Will Shape Your Organization, Your Management Style, and Your Life. Harvard Business School Press, Boston (2004)

Mumford, E.: The Story of Socio-Technical Design: Reflections on its Successes, Failures and Potential. Information Systems Journal (16), 317–342 (2006)

Oates, B.J.: Researching Information Systems and Computing. Sage Publications Ltd., Oxford (2006)

Orlikowski, W.J., Iacono, C.S.: Research Commentary: Desperately Seeking the 'IT' in IT Research—A Call to Theorizing the IT Artifact. Information Systems Research 12(2), 121–143 (2001)

Porter, G., Kakabadse, N.K.: HRM Perspectives on Addiction to Technology and Work. Journal of Management Development 25(6), 535–560 (2006)

Singh, R., Wood-Harper, A.T., Wood, B.: Designing Socio-Technical Systems for the Ubiquitous Information Environments. Scientific Inquiry 9(1), 37–46 (2008)

Sorensen, C.: The Future Role of Trust in Work—The Key Success Factor for Mobile Productivity: Optimizing the Knowledge Supply-Chain, Microsoft (2004), http://stuff.carstensorensen.com/Sorensen2004.pdf

Telia. About Telia HomeRun (2007), http://www.homerun.telia.com/eng/about/ (accessed November 28, 2007)

TeliaSonera. CSR: Flexible Working (2007a), http://www.teliasonera.com/about_teliasonera/csr/workplace/flexible_working (accessed November 28, 2007)

TeliaSonera. CSR: Health and Well-Being (2007b), http://www.teliasonera.com/about_teliasonera/csr/workplace/health_and_wellbeing (accessed November 28, 2007)

TeliaSonera. Markets and Brands: Sweden (2007c), http://www.teliasonera.com/about_teliasonera/markets_and_brands/sweden (accessed November 28, 2007)

## About the Authors

**Ramanjit Singh** recently completed his Ph.D. the at Manchester Business School, University of Manchester. In addition to his doctoral research, he has published a paper in *Scientific Inquiry*, a report at the University of Trento, Italy, and five conference papers. He can be reached by e-mail at raman.si@gmail.com.

**Trevor Wood-Harper** is a professor of Information Systems at the Manchester Business School, University of Manchester. He has authored, coauthored, or coedited 20 books and proceedings, and has published over 200 research articles. He has supervised or co-supervised more than 30 Ph.D. students. He can be reached by e-mail at atwh@mbs.ac.uk.

# Design Science Research for Business Process Design: Organizational Transition at Intersport Sweden

Mikael Lind[1], Daniel Rudmark[2], and Ulf Seigerroth[3]

[1] School of Business and Informatics,
University of Borås,
SE 510 90 Borås, Sweden
[2] Innovation Lab,
University of Borås,
SE 510 90 Borås, Sweden
[3] School of Engineering,
Jönköping University,
SE 551 11Jönköping, Sweden

**Abstract.** Business processes need to be aligned with business strategies. This paper elaborates on experiences from a business process design effort in an action research project performed at Intersport Sweden. The purpose with this project was to create a solid base for taking the retail chain Intersport into a new organizational state where the new process design is aligned with strategic goals. Although business process modeling is concerned with creating artifacts, traditionally information systems design science research has had little impact on research on business process models. In this paper, we address the question of how design science research can contribute to business process design. Three heuristic guidelines for creating organizational commitment and strategic alignment in process design are presented. The guidelines are derived from the successful actions taken in the research project. The development of these guidelines is used as a basis to reflect upon the contribution of design science research to business process design.

**Keywords:** Design science research, business process design, action research, co-design.

## 1 Introduction

A significant part of science has always been to create abstractions for different purposes. Rosenblueth and Wiener (1945) once stated that no substantial part of the universe is so simple that it can be grasped and controlled without making abstractions. A *model* is usually a representation of a phenomenon for a certain purpose (Matthews 2007). In this paper, the role of models and how to design models is elaborated in the context of business process design where process models serve as a transformation vehicle in such a design process. On a scientific level, which also affects process design, there is still a debate about the role of models and the required

J. Pries-Heje et al. (Eds.): IS Design Science Research, IFIP AICT 318, pp. 159–176, 2010.

characteristics of models in order to contribute to peoples' understanding and development of a common knowledge base (Matthews 2007).

Modeling and business process design has been acknowledged as critical for the development of business practices and information systems (Harmon 2010). Business processes have received significant attention in conceiving business practices due to their focus on clients and other stakeholders (e.g., Davenport 1993; Davis 2001; vom Brocke and Thomas 2006). Business process models are used for several purposes (see Bandara et al. 2006; Harmon 2010) such as describing existing practice (AS-IS) and designing the future (TO-BE), as well as determining historical chains of events. Based on this, there is a need to elaborate on the role of models and their usage since this will affect both the design and implementation of the models. This is motivated by the tendency of practitioners within the IS field to engage in conceptual modeling, focusing on business processes for the purpose of analysis, design, and evaluation of information systems (Davies et al. 2006). As an object, business process models can be regarded as tangible patterns of actions performed by people, often supported by artifacts, within and between organizations (Goldkuhl and Lind 2008). Process modeling and process models are often considered a part of the area of enterprise modeling. One way to conceptually describe this area is to divide it into three sections: modeling product (language and notation), modeling process (guidance), and modeling tool (support) (Stirna and Kirikova 2008). Historically, significant emphasis has been given to languages and notations for modeling (e.g., Scheer and Nüttgens 2000; Tolvanen and Lyytinen 1992), but less research has been performed in relation to guidance for how to design models, how to use models, or how the actual modeling should be performed.

Design science research is concerned with the artificial (Simon 1996). The rationale for undertaking design science research is to develop knowledge about how to construct artifacts that address an unsolved problem space. In process design, business process models are central—both as a part of the process and as the product of business process design. Since these process models are artifacts, design science research could be an interesting approach to address *how* to construct process models (e.g., Hevner et al. 2004; van Aken 2004). To our knowledge, the business process modeling research community has yet to adopt and evaluate design science research as a mode of inquiry. The research reported in this paper is consequently driven by how to design business processes by using process models as a transformation vehicle into a future state. Specifically, since the research conducted is concerned with interventional *in situ* design of business processes, the research must handle both the social construction of a possible future as well as the strategic goals of the organization. Hence, the research question posed in this paper is, *how can design science research contribute to business process design?* To explore this question, an action research project has been performed where the design of the business processes of the Swedish part of Intersport has been the focus. One should note that there has been a debate whether action research and design science research is a good blend (Cole et al. 2005) or if their relationship is more complicated (Iivari and Venable 2009). Hence, this research has the potential to yield several contributions. During the Intersport process design project, design guidelines for process design have been developed using the design science research literature. In this paper, we use these guidelines for reflecting upon the use of design science research as a means to develop knowledge about business process design.

The rest of the paper is organized as follows. Following this section, design science research as an approach for business process modeling is introduced, followed by the introduction of used kernel theories in the case. These kernel theories address both pragmatic perspectives on business processes and our view on collaborative business process modeling. This is followed by descriptions of the Intersport case and the evolving guidelines for business process design. The discussion then focuses on experiences made from using design science research in business process design. The paper concludes with some reflections related to performing business process design endeavors in using design science research.

## 2 Design Science Research for Business Process Design

In the design science research paradigm, knowledge and understanding of a problem domain and its solutions are achieved through scientifically grounded design and evaluation of artifacts (Hevner et al. 2004; Gregor and Jones 2007). Thus, at the core of design science lies the generation of knowledge about how to design artifacts that solve problems that so far have not been solved (to some extent), and where these artifact(s) may be used to improve an unwanted situation (Simon 1996).

Since many practitioners in the IS field are concerned with designing (artifacts and/or actions), design science research has been brought forward as a response to the various calls for practitioner relevance (see Benbasat and Zmud 1999; Roseman and Vessey 2008). The usefulness of design science research has been argued in a range of application areas related to information systems: technology-oriented artifacts (Hevner et al. 2004; Nunamaker et al. 1991), socio-technical systems (Markus et al. 2002), organizations (Romme 2003), and managerial action (Van Aken 2004).

A core concept within design science is the artifact. Our conception is that an artifact is something that is created by humans which cannot exist without human involvement, both in design and interpretation, and as something that can be instantiated with physical and/or social properties (Lind et al. 2008).

In the context of this paper, the problem of how to design business processes is conceived as a class of problems addressing questions including

- How can models be used as an essential transformation vehicle to successfully reach a desired state?
- What kind of models should be used?
- Which different versions of models exists during process design?
- What cooperation patterns should be emphasized during such endeavor?

However, this class of problems (business process modeling for business process design) suggests that artifacts alone cannot produce the type of results necessary to achieve the sought-after organizational transition. To be able to put scientific validity claims on such research findings, it must also address the use of other theoretically informed actions in cohesion with the artifacts being constructed. Put in other words, in business process modeling, *actions* (van Aken 2004) and *artifacts* (Hevner et al. 2004; March and Smith 1995; Nunamaker et al. 1991) constitute inseparable parts that the design science researcher is obliged to recognize. This means that design science research should be concerned with two principal parts: developing knowledge about both the constituents of business process models (*artifacts*) and the complementary *actions* that need to accompany these models in order to reach the desired transition. In this paper, we will put stronger focus on the actions than on the constituents of the artifacts (business process models) due to the need for knowledge related to the modeling process (see above).

Design science research is carried out by an ongoing interplay between two major activities: build/design and evaluate. By *building* or *designing* the researchers are inscribing *kernel theories* into the artifact(s) and hence demonstrating that the artifact can be constructed (Gregor 2006; Hanseth and Lyytinen 2004; Walls et al. 1992). In the case of business process design, the researcher must further be concerned with applying principles informed by kernel theories to connected actions (van Aken 2004), as described earlier.

The next principal phase is *evaluating* (Hevner et al. 2004), where the design is measured against some metrics, showing whether (or to what extent) the problem has been solved and which new scientific theories that can be formulated (March and Smith 1995). In the case of business process modeling, we argue that it is necessary to design and evaluate in an authentic environment or, put in words of van Aken (2004), that the design is both *field-tested* and *grounded*. This is true since we believe that performing relevant research on tangible phenomena such as collaborative construction of an organization's future (and the stakes associated with such a process) is a bad fit with a more controlled environment. With this backdrop on our conception of design science research and how business process design may be inquired through it, we next present our case were this research approach has been applied. We start with putting forward used kernel theories.

## 3 Used Kernel Theories for Business Process Design

### 3.1 Transition through Business Process Design: A Pragmatic Perspective

Business process modeling has been acknowledged as a means for management of processes by several scholars (e.g., Günther et al. 2008; van der Aalst et al. 2007). Business process management (BPM) has traditionally adopted a horizontal rather than vertical view on the division of labor  and  has its origin in both total quality management (TQM; Harrington 1991) and business process reengineering (BPR; Davenport 1993; Hammer 1990). Basically, BPM can be seen as an industrial view on business processes, where input (raw material) is transformed into output (finished products). As advocated by Keen and Knapp (1996) there are, however, other conceptions of business processes.

One complementary conceptual base for business processes is a pragmatic foundation (e.g., Recker 2007)—rooted in American pragmatism (see Dewey 1922)—which ontologically puts *action* as the core of business processes. In order to expand the scope beyond transformational dimensions of business processes, the notion of *business acts* is conceived as the basic unit of analysis (see Lind and Goldkuhl 2003).

A business act can be a speech act (communicative act) (e.g., Searle 1969) or a material act.

Business acts build upon the notion of social action. An organization consists of humans, artifacts (along with other resources), and the actions performed. Humans (often supported by artifacts) perform actions on behalf of the organization (Ahrne 1994). Actions are both performed within the organization—internal acts—and toward other organizations (e.g., customers or suppliers)—external acts. Humans act in order to achieve ends (von Wright 1971). Human action often aims at making material changes. However, humans do not only act in the material world; they also act communicatively toward other humans. Human actions are about making a difference, where such a difference can have an impact in the social world as well as in the material world. As described in Lind and Goldkuhl (2003), a business act is defined as the performance of communicative and/or material acts by someone aimed at someone else. By using business acts as the basic unit of business processes, transformative as well as coordinative and interactive dimensions of business processes may be included (Goldkuhl and Lind 2008).

Transformative dimensions denote a focus on the transformation of deliverable products, in structured and sequenced ways, from base products (raw material) to refined products. Coordinative dimensions mean that business processes involve important coordination mechanisms for the establishment, fulfillment, and assessment of agreements between involved stakeholders (e.g., suppliers and customers). Interactive dimensions are the special case of coordination in which the actors' performance of communicative and/or material exchanges is focused. As proposed by Goldkuhl and Lind (2008), these two views need to be combined in an integrative view where coordination (including interaction) and transformation form an integrated texture of actions. In this sense, assignment processes become superior in relation to transformation processes.

The modeling process is constituted of asking questions and giving answers to these questions through documentation in models. Business process models are thus built upon modeling languages (see Schuette and Rotthowe 1998); that is, concepts and notation to be used. The view on business processes, as discussed above, will in this way influence the content of the models being generated. The underlying view on business processes could thus be seen as a reference model (see Thomas 2005) to be used in generating situational models covering particular areas of concern. In this paper, we are especially interested in the use of process models for the purpose of taking a business practice from one state to another—a transition. In such a transition process it is important to focus on essential characteristics of the future in the business practice through the use of a rich repertoire of process concepts. This concerns both *resulting models* to be used for describing a future state (TO-BE) as well as *intermediary models* used to develop an understanding about the characteristics of the future state. The gap between existing practice (AS-IS) and a desired future state described in the resulting models form the basis for specifying an action plan covering overall and detailed actions to arrive at a future desired state.

### 3.2  Collaborative Process Modeling for Strategic Alignment and Organizational Commitment

The models that are produced during business process modeling should be aligned with intended business plans and strategies. To meet this challenge, there is a need to understand and to be able to handle the complexity that exists in terms of different aspects or conceptual domains in the business (Langefors 1973; Lankhorst. 2005; Vernadat 2002).

Lankhorst (2005) exemplifies these multiple enterprise aspects with five hetero-geneous architectural domains (i.e., information architecture, process architecture, product architecture, application architecture, and technical architecture) that are related to each other and the need for them to be aligned in an integrated way. The challenge is not to deal with isolated domains but to go beyond the individual models and to cope with how they are related to each other on different levels and how, as parts in the total picture, they support different strategic goals. One way to achieve alignment between strategies, models, and, in the end, IS/IT architectures is to adopt a co-design approach (Lind et al. 2007; Liu et al. 2002; Rittgen 2007) during the development of the models.

The process of developing models is about capturing different people's knowledge about diverse parts of business processes and different levels. Based on a social-constructive view on knowledge creation, business process models will be an issue of design since the research is concerned with what does not yet exist (Nelson and Stolterman 2003). Knowledge and commitment between people about the future is created through their interaction (i.e., people are acting socially in relation to each other). Throughout the process different versions of models (solutions) coevolve with the understanding of the problem (see Cross 2007; Purao 2002). This means that different roles need to be involved in process design, thereby constructing a joint view of the object in and of the design. One way to conceive such a process is to regard it as a *co-design process* (Lind et al. 2008) in which a number of views of reality coexist to be used for exploring solutions and the problem domain from different viewpoints. This co-innovative approach is closely related to the streams of Web 2.0 (Lind and Forsgren 2008) in which clients are engaged in collaborative processes of design (see Albinsson et al. 2007; Lind et al. 2007). Co-design as a design approach was originally coined by Forsgren (see Lind et al. 2008), who proposed a co-design framework as a multi-stakeholder model in which all stakeholders concerns, related to a certain co-design situation, are taken into consideration by either inviting, or considering, perspectives of diverse stakeholders. Measurement scales and ideals are co-constructed by engaged stakeholders and perspectives driven by future-oriented returns.

The motivation for a co-design approach to process design is to simultaneously work with several different stakeholders in a collaborative way to avoid conceptual deviations between strategic plans and models on different levels. The necessity of such a collaborative approach to process modeling has also been put forward by vom Brocke and Thomas (2006). They claim that relevant stakeholders in a certain modeling situation must be identified and efficient ways of coordination between them needs to be established. Much of the discourse related to strategic alignment is based on the framework by Henderson and Venkatraman (1999), who put forward four dimensions and their strategic fit to each other. Many of these dimensions are elaborated on through modeling and different models are used as an instrument to express how to achieve alignment and competitive advantage. In this paper, our basic assumption is that different types of process models can serve as a vehicle for realization of strategic business plans.

Business process models need to be a part, and the result, of people engaging in co-creating processes that are aligned with business strategies. In this approach an infinite number of views of reality may be designed based on the intention of the participators in the process. This type of collaborative design research is not stressed in the seminal information systems design science research frameworks (Hevner et al. 2004; March and Smith 1995; Nunamaker et al. 1991; van Aken 2004). Such an approach means that people in the environment and researchers jointly create artifacts (business process models) and collaboratively develop an understanding of the problem to be solved.

## 4 Applying Design Science Research in Business Process Design: The Transition at Intersport Sweden

### 4.1 Project Background

In this action research project, the main task has been to design Intersport's future business processes (for a description of the case and models produced, see Lind and Seigerroth 2010a). Intersport is a specialized, franchise-concept retail chain for sports and recreation. Intersport Sweden is part of the Intersport International Corporation (IIC), which is the world's largest sports retail chain with more than 4,900 stores in 32 countries.

The motivation of this project stems from Intersport Sweden initiating an extensive change program to redesign their business model in order to meet future needs and to create a competitive advantage in retail for sports and recreation. The core of the change process at Intersport is the transition from being a wholesale dealer with more or less independent stores to take an overall responsibility for the entire value chain (i.e., to become both retailer and wholesaler). In this sense, the scope of the business process design project covered the value chain spanning several organizations. This change process, called wholesaler–business development–retailer (WBR), describes a new vision for business areas (conceptual, strategic, and operative) that should be up and running in 2013.

The business process design in this case is meant to define Intersport Sweden's business practice for activities, results, prerequisites, work procedures, cooperation procedures, communication principles, roles, and responsibilities on different abstraction levels. The focus for the project has been to design Intersport's business model for 2013. Based on a new business strategy, business process models were designed to involve the people affected by the design. For Intersport, this covers everything—from strategic planning to products and services in use by their customers and ways to satisfy customer needs. Examples of new business principles in WBR are

- The responsibility for supplying and filling the stores with products is moved from the stores to a central organization at Intersport
- A shift in focus from a product structure to concepts that include more than the physical products
- The coordination and distribution of both Intersport's own and external brands should be done in a uniform way
- Intersport should have control of more than 80 percent of the total collections in all stores (base collection and category collections)
- A shift from stores ordering products early to early planning with late central distribution of collections
- A central retail function with responsibility for the total value chain

Through these changes, Intersport wants to strengthen its position by adopting a retail focus with centralized management and coordination. In combination with this Intersport is also moving from a focus on products and purchases to a focus on concepts and sales. The external attraction should increase in the value chain through development and clarification of Intersport's concepts, clarity in marketing, and focus on the customer. The aim is also to increase the internal efficiency through development of logistics and cost programs.

In the following sections, we present how we have developed three guidelines for business process design and how these guidelines are presented.

### 4.2   Research Methodology: The Process of Deriving Guidelines

Our choice of method was action research, a method that has proven to be useful in a certain type of research setting (see Lindgren et al. 2004). Action research has been described as a research method suited to study technology in a human context (Baskerville and Wood-Harper 1996), which is a core focus in the IS discipline. Our aim has been to investigate how design science research can contribute to business process design. We rely on the arguments presented by Lindgren et al. (2004), based on Mathiassen (2002, pp. 441): "Merely studying a real-world problem without assisting to resolve or ameliorate it is perceived as unhelpful. In other words, action researchers see it as their responsibility to assist practitioners by not only developing but also applying knowledge."

Validity claims concerning our contribution to the scientific body of knowledge are in accordance with multi-grounded theory (MGT) (Goldkuhl and Cronholm 2003): that the knowledge becomes internally, empirically, and theoretically validated. MGT is a reaction to grounded theory and it is more a pure inductive approach. MGT is a process for theory development. If a pragmatic view on knowledge is adopted, the result of an MGT process is knowledge as practical theories on the level of scientific body of knowledge. The combination of action research and MGT has made it possible for us to make contributions ("knowing through building," Purao et al. 2008, p. 5) to local practice (process models) in parallel with the development of scientific knowledge (guidelines for business process design).

In the spirit of action research, we have acted as intervening and co-designing observers at Intersport. Observations of the effects of performed acts and people's behavior have been the main sources of empirical input. The total set of empirical sources that act as our base for development of the guidelines are

- Project minutes and research notes from modeling sessions, meetings, and presentations in the practical inquiry at Intersport.
- Project minutes and research notes from other meetings concerning planning, coordination, assessment, and analysis of the practical inquiry.
- Project documentation (text, models, final report, etc.) as a result of actions performed in the practical inquiry in the local practice at Intersport. The final report was a project delivery with the prime purpose of presenting the newly designed business processes.
- Existing organizational documents from Intersport that describe existing and future practices (e.g., the new business, plan, organizational structure, etc.).

In addition, the personal knowledge—the impressions and experiences—we developed during the practical inquiry has been used as an empirical source.

The data collected were used in deriving the guidelines for business process design by conceptualizing experiences from the process design in local practice. The guidelines have been justified as multi-grounded according to Goldkuhl and Cronholm (2003). This means that we, in the development process, have gone through steps of multi-grounded theory in terms of theory generation (formulation of guidelines) and explicit grounding (test and evaluation of the guidelines).

## 4.3   Result: Evolving Design Guidelines for Business Process Design

In this section we present three guidelines for business process design based on the project. These guidelines are the result of a reconstruction of actions performed in this process design endeavor where we conceive these guidelines as the result of successfully conducted actions in the project.

**Guideline 1: Extensive stakeholder involvement for establishing commitments.** The process design described in this paper was performed through collaborative modeling where different organizational roles (stakeholders) have been involved in the design of a future state. The representation of people from Intersport in the project covered both new roles as a result of recruitment based on the new business plan as well as existing roles, which were preserved in the organization. The future design is governed by joint creation of business process models on different levels. The involvement of a multitude of stakeholders in the design conversation is one of the main pillars in co-design (Lind et al. 2008). The involved stakeholders in this case were (1) the CEO and executive management, (2) middle management (head of retail, head of logistics, etc.), and (3) operative personnel within different areas. Based on these categories, there was also a mixture of newly recruited people and personnel representing the existing organizational structure. These different stakeholders were mainly involved in design conversations according to the following division:

- Principle oriented design dialogue together with CEO and executive management.
- Design oriented modeling seminars together with concerned roles of delimited parts of the practice. This was mainly performed with middle management and operative personnel, but also partly with executive management.

- Design oriented modeling seminars together with concerned roles of cross-sectional parts of the practice. This was mainly performed together with middle management and operative personnel, but also partly with executive management.
- Validation as a part of the design dialogue and the modeling seminars and as explicit activities in dedicated meetings/presentations.

In the design project at Intersport, the evolving process models served as common ground for communication where different aspects of the new business logic were elaborated and on which the participating parties created a commitment to the evolving process design. This commitment concerned two aspects: a commitment of how to view the future of the practice (with its different parts), and a commitment from each stakeholder to engage in the realization of the depicted structure. One empirical proof for the first aspect is that all stakeholders signed the final report. By involving different stakeholders, the aim of the co-design process was to determine pros and cons, as well as determine new ideas and views in relation to the design (Lind et al. 2008). The resulting models of the process design are to be regarded as agreements among the involved stakeholders in which different stakeholder views have been taken into consideration and valued in the modeling process.

Engagement in the modeling sessions could differ from being active in discussions to actually, through drawings, giving suggestions for process design on a whiteboard or modeling sheet. In addition to this, and as mentioned earlier, the evolving process design was continuously sent to other stakeholders within Intersport for validation and response.

**Guideline 2: Initial middle-out for organizational engagement**. In this project, three types of models (main, principle, and detailed) have been used to represent process design on different levels of abstraction. The relative distribution over time of these three models is presented in Figure 1.

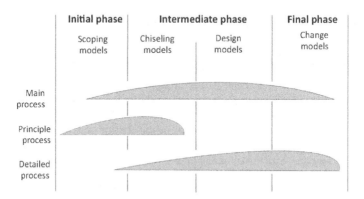

**Fig. 1.** The Roles of Different Artifacts

The final result from the project was to develop process descriptions on two levels, main process and detailed process. However, we did not start the work with these two types of models. During the initial modeling sessions, the main process model was regarded as too abstract, while in the detailed process model we got stuck in details. Hence we started to work with an intermediate level (principle process) that addressed principles in the new business model at the same time that we, during the modeling sessions, were able to understand the major consequences of the principles for further detailed design. This principle process, then, for the first half of the project, served as a bridge between the main process model and the detailed process models. In addition to the modeling sessions, the principle model also became the initial instrument for talks with the CEO and executive management, both for validation and to give new input to the subsequent modeling sessions. As can be seen in Figure 1, the principle model had served its purpose when the other two models evolved to a state where the relation between these two models became clear. At this stage, it became clear how the new business model was instantiated on the main process level and how these principles were instantiated in the detailed process models. The design of the main and detailed processes then evolved in parallel. The case shows that the principle process model (middle-out rather than top-down or bottom-up) is an important vehicle to engage and commit stakeholders in the development of the main process model and the detailed process models. Hence, this principle process model served as a bridging facilitator during the early stages of the project.

**Guideline 3:   Start addressing the core business and the rest will follow.**   As described above, different models on different levels have continuously been designed and refined throughout the project. As claimed earlier, different process models were needed to capture different aspects to pinpoint certain design results (business states) on different levels of granularity. Building on pragmatic (Lind and Goldkuhl 2003) foundations for understanding, the evaluation and design of business processes were elaborated in three essential process dimensions during the process design:

- Transformation—the refinement of the basis for finished products; the core business processes
- Coordination—the governance and management of the transformation
- Interaction—the interplay between people/organizations and artifact

We could empirically validate all three dimensions when we started to work with the translation of Intersport's new business plan into design of new business processes. For instance, during the modeling sessions, when people started to discuss how different matters on an operative level should be performed (transformation), the need to deal with governance, management, and interaction became an issue of the design. These issues (coordination and interaction) were captured in the models and emerged as more and more relevant as the models matured in their transformational dimension.

In the analysis of the case, we explored the three types of models that were designed in the project (main process model, principle process model, and detailed process model) in relation to their role (none, partly, or dominate) during different phases (see Table 1). The table is horizontally divided into the phases and vertically divided into the three core process dimensions.

As can be seen in Table 1, the role of the different dimensions (i.e., transformation, coordination, and interaction) has evolved during the phases of the project. One can note that the transformative dimension has been important during all phases of the project while the interactive dimension of the models is suppressed until the latter phases. This became quite clear when we analyzed different versions of the models and how the content of the models had evolved in the project. The main reason for this evolution of the process dimensions is that we needed to reach very detailed descriptions before it was meaningful to address which organizational roles should be responsible for and involved in different parts of the process. Similarly, the coordinative dimensions were only briefly addressed in the early phases and they were not fully developed until the latter phases of the project. There was a need to develop transformational process knowledge in order to be able to address what to coordinate. It is also important to note that in order to achieve "usable" design, all three dimensions (i.e., transformation, coordination, and interaction) needed to be elaborated and described.

**Table 1.** Different Models and the Roles of Process Dimensions during Different Phases of the Project

| Model Type/ Aspect | Initial Phase Scoping Models | Intermediate Phase Chiseling Models | Design Models | Final Phase Change Models |
|---|---|---|---|---|
| **Transformation** | Main: Part Princ: Dom Detail: Dom | Main: Dom Princ: Dom Detail: Dom | Main: Dom Princ: N/A Detail: Dom | Main: Dom Princ: N/A Detail: Dom |
| **Coordination** | Main: Part Princ: Part Detail: None | Main: Part Princ: Part Detail: Part | Main: Dom Princ: N/A Detail: Dom | Main: Dom Princ: N/A Detail: Dom |
| **Interaction** | Main: None Princ: None Detail: None | Main: Part Princ: None Detail: Part | Main: Part Princ: N/A Detail: Dom | Main: Part Princ: N/A Detail: Dom |

# 5    Discussion: Design Science Research and Business Process Design

## 5.1    The Validity of Suggested Guidelines

As claimed in the introduction of this paper, in BPM a lot of emphasis has historically been put on the constituents of models. In this paper, a stronger focus has instead been put on guidelines to assist in arriving at valid models. In design science research projects, there is a constant movement between the general and the specific (e.g., kernel theory–design–design theory) where the resulting, general design theory is based on the experiences gained in evaluating the more specific design. However, working in a specific and authentic setting, factors other than those reported in this essay influenced the final result, and vice versa. Reuse of these guidelines does not automatically depict commitment and alignment. Nevertheless, we strongly believe the practical utility claims of such knowledge could still be argued: "One might compare this contribution with one of a well-designed route, drawn on a good map for a South Pole expedition. It is a valuable asset to realize eventual success (reaching the South Pole and returning home safely), but success is not guaranteed" (van Aken

2004, p. 12). When addressing guideline validity, they are demonstrated locally as in the case above but we argue that other factors further strengthen their validity.

- *Guideline 1: Extensive stakeholder involvement for establishing commitments.* This guideline stems from previous collaborative design work in other domains, where the co-design approach has proved useful (Lind et al. 2007; Liu et al. 2002; Rittgen 2007). In our case, we wanted to explore whether the approach could be useful in establishing organizational commitment in process design.
- *Guideline 2: Initial Middle-Out for Organizational Engagement.* This guideline emerged through the work during process design and is not directly derived from any kernel theory. This also means that this finding is potentially quite novel, but needs, in the spirit of multi-grounded theory, further grounding both theoretically and empirically.
- *Guideline 3: Start addressing the core business and the rest will follow.* This directive has its roots from prior pragmatic research in business process modeling based on several research projects (Goldkuhl and Lind 2008). However, this knowledge has not been presented previously as heuristic prescriptions in a design science research manner and its temporal dimension was found through the design inquiry.

### 5.2  Framing Business Process Design as Action and Design Science Research

During the design process performed at Intersport, a combination of research components has been applied (design science research being one). The process design has had a focus on design and validation of business models as artifacts, which have evolved, based on business demands and the utilization of essential categories derived from used kernel theories (the knowledge base). Both action research and design science research express the need for performing theoretically informed actions during research. Traditionally, action research has a strong focus on organizational change while design science research puts emphasis on evolving artifacts (properties of the artifacts and actions for arriving at desired artifacts). The action research tradition hence fails to properly address the theory-informed construction of artifacts (see Lindgren et al. 2004) while design science research does not intrinsically cover organizational change. In this setting, we found van Aken (2004) to be a particularly useful bridge between management action research and the more artifact-oriented IS literature in the field. In other words, even though the research performed and reported on in this paper has been performed in an action research setting, we still believe, in the spirit of Walls et al. (1992), that the knowledge presented in IS design science research gave us as researchers a more nuanced toolbox to address process design research. The division between artifact construction and evaluation (March and Smith 1995), the knowledge base, and the environment (Hevner et al. 2004) has helped us in structuring and paying attention to essential processes for this knowledge development and resulted in the three guidelines for business process design presented above.

## 6  Conclusions

In this paper, we have presented findings based on a process design project performed in a retail chain setting with the purpose of engaging people in describing and becoming committed to a future state as a means for the implementation of a new business model. In this setting, a business process design was performed as a step to transform a new business plan into detailed and comprehensive business process models.

On the basis of experiences gained from conducting this project as an action research endeavor, we have addressed the question of *how design science research can contribute to business process design.* From our experiences in this project, we believe the contribution of design science research is two-fold.

1. Since we believe that the nature of the problem domain in this paper (process design for organizational commitment and strategic alignment) requires that the design and evaluation of artifacts is performed in a naturalistic environment (Iivari and Venable 2009), iterating different versions of artifacts requires intervention. However, since action research is not designed to construct artifacts, importing such research constructs (e.g., kernel theory–design–evaluate) from the design science research approach makes the design process researcher more versatile. It does so by providing the researcher the ability to develop artifact-oriented knowledge through theory-ingraining, as demonstrated in the case. By using these design science research components, new knowledge dimensions on process design can be developed, such as guideline 2 and the temporal dimension of guideline 3.

2. As stated at the beginning of the paper, research on process design has mainly focused on the constituents of models. Considering the three guidelines put forward in this paper, we have found clear indications that research on process design in a design science mode might serve as a vehicle in addressing both the gap in the theoretical body of knowledge (how to produce models) as well as practitioner relevance through practical guidelines. These validity guidelines remains to be evaluated by practitioners in future studies.

The knowledge endeavor reported in this paper is to be seen as a step toward combining action research and design science research for collaborative modeling using co-design with the purpose of supporting organizations in their transition by using business process modeling. This approach has also been shown to be useful as a mean to ensure alignment between the new strategic business plan and the actual design of the new business process(es). This alignment dimension will be elaborated in a forthcoming article.

## References

Ahrne, G.: Interaction Inside, Outside and Between Organization. Sage Publications, London (1994)

Albinsson, L., Lind, M., Forsgren, O.: Co-Design: An Approach to Border Crossing, Network Innovation. In: Cunningham, P., Cunningham, M. (eds.) Expanding the Knowledge Economy: Issues, Applications, Case Studies, vol. 4, Part 2, pp. 977–983. IOS Press, Amsterdam (2007)

Bandara, W., Gable, G., Rosemann, M.: Business Process Modeling Success: An Empirically Tested Measurement Model. In: Proceedings of the 27th International Conference on Information Systems, Milwaukee, WI (2006)

Baskerville, R.L., Wood-Harper, A.T.: A Critical Perspective on Action Research as a Method for Information Systems Research. Journal of Information Technology (11), 235–246 (1996)

Benbasat, I., Zmud, R.W.: Empirical Research in Information Systems: The Practice of Relevance. MIS Quarterly 23(1), 3–16 (1999)

Cole, R., Purao, S., Rossi, M., Sein, M.K.: Being Proactive: Where Action Research Meets Design Research. In: Avison, D., Galletta, D., DeGross, J.I. (eds.) Proceedings of the 26th International Conference on Information Systems, Las Vegas, pp. 325–336 (2005)

Cross, N.: Understanding Design Cognition. In: Cross, N. (ed.) Designerly Ways of Knowing, pp. 72–95. Birkhäuser, Basel (2007)

Davenport, T.H.: Process Innovation: Reengineering Work Through Information Technology. Harvard Business School Press, Boston (1993)

Davis, R.: Business Process Modeling with ARIS: A Practical Guide. Springer, London (2001)

Davies, I., Green, P., Rosemann, M., Indulska, M., Gallo, S.: How Do Practitioners Use Conceptual Modeling in Practice? Data and Knowledge Engineering 58(3), 358–380 (2006)

Dewey, J.: Human Nature and Conduct. Henry Holt, New York (1922)

Goldkuhl, G.: Design Theories in Information Systems: A Need for Multi-Grounding. Journal of Information Technology Theory and Application 6(2), 59–72 (2004)

Goldkuhl, G., Cronholm, S.: Multi-Grounded Theory: Adding Theoretical Grounding to Grounded Theory. In: Proceedings of the Second European Conference on Research Methods in Business Reading, UK (2003)

Goldkuhl, G., Lind, M.: Coordination and Transformation in Business Processes: Towards an Integrated View. Business Process Management Journal 14(6), 761–777 (2008)

Gregor, S.: The Nature of Theory in Information Systems. MIS Quarterly 30(3), 611–642 (2006)

Gregor, S., Jones, D.: The Anatomy of a Design Theory. Journal of the Association for Information Systems 8(5), 312–335 (2007)

Günther, C., Rinderle-Ma, S., Reichert, M., Van der Aalst, W.M.P., Recker, J.: Using Process Mining to Learn From Process Changes in Evolutionary Systems. International Journal of Business Process Integration and Management 3(1), 61–78 (2008)

Hammer, M.: Reengineering Work: Don't Automate, Obliterate. Harvard Business Review 68(4), 104–112 (1990)

Hanseth, O., Lyytinen, K.: Theorizing about the Design of Information Infrastructures: Design Kernel Theories and Principles. Sprouts: Working Papers on Information Environments, Systems and Organizations 4(12) (2004)

Harmon, P.: The Scope and Evolution of Business Process Management. In: vom Brocke, J., Rosemann, M. (eds.) Handbook on Business Process Management. Springer, Berlin (forthcoming, 2010)

Harrington, H.J.: Business Process Improvement: The Breakthrough Strategy for Total Quality, Productivity and Competitiveness. McGraw-Hill, New York (1991)

Henderson, J.C., Venkatraman, N.: Strategic Alignment: Leveraging Information Technology for Transforming Organizations. IBM System Journal 38(2-3), 472–485 (1999)

Hevner, A.R., March, S.T., Park, J., Ram, S.: Design Science in Information Systems Research. MIS Quarterly 28(1), 75–105 (2004)

Iivari, J., Venable, J.: Action Research and Design Science Research: Seemingly Similar But Decisively Dissimilar. In: Proceedings of the 2009 European Conference on Information Systems, Verona, Italy, June 8-10 (2009)

Keen, P.G.W., Knapp, E.M.: Every Manager's Guide to Business Processes: A Glossary of Key Terms and Concepts for Today's Business Leaders. Harvard Business School Press, Boston (1996)

Langefors, B.: Theoretical Analysis of Information Systems, 4th edn. Studentlitteratur, Lund (1973)

Lankhorst, M.: Enterprise Architecture at Work: Modeling, Communication, and Analysis. Springer, Berlin (2005)

Lind, M., Albinsson, L., Forsgren, O., Hedman, J.: Integrated Development, Use and Learning in a Co-design Setting: Experiences from the Incremental Deployment of e-Me. In: Cunningham, P., Cunningham, M. (eds.) Expanding the Knowledge Economy: Issues, Applications, Case Studies, pp. 773–780. IOS Press, Amsterdam (2007)

Lind, M., Forsgren, O.: Co-design and Web 2.0: Theoretical Foundations and Application. In: Cunningham, P., Cunningham, M. (eds.) Collaboration and the Knowledge Economy: Issues, Applications, Case Studies, pp. 1105–1112. IOS Press, Amsterdam (2008)

Lind, M., Goldkuhl, G.: The Constituents of Business Interaction: Generic Layered Patterns. Data and Knowledge Engineering 47(3), 327–348 (2003)

Lind, M., Seigerroth, U.: Collaborative Process Modeling: The Intersport Case Study. In: vom Brocke, J., Rosemann, M. (eds.) Handbook on Business Process Management. Springer, Berlin (2010a) (forthcoming)

Lind, M., Seigerroth, U.: A Multi-Layered Approach to Business and IT Alignment. In: Proceedings of the 43rd Hawaii International Conference on System Sciences. IEEE Computer Society Press, Los Alamitos (2010b)

Lind, M., Seigerroth, U., Forsgren, O., Hjalmarsson, A.: Co-design as Social Constructive Pragmatism. Paper presented at the inaugural meeting of the AIS Special Interest Group on Pragmatist IS Research (SIGPrag 2008), Paris (2008)

Lindgren, R., Henfridsson, O., Schultze, U.: Design Principles for Competence Management Systems: A Synthesis of Action Research Study. MIS Quarterly 28(3), 435–472 (2004)

Liu, K., Sun, L., Bennett, K.: Co-Design of Business and IT Systems. Information Systems Frontiers 4(3), 251–256 (2002)

March, S.T., Smith, G.: Design and Natural Science Research on Information Technology. Decision Support Systems 15(4), 251–266 (1995)

Markus, M.L., Majchrzak, A., Gasser, L.: A Design Theory for Systems That Support Emergent Knowledge Processes. MIS Quarterly 26(3), 179–212 (2002)

Mathiassen, L.: Collaborative Practice Research. Information Technology and People 14(1), 321–345 (2002)

Matthews, M.R.: Models in Science and in Science Education: An Introduction. Science and Education 16(7-8), 647–652 (2007)

Nelson, H.G., Stolterman, E.: The Design Way: Intentional Change in an Unpredictable World. Educational Technology Publications, Englewood Cliffs (2003)

Nunamaker, J., Chen, M., Purdin, T.D.M.: Systems Development in Information Systems Research. Journal of Management Information Systems 7(3), 89–106 (1991)

Purao, S.: Design Research in the Technology of Information Systems: Truth or Dare. Unpublished paper, School of Information Sciences and Technology, Pennsylvania State University (2002)

Purao, S., Baldwin, C.Y., Hevner, A., Storey, V.C., Pries-Heje, J., Smith, B.: The Sciences of Design: Observations on an Emerging Field. Working Ppaer No. 09-056. Harvard Business School (2008)

Recker, J.: A Socio-Pragmatic Constructionist Framework for Understanding Quality in Process Modeling. Australiasian Journal of Information Systems 14(2), 43–63 (2007)

Rittgen, P.: Co-designing Models for Enterprises and Information Systems: A Case for Language Integration. In: Magyar, G., Knapp, G., Wojtkowski, W.G., Zupancic, J. (eds.) Advances in Information Systems Development: New Methods and Practice for the Networked Society, vol. 1, pp. 73–83. Springer, Berlin (2007)

Romme, A.G.L.: Making a Difference: Organization as Design. Organization Science 14(5), 558–573 (2003)

Roseman, M., Vessey, I.: Toward Improving the Relevance of Information Systems Research to Practitioners: The Role of Applicability Checks. MIS Quarterly 32(1), 1–22 (2008)

Rosenblueth, A., Wiener, N.: The Role of Models in Science. Philosophy of Science 12(4), 316–321 (1945)

Scheer, A.-W., Nüttgens, M.: ARIS Architecture and Reference Models for Business Process Management. In: van der Aalst, W.M.P., Desel, J., Oberweis, A. (eds.) Business Process Management. LNCS, vol. 1806, pp. 376–389. Springer, Heidelberg (2000)

Schuette, R., Rotthowe, T.: The Guidelines of Modeling: An Approach to Enhance the Quality in Information Models. In: Ling, T.-W., Ram, S., Li Lee, M. (eds.) ER 1998. LNCS, vol. 1507, pp. 240–254. Springer, Heidelberg (1998)

Searle, J.R.: Speech Acts: An Essay in the Philosophy of Language. Cambridge University Press, London (1969)

Simon, H.A.: The Sciences of the Artificial, 3rd edn. MIT Press, Cambridge (1996)

Stirna, J., Kirikova, M.: How to Support Agile Development Projects with Enterprise Modeling. In: Johannesson, P., Söderström, E. (eds.) Information System engineering: From Data Analysis to Process Networks, pp. 159–185. IGI Publishing, London (2008)

Thomas, O.: Understanding the Term Reference Model in Information Systems Research: History, Literature Analysis and Explanation. In: Kindler, E., Nüttgens, M. (eds.) Business Process Reference Models, Proceedings of the Workshop on Business Process Reference Models, Nancy, France (2005)

Tolvanen, J.-P., Lyytinen, K.: Flexible Method Adaptation in CASE Environments: The Metamodeling Approach. Scandinavian Journal of Information Systems (5), 51–77 (1992)

Van Aken, J.E.: Management Research Based on the Paradigm of the Design Sciences: The Quest for Field-Tested and Grounded Technological Rules. Journal of Management Studies 41(2), 219–246 (2004)

van der Aalst, W.M.P., Rosemann, M., Dumas, M.: Deadline-Based Escalation in Process-Aware Information Systems. Decision Support Systems 43(2), 492–511 (2007)

Vernadat, F.B.: Enterprise Modeling and Integration (EMI): Current Status and Research Perspectives. Annual Reviews in Control 26(1), 15–25 (2002)

Vom Brocke, J., Thomas, O.: Reference Modeling for Organizational Change: Applying Collaborative Techniques for Business Engineering. In: Proceedings of the 12th Americas Conference on Information Systems, Acapulco, Mexico, pp. 680–688 (2006)

von Wright, G.H.: Explanation and Understanding. Rouledge and Kegan Paul, London (1971)

Walls, J.G., Widmeyer, G.R., El Sawy, O.A.: Building an Information System Design Theory for Vigilant EIS. Information Systems Research 3(1), 36–59 (1992)

## About the Authors

**Mikael Lind** is an associate professor with the University of Borås, the Viktoria Institute, and Linköping University, Sweden. He is the director of the informatics department and the founder of the InnovationLab at the school of Business and Informatics in Borås. He is also the co-founder of the Swedish GSI (Graduate School of Informatics). He is associated with the research network VITS in Sweden and is active in different international communities such as Language/action and Pragmatic Web. He is also part of the management board for the AIS special interest group SIGPrag (www.sigprag.org). His research focus is on pragmatist IS research on co-design of business and IT. The research is divided into four research areas: business process management, e-service innovation, method engineering, and research methods for information systems development. His research is mainly characterized by empirically driven theory and method development, action research, design science, multi-grounded theory, and practical theory. He is also the project manager of the citizen-centric e-service project e-Me— turning the Internet around (www.e-me.se) as well as associate editor for the open journal *Systems, Signs & Actions* (www.sysiac.org). He can be contacted by e-mail at mikael.lind@hb.se.

**Daniel Rudmark** is pursuing his Ph.D. at the InnovationLab, University College of Borås, where he practices modern systems development. He is also a part of the Graduate School of Informatics and the AIS special interest group SIGPrag (www.sigprag.org). Prior to joining University College of Borås, he spent more than 10 years as a developer, architect, project manager, and CTO. His research interests are primarily in the areas of design science in organizational settings and the role of the developer in modern systems development. He is currently involved in two design science research projects and is managing project development activities for the next generation of e-me. He can be contacted by e-mail at daniel.rudmark@hb.se.

**Ulf Seigerroth** is an assistant professor with Jönköping University, Sweden. Ulf is the co-director and co-founder of CenIT (Centre of Evolving IT in Networked organizations) (www.hj.se/cenit). From 2004 to 2007, he was head of the Department of Informatics. Ulf is one of the co-founders of GSI (Graduate School of Informatics) that was launched in April 2008. He is also part of the AIS special interest group SIGPrag (www.sigprag.org). His current research is directed at issues concerning business and IT-alignment and transformation. Within this area, specific issues of interest are enterprise modeling, enterprise architecture, information logistics, method engineering, co-design, and IT economics. His research is characterized by empirically driven and theory- and method-informed development (action research). He is involved in different action research projects focusing on alignment of business processes and information systems and information logistics. He can be contacted by e-mail at ulf.seigerroth @jth.hj.se.

# Part 4

# Designing Adoption

# An Adoption Diffusion Model of RFID-Based Livestock Management System in Australia

Mohammad Alamgir Hossain and Mohammed Quaddus

Graduate School of Business,
Curtin University of Technology,
Perth, WA, Australia

**Abstract.** Many countries, like Australia, have introduced a radio frequency identification (RFID) based livestock identification and management system,which can be used for condition monitoring and fault prognosis during an outbreak situation. This paper examines the adoption process and its subsequent diffusion and extended usage of RFID in Australian livestock management practices, and proposes a research model. The model is primarily built on Rogers' innovation-diffusion theory and Oliver's expectation–confirmation theory, with some logical modifications. It posits that while adoption of RFID may be the result of legislative pressure, its further diffusion is an evaluative process, which is judged against "satisfaction" and "performance" derived from RFID systems. The implications of these and other related concepts are also discussed. Hypotheses are developed which can be tested via empirical study. The proposed model has both theoretical and practical implications. Although it is developed on the basis of the Australian livestock industry, it can be used in other countries and also in other applications with some industry-specific modifications.

**Keywords:** RFID, adoption, diffusion, extended use, livestock industry, Australia.

## 1 Introduction

Radio frequency identification (RFID) technology is one of the most effective enabling technologies in identifying an object uniquely and keeping the desired data as long as required, which can later be retrieved as information. Along with tens of other applications, RFID is a very efficient method of identifying animals and collecting data more quickly, and is potentially a revolutionary innovation for the food industry. For livestock markets, the data and information serve as the "certificate" of the product and the international livestock market is increasingly demanding an RFID-generated data and information system from the livestock and livestock products supplying countries that can be used for condition monitoring and fault prognosis in the event of an outbreak situation (Sullivan 2004). The pressure intensified with the scrutiny of various government agencies. To this end, some countries such as Canada, Australia, and Uruguay, as well as numerous European countries, passed legislation on mandatory use of auto- identification, while other

J. Pries-Heje et al. (Eds.): IS Design Science Research, IFIP AICT 318, pp. 179–191, 2010.

countries such as the United States, Malaysia, and Japan are implementing the system on a volunteer basis (Patent et al. 2006). Australia has the world's first and largest RFID-enabled national livestock identification system, called NLIS (Tonsor and Schroeder 2006). When integrated with post-slaughter tracking systems, the NLIS database allows for rapid and accurate tracing of cattle in the event of a disease outbreak or residue incident and saves the industry from more losses than would otherwise be the case. For example, in July 2008, Russia, Australia's fourth largest beef export market, banned three kangaroo processing plants and a beef facility because of microbial contamination (ABC 2008). If NLIS could not track the sources of the contamination quickly, the entire Australian meat industry would have suffered from this ban.

The Australian meat and livestock industry is regarded as one of the largest in the world and is renowned for its "clean and green" beef. Australia is the second-largest exporter of beef, mutton, and lamb in the world, exporting to more than 100 countries (Tonsor and Schroeder 2006), and world's largest exporter of beef (ABARE 2008). During 2007-2008, the gross value of livestock production was $41.5 billion, contributing 63 percent of the gross value of agricultural product ($65.4 billion). A significant portion of this products was exported, contributing 53 percent of the agribusiness's export in 2007-2008, $14.5 billion of the total $27.5 billion (ABARE 2008).

Most studies on RFID have dealt with technology issues (frequency standardization, tag orientation), security, privacy, and implementation issues primarily in supply chain and logistics management, although several studies have been undertaken in the RFID adoption diffusion area (Chang et al. 2008; Cheng and Yang 2007; Huyskens and Loebbecke 2007; Krasnova et al. 2008; Lee and Shim 2007; Matta and Moberg 2006, 2007; Ranganathan and Jha 2005; Schmitt et al. 2008; Schmitt et al. 2007; Sharma and Citurs 2005). The adoption of RFID in the Australian livestock industry is, however, a special type of adoption as the government imposed the legal requirement of using this technology for cattle identification. However, farmers may also use RFID voluntarily for identifying other animals or in other livestock applications. Therefore, it would seem to be interesting to examine how farmers embraced this technology and whether they got what they expected. It is likely that if they are satisfied they would diffuse this technology and possibly use it for other applications. Alternatively, if they are not satisfied, they are likely to use this technology only for mandated purposes. However, unfortunately, no significant work has been performed to explain the farmers' adoption and diffusion behavior in RFID-based livestock identification and management field. This paper addresses and attempts to close this research gap. Equipped with a background of adoption and diffusion of innovation, this paper develops a research model to examine and identify the factors affecting the adoption-diffusion and extended use of RFID in the livestock industry. The two dominant research questions of this study are

1.   What are the factors that influence the farmers' adoption decision of RFID technology in their livestock identification operation?
2.   What are the factors influencing the diffusion and extended use decision of RFID in livestock management operations?

## 2 Background

Adoption diffusion of an innovation has been studied primarily with three theories: innovation-diffusion theory (IDT), theory of reasoned action (TRA), and technology acceptance model (TAM). While IDT focuses on the diffusion processes of an innovation, the TRA and TAM models explain the relationship between actual use of a technology and user attitudes, perceptions, and beliefs (Xu and Quaddus 2007). RFID adoption is more or less imposed rather than voluntary, which is based on the attitude of the users or perceived usefulness, while RFID diffusion is believed to be more dependent on performance evaluation rather than belief or attitude. Bhattacherjee (2001) argues that not only adoption but continued use is necessary for an innovation's ultimate success and has used expectation confirmation theory (ECT) in explaining IS continuance, although ECT is primarily used in consumer behavior literature. This study, based on IDT and ECT, develops a theoretically grounded, comprehensive framework to investigate the antecedents of RFID adoption, diffusion, and extended use, which is further refined using theoretical and empirical findings from prior literature. The following subsections discuss the two underlying theories as they relate to adoption diffusion and continued use of an innovation.

### 2.1 Innovation Diffusion Theory (IDT)

An "innovation is the adoption of a change which is new to an organization and to the relevant environment" (Knight 1967, p. 467). Diffusion is "the process by which an innovation is communicated through certain channels over time among the members of a social system" (Rogers 1995, p. 5). Therefore, RFID can certainly be examined by IDT.

IDT proposes that potential adopters of an innovation must gain some knowledge about the innovation, then be persuaded of its value, decide to adopt and implement it, and confirm the decision to adopt the innovation. For pursuing the maximum benefits, however, mere adoption of RFID is not sufficient; rather, it is necessary to institutionalize this technology into routine operations and practices and extend its use to different applications, where possible, suitable, or profitable. The continued and extended use behavior is different from and possibly more important than its initial adoption because many RFID adopters are initially driven by mandatory pressure and later choose different level of use depending on their internal judgment. IDT is silent, not explaining how adopters go to the next stage of diffusion and to further innovative applications. Moreover, IDT is primarily based on individual-level adoption decisions (Eveland and Tornatzky 1990), but RFID adoption needs to be examined from government and organizational perspectives because it involves many national policies and requires modification of organizational structures and operations.

### 2.2 Expectation–Confirmation Theory

Expectation–confirmation theory (ECT) is widely used in the consumer behavior literature to study consumer satisfaction and post-purchase behavior. Post-purchase behavior is somewhat related to the continued and extended use characteristics of an innovation. The process by which consumers reach repurchase intentions in an ECT

framework is as follows (Oliver 1980, p. 462):    First, buyers form an initial
expectation of a specific product or service prior to purchase. Second, consumption
reveals a perceived quality level, which is influenced by expectations.    Third, they
determine the extent to which their expectation is confirmed. Fourth, they form a
satisfaction based on their confirmation level and expectation. Finally, satisfied
consumers form a repurchase intention, while dissatisfied consumers discontinue its
subsequent use.

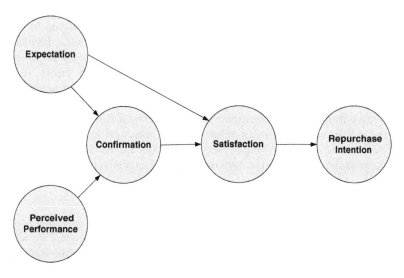

**Fig. 1.** Expectation–Confirmation Theory (Adapted from Figure 1 in A. Bhattacherjee,
"Understanding Information Systems Continuance: An Expectation-Confirmation Model," *MIS
Quarterly* (25:3), pp. 351-370. Copyright © 2001, Regents of the University of Minnesota.
Used with permission.)

In ECT, *expectation* acts as the frame-of-reference to measure *confirmation* and
*satisfaction*. ECT, however, does not explain the basis of expectations and ignores the
driving forces behind adopting a product, service, or innovation. It ignores the mandatory introduction of a product or service; rather, it is based on voluntary decisions. In
a mandatory system, the expectations are shaped and biased by the imposing authority
and, therefore, not an independent variable as proposed in ECT.

### 2.3  Conceptual Framework

This study suggests that farmers, driven by the market and/or legislative requirements,
gather and utilize all available information (from internal and external sources), share
information, and develop and adjust their expectations in developing *rational
expectations* (Au and Kauffman 2003) before they adopt RFID. Adoption drives
RFID to further diffusion. Meanwhile, the expectations are modified. Eventually the
satisfied farmers diffuse RFID into their routine operations while dissatisfied farmers
may use it for limited operation(s). Farmers in Australia do not have the choice to
reject RFID use as it is mandatory for cattle identification. Moreover, some satisfied

farmers may voluntarily use RFID for extended use. *Satisfaction*, however, is measured against the level of *confirmation* of the expectations, and the *performance* of RFID. Thus the framework is presented in two parts: *External factors* → *Knowledge* → *Adoption;* and *Expectations* → *Satisfaction* → *Diffusion and Extended Use.* We use this conceptual framework for the development of the RFID adoption–diffusion[+] model, which is discussed in the following section.

## 3 The Research Model and Hypotheses Development

Figure 2 depicts the proposed model. The following section describes the constructs of the research model.

### 3.1 RFID Knowledge

*RFID knowledge* describes the amount of knowledge in the field of RFID that a farmer accumulates in theory and practice. In this study, the *RFID knowledge* construct consists of basic, technical, and technological RFID knowledge. *Basic RFID knowledge* refers to knowledge about the existence and potential benefits of RFID. *Technical RFID knowledge* is knowledge about the state-of-the-art of RFID technology. *Technological RFID knowledge* is about technological laws (scientific and IT mathematics), functional rules (RFID standard and frequency use), structural rules (depth of integration), and socio-technical understanding (such as ethics, privacy, etc.) of RFID. *RFID knowledge* itself is dependant of *external information sources* and the *organization's internal information sources* (Tellkamp et al. 2009).

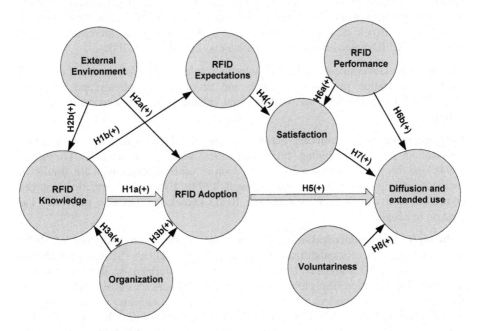

**Fig. 2.** The Proposed Research Model of RFID Adoption–Diffusion[+]

Furthermore, the amount of RFID knowledge influences the likelihood of RFID adoption(Lee and Shim 2007; Ranganathan and Jha 2005; Tellkamp et al. 2009) and generates more realistic and rational RFID expectations (Au and Kauffman 2003).

*Hypothesis 1a:* **RFID knowledge** *positively influences the speed and extent of* **RFID adoption***.*

*Hypothesis 1b:* **RFID knowledge** *positively influences* **RFID expectations** *in livestock farms.*

### 3.2 External Environment

The external environment is the global control where the organization operates and it is beyond the organization's control but is important in decision-making behavior (Quaddus and Hofmeyer 2007). *External environment* has been recognized as playing a very significant role in adoption–diffusion research, including RFID adoption (Sharma and Citurs 2005). Related to RFID adoption, the external environment consists of *external pressure* (Matta and Moberg 2007), *government* (Matta and Moberg 2007; Zhu et al. 2003), *external information sources* (Jeyaraj et al. 2006 ; Matta and Moberg 2007), and *industry-wide standardization and cost* (Brown and Russell 2007; Cheng and Yang 2007; Juban and Wyld 2004).

**External pressure:** External pressure consists of *government pressure* (Kuan and Chau 2001) and *market pressure* (Chang et al. 2008; Ranganathan and Jha 2005). A practical reason for livestock farmers to adopt RFID is government policy and regulations. Like Australia, a growing number of animal exporting countries have introduced legislation on compulsory RFID-based livestock management systems. Therefore, farmers do not have any choice but to adopt RFID technology. Another reason for livestock farmers to adopt RFID is because of the increasing market pressure for RFID-based animal tracking systems (Li and Visich 2006).

**Government:** Government can play an important role in RFID adoption and diffusion through information provision, research and development policies and facilities, incentives for the adopters, and building and enhancing the infrastructure (Scupola 2003).

**External information sources:** Farmers acquire RFID information from external information sources, including farm magazines, government agencies (Kettinger 1994), and through interpersonal channels such as other adopters who are similar in socioeconomic status (Ghadim and Pannell 1999). External information sources contribute to livestock farmers acquiring RFID knowledge and also motivates the farmers to adopt RFID.

**Industry-wide standardization and cost:** One of the main inhibitors of RFID adoption is the lack of standardization and the cost of RFID tags (Schmitt et al. 2008). Although the RFID standards (ISO11784/11785) are defined by the International Standards Organization (ISO) to use LF 134.2 KHz, farmers are easily confused when they find too many providers with many different types of tags and readers. They are afraid of buying tags and readers from different providers because they think that the tags might not be read by readers from a different company (readability). That brings the fear of not being able to read the tags in different countries and hinders the process of a global system of livestock identification (interoperability). Therefore, adopters are looking for an industry-wide standard system (Brown and Russell 2007; Cheng and Yang 2007; Juban and Wyld 2004; Sharma and Citurs 2005) and the tags need be cheaper (Schmitt et al. 2008; Sharma and Citurs 2005; Sharma et al. 2007). As a whole,

Hypothesis 2a: **External environment** positively influences **RFID adoption**.
Hypothesis 2b: **External environment** positively influences **RFID knowledge**.

### 3.3 Organizational Factors

Tornatzky and Fleischer (1990) argued that organizational factors must be considered in any organizational innovation adoption research. Organizational variables such as *(top) management attitude* towards adoption of RFID with adequate funding and expertise ensures RFID adoption (Brown and Russell 2007; Huyskens and Loebbecke 2007; Krasnova and Weser 2008; Ranganathan and Jha 2005; Schmitt et al. 2007; Sharma and Citurs 2005; Sharma et al. 2007). *Organizational size* also is an important factor as the RFID integration-depth comes with the physical, financial, and techno-logical resources of the farm (Brown and Russell 2007; Huyskens and Loebbecke 2007; Matta and Moberg 2006, 2007). Organizational size facilitates knowledge acquisition (and/or knowledge generation). Infrastructure-related facilities (IS/IT/ICT) available in the organization influence RFID adoption (Ranganathan and Jha 2005; Sharma and Citurs 2005; Sharma et al. 2007). As a whole,

Hypothesis 3a: **Organizational factors** positively influence **RFID knowledge** for its adoption and diffusion among livestock farmers.

Hypothesis 3b: **Organizational factors** positively influence **RFID adoption** in livestock farms.

### 3.4 RFID Expectations

*RFID expectations* are the expected attributes of RFID that are derived during the knowledge gathering phase, and are similar to the perceived characteristics of an innovation in IDT. This study differentiates *expectation* from *attributes* as some expectations are developed during the knowledge gathering phase, while some expectations are formed, or past expectations are modified, after the initial adoption, which means *expectation* is a continuous process rather than an initial and complete stage. Among the main attributes of an innovation in IDT (e.g., trialability, observability, relative advantage, complexity, and compatibility), empirical research and theoretical analysis found that relative advantage (Brown and Russell 2007; Krasnova et al. 2008), complexity (Chang et al. 2008; Schmitt et al. 2007), and compatibility (Schmitt et al. 2007) are consistently used attributes. Some other attributes, including profitability (Lindner 1987), cost (Sharma and Citurs 2005), market penetration, and risk and uncertainty (Ghadim et al. 2005) are also important for RFID study. However, adopters' *expectations* have a direct negative influence on *satisfaction*(Bearden and Teel 1983; Churchill and Surprenant 1982; Oliver 1980; Westbrook and Oliver 1981) as *satisfaction* is the difference between *performance* and *expectations*.

*Hypothesis 4: **RFID expectations** negatively influence the level of **satisfaction**.*

### 3.5  RFID Adoption

Mandatory RFID adoption drives farmers to identify their cattle with RFID tags. Successful RFID adoption motivates farmers to further diffuse the technology.

*Hypothesis 5: **RFID adoption** positively influences **RFID diffusion and extended use** in livestock industry.*

### 3.6  Performance

Performance is the manner of functioning or operating. Once the system is implemented, the performance of the RFID system is measured, including general (works as designed), financial (on-budget, return-on-investment, etc.), and technical (complexity, maintenance, data recovery) performance of the system. Churchill and Surprenant (1982) and Oliver and DeSarbo (1988) showed that *performance* has a direct and significant effect on *satisfaction*. However, Bhattacherjee (2001) and Schmitt et al. (2007) found that *performance* influences RFID diffusion.

*Hypothesis 5a:  **RFID performance** positively influences **satisfaction** of RFID use.*

*Hypothesis 5b:  **RFID performance** positively influences **diffusion and extended use** of RFID system.*

### 3.7  Satisfaction

Satisfaction is defined as "the summary of psychological state resulting when the emotion surrounding disconfirmation expectations is coupled with the consumer's prior feelings about the consumption experience" (Oliver 1981, p. 27). It is an evaluative response concerning the perceived outcomes of experience from that product or service. The *satisfaction* construct is composed of the *presence of affect* and the *notion of satisfaction*. Presence of affect is central to satisfaction, which is the evaluation of outcomes such as happy or regretful and so on. The notion of satisfaction is the degree of affect that the adopter is more or less inclined to continue use of the product. ECT holds that *satisfaction* has a direct effect on consumers' intention to repurchase a product or continue use (Anderson and Sullivan 1993; Oliver 1980).

*Hypothesis 6: **Satisfaction** positively influences **diffusion and extended use** of the RFID system.*

## 3.8  RFID Diffusion and Extended Use

Diffusion and extended use is the only dependent variable of this study. This variable refers to the degree of use of the RFID systems in livestock management. Here, farmers do not have the luxury to decide not to continue RFID use as its use is mandatory in Australia (for cattle identification). However, farmers can decide the degree or de*pth* of its use. Voluntarily, farmers may identify other animals and/or apply RFID for livestock operations including herd management and dairy management.

## 3.9  Farmers' Voluntariness

Farmers' RFID voluntariness is the degree to which farmers decide to implement RFID in livestock management operations of their own free will. It is the willingness to take initiative to try out RFID in livestock applications other than identification. Voluntariness is considered as one of the perceived characteristics for the diffusion of an innovation (Agarwal and Prasad 1997). Voluntariness may be varied with required investment and slack resources. However, this study postulates that farmers with more voluntariness would show interest and implement RFID in extended livestock-management application(s) than other farmers who are not volunteers.

*Hypothesis 7:  **Farmers' voluntariness** positively influences **RFID diffusion and extended use** in livestock management processes.*

## 3.10  Measurement Scale

The variables of this study will be measured by adapting measurement scales from previous studies: *organizational factors* will be adapted from Patterson et al.'s (2003) organizational characteristics scale; *satisfaction* measure will be adapted from Westbrook and Oliver's (1981) satisfaction scale; *competition* measure will be adapted from Kuan and Chau (2001). The measure for attributes of *RFID expectations* will be adapted from the innovation–diffusion literature. Adapted measurement scales will be subjected to rigorous reliability and validity tests.

# 4  Future Directions and Conclusion

This article presents a research model for investigating the factors influencing the adoption, diffusion, and extended use of RFID technology—a subject that has not been well explored in the literature. Future research could test the entire research model. Parts of the model could also be extracted and investigated in detail. As the model is divided into two parts, future study could be conducted using different types of adopters. The model, including both of its main constructs and subfactors, can be taken as-is or fine-tuned for a comprehensive survey. Organizations embarking on RFID use can use the constructs and factors of the study to perform an internal audit to find out how they vary. The proposed model also provides guidelines for RFID adoption-diffusion practitioners and consultants. Therefore, this study will make two main contributions. First, it will test the theories in a new setting. Second, it will give practitioners new insights at the operational level as well assist with strategic decisions about effective diffusion policies and further RFID investments in the Australian livestock industry.

# References

ABARE. Australian Commodities, December Quarter, ABARE Project 1163, Commonwealth of Australian, pp. 631–776 (2008), http://www.abareconomics.com/interactive/08ac_Dec/htm/beef.htm (accessed November 12, 2009)

ABC. Australia's Livestock Industry Meets Over Russia Ban, Radio Australia News (2008), http://www.radioaustralia.net.au/news/stories/200807/s2313053.htm (accessed November 16, 2009)

Agarwal, R., Prasad, J.: The Role of Innovation Characteristics and Perceived Voluntariness in the Acceptance of Information Technologies. Decision Sciences 28(3), 557–582 (1997)

Anderson, E.W., Sullivan, M.W.: The Antecedents and Consequences of Customer Satisfaction for Firms. Marketing Science 12(2), 125–143 (1993)

Au, Y.A., Kauffman, R.J.: What Do You Know? Rational Expectations in Information Technology Adoption and Investment. Journal of Management Information Systems 20(2), 49–76 (2003)

Bearden, W.O., Teel, J.E.: Selected Determinants of Consumer Satisfaction and Complaint Reports. Journal of Marketing Research (20), 21–28 (1983)

Bhattacherjee, A.: Understanding Information systems Continuance: An Expectation–Confirmation Model. MIS Quarterly 25(3), 351–370 (2001)

Brown, I., Russell, J.: Radio Frequency Identification Technology: An Exploratory Study on Adoption in the South African Retail Sector. International Journal of Information Management 27(4), 250–265 (2007)

Chang, S.-I., Hung, S.-Y., Yen, D.C., Chen, Y.-J.: The Determinants of RFID Adoption in the Logistics Industry: A Supply Chain Management Perspective. Communications of the Association for Information Systems 23(12), 197–218 (2008)

Cheng, Y.-H., Yang, A.S.: Investigating Key Factors of Deciding RFID's Adoption in Logistics Service Providers. Paper presented at the 11th International Conference on Computer Supported Cooperative Work in Design, Melbourne, Australia, April 26-28 (2007)

Churchill, J.G.A., Surprenant, C.: An Investigation into the Determinants of Customer Satisfaction. Journal of Marketing Research 19(4), 491–504 (1982)

Eveland, J.D., Tornatzky, L.G.: The Deployment of Technology. In: Tornatzky, L., Fleischer, M. (eds.) The Processes of Technological Innovation, pp. 117–147. Lexington Books, Lexington (1990)

Ghadim, A.K.A., Pannell, D.J.: A Conceptual Framework of Adoption of an Agricultural Innovation. Agricultural Economics (21), 145–154 (1999)

Ghadim, A.K.A., Pannell, D.J., Burton, M.P.: Risk, Uncertainty, and Learning in Adoption of a Crop Innovation. Agricultural Economics (33), 1–9 (2005)

Huyskens, C., Loebbecke, C.: RFID Adoption: Theoretical Concepts and Their Practical Application in Fashion. In: McMaster, T., Wastell, D., Ferneley, E., DeGross, J.I. (eds.) Organizational Dynamics of Technology-Based Innovation: Diversifying the Research Agenda, pp. 345–361. Springer, Boston (2007)

Jeyaraj, A., Rottman, J., Lacity, M.C.: A Review of the Predictors, Linkages, and Biases in IT Innovation Adoption Research. Journal of Information Technology 21(1), 1–23 (2006)

Juban, R.L., Wyld, D.C.: Would You Like Chips With That? Consumer Perspectives of RFID. Management Research News 27(11/12), 29–44 (2004)

Kettinger, W.: National Infrastructure Diffusion and the US Information Super Highway. Information and Management 27(6), 357–368 (1994)

Knight, K.E.: A Descriptive Model of the Intra-Firm Innovation Process. The Journal of Business 40(4), 478–496 (1967)

Krasnova, H., Weser, L., Ivantysynova, L.: Drivers of RFID Adoption in the Automotive Industry. In: Proceedings of the 14th Americas Conference on Information Systems, Toronto, Canada, August 14-17 (2008)

Kuan, K., Chau, P.: A Perception-Based Model of EDI Adoption in Small Businesses Using a Technology–Organizational–Environmental Framework. Information and Management 38(3), 507–521 (2001)

Lee, C.-P., Shim, J.P.: An Exploratory Study of Radio Frequency Identification (RFID) Adoption in the Healthcare Industry. European Journal of Information Systems (17), 712–724 (2007)

Li, S., Visich, J.K.: Radio Frequency Identification: Supply Chain Impact and Implementation Challenges. International Journal of Integrated Supply Management 2(4), 407–424 (2006)

Lindner, R.K.: Adoption and Diffusion of Technology: An Overview. Technological Change in Postharvest Handling and Transportation of Grains in the Humid Tropics, Canberra, Australian Centre for International Agricultural Research (1987)

Matta, V., Moberg, C.: The Development of a Research Agenda for RFID Adoption and Effectiveness in Supply Chains. Issues in Information Systems 7(2), 246–251 (2006)

Matta, V., Moberg, C.: Defining the Antecedents for Adoption of RFID in the Supply Chain. Issues in Information Systems 8(2), 449–453 (2007)

Oliver, R.L.: A Cognitive Model for the Antecedents and Consequences of Satisfaction Decisions. Journal of Marketing Research 17, 460–469 (1980)

Oliver, R.L.: Measurement and Evaluation of Satisfaction Process in Retail Settings. Journal of Retailing 57, 25–48 (1981)

Oliver, R.L., DeSarbo, W.S.: Response Determinants in Satisfaction Judgements. Journal of Consumer Research 14(4), 495–507 (1988)

Patent, K., Roe, B., Fluharty, F.: Awareness and Intended Compliance of Beef Cattle Exhibitors in the National Animal Identification System. Journal of Extension 44(5) (2006), http://www.joe.org/joe/2006october/rb7.php

Patterson, K.A., Grimm, C.M., Corsi, T.M.: Adopting New Technologies for Supply Chain Management. Transportation Research Part E: Logistics and Transportation Review 37(2), 95–121 (2003)

Quaddus, M., Hofmeyer, G.: An Investigation into the Factors Influencing the Adoption of B2B Trading Exchanges in Small Business. European Journal of Information Systems 16, 202–215 (2007)

Ranganathan, C., Jha, S.: Adoption of RFID Technology: An Exploratory Examination from Supplier's Perspective. In: Proceedings of the 11th Americas Conference on Information Systems, Omaha, Nebraska, August 11-14 (2005)

Rogers, E.M.: Diffusion of Innovation. Free Press, New York (1995)

Schmitt, P., Michaelles, F., Fleisch, E.: Why RFID Adoption and Diffusion Takes Time: The Role of Standards in the Automotive Industry. AUTO-ID Labs (2008), http://www.autoidlabs.org/single-view/dir/article/6/307/page.html (accessed November 11, 2009)

Schmitt, P., Thiesse, F., Fleisch, E.: Adoption and Diffusion of RFID Technology in the Automotive Industry. In: Proceedings of the 15th European Conference on Information Systems, St. Gallen, Switzerland (2007)

Scupola, A.: The Adoption of Internet Commerce by SMEs in the South of Italy: An Environmental, Technological and Organizational Perspective. Journal of Global Information Technology Management 6(1), 51–71 (2003)

Sharma, A., Citurs, A.: Radio Frequency Identification (RFID) Adoption Drivers: A Radical Innovation Adoption Process. In: Proceedings of the 11th Americas Conference on Information Systems, Omaha, Nebraska, August 11-14 (2005)

Sharma, A., Citurs, A., Konsynski, B.: Strategic and Institutional Perspectives in the Adoption and Early Integration of Radio Frequency Identification (RFID). In: Proceedings of the 40th Hawaii International Conference on System Sciences, Big Island, Hawaii, January 3-6. IEEE Computer Society, Los Alamitos (2007)

Sullivan, L.: RFID Technology Could Be Used to Build a National Livestock-Tracking System. Information Week, January 12 (2004), http://www.informationweek.com/news/management/showArticle.jhtml?articleID=17300330 (accessed November 11, 2009)

Tellkamp, C., Wiechert, T., Thiesse, F., Fleisch, E.: The Adoption of RFID-Based Self-Check-Out-Systems at the Point-of-Sale: An Empirical Investigation. In: Proceedings of the 6th International Federation for Information Processing Conference on e-Commerce, e-Business, and e-Government, Turku, Finland, pp. 153–165. Springer, Boston (2009)

Tonsor, G.T., Schroeder, T.C.: Livestock Identification: Lessons for the U.S. Beef Industry from the Australian System. Journal of International Food and Agribusiness Marketing 18(4), 103–118 (2006)

Tornatzky, L.G., Fleischer, M.: Process of Technological Innovation. Lexington Books, Lexington (1990)

Westbrook, R.A., Oliver, R.L.: Developing Better Measures of Consumer Satisfaction: Some Preliminary Results. Advances in Consumer Research 8(1), 94–99 (1981)

Xu, J., Quaddus, M.: Exploring the Factors Influencing End Users' Acceptance of Knowledge Management Systems: Development of a Research Model of Adoption and Continued Use. Journal of Organizational and End User Computing 19(4), 57–79 (2007)

Zhu, K., Kraemer, K., Xu, S.: Electronic Business Adoption by European Firms: A Cross-Country Assessment of the Facilitators and Inhibitors. European Journal of Information Systems 12(4), 251–268 (2003)

## About the Authors

**Mohammad Hossain** received a Bachelor of Science in Metallurgical Engineering from Bangladesh University of Engineering and Technology (BUET), a Master's in Advanced Engineering Management from BUET, and a Master's in e-Business from Edith Cowan University, Perth, Western Australia. He is currently working on his Ph.D. at Curtin University of Technology, Perth, Western Australia. Mohammad has varied work experience in engineering and IT administration and management in Australia and Bangladesh. His research interests are generally in the diffusion of IS/ICT, mathematical modeling, decision support systems, and electronic business and electronic commerce. Mohammad can be contacted at mohammad.hossain@postgrad.curtin.edu.au.

**Mohammed Quaddus** received his Ph.D. from the University of Pittsburgh, and an MS from the University of Pittsburgh and the Asian Institute of Technology. His research interests are in information and knowledge management, decision support systems, group decision and negotiation support systems, multiple criteria decision making, business research methods, and the theories and applications of innovation diffusion process. Mohammed has published in a number of journals and contributed to several books and monographs. In 1996 and 2005, he received the "Researcher of the Year" award from the Curtin Business School, Curtin University of Technology, Australia. Currently he is a professor in the Department of Information and Decision Systems with the Graduate School of Business, Curtin University of Technology, Australia. Prior to joining Curtin, he was with the University of Technology-Sydney and with National University of Singapore. He also spent a year at the Information Management Research Centre, Nanyang Technological University, Singapore, and six months with the Asian Institute of Technology, Bangkok, Thailand. Mohammed can be contacted at mohammed.quaddus@gsb.curtin.edu.au.

# Developing a Broadband Adoption Model in the UK Context

Yogesh K. Dwivedi[1], Navonil Mustafee[1], Michael D. Williams[1], and Banita Lal[2]

[1] School of Business & Economics,
Swansea University,
Swansea, United Kingdom
[2] Nottingham Business School,
Nottingham Trent University,
Nottingham, United Kingdom

**Abstract.** This research examines the factors affecting the consumer adoption of broadband in the United Kingdom. A conceptual model of broadband adoption was developed by selecting and justifying a number of relevant constructs from the technology adoption literature. The model was then empirically tested by employing survey data that was randomly collected from 358 UK broadband consumers. The findings suggest that, with the exception of one construct that was included in the conceptual model (namely, knowledge), all of the constructs significantly influence consumers when adopting broadband in a UK household. The significant constructs include relative advantage, utilitarian outcomes, hedonic outcomes, primary influence, facilitating conditions resources, and self-efficacy. Furthermore, when considering the behavioral intention and facilitating conditions resources constructs together, they significantly explain UK broad band adoption behavior. The theoretical contribution of this research is that it determines and integrates the appropriate constructs from the technology adoption literature in order to enhance the knowledge of technology adoption from the consumer's perspective. This research has implications for policy makers and broadband providers since the results of this study can be exploited by the aforementioned stakeholders in order to encourage and promote the adoption and usage of broadband among the general population.

**Keywords:** Broadband, adoption, consumer, TPB, DTPB, UK.

## 1 Introduction

Broadband offers several advantages to the public and to private sector organizations in terms of cost savings, efficiency, and competitiveness at a macro level (Oh et al. 2003; Sawyer et al. 2003). Broadband diffusion is regarded as a measure of international competitiveness (BSG 2004; Langdale 1997; Oh et al. 2003; Sawyer et al. 2003) and governments around the world have set ambitious targets for the deployment of broadband services (National Broadband Task Force 2001; Office of the e-Envoy 2001; Office of Technology Policy 2002). This is because a high

J. Pries-Heje et al. (Eds.): IS Design Science Research, IFIP AICT 318, pp. 192–208, 2010.

penetration rate of broadband is perceived to have a positive impact on the growth and development of the Internet, electronic commerce, and the information economy (Lee et al. 2003; Sawyer et al. 2003).

Broadband technologies can also improve the quality of life in various ways. For example, they facilitate home working/telecommuting (Suomi and Pekkola 1998), thereby contributing to flexibility of life style for individuals, permitting space savings for organizations, and helping to decrease carbon footprints by reducing travel between home and the workplace. Similarly, broadband is essential to implement telemedicine-enabled health service delivery, particularly for older people and for dispersed populations located in remote areas. Yet another important use of the technology is support for e-Learning and distance learning. e-Learning both complements face-to-face classroom education with computer-aided teaching (so called *blended learning*), and enables those who are unable to attend a formal educational environment (e.g., people in remote areas) to learn and gain knowledge by accessing online resources through an Internet connection (distance learning). Many governments have realized the potential of broadband technologies and have made available an increasing number of government services for citizens to access online. Broadband can be utilized by household consumers/users in various other ways and the reader is referred to Dwivedi et al. (2006a) for further examples.

Governments in a number of countries, including South Korea, Japan, Hong Kong, Sweden, Australia, Canada, the United Kingdom, and the United States, have made large investments for developing a broadband infrastructure that will deliver high-speed Internet access to end users, including household consumers and small and medium enterprises (BSG 2004; OECD 2001; Oh et al. 2003; Sawyer et al. 2003). In recent times, some of these broadband pioneers have rejuvenated their efforts to provide broadband access to all citizens. For example, the USA has formulated the National Broadband Plan that "shall seek to ensure that all people of the United States have access to broadband capability."[1] Similarly, the prime minister of Australia has announced plans to build a new national broadband network that will aim to reach 90 percent of Australian households at a cost of $30 billion (Radio Australia News[2]). Such initiatives indicate that the development, deployment, and diffusion of broadband infrastructure and technologies requires continued and long-term planning and strategic thinking.

Although broadband offers several benefits for both individual consumers and businesses (some of these benefits being mentioned earlier), in many countries its demand has not increased in line with expectation. Previous studies have argued that the provision of broadband is more "demand constrained" than "supply constrained" (Crabtree 2003; Oh et al. 2003; Stanton 2004). Thus it may be argued that in order to enhance the widespread adoption and use of broadband, it is essential to focus on understanding the factors influencing the decisions of household consumers. Previous research undertaken on the adoption of technology (e.g., adoption of personal computers by residential consumers) has also emphasized the role of the demand perspective (see, for instance, Venkatesh and Brown 2001). Similarly, initial studies on consumer adoption of broadband have also argued the issue of demand constraint,

---

[1] http://www.broadband.gov
[2] http://www.radioaustralianews.net.au/stories/200904/2538028.htm

and these studies have attempted to study consumer attitude and behavior toward broadband adoption. Some of these studies are briefly described here. An initial study by Oh et al. (2003) examined individual-level factors affecting the adoption of broadband access in South Korea by combining factors taken from Rogers' (1995) diffusion theory and the technology acceptance model (Davis 1989; Davis et al. 1989). The findings of this study suggest that congruent experiences and opportunities in adopting a new technology affect user attitudes through the three extended technology acceptance model constructs; namely, *perceived usefulness, perceived ease of use*, and *perceived resources* (Oh et al. 2003). Stanton (2004) analyzed the secondary data pertaining to U.S. broadband consumers with the objective of studying the digital divide. This study highlighted an urgent need to better understand the demography and other factors of broadband adopters and non-adopters in order to increase the growth rate of broadband and to bridge the digital divide. The research presented in this paper forms a part of a larger project; some of the findings having already been published (see Choudrie and Dwivedi 2005, 2006, 2007; Dwivedi and Irani 2009; Dwivedi et al. 2006a; Irani et al. 2009). However, the initial studies resulting from this project had several limitations; they either adopted a parsimonious theoretical framework to analyze and interpret the data (Irani et al. 2009) or they were of an overly descriptive nature (Dwivedi and Irani 2009). With the objective of overcoming these limitations, this paper adopts a broad theoretical framework by integrating constructs (see section two) from dominant theories and models and then utilizes statistical techniques including factor analysis, regression analysis, and logistic regression analysis to measure the influence of independent variables on dependent variables.

Bearing the aforementioned discussion in mind, the aim of this study is to *investigate factors affecting the consumer adoption of broadband in the UK context*. The aim has been achieved by developing a conceptual model by identifying and integrating constructs from extant literature on IT/IS adoption and validating/testing it by utilizing empirical data. The remainder of the paper is structured as follows. The next section briefly describes the proposed conceptual model. Section three discusses the research methodology. The findings are presented in section four while the conclusions and implications of the work are discussed in section five.

## 2   A Conceptual Model of Broadband Adoption

Our proposed conceptual model of broadband adoption (Figure 1) is based on the underlying principle of the decomposed theory of planned behavior (DTPB) and utilizes constructs from the model of adoption of technology in households (MATCH) and diffusion of innovation (DoI) theory. In keeping with the works of Ajzen (1991), Rogers (1995), Taylor and Todd (1995), and Venkatesh and Brown (2001) among others, our proposed adoption model postulates that *behavioral intentions* (BI) to adopt broadband are determined by the following three forms of construct: (1) **attitudinal constructs** (*relative advantage, utilitarian outcomes*, and *hedonic outcomes*) that represent consumers' favorable or unfavorable evaluation of the behavior in question (in this case, adoption of broadband); (2) **normative constructs** (*primary influence* and *secondary influence*) that represent perceived social pressure to perform the behavior in question (i.e., adoption of broadband); (3) **control constructs** (*knowledge, self-efficacy,* and *facilitating conditions resources*) that represent perceived control over personal or external factors that may facilitate or constrain behavioral performance. The predictor variables from the aforementioned three categories are expected to determine and explain the BI to adopt broadband, which in turn is expected to predict actual *broadband adoption behavior* (BAB). The proposed model also includes two independent constructs, namely *service quality* and *secondary influence*, that examine sustained adoption of broadband. Figure 1 illustrates the relationship between independent and dependent constructs (readers should note that word limits preclude the description and justification of each individual construct).

## 3   Research Methodology

The survey research method, employing self-administered questionnaires, is considered an appropriate method to examine the adoption of broadband. The empirical data for this study was randomly collected from citizens of the UK by utilizing "UK-Info Disk V11" as a sampling frame. The structure of the sampling frame necessitated the adoption of the stratified random sampling approach for selection of respondents.

Development of the survey instrument comprised three stages: exploratory survey, content validity testing, and instrument testing. The development and validation of the survey instrument, together with a full discussion of the results of the three aforementioned stages, is reported in Dwivedi et al. (2006b). The final questionnaire used in this research consisted of 17 questions. These questions were divided into two categories: (1) *multiple-choice questions* addressing socio-economic characteristics such as age, gender, education, occupation and income, and type of Internet connections the respondents had access to at home, and (2) *seven-point Likert scale questions* addressing issues relating to the attitudinal, normative and control factors of broadband adoption. See Dwivedi et al. (2006b) for the list of constructs and corresponding Likert scale items utilized in this study.

Being mindful of the statistical analysis plan, it was decided that the total sample size should be large enough to obtain a minimum of 300 responses. A sample size of 1,500 was estimated to achieve 300 responses. To compensate for any shortfalls in the 300 responses that may occur due to undelivered and partially completed responses, the sample size was duly increased from 1,500 to 1,600. Thus, a total sample size of 1,600 was considered for this study. In the period between January 2005 and March 2005, a questionnaire pack consisting of a cover letter, a copy of the survey instrument, and a self-addressed prepaid return envelope was posted to a total of 1,600 household consumers in the UK.

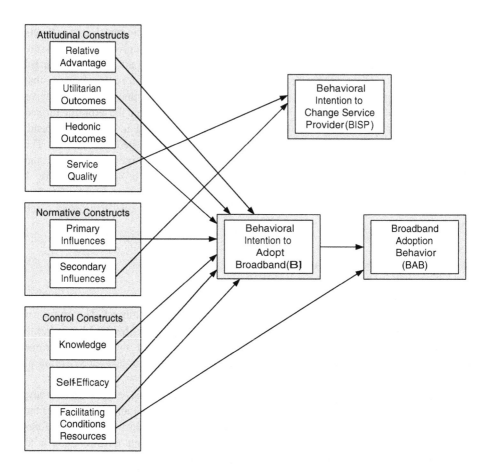

**Fig. 1. Conceptual Model of Broadband Adoption (MBA)** (Adapted from Ajzen 1991, Rogers 1995, Taylor and Todd 1995, and Venkatesh and Brown 2001)

**Table 1.** *t* -Test to Examine Non-Response Bias

| Variables | t | df | p |
|---|---|---|---|
| Age | .766 | 355 | .444 |
| Gender | .557 | 353 | .578 |
| Internet access at home | .646 | 356 | .519 |
| Type of connection | -1.609 | 306 | .109 |

From the total of 1,600 questionnaires distributed, 300 replies were received within the specified period (January 2005 to March 2005). Of these, 280 questionnaires were usable with the remaining 20 being incomplete, providing a response rate of 17.5 percent. In order to test the non-response bias (Fowler 2002), an additional 200 questionnaires were sent to randomly selected non-respondents from the original sample in mid-March 2005. Of these, 40 replies were received, 38 of which were usable with two being partially completed. Findings obtained from the non-response bias test are illustrated in Table 1. Data presented in Table 1 reveals that there were no significant differences in the number of demographic variables between the original respondents and a sample of non-respondents. Responses received from non-respondents were added to the original responses. It should be further noted that since no substantial changes were made to the final questionnaire after the pilot, it was decided to include pilot responses in the main study. This approach has been followed by other studies (for example, Fowler 2002). Thus, the total number of responses included in the final analysis was 358.

The data collected was subjected to the following statistical tests. Factor analysis and reliability tests were employed to examine construct validity and internal consistency of the survey instrument. In order to explain the relationship between independent and dependent variables, linear regression analysis and logistic regression analysis were utilized. Logistic regression analysis was also employed in this work to explain the relationship between aggregate measure of independent variables (i.e., behavioral intention and facilitating conditions resources) and the categorical dependent variable (i.e., broadband adoption).

## 4 Research Findings

### 4.1 Respondents' Profile

A profile of the survey respondents is presented in Table 2. Of the 358 responses, 26.1 percent of respondents belonged to the 25 to 34 years age group which formed the largest response category. The category with the least number of responses was the 65 years and above age group with 3.9 percent. In terms of gender, the break was 51 percent males and 49 percent females. The majority of respondents possessed educational qualifications, with 34.6 percent having gained an undergraduate degree and 29.3 percent educated to postgraduate level. The educational category with the least number of responses was the GNVQ/diploma group, with an 8.8 percent response rate. Of the 358 respondents, 308 (86 percent) had Internet access at home, the remaining 50 (14 percent) respondents did not have any Internet connectivity. Of the 308 respondents who possessed Internet access at home, 101 (32.8 percent) had a narrowband connection and the remaining 207 (67.2 percent) respondents had a broadband connection.

### 4.2 Reliability of the Measurement

Before presenting the findings, the research instrument was tested for reliability and construct validity. Table 3 illustrates the Cronbach's coefficient alpha values that were obtained to examine internal consistency. Cronbach's α varied between 0.91 for the utilitarian construct and 0.79 for the two constructs *hedonic outcomes* and *service quality*. Following Hinton et al.'s (2004) suggestion for cut-off points for reliability, it can be seen from Table 3 that of the seven constructs, two possess excellent

**Table 2.** Profile of Survey Participants

| Variable Category | Percent | Variable Category | Percent |
|---|---|---|---|
| Age | | Occupation* | |
| ≤ 24 | 21.0 | A | 10.6 |
| 25–34 | 26.1 | B | 27.4 |
| 35–44 | 21.6 | C1 | 19.0 |
| 45–54 | 19.0 | C2 | 2.0 |
| 55–64 | 8.4 | D | 1.7 |
| ≥ 65 | 3.9 | Others | 41.0 |
| Gender | | Annual Income | |
| Male | 50.6 | ≤ 10 K | 9.2 |
| Female | 48.6 | 10–19 K | 16.8 |
| Education | | 20–29 K | 17.3 |
| GCSC (O Level/High School) | 11.2 | 30–39 K | 16.8 |
| GNQV | 8.4 | 40–49 K | 10.6 |
| A Level (10+2/Intermediate) | 14.8 | 50–59 K | 7.0 |
| Degree (B.Sc./BA) | 33.0 | 60–69 K | 9.2 |
| PG (M.Sc./MA/Ph.D.) | 27.9 | ≥ 70 K | 10.1 |
| Internet Access at Home | | Type of connection at Home | |
| Yes | 86.0 | Narrowband | 28.2 |
| No | 14.0 | Broadband | 57.8 |

*Mainstream professionals such as doctors, lawyers, and judges with responsibility for 25 or more staff members belonged to social class "A," with the same occupations with responsibility for fewer than 25 staff, along with academics, being grouped into social class "B." Skilled, non-manual workers were categorized as social class "C1" and social class "C2," with unskilled manual workers belonging to social class "D." Respondents from the "other" category were unemployed and students.

**Table 3.** Reliability of Measurements

| Constructs | N | Number of Items | Cronbach's Alpha (α) | Type |
|---|---|---|---|---|
| Behavioral Intention (BI) | 358 | 2 | .8790 | High Reliability |
| BISP | 308 | 1 | — | — |
| Relative Advantage (RA) | 358 | 4 | .8481 | High Reliability |
| Utilitarian Outcomes (UO) | 358 | 10 | .9131 | **Excellent Reliability** |
| Hedonic Outcomes (HO) | 358 | 4 | .7968 | High Reliability |
| Service Quality (SQ) | 308 | 4 | .7912 | High Reliability |
| Primary Influence (PI) | 358 | 3 | .8420 | High Reliability |
| Secondary Influence (SI) | 358 | 2 | .9034 | **Excellent Reliability** |
| Facilitating Conditions Resources (FCR) | 358 | 4 | .8114 | High Reliability |
| Knowledge (K) | 358 | 3 | .8193 | High Reliability |
| Self-efficacy (SE) | 358 | 3 | .9026 | **Excellent Reliability** |
| LEGEND: BISP = Behavioral Intention to change Service Provider; N = Sample Size | | | | |

**Table 4.** Factor Analysis: Rotated Component Matrix

| Items | Component | | | | | | | | |
|---|---|---|---|---|---|---|---|---|---|
| | 1(UO) | 2 (FCR) | 3 (SQ) | 4 (RA) | 5 (SE) | 6 (HO) | 7 (PI) | 8 (K) | 9 (SI) |
| UO1 | **.788** | .094 | .102 | .041 | .070 | .025 | .087 | -.021 | -.069 |
| UO6 | **.783** | .116 | .060 | .095 | .086 | .057 | -.016 | .136 | -.051 |
| UO8 | **.758** | .106 | .054 | .053 | .035 | .062 | .121 | -.038 | .093 |
| UO5 | **.740** | .079 | .025 | .041 | .070 | .146 | -.034 | .077 | .118 |
| UO4 | **.682** | .121 | .094 | .194 | .027 | .084 | .041 | .153 | .014 |
| UO2 | **.679** | .041 | .028 | .107 | .019 | -.071 | .079 | .174 | .168 |
| UO3 | **.663** | .124 | .035 | .188 | .261 | .096 | .132 | .028 | -.063 |
| UO10 | **.564** | .240 | .179 | .347 | .143 | .100 | .227 | .184 | -.006 |
| UO7 | **.520** | -.002 | -.078 | .368 | .169 | -.038 | .134 | .109 | .021 |
| UO9 | **.519** | .309 | .139 | .246 | .058 | .021 | .227 | .227 | .096 |
| FCR3 | .171 | **.780** | .190 | .079 | .130 | .103 | .024 | .022 | .020 |
| FCR1 | .133 | **.768** | .133 | .073 | .228 | -.037 | .084 | .201 | .020 |
| FCR4 | .107 | **.687** | .029 | .056 | .238 | -.026 | .067 | .212 | .102 |
| FCR2 | .234 | **.649** | .016 | .206 | -.089 | .058 | .042 | -.016 | -.070 |
| SQ4 | .087 | .068 | **.858** | .053 | .134 | .017 | .041 | .014 | -.048 |
| SQ1 | .057 | .132 | **.794** | .063 | -.083 | .024 | .011 | .024 | .007 |
| SQ3 | .041 | .017 | **.769** | .013 | .225 | .068 | .183 | .094 | .032 |
| SQ2 | .111 | .081 | **.650** | -.047 | -.027 | .089 | .097 | .038 | .102 |
| RA4 | .137 | .153 | .038 | **.728** | .125 | .022 | .001 | -.073 | .105 |
| RA2 | .197 | .124 | .053 | **.706** | .129 | .118 | .017 | .308 | .022 |
| RA1 | .222 | .026 | -.039 | **.683** | .165 | -.054 | .048 | .256 | .017 |
| RA3 | .373 | .175 | .054 | **.589** | .112 | .022 | -.013 | .196 | -.080 |
| SE2 | .120 | .115 | .095 | .117 | **.844** | .055 | -.035 | .178 | .003 |
| SE3 | .230 | .188 | .088 | .179 | **.795** | .013 | .016 | .262 | .032 |
| SE1 | .172 | .183 | .045 | .241 | **.771** | -.005 | .095 | .139 | -.023 |
| HO2 | .048 | .010 | .024 | .135 | .099 | **.853** | .111 | -.063 | -.011 |
| HO3 | .081 | .030 | .109 | -.151 | -.049 | **.793** | .133 | .099 | .135 |
| HO1 | .226 | .090 | .038 | .116 | .148 | **.767** | .187 | -.057 | .047 |
| HO4 | -.028 | -.013 | .060 | -.015 | -.138 | **.600** | -.055 | .208 | .268 |
| PI1 | .092 | -.010 | .093 | .036 | .005 | .132 | **.897** | .063 | .108 |
| PI2 | .123 | .067 | .065 | -.017 | .058 | .163 | **.864** | .015 | .117 |
| PI3 | .298 | .216 | .271 | .077 | -.008 | .064 | **.654** | .033 | .036 |
| K3 | .215 | .123 | .115 | .255 | .192 | .054 | .011 | **.758** | -.021 |
| K2 | .182 | .064 | .067 | .163 | .311 | .020 | -.025 | **.754** | -.010 |
| K1 | .173 | .314 | .015 | .147 | .130 | .108 | .177 | **.615** | .033 |
| SI1 | .065 | .034 | .034 | .112 | .011 | .143 | .160 | -.049 | **.910** |
| SI2 | .108 | .026 | .061 | -.021 | .005 | .193 | .091 | .039 | **.903** |

**Extraction Method**: principal component analysis.
Rotation Method: Varimax with Kaiser normalization.

reliability and the remaining five illustrate high reliability. High Cronbach's α values for all constructs imply that the measures are internally consistent. This in turn suggests that all items of each of the constructs are measuring the same content universe (i.e., construct).

### 4.3 Construct Validity Using Factor Analysis

In order to verify the construct validity (convergent and discriminant validity), a factor analysis was conducted utilizing principal component analysis (PCA) with Varimax as an extraction method, and Kaiser normalization as a rotation method. The results of the PCA are presented in Table 4. All constructs had Eigenvalues greater than one and in combination accounted for a total of 67.13 percent variance in data. The rotated component matrix presented in Table 4 shows the factor loadings for all nine independent constructs, which clearly suggest that the nine components are loaded. All items loaded above 0.40, which is the minimum recommended value in IS research (Straub et al. 2004). Also, cross loading of the items was not found above 0.40. The aforementioned description suggests that the items were properly loaded on each factor, as was expected. The factor analysis results satisfied the criteria of construct validity including both the discriminant validity (loading of at least 0.40, no cross-loading of items above 0.40) and convergent validity (Eigenvalues of 1, loading of at least 0.40, items that load on posited constructs) (Straub et al. 2004, p. 410). This confirms construct validity (both discriminant validity and convergent validity) in the instrument measures utilized for data collection in this research. This suggests that the data collected and findings obtained from this instrument are reliable.

### 4.4 Regression Analysis

A regression analysis was performed with *behavioral intention (BI)* as the dependent variable and *relative advantage (RA), utilitarian outcomes (UO), hedonic outcomes (HO), primary influence (PI), facilitating conditions resources (FCR), knowledge (K), and self-efficacy (SE)* as the predictor variables. A total of 358 cases were analyzed. From the analysis, a significant model emerged ($F$ (7, 358) = 40.576, $p < 0.001$) with the adjusted R square being 0.437. Significant variables include $FCR$ ($\beta$ = .169, $p < .001$), $HO$ ($\beta$ = .094, $p = .027$), $PI$ ($\beta$ = .196, $p < .001$), $SE$ ($\beta$ = .139, $p = .005$), and $RA$ ($\beta$ = .230, $p < .001$). $K$ ($\beta$ = .086, $p = .121$) and $UO$ ($\beta$ = .098, $p = .072$) were not considered to be significant predictors in this model. The $p$ value of the $UO$ construct was close to the significance level but for the $K$ construct it was not. Therefore, it was decided to undertake another regression analysis cycle, keeping the other settings as above but removing the $K$ construct from the predictors list. In the second regression cycle, the number of predictor variables was reduced to six, with *knowledge (K)* being eliminated from the list. A total of 358 cases were analyzed. From the analysis, a significant model emerged ($F$ (6, 358) = 46.749, $p < .001$). The adjusted R square was 0.435. This time all six, including the *utilitarian outcomes (UO)* predictor variables, were found to be significant. These include $FCR$ ($\beta$ = .169, $p < .001$), $HO$ ($\beta$ = .100, $p = .018$), $PI$ ($\beta$ = .195, $p < .001$), $SE$ ($\beta$ = .165, $p < .001$), $RA$ ($\beta$ = .255, $p < .001$), and $UO$ ($\beta$ = .113, $p = .035$).

As illustrated in Table 5, the constructs are arranged according to their size of β values in decreasing order. The size of β suggests that *RA* construct has the largest impact in the explanation of variations of *BI*. This is followed by the *PI* construct and then *FCR*. This suggests that the three constructs that have the largest impact in explaining variance of *BI* belong to all three categories (i.e., attitudinal, normative, and control constructs).

When performing a regression analysis, an important cause of concern is the existence of multicolinearity amongst independent variables such as *RA*, *PI*, *FCR*, *SE*, *UO*, and *HO*. It is likely to exist when the independent variables included in the analysis are not truly independent and measure redundant information (Myers 1990). SPSS provides two options to estimate the tolerance and variance inflation factor (VIF) to trace if data suffers with the problem of multicolinearity (Brace et al. 2003; Myers 1990). In order to detect multicolinearity in this research, both VIF and tolerance estimated are shown in Table 5. Values obtained for both VIF and tolerance indicate that multicolinearity was not a problem in this work. Table 5 illustrates that the VIF for this model varied between 1.80 for *PI* constructs and 1.12 for *HO* constructs, which is within recommended levels (Brace et al. 2003; Myers 1990; Stevens 1996).

**Table 5.** Regression Analysis: Coefficients[†]

| | Unstandardized Coefficients | | Standardized Coefficients | | | | Colinearity Statistics | |
|---|---|---|---|---|---|---|---|---|
| | B | Std. Error | β | t | p | Partial Correlations | Tolerance | VIF |
| (Constant) | -.904 | .432 | | -2.093 | .037 | | | |
| RA | .384 | .077 | .255 | 4.962 | .000 | .256 | .601 | 1.664 |
| PI | .196 | .045 | .195 | 4.362 | .000 | .227 | .789 | 1.267 |
| FCR | .191 | .049 | .180 | 3.916 | .000 | .205 | .749 | 1.335 |
| SE | .206 | .058 | .165 | 3.582 | .000 | .188 | .742 | 1.347 |
| UO | .153 | .072 | .113 | 2.116 | .035 | .112 | .555 | 1.801 |
| HO | .097 | .041 | .100 | 2.382 | .018 | .126 | .890 | 1.124 |

[†]Dependent Variable: BI

### 4.5  Logistic Regression Analysis

A logistic regression analysis was performed with broadband adoption as the dependent variable and *BI* and *FCR* as the predictor variables. A total of 358 cases were analyzed and the full model was considered to be significantly reliable ($\chi^2$ (2, $N = 358$) = 128.559, $p < .001$). This model accounted for between 30.2 percent and 40.6 percent of the variance in broadband adoption (Table 6), with 88.4 percent of broadband adopters being successfully predicted. However, only 58.9 percent of predictions for non-adopters were accurate. Overall, 76.0 percent of predictions were accurate.

Table 7 illustrates coefficients, Wald statistics, associated degrees of freedom, and probability values for each of the predictor variables. This reveals that both *BI* and *FCR* constructs reliably predicted broadband adoption. Values of the coefficients suggest that each unit increases in *BI* and the *FCR* score is associated with an increase in the odds of broadband adoption by a factor of 2.50 and 1.58 respectively (Table 7). This means that *BI* has a larger part in explaining actual adoption than *FCR*.

## 4.6 The Relationship between Service Quality (SQ), Secondary Influence (SI) and Behavioral Intention to Change Service Provider (BISP)

A further regression analysis was conducted with *BISP* as the dependent variable and *SI and SQ* as predictor variables. A total of 308 cases were analyzed. From the analysis, a significant model emerged ($F$ (2, 308) = 13.239, $p < .001$), with an adjusted R square of 0.074. Both predictor variables were found to be significant (Table 8): *SI* ($\beta = .153$  $p = .006$) and *SQ* ($\beta = -.255$, $p < .001$). Thus *SQ* is negatively correlated with *BISP*, which indicates that the lower the quality of the service provided, the higher the chance that consumers will change service providers. However, it is important to note that since the adjusted R square is very low, *SQ* and *SI* have limited explanatory prowess in terms of variation in *BISP*, which in turns indicates the possibility of other constructs that should be reexamined in the context of continued adoption of broadband.

**Table 6.** Logistic Regression: Model Summary

| Step | Cox & Snell R$^2$ | Nagelkerke R$^2$ |
|------|-------------------|------------------|
| 1    | .302              | .406             |

**Table 7.** Logistic Regression:  Variables in the Equation

|  |  | B | S.E. | Wald | df | p | Exp (B) |
|---|---|---|------|------|----|----|---------|
| Step 1[†] | BI | .916 | .141 | 42.021 | 1 | .000 | 2.500 |
|  | FCR | .455 | .109 | 17.471 | 1 | .000 | 1.576 |
|  | Constant | -7.529 | .954 | 62.222 | 1 | .000 | .001 |
| [†]Variable(s) entered on step 1:  BI, FCR. | | | | | | | |

**Table 8.** Regression Analysis: Coefficients[†]

| Model | Predictors | Un standardized Coefficients | | Standardized Coefficients | t | p |
|-------|-----------|------|-----------|-----|--------|------|
|  |  | B | Std.  Error | β |  |  |
| 1 | (Constant) | 4.495 | .415 |  | 10.843 | .000 |
|  | SQ | -.359 | .078 | -.255 | -4.619 | .000 |
|  | SI | .166 | .060 | .153 | 2.774 | .006 |
| [†]Dependent Variable:  *BISP* | | | | | | |

Table 5 suggest that the paths from relative advantage, *UO* and *HO* toward the *behavioral intention (BI)* to adopt broadband are significant. Consistent with the proposed model, the fourth attitudinal construct *(SQ)* significantly explained the *BISP*. As was expected, the path from *PI* to *BI* is significant. The second normative construct (*SI*) is significantly related to *BISP*. Of the three control constructs, two (*SE* and *FCR*) are significantly related to *BI*. However, the path from the third control construct (*K*) to *BI* is not significant. Finally, both *BI* and *FCR* are significant determinants of the actual behavior of adopting broadband.

It is not possible to directly compare the predictability of our broadband adoption model with the study by Oh et al. (2003) as both studies examined different independent and dependent constructs. For instance, this study employed *BI* and actual behavior as dependent constructs, but in Oh et al.'s study the dependent construct was attitude. However, the predictive power of our broadband adoption model can be compared to models such as TAM, TPB, and DTPB as the behavior and structure of our broadband adoption model are similar to TAM, TPB, and DTPB. Table 9 illustrates the comparison of previous studies for the adjusted $R^2$ obtained for both Behavioral intention and actual behavior. The comparison clearly demonstrates that the broadband adoption model performed well when compared to previous studies.

Table 9 illustrates that the *BI* value of the adjusted $R^2$ varied between 0.20 (Gefen and Straub 2000) and 0.57 (Taylor and Todd 1995), with the adjusted $R^2$ for this study being 0.43, which suggests an appropriate level of explained variance. This suggests that the independent variables considered in this study are important for understanding consumers' Behavioral intention to adopt broadband. In terms of behavior, the adjusted $R^2$ reported in previous studies varied between 0.32 (Davis et al. 1989) and 0.51 (Davis 1989). Since the adjusted $R^2$ value in this study for variance in behavior was 0.40, it falls within the range of previous works.

**Table 9.** Comparison of Intention and Behavior in Terms of Adjusted $R^2$

| Study | Theory | Adjusted R2 | |
|---|---|---|---|
| | | Behavioral Intention | Behavior |
| Davis et al. (1989) | TAM | — | 0.45 |
| Davis et al. (1989) | TRA | — | 0.32 |
| Davis (1989) | TAM | — | 0.51 |
| Taylor and Todd (1995) | DTP | 0.57 | 0.34 |
| Taylor and Todd (1995) | TPB | 0.57 | 0.34 |
| Taylor and Todd (1995) | TAM | 0.52 | 0.34 |
| Karahanna et al. (1999) | TRA + TAM | 0.38 | — |
| Agarwal and Karahanna (2000) | TAM & Cognitive Absorption | 0.50 | — |
| Gefen and Straub (2000) | TAM | 0.20 | — |
| Brown et al. (2002) | TAM | 0.52 | — |
| Koufaris (2002) | TAM + Flow Theory | 0.54 | — |
| **This Study** | **TPB + DTPB + MATH** | **0.43** | **0.40** |
| **Recommended level (Straub et al. 2004)** | **—** | **0.40 or above** | **0.40 or above** |

# 5  Conclusions and Implications

A total of seven constructs from attitudinal (*relative advantage, utilitarian outcomes, and hedonic outcomes*), normative (*primary influence*) and control (*knowledge, self-efficacy, and facilitating conditions resources*) categories were expected to influence *behavioral intention* (*BI*) of consumers when adopting broadband in the UK household. Our study revealed that all of the aforementioned constructs except knowledge significantly influenced the *BI* of UK consumers when adopting broadband. In terms of the size of the effect of these significant constructs *relative advantage* exhibited the largest and *hedonic outcomes* the least variance of *BI*. *Primary influence* explained the second largest variance, which was followed by *facilitating conditions resources*. The fourth strongest construct was *self-efficacy*, and the fifth was *utilitarian outcomes*. Both *BI* and the control construct appear to significantly influence broadband adoption behavior in UK households. In terms of the relative impact of the two aforementioned constructs that contributed significantly to the *broadband adoption behavior* (*BAB*), BI had much higher impacts than the control construct.

## 5.1  Contributions to Theory

The first contribution of this research toward theory is that it integrates the appropriate IS literature in order to enhance the knowledge of IT/IS adoption from the consumer perspective. That is, it assimilates previous research findings to develop a coherent and comprehensive picture of the technology adoption research conducted in the IS field.  By doing so, this work introduces a *conceptual model of broadband adoption* that integrates factors from different technology adoption models with the objective of studying technology diffusion in the home environment from a consumer's perspective. The second contribution is to empirically confirm the appropriateness of various constructs and validate the conceptual model in the context of household consumers. Considering the above points, this study has made distinct contributions to the area of technology adoption and diffusion in general and broadband adoption in particular.

## 5.2  Implications for the Industry and Policy

It was found that *relative advantage* was most important and *hedonic outcomes* least important in terms of influencing *behavioral intention* when adopting broadband in UK households. Other important constructs that fall within these two extremes were *primary influence, facilitating conditions resources, self-efficacy*, and *utilitarian outcomes*. The findings of this research raise a number of issues that may assist both policy makers and ISPs for understanding consumer adoption of broadband. For example, since *relative advantage* is found to be the most influential construct, it indicates that ISPs have to provide broadband services to consumers by offering a package that demonstrates clear advantage over narrowband facilities or existing broadband arrangements. *Facilitating conditions resources* is the third most important factor in terms of influencing *BI* to adopt broadband. This has implications for both ISPs and policy makers as, for instance, ISPs need to think about more consumer-centric services and alternative price plans so that all consumers who want to subscribe to broadband are able to do so. Policy makers have to provide alternative places for broadband access where lower income groups or those who cannot afford it can use it, as this may help increase Behavioral intention to adopt broadband and therefore encourage overall adoption and diffusion of broadband. As mentioned above, *self-efficacy* is also an important influencing factor which touches upon policy-related issues, suggesting that there is a need to equip citizens with the skills required to use computers and the Internet. Since both *utilitarian outcomes* and *hedonic outcomes* are important factors for explaining Behavioral intentions, it is important to provide more content and applications for the purpose of household utility and entertainment.

### 5.3   Research Limitations and Future Research Directions

This study provides a snapshot of adoption of broadband in UK households. The findings may change as the technology becomes established, and as consumers become more experienced in its use. The findings would also have been reinforced had the research been longitudinal. Our study employed a quantitative approach, and we acknowledge that this may have limited the ability to obtain an in-depth view of household technology adoption. The questionnaire findings would have been strengthened had they been supplemented by interview data; however, time and resource restrictions dictated that it was not possible to conduct both qualitative and quantitative investigations. With regard to broadband adoption in the future, we intend to examine whether the findings from this study are specific to UK consumers or whether the results will be transportable to other countries, particularly in developing nations where broadband adoption is still at an embryonic stage.

# References

Agarwal, R., Karahanna, E.: Time Flies When You're Having Fun: Cognitive Absorption and Beliefs about Information Technology Usage. MIS Quarterly 24(4), 665–694 (2000)

Ajzen, I.: The Theory of Planned Behavior. Organizational Behavior and Human Decision Processes 50, 179–211 (1991)

Brace, N., Kemp, R., Snelgar, R.: SPSS for Psychologists: A Guide to Data Analysis Using SPSS for Windows. Palgrave Macmillan, New York (2003)

Brown, S.A., Massey, A.P., Montoya-Weiss, M.M., Burkman, J.R.: Do I Really Have To? User Acceptance of Mandated Technology. European Journal of Information Systems 11(4), 267–282 (2002)

BSG Briefing Paper. The Impact of Broadband-Enabled ICT, Content, Applications and Services on the UK Economy and Society to 2010, London (2004), http://www.broadbanduk.org/news/news_pdfs/Sept%202004/ BSG_Phase_2_BB_Impact_BackgroundPaper_Sept041.pdf (accessed October 30, 2004)

Choudrie, J., Dwivedi, Y.K.: The Demographics of Broadband Residential Consumers of a British Local Community: The London Borough of Hillingdon. Journal of Computer Information Systems 45(4), 93–101 (2005)

Choudrie, J., Dwivedi, Y.K.: Investigating Factors Influencing Adoption of Broadband in the Household. Journal of Computer Information Systems 46(4), 25–34 (2006)

Choudrie, J., Dwivedi, Y.K.: Broadband Impact on Household Consumers: Online Habits and Time Allocation Patterns on Daily Life Activities. International Journal of Mobile Communications 5(2), 225–241 (2007)

Crabtree, J.: Fat Pipes, Connected People—Rethinking Broadband Britain. iSOCIETY Report, London (2003), http://www.theworkfoundation.com/pdf/1843730146.pdf (accessed March 30, 2004)

Davis, F.D.: Perceived Usefulness, Perceived Ease of Use, and User Acceptance of Information Technology. MIS Quarterly 13(3), 319–340 (1989)

Davis, F.D., Bagozzi, R.P., Warshaw, P.R.: User Acceptance of Computer Technology: A Comparison of Two Theoretical Models. Management Science 35(8), 982–1003 (1989)

Dwivedi, Y.K., Irani, Z.: Understanding the Adopters and Non-adopters of Broadband. Communications of the ACM 52(1), 122–125 (2009)

Dwivedi, Y.K., Choudrie, J., Brinkman, W.P.: Consumer Usage of Broadband in British Households. International Journal of Services and Standards 2(4), 400–416 (2006a)

Dwivedi, Y.K., Choudrie, J., Brinkman, W.P.: Development of a Survey Instrument to Examine Consumer Adoption of Broadband. Industrial Management and Data Systems 106(5), 700–718 (2006b)

Fowler Jr., F.J.: Survey Research Methods. SAGE Publications Inc., London (2002)

Gefen, D., Straub, D.W.: The Relative Importance of Perceived Ease of Use in IS Adoption: A Study of E-Commerce Adoption. Journal of the Association for Information Systems (1), 1–28 (2000)

Hinton, P.R., Brownlow, C., McMurray, I., Cozens, B.: SPSS Explained. Routledge Inc., East Sussex (2004)

Irani, Z., Dwivedi, Y.K., Williams, M.D.: Understanding Consumer Adoption of Broadband: An Extension of Technology Acceptance Model. Journal of Operational Research Society 60(10), 1322–1334 (2009)

Karahanna, E., Straub, D.W., Chervany, N.L.: Information Technology Adoption Across Time: A Cross-Sectional Comparison of Pre-Adoption and Post-Adoption Beliefs. MIS Quarterly 23(2), 183–213 (1999)

Koufaris, M.: Applying the Technology Acceptance Model and Flow Theory to Online Consumer Behavior. Information Systems Research 13(2), 205–223 (2002)

Langdale, J.V.: International Competitiveness in East Asia: Broadband Telecommunications and Interactive Multimedia. Telecommunications Policy 21, 235–249 (1997)

Lee, H., O'Keefe, B., Yun, K.: The Growth of Broadband and Electronic Commerce in South Korea: Contributing Factors. The Information Society 19, 81–93 (2003)

Myers, R.H.: Classical and Modern Regression with Applications. PWS-KENT Publishing Company, Boston (1990)

National Broadband Task Force, The New National Dream: Networking the Nation for Broadband Access, Ottawa Industry, Canada (2001)

OECD. Working Party on Telecommunication and Information Services Policies: The Development of Broadband Access in OECD Countries, OECD, Paris (2001), http://www.oecd.org/dataoecd/48/33/2475737.pdf (accessed March 12, 2003)

Office of the e-Envoy. UK Online: The Broadband Future (2001), http://archive.cabinetoffice.gov.uk/e-envoy/reports-broadband/$file/ukonline.pdf (accessed July 15, 2003)

Office of Technology Policy. Understanding Broadband Demand: A Review of Critical Issues, U.S. Department of Commerce, Washington, DC (2002)

Oh, S., Ahn, J., Kim, B.: Adoption of Broadband Internet in Korea: The Role of Experience in Building Attitude. Journal of Information Technology 18(4), 267–280 (2003)

Rice, C.: Understanding Customers. Butterworth-Heinemann, Oxford (1997)

Rogers, E.M.: Diffusion of Innovations. Free Press, New York (1995)

Sawyer, S., Allen, J.P., Heejin, L.: Broadband and Mobile Opportunities: A Socio-Technical Perspective. Journal of Information Technology 18(4), 121–136 (2003)

Stanton, L.J.: Factors Influencing the Adoption of Residential Broadband Connections to Internet. In: Proceedings of the 37th Hawaii International Conference on System Sciences. IEEE Computer Society Press, Los Alamitos (2004)

Stevens, J.: Applied Multivariate Statistics for the Social Sciences. Lawrence Erlbaum Associates, Inc., Mahwah (1996)

Straub, D.W., Boudreau, M.-C., Gefen, D.: Validation Guidelines for IS Positivist Research. Communications of the Association for Information Systems 13, 380–427 (2004)

Suomi, R., Pekkola, J.: Inhibitors and Motivators for Tele-work: Some Finnish Experiences. European Journal of Information Systems 7(4), 221–231 (1998)

Taylor, S., Todd, P.A.: Understanding Information Technology Usage: A Test of Competing Models. Information Systems Research 6(1), 44–176 (1995)

Venkatesh, V., Brown, S.: A Longitudinal Investigation of Personal Computers in Homes: Adoption Determinants and Emerging Challenges. MIS Quarterly 25(1), 71–102 (2001)

## About the Authors

**Yogesh K. Dwivedi** is a senior lecturer in Information Systems at the School of Business and Economics, Swansea University, UK. His research focuses on the adoption and diffusion of ICT in organizations and society. He has coauthored several papers which have appeared in international referred journals such as *Communications of the ACM, DATA BASE, European Journal of Information Systems, Information Systems Journal, Information Systems Frontiers, Journal of Computer Information Systems, Journal of Information Technology, Journal of the Operational Research Society,* and *Industrial Management & Data Systems.* He has authored, coauthored, or coedited eight books on a variety of IS topics. He is senior editor of *DATA BASE,* assistant editor of *Transforming Government: People, Process and Policy,* and managing editor of *Journal of Electronic Commerce Research.* He is a member of the Association for Information Systems, IFIP WG8.6, and the Global Institute of Flexible Systems Management, New Delhi. He can be reached at ykdwivedi@gmail.com.

**Navonil Mustafee** is a lecturer in Information Systems at the School of Business and Economics, Swansea University, UK. Previously he worked as a research fellow in Grid Computing and Simulation in the School of Information Systems, Computing and Mathematics, Brunel University (UK). He received his M.Sc. in Distributed Information Systems and Ph.D. in Information Systems and Computing from Brunel University (UK). His research interests are in grid computing, parallel and distributed simulation, and healthcare simulation and information systems. His e-mail address is Navonil.Mustafee@gmail.com

**Michael D. Williams** is a arofessor in the School of Business and Economics at Swansea University in the UK. He holds a BSc from the CNAA, an M.Ed. from the University of Cambridge, and a Ph.D. from the University of Sheffield. He is a member of the British Computer Society and is registered as a Chartered Engineer. Prior to entering academia Professor Williams spent 12 years developing and implementing ICT systems in both public and private sectors in a variety of domains including finance, telecommunications, manufacturing, and local government, and since entering academia, has acted as consultant for both public and private organizations. He is the author of numerous fully refereed and invited papers within the ICT domain, has editorial board membership with a number of academic journals, and has obtained external research funding from sources including the European Union, the Nuffield Foundation, and the Welsh Assembly Government. He can be reached at m.d.williams@swansea.ac.uk

**Banita Lal** is a lecturer in the Nottingham Business School, Nottingham Trent University, UK. She obtained her Ph.D. and M.Sc. in Information Systems from Brunel University. Her research interests involve examining the individual and organizational adoption and usage of ICTs and technology-enabled alternative forms of working. She has published several research papers in internationally refereed journals such as *Journal of Information Technology, Industrial Management & Data Systems, Information Systems Frontiers, Electronic Government, International Journal of Mathematics and Computation,* and *Transforming Government: People, Process and Policy,* and has presented several papers at several international conferences. She can be reached at banita.lal@ntu.ac.uk

# The Uneven Diffusion of Collaborative Technology in a Large Organization

Gasparas Jarulaitis

Department of Computer and Information Science,
Norwegian University of Science and Technology,
Trondheim, Norway

**Abstract.** This paper investigates the large-scale diffusion of a collaborative technology in a range of different business contexts. The empirical data used in the article were obtained from a longitudinal (2007–2009) case study of a global oil and gas company (OGC). Our study reports on ongoing efforts to deploy an integrated collaborative system that uses Microsoft SharePoint (MSP) technology. We assess MSP as a configurational technology and analyze the diffusion of a metadata standard developed in-house, which forms an embedded component of MSP. We focus on two different organizational contexts, namely research and development (R&D) and oil and gas production (OGP), and illustrate the key differences between the ways in which configurational technology is managed and used in these contexts, which results in an uneven diffusion. In contrast with previous studies, we unravel the organizational and technological complexity involved, and thus empirically illustrate the flexibility of large-scale technology and show how the trajectories of the various components are influenced by multiple modes of ordering.

**Keywords:** Uneven diffusion, multi-sited study, large-scale collaborative technologies, integration.

## 1 Introduction

The nature of diffusion of large-scale technologies is different from that of the diffusion of self-contained artefacts (i.e., products). A critical mass must be reached in order to diffuse a product successfully, and over time the diffusion of a product stabilizes. In contrast, large-scale technologies are not self-contained artefacts, and their attractiveness (and thus their diffusion) depends on whether or not the technology becomes integrated with other existing technologies. The more users become engaged with a system, the more complementary products are attracted to it, and the diffusion of large-scale technologies may thus be described by reinforcement mechanisms (Hanseth 2000). Because the diffusion of large-scale technologies, such as enterprise resource planning (ERP), customer relationship management (CRM), or the collaborative technologies is becoming more widespread (Pollock and Williams 2009), the discussion of why, how and with what consequences such technologies diffuse is becoming more intense.

J. Pries-Heje et al. (Eds.): IS Design Science Research, IFIP AICT 318, pp. 209–224, 2010.
© IFIP International Federation for Information Processing 2010

A number of studies have identified some of the challenges entailed in diffusing such technologies. According to Davenport (1998), the diffusion of such technologies inevitably entails some form of change, either organisational or technological, or a combination of both. Large-scale technologies have been described as being standardised and rigid, and as being responsible for imposing certain logical structures on established work practices. As a result, in order to put such technologies to work, appropriations (i.e., workarounds) by individual users must be carried out (Soh et al. 2000). In short, such technologies do not diffuse in the same way as stable artefacts; instead, they are continually modified during their diffusion.

In contrast to the view of large-scale technologies as being rigid and resistant to change, Fleck (1994) proposed that such technologies may be better understood as being configurational, consisting of multiple components that can be modified, removed, or added. Such technologies then provide a spectrum of various adjustment strategies (Pollock and Williams 2009, pp. 42-43). However, few studies have analysed large-scale technologies along these lines (but see de Laet and Mol 2000). We thus argue that there are few studies that unravel both the organisational and technological complexities involved and empirically illustrate the flexibility of large-scale technologies and show how the trajectory of the various components is influenced by multiple modes of ordering (Law 1994).

The main aim of this paper is to explore the large-scale diffusion of technology across a range of contexts. The empirical data used in our paper are obtained from a longitudinal (2007–2009) case study of a global oil and gas company (OGC, a pseudonym to maintain anonymity). Our study reports ongoing efforts to deploy an integrated collaborative system based on Microsoft SharePoint (MSP). We assess MSP as a configurational technology and analyze the diffusion of a metadata standard, an embedded component that was developed in-house. We focus on two different organizational contexts, namely research and development (R&D) and oil and gas production (OGP), and illustrate the various ways in which configurational technology is managed and used in different contexts, resulting in an uneven diffusion.

The remainder of this paper is organized as follows. In the next section, we conceptualize the diffusion of large-scale collaborative technologies. We then outline our research approach, introduce the historical context, and describe the intention of OGC to change its collaborative infrastructure. Thereafter, we illustrate and discuss the ways in which configurational technology is diffusing unevenly in different contexts. Finally, we provide some analytical and practical implications for the study and management of the diffusion of large-scale configurational technologies.

## 2   Conceptualizing the Diffusion of Large-Scale Collaborative Technologies

The transfer and diffusion of information technology is currently conceptualized in two distinct ways, namely as a product or as a process (Baskerville and Pries-Heje 2003). While the former conceptualization considers diffusion in a rather mechanical manner, the latter emphasizes the continuous effort required to sustain the diffusion. Studies of the process of diffusion often draw on process theories such as the actor–network–theory or Walsham's interpretive framework (Henriksen and Kautz 2006). Our study builds on the latter perspective.

The ways in which collaborative technologies are diffused in various settings is an important topic that is discussed widely in the computer-supported cooperative work (CSCW) literature (Munkvold 2003). Ciborra (1996) suggested that collaborative technologies are fragile and that when they fail, users tend to switch to other alternative media nearby. Indeed, the core findings of the CSCW suggest that "users appear to use groupware in another way than the groupware designers intended or IT departments expected. Users tend to 're-invent' the technology by developing novel uses" (Andriessen et al. 2003, p. 367). Collaborative technologies are not single-user applications and their primary function is to improve collaboration between and within groups. As a result, collaborative work should be based on an agreed set of rules for interaction (Mark 2002). At the same time, groupware systems should be flexible and should "encourage unanticipated and innovative patterns of use" (Andriessen et al. 2003, p. 367).

Lyytinen and Damsgaard (2001) argued that the diffusion of large-scale technologies is somewhat different to the process described above. Large-scale technologies consist of multiple interconnected components, which may also be reconfigured by adding or removing particular components. In short, such technology is not self-contained. The diffusion of large-scale technology is not determined by gaining a critical mass of users and reaching a saturation point, but rather by the continual improvement of the technology by adding and improving individual components. In that sense, "diffusion of innovation results from a series of innovations" (Baskerville and Pries-Heje 2003, p. 252).

Diffusion is unpredictable and does not occur automatically (Monteiro and Hepsø 1998). More importantly, diffusion is not complete when a particular technology is implemented and all the users trained. Technologies must be continually (re)enacted in local contexts(Orlikowski 2000). According to Fleck (1994), such a process is better described as *innofusion*, indicating that significant innovation takes place during its implementation. Local improvisations are required for the technology to diffuse: "without successful adaptation of particular components, no innovative configuration can result and no diffusion takes place" (Fleck 1994, p. 649).

The diffusion of large-scale technologies is not accomplished by a single centralized IT department, but requires a rather more distributed effort. As suggested by Law (1994), an organization does not follow a single system of logic, but its development is instead determined by multiple modes of ordering. According to Law, ordering is a continuous process, with multiple ordering activities running in parallel and interacting.

The way in which the same or similar technologies are diffused (i.e., implemented and used) within various different kinds of organizations is recognized to be an important research area within the field of Information Systems. A number of authors have acknowledged the situated nature of information systems (Orlikowski 2000) and have discussed various misfits (Soh et al. 2000) that occur when technology cuts across divergent contexts. Robey and Boudreau (1999) employed the logic of opposition and argued that either the same or similar technologies produce different outcomes both within the same organization or between different organizations. While exact workarounds (i.e., local appropriations) vary between contexts, large-scale technologies do possess similarities (Leonardi and Barley 2008), because their diffusion processes are themselves similar.

## 3  Method

We report on an ongoing longitudinal research project that began in January 2007. Our research approach can be thought of as an interpretive case study (Walsham 2006) because of our "attempts to understand phenomena through the meanings that people assign to them" (Klein and Myers 1999, p. 69).

Data collection began in early 2007 and had the primary aim of exploring the nature of the changes associated with the implementation of MSP technology. The study was multi-contextual, and aimed at analyzing the ways in which a collaborative technology diffuses in a variety of contexts. Two different business units of the same organization were studied. One of them was R&D, where we engaged in conversations with various engineers working in technology development, and other researchers who were studying organizational issues. The second was OGP, where we aimed to cover the various disciplines involved in oil and gas production activities.

We employed three modes of data gathering, namely the use of formal and informal interviews, observation, and the use of documentary evidence. In total, 64 in-depth formal interviews, each lasting between 1 and 3 hours, were conducted. The first interviews were open-ended and aimed to identify the strategic IT visions and implementation activities related to MSP. During later interviews, we analyzed specific infrastructural components, work practices, or individual engagements with technology. The technological complexity and purpose of new infrastructure were discussed with developers, administrators, and managers of the collaborative infrastructure. We conducted 14 formal interviews with actors in this group. The use of collaborative infrastructure was explored with actors from several organizational units. A total of 23 formal interviews were conducted with various engineers and senior researchers in the R&D department; 27 interviews were conducted with personnel in OGP, where we interviewed drilling, well, production, and process engineers.

Participatory observation and informal discussions were mainly carried out in one of the OGC research centers, to which the author had been granted access from the beginning of the data collection period. In January 2008, the author was granted office space, as well as access to the building and to the OGC IT network. A researcher then spent two or three days per week in the research center. The significant amount of time spent on site helped to form an understanding of how work was carried out in practice and the nature of the problems and frustrations that were experienced. In addition, being on site afforded the opportunity for informal but informative chats around a coffee machine or during lunch breaks.

The third major empirical source of data were the internal OGC documents. We carried out an extensive study of the strategic documents that related to the planning and implementation activities of MSP. In addition, we analyzed the technical descriptions, formal presentations and training materials of various infrastructural components. A number of policy documents, which defined how particular technology should be used or how specific work should be carried out, were studied in detail. Finally, OGC's intranet portal provided extensive contextual information on the diverse activities of OGC.

The data analysis procedures are ongoing and iterative. In our faculty, there are several actors (not only the author of this paper) who are currently exploring the ways in which collaborative technologies are used in OGC. We often meet and discuss. A significant part of the data analysis and validation process is in fact occurring with the help of OGC employees. During both informal and formal meetings, we frequently present our findings to various OGC employees. We are then challenged, supported, or directed to issues that require our further attention. For example, several record information managers (RIMs) supported our early findings on the use of metadata in R&D, but we received extensive comments and suggestions for the study of other organizational contexts. We made adjustments to some of our generalizations. More importantly, we began to study the implementation of MSP in OGP.

In general, the empirical data are classified into broad themes that reflect a specific organizational project, practice, or technical component. Such a classification is neither all-encompassing nor exhaustive; it is rather characterized by overlapping and continual change. Theoretical considerations have an important role to play in the analysis by providing an analytical means to order and reclassify the empirical data. For example, in this paper we have analyzed the differences and similarities (Leonardi and Barley 2008) between different contexts. Our analysis is also inspired by STS studies, which emphasize multiplicities (Law 1994).

## 4  Case Study

### 4.1  Oil and Gas Company

Established in the 1970s, OGC has grown from a small, regional operator in northern Europe to a significant energy company, currently employing some 30,000 people with activities in about 40 countries across four continents. OGC has grown largely organically, but also by means of a few important national and international acquisitions. Facing limited growth potential in its region of origin, OGC is now actively pursuing a strategy of global growth. In order to boost its financial capacity and flexibility, in the 1990s OGC diversified and expanded its shareholder ownership including becoming listed on the New York Stock Exchange.

Aside from its growth in size, geography, and business area, OGC has been engaged in a number of corporate initiatives in order to improve communication and collaboration. These initiatives have relied heavily on the use of information systems. The first comprehensive effort to establish a corporate, collaborative infrastructure in this regard took place in the early 1990s, at a time of recession in the oil industry, falling oil prices, and low dollar exchange rates. The centralization, standardization, and market orientation of IT services was the direct outcome of several projects whose primary aim was to solve the problems of fragmented and incompatible IT. The outcome of these standardization activities led to the establishment of a collaborative infrastructure that used Lotus Notes.

The Lotus Notes infrastructure has proved successful inasmuch as it has been widely used for a range of different purposes. A key vehicle for facilitating collaboration within projects in OGC has been the Lotus Notes Arena (hereafter Arena) databases for the collective storing and dissemination of documents. However, the main challenge for this infrastructure has been to promote communication across the project-defined boundaries of the Arena databases. The Arena databases had no central indexing functionality, meaning that it was impossible to retrieve a document by searching if one did not know which database to search. With the existence of Arena databases that were thriving, apparently out of control (there were estimated to be some 5,000 databases at the latest count), locating relevant information stored outside the immediate scope of one's own project was far from being a trivial matter. Each user also had access to both personal (F disk) and departmental (G disk) storage areas. In short, information was scattered and duplicated over many storage areas.

## 4.2 New Collaborative Infrastructure

In order to overcome the problems associated with Lotus Notes and to establish more effective means of collaboration, coordination, and experience transfer, in 2001 OGC formulated a new strategy. According to this strategy, although OGC already possessed a set of general collaborative tools, "these tools [were] poorly integrated" and "there [was] a particular need for better and more integrated coordination tools, better search functionality and improved possibilities for sharing information with external partners" (OGC strategy documents). Accounting regulations enacted in the aftermath of the Enron affair increased the pressure to ensure a more systematic and consistent documentation of business decisions to better inform the stock market and the public at large.

The selection of the technology that would support the new collaborative strategy followed a long, rigorous process. A feasibility study was carried out in late 2002. During 2003, several solution scenarios were developed, requirements specified, and vendors selected. In December 2003, a contract with a vendor was signed and at the beginning of 2004, the first pilot using an MSP[1] out-of-the-box solution was launched. Early experiences of this technology evoked multiple user requests for improvements. In addition, numerous technical components had to be developed in order to achieve better integration between MSP and the existing installed base systems. By the end of 2004, version 1.0 was released, but even so multiple improvements were again required.

The beginning of 2005 saw the release of version 1.1 and, as one manager explained, "we were ready to roll-out the solution." The role-out process was fairly fast, and by the end of October 2005 the final 5,000 users had been added. The technical part of the diffusion (i.e., adding some 25,000 users to the new system) was thus to a large extent problem-free and took less than a year.

MSP is a core element of OGC's new collaborative infrastructure. The central element of MSP is the so-called Team Site (TS), the virtual area for collaboration. TS provides the functionality for checking-in and checking-out documents, posting announcements, sharing links, and creating discussion boards. While MSP is mainly used for the management of documents, the technology is integrated with a corporate-wide search engine, an archive system, and MS Exchange. The technology itself (MSP) is customizable; however, the OGC decided to make the solution as generic as possible so that it would fit all contexts (internally it is referred to as a one-size-fits-all strategy). As a result, all TSs have a common interface and functionality.

---

[1] http://sharepoint.microsoft.com/Pages/Default.aspx

## 4.3   Developing a Custom Component: The Metadata Standard

According to IT managers, MSP was rather an immature solution and needed to be customized to comply with OGC's regulations. During pilot testing, it became apparent that MSP was unable to support complex folder hierarchies due to URL length limitations. The MSP implementation team also found it difficult to develop a common and controlled folder structure that would comply with corporate requirements. It implied that documents would be stored in TSs in a flat structure. In order to improve information retrieval and retention, the MSP implementation team decided to utilize the metadata of documents. Two options for metadata were defined, namely the automatic selection of metadata from documents and the implementation of a controlled vocabulary. The latter alternative was chosen. The metadata standard was collaboratively developed by the MSP project team, RIMs and process owners (PO). RIMs would define and maintain metadata structure and POs would primarily be responsible for developing the values of the metadata. The structure of the metadata standard was inspired by the Dublin Core Metadata Initiative[2] (DCMI). DCMI defines a simple set of elements for describing document-like objects. OGC made significant customization and the current metadata structure has 13 elements with corresponding sub-elements (see Table 1). In total, there are fewer than 100 sub-elements. Our analysis primarily focuses on the *activity* and *category* sub-elements from the element *subject*. While some of the metadata values are captured automatically, such as the date or document format, others need to be defined and assigned manually. *Category* and *activity* sub-elements values are pre-defined by POs and users must assign each value as they create a new document in a TS (see Figure 1). The *activity* sub-element indicates a specific activity to which a document is related and the *category* sub-element is intended to describe the outcome of that activity.

**Table 1.** The Metadata Standard Structure

| | | | |
|---|---|---|---|
| 1. | People and roles | 5. | Description |
| 2. | Rights management | 6. | Language |
| 3. | Title | 7. | Relation |
| **4.** | **Subject** | 8. | Coverage |
| 4.1 | BICS 1 | 9. | Date |
| 4.2 | BICS 2 | 10. | Status |
| 4.3 | **Category** | 11. | Format |
| 4.4 | **Activity** | 12. | Identifier |
| 4.5 | **Keyword** | 13. | Preservation history |

Metadata values are stored in a so-called metadata repository, which is technically part of MSP; however, the metadata is utilized in the corporate-wide search engine and the archive system as well. In that sense, metadata is an integrated component of

---

[2] http://dublincore.org/

the collaborative infrastructure. As discussed previously, TS functionality and user interface are standardized for all users, thus the metadata is the only element that makes the TSs different. In contrast with Lotus Notes, MSP is configured to impose more standardization between geographical locations. Metadata value sets are standardized, which means, for example, that drilling engineers work with the same set of metadata irrespective of their geographical location or the specific characteristics of the particular oil and gas field. In that sense, the metadata standard not only provides a controlled vocabulary for the classification of documents, but also aims to improve the process of information retrieval. Since the metadata standard is integrated with the search engine, all users have the functionality required to search and filter information according to the metadata values. An implicit, but crucial, aspect of this functionality is that the same "common" metadata values be used in all contexts. In addition, the metadata standard may be considered as an initiative for improving the retrieval of long-term information and for ensuring compliance with external laws and regulations.[3] The metadata standard is integrated with the corporate archive solution (i.e., the document is archived with its associated metadata and may be found later on using the search engine).

Both the current structure and values of the metadata standard are subject to continual change. RIMs explained it as a "fumbling start":

*In the first release users had very few and too generic metadata values. The process of defining metadata was new to process owners…in some cases it took a couple years before more and better metadata values were developed.*

The initial versions of the metadata standard were experienced as a top-down solution for users, because both the structure and the values were defined beforehand. Recently, a free text sub-element called *keyword* was added in order to provide greater flexibility. The metadata values are subject to continual change as well. Despite the common character of the metadata standard, the nature of the diffusion thus varies greatly between contexts.

## 5    Analysis: How Does the Metadata Standard Diffuse in Different Contexts?

In this section we analyze and compare the diffusion of the metadata standard between different contexts. Two distinct organizational units are compared: R&D and OGP. The analysis highlights differences in the development of metadata and their patterns of use (see Table 2 for a summary).

### 5.1    Metadata in R&D:  Developing Specific Values That Fit the Local Context

R&D is an organizational unit that conducts research in special laboratories within the fields of materials technology, energy and environmental analysis, oil refining, gas

---

[3] Being listed on the New York Stock Exchange, OGC must comply with U.S. laws and regulations. The Sarbanes-Oxley act (SOX) of 2002 is a United States federal law enacted on July, 30, 2002, as a reaction to a number of major corporate and accounting scandals. The primary intention of SOX is to ensure the accuracy and transparency of financial statements.

and oil processing, gas conversion and petrochemicals, and biotechnology. Other research covers softer issues including, for example, the analysis of work practices in order to improve collaboration. Some research projects are conducted in specific areas (like the one mentioned above), while in other cases research projects are innovative and may cut across a variety of disciplines. The "newness" of R&D activities has implications for the development of metadata. It implies that a new set of metadata values should be developed whenever an innovative project is launched. The idea of the metadata values in OGC, on the other hand, was to engender a more static and less responsive process of change. Although the diffusion of MSP began in 2005, R&D is not thought of as a valid business process and currently (i.e., mid 2009), metadata values have not been developed. During a formal interview in late 2008, a RIM explained that development is in progress and a group of people from R&D are working on this in collaboration with process owners and RIMs. The core question then becomes one of how users are to classify documents without the use of metadata.

Some R&D projects aim to develop specific technology that could improve reservoir modeling, drilling, or other core oil and gas production activities. In that sense, some metadata values can be borrowed from other processes:

**Table 2.** Comparison of Diffusion of the Metadata Standard between Contexts

| Research and Development | Oil and Gas Production |
|---|---|
| *Metadata development* | |
| • Lagging development of metadata values<br>• Non-engaged process owners | • Active development and maintenance of metadata values<br>• Active process owners and engaged users |
| *Metadata use patterns* | |
| • Navigating by name or date<br>• Borrowing metadata values from other processes<br>• Inevitable working-around (replacing default values)<br>• Side-stepping MSP (using file-servers) | • Inconsistent (or wrong) use of metadata values<br>• Working-around (creating portals with links to documents)<br>• Using sorting and filtering functionality |

> *When we create a new team site, we have to define, which metadata we will use, but there is no metadata set for R&D...so I choose from other processes, for instance "petroleum technology."* (Researcher).

Even where metadata values are borrowed from other processes, they are quite generic and do not reflect actual activities:

> *The project I am working on is quite local, some 10 engineers are located in this building....we meet once a week to discuss the status of the project and plan the work ahead. I do not use metadata since many values are very generic. I have a good overview of the project, I know who is working with what and when certain deliveries have to be produced... it is easy to find documents, most often I sort documents by name or by date.* (Researcher)

OGC policy states that users should use the metadata values provided, however TS administrators are given the permissions required to change metadata values. While some use generic values, others question the rationale behind the use of generic values: *"We cannot change values, but what is the reason for using values that are meaningless in the project?"* (Researcher). Accordingly, some of them think that it is better to replace the metadata values provided rather than to use ones that do not fit. Figure 1, for example, illustrates the use of a TS with replaced values. Initially, the TS contained such generic values as accounting and control, best practice, manage coordination, network and competence, target setting and planning, experience and lessons learned, external document, publication, and report. The project team did not see the reason for using such values, and replaced them with ones that reflected actual activities (i.e., video, Canada, and needs).

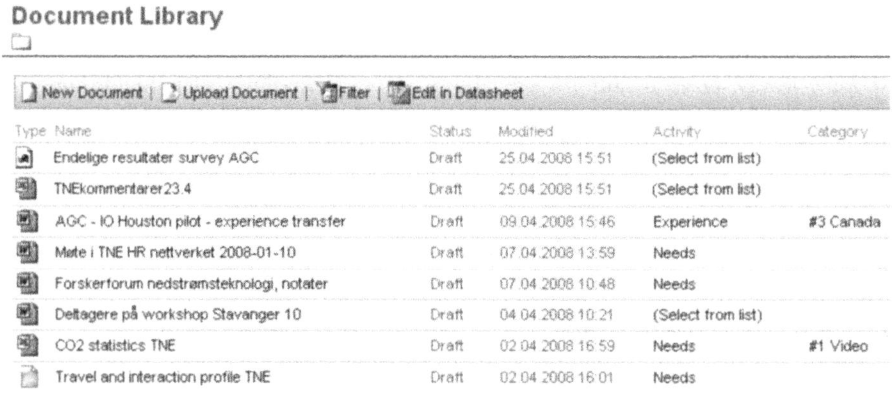

### Document Library

| Type | Name | Status | Modified | Activity | Category |
|---|---|---|---|---|---|
| | Endelige resultater survey AGC | Draft | 25.04.2008 15:51 | (Select from list) | |
| | TNEkommentarer23.4 | Draft | 25.04.2008 15:51 | (Select from list) | |
| | AGC - IO Houston pilot - experience transfer | Draft | 09.04.2008 15:46 | Experience | #3 Canada |
| | Møte i TNE HR nettverket 2008-01-10 | Draft | 07.04.2008 13:59 | Needs | |
| | Forskerforum nedstrømsteknologi, notater | Draft | 07.04.2008 10:48 | Needs | |
| | Deltagere på workshop Stavanger 10 | Draft | 04.04.2008 10:21 | (Select from list) | |
| | CO2 statistics TNE | Draft | 02.04.2008 16:59 | Needs | #1 Video |
| | Travel and interaction profile TNE | Draft | 02.04.2008 16:01 | Needs | |

New Document | Upload Document | Filter | Edit in Datasheet

**Fig. 1.** Use of Metadata Values in R&D

We have observed many users during our research, and many of them know, or get to know, that changing metadata values quite often allows such a workaround. One engineer's expression illustrates the situation well: *"Someone recently told me that it is possible to change values...it is much better now."*

In some extreme cases, our respondents knew nothing or very little about the metadata:

> *We are working in laboratories with some specialized systems. Some files are very large and some formats are not actually supported by MSP. So it is much easier for us to use file servers with common folders. We have TSs in parallel, but most of the things [i.e., files] are not there.* (Researcher)

As explained by a RIM involved in R&D activities, the greatest challenge occurs when R&D projects cut across multiple disciplines:

> *It is difficult to define what new and innovative projects there will be in the future. In particular, it is a big challenge when a single project cuts across multiple processes. I don't know in detail how it is in other places [other OGC organizational units], but here [in R&D] it is difficult.* (RIM).

## 5.2  Metadata in OGP:  Learning How to Navigate in an Imperfect Information Space

OGP is a distinct business unit within OGC. OGP may be characterized as an interdisciplinary, heterogeneous, and distributed work activity. The oil and gas value chain spans such activities as exploration, well drilling, and the optimization of production. The central object in OGP is a well. Geophysicists, petrophysicists, and drilling and reservoir engineers are all involved in the planning of new wells. While the drilling is primarily controlled by drilling engineers, production engineers observe well performance and initiate well interventions during production, which are then performed by well engineers. These activities are interdependent and distributed in time and space as the different disciplines work with the same well over a period of many years.  Multiple specialist technologies are used to visualize well data and observe its performance.  Other information related to planning and administration is stored using collaborative technologies such as MSP.

Metadata was introduced in OGP at the same time as in R&D and other parts of the company. However, the development of metadata has received a greater level of attention in OGP than in other parts of the company. Several managers and users participated in the project to develop metadata values. The prioritization of the project may be explained by several factors. First, the activities of OGP generate a large number of documents; during well planning alone, several hundred documents can be produced. Second, OGP is a core OGC activity, where certain policies on document retention must be followed. Third, engineers, who are used to building abstractions, constitute the large majority of OGP workers. As one manager explained, *"We [OGP] rather quickly understood that things would go wrong if we did nothing.  So right from the beginning several managers and engineers started to work on metadata."*

The comments made by the users in OGP are divergent, yet a majority have had positive experiences.

> *We [OGP] are quite good at classifying, because we have many values to choose from....The metadata does not actually fit all the documents, but for the large majority [of documents] values are good.*  (Drilling engineer)

Other engineers emphasize that fewer, but more precise. values would perhaps be easier to use.

> *The people who made this were very enthusiastic and thought that this would be a very good 'system' and specified as you can see many words [metadata values].  But when people begin to use this...if people don't know which value to use then they will use "none"...so it is important to have a rigid process with few words so it will be much easier for people to use it.* (Engineer)

The navigation and organization of overwhelming numbers of documents in a single TS is time consuming and not always successful, and many engineers appreciate the ability to filter and sort documents in a variety of ways.  In particular, predefined filters (so-called *views*), which allow the sorting of documents according to certain criteria, is considered to be a very helpful functionality (see Figure 2).

The success of common classification implies that the different actors who use the classification have the same (or similar, but not different) interpretation of values and use them in a consistent manner. This is not always the case in OGP, however. Some documents are not classified, and some are classified incorrectly. In contrast to the R&D example discussed in the previous section, it is quite rare in OGP to have a good overview of who is working with what.

**Fig. 2.** The Filtering of Documents According to Multiple Criteria in OGP

*It is great if you know who has produced or uploaded a specific document, but it is not always the case....If you use a specific team site a lot, then it is easier, because you know what to look for...but sometimes I just go and ask people where a specific document is.* (Drilling engineer)

The difficulties of using metadata are especially acute for engineers working offshore, and thus onshore engineers have invented a way in which offshore engineers can side-step the use of metadata.

*Sometimes I get a call in the evening from offshore people saying that they have been searching for a specific document for an hour or so with no success...to avoid this we have developed a practice [which is unofficial, i.e., a workaround] that for every new drilling program, a drilling engineer [working onshore] creates an Excel document containing links to documents that are the most important ones for drilling engineers working offshore. It is additional work as we [engineers working onshore] have to update those excel documents during drilling, but then offshore people have a much better overview.* (Drilling engineer working onshore).

Engineers who are working on a range of different oil and gas fields are exposed to inconsistency and difficulty using the activity and category values.

*The most important metadata for me is wellbore [well number, which is rather unambiguous], the rest has little value. The main thing I do is I sort documents according to a specific well [see Figure 2, top left corner] and then navigate... we [engineers conducting well interventions] also have internally decided document naming logic and agreed that all documents should start with a well number so that it would be easier to navigate.* (Well engineer).

## 6  Discussion and Conclusions

Our discussion relates to how a large-scale technology diffuses across contexts. The core findings of different studies suggest that the use of the same or similar technology produces different results in different contexts. The different outcomes arise due to the openness of the technologies (in particular the collaborative ones) (Ciborra 1996), which are subsequently interpreted and enacted differently by the various groups of users (Orlikowski 2000). We contribute to this body of literature by providing some of the analytical and practical implications of this statement.

In contrast to studies of the diffusion of a particular technology as a whole, our study recognizes that large-scale systems are best conceptualized as configurational technologies (Fleck 1994). This conceptualization emphasizes the fact that the technology consists of multiple components rather than a fixed set of modules or functionalities. Configurational technologies are "built from a combination of standard and custom technology components from different suppliers, selected and adapted to the user's context and purposes" (Pollock and Williams 2009, p. 47).

Technology does not diffuse as a whole; instead multiple components are continually modified and subsequently appropriated in a variety of ways. MSP, then, is not a rigid and unchangeable technology, on the contrary, it is rather flexible and offers a spectrum of various configurations (Pollock and Williams 2009, pp. 42-43). MSP is a configurational technology and the metadata standard is an internally developed component aimed at improving information retrieval and retention. The metadata standard is an embedded component of MSP, which implies that the trajectory of the metadata standard is influenced by its interactions with other components. More importantly, the metadata standard also influences the trajectory of the collaborative infrastructure. For example, the structure and rigidity of the metadata standard was influenced by the fact that MSP could not support complex folder hierarchies. The incorrect classification of documents, on the other hand, makes it difficult or sometimes impossible to find documents using the corporate-wide search engine.

While the concept of configurability was originally associated with the modification of technical parameters, recent contributions have extended this concept and illustrate how the politics of a small software supplier need to be configured according to changing circumstances (Sahay et al. 2009). Similarly, we suggest that successful configuration not only specifies technical parameters, but also involves multiple modes of ordering (Law 1994).

Since the technology consists of multiple components, it is quite often the case that certain communities are responsible for managing a particular component. In that sense, the diffusion of the same technology is a collective, yet distributed, effort. In the case of OGC, a certain community defines the overall strategy for the collaborative infrastructure but others have particular responsibility for the search engine, for document archiving, or for messaging services. The metadata standard is managed by several communities. RIMs maintain the structure and POs define the metadata values. In addition, there are multiple user communities, only a few of which we have illustrated herein. The core message then, is that the trajectory of either the metadata standard or MSP does not follow a single pathway; instead, multiple modes of ordering (Law 1994) continually apply. As illustrated for OGC, MSP had been technically rolled-out by the IT department by late 2005; however, tensions among communities are still present. RIMs, for example, are working closely with users, but their perspectives are not necessarily aligned with those of POs: *"Even if the users and I [RIM] know which metadata values would work better in particular contexts, we should not change them, it is the POs' responsibility to define them. We can suggest values for improvements, but it will not necessarily happen"* (RIM). Collaboration between POs and users is also quite problematic, especially in R&D. Users are not involved in the process of defining metadata values, thus their dissatisfaction is not surprising. In short, it is not only the technical aspects that should be configurable, but so should the modes of ordering. In OGC, for example, we find that the POs represent a bottleneck in the current configuration.

The practical implications of this study relate to the management of configurational technologies. Our study shows how configurational technology diffuses unevenly, a finding that supports the process perspective of diffusion (Henriksen and Kautz 2006). It requires different amounts of work from users and managers across different organizational contexts to make the technology work. As result, the diffusion of the technology occurs at different rates. Configurational technologies are not single-user applications; instead, they aim to provide collective benefits and require similar management and use across different contexts. Our study shows how the different ways of managing the same component has significant unwanted consequences. The owners of the processes did not develop the metadata values for R&D and, in consequence, some 1,000 engineers working in R&D had to use TSs with inappropriate metadata. As a result, documents were archived using incorrect metadata. Investigating the activities of the R&D department over the last 5 years is rather difficult, either using a corporate-wide search engine or an archive. The successful retrieval of information, therefore, becomes dependent on personal networks rather than on IT tools.

Mark (2002) emphasized the fact that collective work should be guided by agreed rules of interaction. Our empirical case shows that it is important not only to understand how technology is used, but it is equally important to monitor whether technology is managed according to agreed rules. The use of configurational technology imposes certain challenges on managers. Such technologies do not have distinct stages of design and use. These stages are intertwined as continuous configurations are made over time. Thus, the gap between designer and user needs to be bridged continuously. The metadata standard in OGC is an example of one particular configuration. While RIMs defined the metadata structure, POs were neither familiar with the concept of metadata nor with the process of the development of metadata values. In addition, POs have many different responsibilities and work related to the improvement of metadata does not currently enjoy a high priority. Thus, the interests of RIMs and POs are not currently aligned. The practical implication of this, then, is that it is not sufficient to define guidelines for the management of use of a configurational technology. The continuous assessment and improvement of both management and use are required. In essence, configurational technology requires significant resources.

## Acknowledgments

I would like to thank Eric Monteiro, Hans Hysing Olsen, and the anonymous reviewers for their very helpful comments during the revision of the paper. This research was supported by the AKSIO project, which is funded by the Norwegian Research Council (PETROMAKS, pr.nr. 163365/S30).

## References

Andriessen, J.H.E., Hettinga, M., Wulf, V.: Introduction to Special Issue on Evolving Use of Groupware. Computer Supported Cooperative Work (CSCW) 12(4), 367–380 (2003)

Baskerville, R., Pries-Heje, J.: Diversity in Modeling Diffusion of Information Technology. Journal of Technology Transfer 28(3-4), 251–264 (2003)

Ciborra, C.U.: Groupware and Teamwork: Invisible Aid or Technical Hindrance? John Wiley, Chichester (1996)

Davenport, T.H.: Putting the Enterprise into the Enterprise System. Harvard Business Review 76(4), 121–131 (1998)

de Laet, M., Mol, A.: The Zimbabwe Bush Pump: Mechanics of a Fluid Technology. Social Studies of Science 30(2), 225–263 (2000)

Fleck, J.: Learning by Trying: The Implementation of Configurational Technology. Research Policy 23(6), 637–652 (1994)

Hanseth, O.: The Economics of Standards. From Control to Drift. In: Ciborra, C.U., Braa, K., Cordella, A., Dahlbom, B., Failla, A., Hanseth, O., Hepso, V., Ljungberg, J., Montrero, E. (eds.) The Dynamics of Corporate Information Infrastructures, pp. 56–71. Oxford University Press, Oxford (2000)

Henriksen, H.Z., Kautz, K.: An Analysis of IFIP TC 8 WG 8.6 – In Search for a Common Theoretical Denominator. In: Avison, D., Elliot, S., Krogstie, J., Pries-Heje, J. (eds.) The Past and Future of Information Systems: 1976–2006 and Beyond, pp. 143–152. Springer, New York (2006)

Klein, H.K., Myers, M.D.: A Set of Principles for Conducting and Evaluating Interpretive Field Studies in Information Systems. MIS Quarterly 23(1), 67–94 (1999)

Law, J.: Organizing Modernity. Blackwell, Oxford (1994)

Leonardi, P.M., Barley, S.R.: Materiality and Change: Challenges to Building Better Theory About Technology and Organizing. Information and Organization 18(3), 159–176 (2008)

Lyytinen, K., Damsgaard, J.: What's Wrong with the Diffusion of Innovation Theory? In: Ardis, M.A., Marcolin, B.L. (eds.) Proceedings of the IFIP TC8 WG8.1 Fourth Working Conference on Diffusing Software Products and Process Innovations, pp. 173–190. Kluwer, Boston (2001)

Mark, G.: Conventions and Commitments in Distributed CSCW Groups. Computer Supported Cooperative Work 11(3), 349–387 (2002)

Monteiro, E., Hepsø, V.: Diffusion of Infrastructure: Mobilization and Improvisation. In: Larsen, T.J., Levine, L.L., DeGross, J.I. (eds.) Information Systems: Current Issues and Future Challenges, pp. 255–274. IFIP, Laxenburg (1998)

Munkvold, B.E.: Implementing Collaboration Technologies in Industry Case Examples and Lessons Learned. Springer, London (2003)

Orlikowski, W.J.: Using Technology and Constituting Structures: A Practice Lens for Studying Technology in Organizations. Organization Science 11(4), 404–428 (2000)

Pollock, N., Williams, R.: Software and Organizations: The Biography of the Enterprise-Wide System or How SAP Conquered the World. Routledge, London (2009)

Robey, D., Boudreau, M.-C.: Accounting for the Contradictory Organizational Consequences of Information Technology: Theoretical Directions and Methodological Implications. Information Systems Research 10(2), 167–185 (1999)

Sahay, S., Monteiro, E., Aanestad, M.: Configurable Politics and Asymmetric Integration: Health e-Infrastructures in India. Journal of the Association for Information Systems 10(5), 399–414 (2009)

Soh, C., Kien, S.S., Yap, T.J.: Cultural Fits and Misfits: Is ERP a Universal Solution? Communications of the ACM 43(4), 47–51 (2000)

Walsham, G.: Doing Interpretive Research. European Journal of Information Systems 15(3), 320–330 (2006)

## About the Author

**Gasparas Jarulaitis** is a research fellow in the Department of Computer and Information Science at the Norwegian University of Science and Technology. His research interests focus on the implementation and use of large-scale information systems in organizations. He has published in the proceedings of international IS conferences. Gasparas can be reached at gasparas@ idi.ntnu.no.

# Toward an Understanding of the Evolution of IFIP WG 8.6 Research

Yogesh K. Dwivedi[1], Linda Levine[2], Michael D. Williams[3], Mohini Singh[4], David G. Wastell[5], and Deborah Bunker[6]

[1] School of Business & Economics,
Swansea University,
Swansea, United Kingdom
[2] Software Engineering Institute,
Carnegie Mellon University,
Pittsburgh, Pennsylvania, U.S.A.
[3] School of Business & Economics,
Swansea University,
Swansea, United Kingdom
[4] School of Business Information Technology,
RMIT University,
Melbourne, Australia
[5] Nottingham University Business School,
Nottingham, United Kingdom
[6] Faculty of Economics and Business,
University of Sydney,
Sydney, NSW, Australia

**Abstract.** This article analyses research published in the previous 11 IFIP TC8 WG 8.6 conferences held between 1993 and 2008. Analysis of the published material includes examining variables such as most active authors, citation analysis, universities associated with the most publications, geographic diversity, and authors' backgrounds. The keyword analysis suggests that IFIP WG 8.6 research has evolved from examining basic issues such as organizational impact of technology adoption and technology transfer to contemporary issues such as open innovation. We suggest this research has implications for researchers, conference organizers, and research institutions.

**Keywords:** Adoption, diffusion, IFIP TC8 WG 8.6, IS research, profile.

## 1 Introduction

Information systems/information technology adoption and diffusion research is considered to be among the more mature areas of exploration within the IS discipline (Dwivedi, Williams, and Lal 2008). Such research has been published in a range of IS journals (Dwivedi, Williams, and Lal 2008; Williams et al. 2009) and has appeared in the proceedings of numerous IS conferences. Apart from these generic outlets for

J. Pries-Heje et al. (Eds.): IS Design Science Research, IFIP AICT 318, pp. 225–242, 2010.

publishing research in the area, there are also some specialized fora devoted to the discussion and publication of adoption and diffusion research. In this category, IFIP WG 8.6 is considered a prime venue and publishing outlet for researchers focusing on the adoption and diffusion of IS/IT. Since its inception in 1993 in Pittsburgh, Pennsylvnia, IFIP WG 8.6 has taken place in a number of venues in North America, Europe, and the Asia-Pacific region. During its 16 years of existence, it has evolved across a number of dimensions, including research topics addressed and the community of researchers who participate and contribute.

In order to understand the multidimensional evolution occurring between the Pittsburgh and Madrid events, it is useful to analyze the publications appearing in the various proceedings in order to examine if any trends exist. Bearing in mind the potential usefulness of such an analysis for both audience and editorial/organizing teams, similar efforts have been made to analyze well established conferences such as the European Conference on Information Systems (ECIS) (Whitley and Galliers 2007), and numerous IS journals including the *European Journal of Information Systems (EJIS)* (Dwivedi and Kuljis 2008), *Information & Management (I&M)* (Palvia et al. 2007), *Information Systems Frontiers* (Dwivedi et al. 2009), *Information Systems Journal (ISJ)* (Avison et al. 2008), and *Journal of Electronic Commerce Research (JECR)* (Dwivedi, Kiang et al. 2008).

The aim of this paper is to provide a systematic review of the literature pertaining to IS/IT adoption and diffusion research published in the proceedings of the IFIP WG 8.6 conferences. This overall aim is realized by means of the following three objectives: (1) to identify and determine the various demographic variables (such as most active authors, institutions, countries, number of coauthors, etc.) associated with IFIP WG 8.6 publications; (2) to undertake citation analysis to analyze the perceived impact of published studies and authors; and (3) to undertake keyword analysis to identify the most frequently examined issues.

The analysis presented in this study offers several contributions. The findings of such an analysis can be used as a basis for comparison (Whitley and Galliers 2007) with other outlets. For instance, the findings of this study can be used as the basis for comparison with other groups focusing on diffusion research (such as DIGIT), and with adoption and diffusion research published in IS journals and conferences. This can assist with overall trend analysis in order to observe changes in focal, theoretical, and methodological practices prevalent in IS/IT diffusion research. There are several benefits to be associated with the analysis of demographic variables (such as most active authors, institutions, countries, number of coauthors, etc.), particularly as such findings can provide readers with ideas for formal and informal collaboration or assistance. The "most active author" list can also provide editors, associate editors, and conference organizers with ideas for potential reviewers and groups where they can target calls for papers for publishing such research. Similarly, exploring geographical disparity may help in determining suitable venues for future conferences and for creating and sustaining improved regional and continental balance within the IFIP WG 8.6 research community. Finally, keyword analysis can provide new researchers with useful indications as to potentially fruitful topics for examination, and expert and more experienced researchers with an overview of the changing nature of research focus, and methods and theories employed in order to assist with the making of relevant and timely decisions within their own work.

In order to realize the above objectives, a systematic review of 271 articles appearing in the proceedings of the 11 IFIP WG 8.6 conferences (see Table 1) during the period 1993–2008 was conducted. The remainder of this paper is structured as follows. In section 2 we provide a brief account on origin and evolution of IFIP WG 8.6, followed in section 3 by a discussion of the method employed in the analysis. Our findings are presented and discussed in section 4, and finally, section 5 presents conclusions from this work and the limitations of our approach.

## 2   Background: The Origin and Evolution of IFIP WG 8.6

In 1991, Priscilla Fowler and Linda Levine, both of the Software Engineering Institute (SEI) at Carnegie Mellon University (CMU), became engaged in dialogue with two SEI senior staff members about IFIP, its role, technical committees, and how IFIP accomplished its work through working groups. These conversations were with Len Bass and Mario Barbacci, both of whom were active in IFIP, specifically with TC 2 on Software. Both Fowler and Levine were working on an SEI research and development project on technology transfer and diffusion of innovations, and Bass and Barbacci duly encouraged them to propose a new IFIP working group in this area. At that time, Fowler and Levine were committed to attend and present a paper at the upcoming IFIP World Congress in Madrid, and so they considered how to approach this challenge, and to explore the possibilities and make contact with potential sponsors at the event. Fowler and Levine then identified several stakeholders. First, they discovered that Brian Oakley (Logica) was presenting a workshop on cooperative R&D, and so they sent an advance e-mail to make contact, highlight shared interests, and arranged to attend Oakley's session and meet.  Second, they identified two technical committees where a proposed group on Diffusion and Transfer might be of interest—TC2 (Software) and TC8 (Information Systems)—and sent advance e-mails to communicate their interest and request meetings with the respective TC chairs, Peter Poole and Gordon Davis. At the Madrid IFIP World Congress, they met with both Poole and Davis. In the case of TC8, they were invited to a working meeting to discuss their proposal for a new WG on Diffusion, Transfer, and Implementation of Information Technology. The discussion was lively and energetic, exploring shared interests, the overlap with WG 8.2 (Information Systems and Organizations), and how a new WG on diffusion might bring more practitioners to the largely academic IFIP forum. This was in keeping with the SEI's mission of improving the state of the practice of software engineering. It eventually became apparent that TC8 was a better match for the proposal than TC2, and Fowler and Levine duly received approval to hold a working conference that would ideally, demonstrate interest in this area. If the conference was successful in demonstrating interest in, and the importance of, the subject area, then IFIP would consider supporting the establishment of a new working group. This process is typically how IFIP formally charters its new groups.

Over the following 18 months, an IFIP working conference was planned on Diffusion, Transfer, & Implementation of Information Technology, in cooperation with the SEI and the IEEE Computer Society Committee on Software Engineering. This event was held on October 10-13, 1993, at Champion, PA, in the area also referred to as Seven Springs. The event was very successful, attracting over 120 academics and practitioners from around the globe. Gordon Davis welcomed the attendees and Priscilla Fowler (Program Chair) opened the event. Three presentation tracks ran concurrently throughout; however, the format was atypical in allowing for afternoon outdoor activity: scheduled breaks were held from 3:30 p.m. to 6:00 p.m. so participants might admire the fall foliage, followed by dinner, and then six working sessions were held on both evenings. Keynotes were given by-Larry Lien (Training and Operations, US), Bernard Glasson (Curtin University, AU), and Rainer Zimmerman (ESSI, EU). All attendees received a conference binder with all submissions. However, the proceedings (see Levine 1994) were distributed some time after the event, early the following year, in order that written summaries of the working group sessions could be included. Shortly afterward, in 1994, the new IFIP WG 8.6 on Diffusion, Transfer, and Implementation was chartered by Technical Committee 8 and the IFIP General Assembly.

The first official working conference on Diffusion and Adoption of Information Technology was held October 14-17, 1995, at Leangkollen, Oslo, Norway, organized by Karlheinz Kautz, Jan Pries-Heje, Tor J Larsen, and Pal Sorgaard. The first Working Group 8.6 Chair was Priscilla Fowler, who served just short of two terms. She was followed by Karlheinz Kautz, who also served two terms. Kautz was followed by Linda Levine, currently serving her first term as Chair. The current website for the group, with additional history on past events, is available at http://www.ifipwg86.org/.

## 3   Research Method

In order to create a profile of the most active authors, universities, and countries, the study thoroughly examined all papers appearing in proceedings of IFIP WG 8.6 conferences held between 1993 and 2008. The authors reviewed a total of 271 published papers (see Table 1 for a breakdown of numbers of papers from different conferences) in order to capture data on these variables. Such an approach for the systematic classification of research published in a particular journal or conference is termed a *meta-study* or *longitudinal literature review* (Palvia et al. 2007; Dwivedi et al. 2009; Dwivedi, Williams, and Lal 2008). Since this approach has been successfully employed previously to profile a number of IS and related journals (Avison et al. 2008; Dwivedi, Kiang et al. 2008; Dwivedi and Kuljis 2008; Dwivedi et al. 2009; Palvia et al. 2007), we also utilized it to profile IFIP WG8.6 conference publications.

Various items were recorded for each article including the citations of selected articles, geographic regions, authors' backgrounds, and the keywords used by the authors. The impact of the research was assessed using Google Scholar citation counts. Institutional contributions/productivity were examined by utilizing normal count approach in which one count was allocated to each authors even if they were from the same institution. Both the authors' backgrounds and geographic location variables were adapted from previous studies (Avison et al. 2008; Dwivedi, Kiang et al. 2008; Dwivedi et al. 2009). It is important to emphasize at this point that, like previous profiling studies (Palvia et al. 2007), the findings of this study, in terms of universities with the most contributors and authors with the most publications, should be regarded as indicative and not an authoritative declaration.

# 4 Findings and Discussion

## 4.1 Most Active Authors

An analysis is conducted to identify those authors who published the most in previous IFIP 8.6 (1993–2008) conferences. For presenting the findings of this study, only those authors who have published three or more articles during the period studied are included in the list. A total of 429 authors contributed to the 271 articles. Table 2 lists the 30 most active authors, ordered according to the number of articles published in IFIP 8.6 conferences. The findings show that the largest number of contributions by any author was 15, followed by two authors contributing 10 publications each. A further five authors contributed seven articles, then two authors with six publications each. All of the most active authors and their associated number of publications are listed in Table 2. Although not listed in the table, 45 authors contributed to two articles each and, finally, the largest number of authors (C = 354) contributed to one article each.

**Table 1.** List of IFIP WG8.6 Conferences and Number of Papers Analyzed

| SN | Conference | Year | # of Papers |
|----|-----------|------|-------------|
| 1 | Pittsburgh, USA | 1993 | 30 |
| 2 | Oslo, Norway | 1995 | 14 |
| 3 | Ambleside, UK | 1997 | 22 |
| 4 | Helsinki, Finland | 1998 | 36 |
| 5 | Banff, Canada | 2001 | 18 |
| 6 | Sydney, Australia | 2002 | 13 |
| 7 | Copenhagen, Denmark | 2003 | 15 |
| 8 | Atlanta, USA | 2005 | 24 |
| 9 | Galway, Ireland | 2006 | 22 |
| 10 | Manchester, UK | 2007 | 44 |
| 11 | Madrid, Spain | 2008 | 33 |
| **Total Number of Papers Analyzed** | | | **271** |

In terms of active authors, it is interesting to correlate publishing behaviors across publishing outlets. For this purpose, we compared outputs in IFIP WG8.6 proceedings with a previous profiling study of authors disseminating adoption and diffusion research in various outlets (Dwivedi, Williams, and Lal 2008). Interestingly, only a small number of authors (Damsgaard, Lyytinen, Pries-Heje, Fichman, and Dwivedi), appear in both studies. This neatly indicates that different publication outlets have their specific author populations for contributing scholarly articles. While the overall author population is large, the dominant behavior is of loyal authors who prefer to concentrate on specific outlets. We surmise that such authors understand the editorial policy, quality criteria, and review process of their preferred outlet well enough that they manage to publish more than two or three articles in the same outlet (Dwivedi et al. 2009; Palvia et al. 2007). In conferences, researchers may have developed a

**Table 2.** The Most Active Authors

| Author | # of Papers | Author | # of Papers |
|---|---|---|---|
| Kautz, K. | 15 | Leon, G. | 4 |
| McMaster, T. | 10 | Swanson, E. B. | 4 |
| Pries-Heje, J. | 10 | Zmud, R. W. | 4 |
| Wastell, D. G. | 9 | Baskerville, R. L. | 3 |
| Levine, L. | 8 | Costello, G. J. | 3 |
| Damsgaard, J. | 7 | Donnellan, B. | 3 |
| Fitzgerald, B. | 7 | Dwivedi, Y. K. | 3 |
| Lyytinen, K. | 7 | Feller, J. | 3 |
| Larsen, T. J. | 6 | Fichman, R. G. | 3 |
| Mathiassen, L. | 6 | Fowler, P. | 3 |
| Bunker, D. | 5 | Ginn, M. L. | 3 |
| Borjesson, A. | 4 | Nielsen, P. A. | 3 |
| Chiasson, M. W. | 4 | Sambamurthy, V. | 3 |
| Finnegan, P. | 4 | Sauer, C. | 3 |
| Henriksen, H. Z. | 4 | Vidgen, R. T. | 3 |

social network among a community of academics and scholars with whom they wish and prefer to share their ideas, thoughts, and findings.

## 4.2  Gender of Authors

Gender information of a total of 548 contributors was extracted from authors' biographies; however, it was not possible to determine the gender of 50 authors due to a lack of such information in their biographies or due to complete lack of biography in certain articles. The analysis presented in Table 3 suggests that the proportion of male authors is much higher than females. A total of 416 (69.56 percent) male authors contributed articles in IFIP 8.6. A much lower proportion of female authors (22.07 percent) made intellectual contributions to the proceedings. Table 3 also presents the trend of gender proportion from 1993 to 2008, which suggests that female contributors' proportion varies between 11.8 percent and 31.4 percent and male authors' proportion varies between 68.6 percent and 88.2 percent. This suggests that the gender proportion is slightly skewed toward the male side.

## 4.3  Occupation of Authors

The data presented in Table 4 suggests that the highest proportion of IFIP 8.6 authors hold professorship positions. An almost equal number of authors were practitioners in various roles. This is then followed by lecturer (10.54 percent) and doctoral candidates (9.70 percent). Other categories are listed in Table 4. For 122 authors, it was not possible to determine their position or job roles from the biography provided with the paper.

## 4.4   Background of Authors: Academia Versus Industry

Table 5 illustrates the number of authors/contributors from academia or industry. The largest number of contributors were from academia (85.3 percent) and a comparatively small proportion of authors were based in industry (13.4 percent) and the public sector (1.3 percent) (Table 5).

**Table 3.** Gender of Authors

| Year | Female | | Male | | Total |
|---|---|---|---|---|---|
| | Count | % | Count | % | |
| 1993 | 4 | 11.8 | 30 | 88.2 | 34 |
| 1995 | 8 | 30.8 | 18 | 69.2 | 26 |
| 1997 | 12 | 25.0 | 36 | 75.0 | 48 |
| 1998 | 18 | 25.0 | 54 | 75.0 | 72 |
| 2001 | 5 | 29.4 | 12 | 70.6 | 17 |
| 2002 | 3 | 15.8 | 16 | 84.2 | 19 |
| 2003 | 7 | 19.4 | 29 | 80.6 | 36 |
| 2005 | 9 | 14.8 | 52 | 85.2 | 61 |
| 2006 | 12 | 23.1 | 40 | 76.9 | 52 |
| 2007 | 33 | 31.4 | 72 | 68.6 | 105 |
| 2008 | 21 | 26.9 | 57 | 73.1 | 78 |
| **Total** | **132** | **22.07** | **416** | **69.56** | **548** |

**Table 4.** Occupation of Authors

| Position/Job Role | Count | % |
|---|---|---|
| Professor | 81 | 13.55 |
| Practitioner | 80 | 13.38 |
| Lecturer | 63 | 10.54 |
| PhD Candidate | 58 | 9.70 |
| Associate Professor | 44 | 7.36 |
| Other Research Staff | 42 | 7.02 |
| Senior Lecturer | 35 | 5.85 |
| Assistant Professor | 24 | 4.01 |
| Head/Chair | 22 | 3.68 |
| Public Sector Employee | 8 | 1.34 |
| Member of the Technical Staff | 8 | 1.34 |
| Scientist | 7 | 1.17 |
| Reader | 4 | 0.67 |
| **Total** | **476** | **79.60** |
| Not Known | 122 | 20.40 |
| **Total** | **598** | **100.00** |

**Table 5.** Authors' Background

| Background | Count | % |
|---|---|---|
| Academic | 510 | 85.3 |
| Industry | 80 | 13.4 |
| Public Sector | 8 | 1.3 |
| **Total** | **598** | **100.00** |

### 4.5  Coauthor Analysis

In terms of the number of coauthors who contributed to each article, 32.1 percent of the articles were written by one author. Articles produced by multiple authors form the following categories: 35.1 percent of articles were coauthored by two authors, forming the largest category, 21.8 percent of articles were by three authors, 5.9 percent of articles were by four authors, 3.3 percent of articles were by five authors, three articles were coauthored by six authors, one article was coauthored by seven authors, and another one by ten authors each (see Table 6).

### 4.6  Leading Research Universities

Authors/contributors from 210 organizations/universities contributed to one or more articles in IFIP 8.6 proceedings between 1993 and 2008. Table 7 presents the top 30 universities having four or more contributors that participated and published IFIP 8.6 conference proceedings. The following is a breakdown of the frequency of contributors/ authors affiliated with a particular organization or university. Copenhagen Business School is ranked first, with a total of 31 contributors. This is followed by two universities with 22 contributors each (Manchester and Salford), and then Carnegie Mellon University with 19 and Georgia State University with 17 contributors. A large number of organizations/universities that are not listed in the table, including 12 universities with four contributors each, 26 organizations/universities with three contributors each, followed by 28 organizations/universities with two contributors each. Finally, the remaining organizations/universities from (210) had affiliations with one contributor from each.

**Table 6.** Coauthor Analysis

| Coauthor | Count | % |
|---|---|---|
| 2 | 95 | 35.1 |
| 1 | 87 | 32.1 |
| 3 | 59 | 21.8 |
| 4 | 16 | 5.9 |
| 5 | 9 | 3.3 |
| 6 | 3 | 1.1 |
| 7 | 1 | 0.4 |
| 10 | 1 | 0.4 |
| **Total** | **271** | **100.0** |

**Table 7.** Top 30 Universities (With Five or More Contributors)

| University | Count | University | Count |
|---|---|---|---|
| Copenhagen Business School | 31 | Norwegian Computing Centre | 6 |
| University of Manchester | 22 | Norwegian School of Management | 6 |
| University of Salford | 22 | Nottingham University | 6 |
| Carnegie Mellon University | 19 | Technical University of Madrid | 6 |
| Georgia State University | 17 | University of California at Los Angeles | 6 |
| Aalborg University | 14 | Brunel University | 5 |
| University of Lancaster | 14 | Erasmus University | 5 |
| University College Cork | 13 | Hong Kong Polytechnic | 5 |
| National University of Singapore | 12 | IT University of Copenhagen | 5 |
| University of New South Wales | 12 | Liverpool University | 5 |
| University of Limerick | 10 | Macquarie University | 5 |
| Ericsson AB | 9 | Swansea University | 5 |
| National University of Ireland | 9 | University of Oslo | 5 |
| University of Jyvaskyla | 8 | University of Turku | 5 |
| University of Wollongong | 7 | University of Warwick | 5 |

An observation similar to the most active authors has been made in terms of most active institutions. Only a limited number of institutions appear both in the previous list (Dwivedi, Williams, and Lal 2008) and in this research, including Carnegie Mellon University from North America, National University of Singapore from Asia, and Brunel University from Europe. This supports the argument provided in the methodology section that the findings of such studies in terms of institutional productivity should be regarded as indicative and not an authoritative declaration.

## 4.7  Country and Geographical Regions

A total of 26 countries had authors that published in IFIP 8.6 between the years 1993 and 2008 (Table 8). In terms of the number of authors/contributors from different countries, the largest number of contributors were located in the United States (20.7 percent), closely followed by the United Kingdom (20.5 percent). The third largest category (10.3 percent) was formed by Danish authors, with Australia (9.8 percent) in fourth place. Table 8 illustrates the proportion of contributors from the 26 countries.

In terms of the number of authors from different geographical regions (as per the Association of Information Systems, the largest number of authors were from the AIS Region 2 (Europe, Middle East, and Africa) with Europe and the United Kingdom providing 61.6 percent of the authors, followed by the AIS Region 1 (North, Central, and South America) with the United States and Canada providing 21.5 percent of authors. The third largest category was formed by the AIS Region 3 (Asia and the Pacific Rim), with Australia and New Zealand providing 10.6 percent of the authors, followed by South Korea, Singapore, Hong Kong, Taiwan, China, Japan, and India (also in AIS Region 3) providing 5.2 percent of the authors (Table 9).

Avison et al.'s (2008) research review *ISJ*, Dwivedi, Kiang et al.'s (2008b) review of *JECR*, and Dwivedi et al.'s (2009) review of *ISF* show that a number of geographical regions (such as South America, the Middle East, the former Soviet Union, and many underdeveloped countries of Asia) are under-represented in terms of undertaking and publishing information systems and electronic commerce research. This investigation also reveals highly under-represented levels of adoption and diffusion research from AIS Region 1 (South and Central America) and no representation from a large sector of AIS Region 3 (countries such as Afghanistan, Bangladesh, Cambodia, Indonesia, Malaysia, Nepal, Pakistan, Sri Lanka, and Thailand) (see Tables 8 and 9). This highly unbalanced picture certainly raises an important research agenda for both IS researchers and for researchers from the adoption and diffusion community to investigate: Is this situation a consequence of a global IS digital divide, or is it is due to a lack of interest or lack of necessary expertise and facilities to undertake IS research within such countries? Since such a geographical imbalance is reported in many studies, it deserves academic attention to form a suitable strategy and effort to reduce it.

**Table 8.** Contributors' Geographical Location

| Country | Count | % | Country | Count | % |
|---------|-------|-----|---------|-------|-----|
| USA | 123 | 20.7 | The Netherlands | 6 | 1.0 |
| UK | 122 | 20.5 | Canada | 5 | 0.8 |
| Denmark | 61 | 10.3 | Hong Kong | 5 | 0.8 |
| Australia | 58 | 9.8 | New Zealand | 5 | 0.8 |
| Ireland | 50 | 8.4 | Malaysia | 4 | 0.7 |
| Sweden | 34 | 5.7 | Switzerland | 4 | 0.7 |
| Finland | 28 | 4.7 | Israel | 3 | 0.5 |
| Norway | 22 | 3.7 | Jordan | 2 | 0.3 |
| Spain | 20 | 3.4 | France | 1 | 0.2 |
| Singapore | 13 | 2.2 | India | 1 | 0.2 |
| Germany | 9 | 1.5 | Japan | 1 | 0.2 |
| Italy | 8 | 1.3 | Saudi Arabia | 1 | 0.2 |
| China | 7 | 1.2 | Slovenia | 1 | 0.2 |
| **Total** | | | | **594** | **100.0** |

**Table 9.** Geographical Regions of Authors

| Association for Information Systems (AIS) Region | Count | % |
|---|---|---|
| AIS-R2 – Europe & UK | 366 | 61.6 |
| AIS-R1 – USA & Canada | 128 | 21.5 |
| AIS-R3 – Australia & New Zealand | 63 | 10.6 |
| AIS-R3 – South Korea, Singapore, Hong Kong, Taiwan, China, Japan, India, Malaysia | 31 | 5.2 |
| AIS-R2 – Middle East & Africa | 6 | 1.0 |
| **Total** | **594** | **100.0** |

## 4.8  Citation Analysis

A citation analysis was conducted to determine the research impact of the most influential authors and studies based on the number of IFIP 8.6 publication citations.

**Table 10.** Most Cited Articles from IFIP WG8.6 Proceedings (Retrieved form Google Scholar on May 1, 2009)

| Study | GS-Citation | Article Title |
|---|---|---|
| **Pittsburgh, USA –1993** | | |
| Saga & Zmud (1993) | 103 | The Nature and Determinants of IT Acceptance, Routinization, and Infusion |
| Fichman & Kemerer (1993) | 30 | Toward a Theory of the Adoption and Diffusion of Software Process Innovations |
| **Oslo, Norway – 1995** | | |
| Moore & Benbasat (1995) | 83 | Integrating Diffusion of Innovations and Theory of Reasoned Action Models to Predict Utilization of Information Technology by End-Users |
| Thong & Yap (1995) | 28 | Information Technology Adoption by Small Business: An Empirical Study |
| **Ambleside, UK – 1997** | | |
| McMaster et al. (1997) | 43 | Technology Transfer: Diffusion or Translation? |
| Buscher & Mogensen (1997) | 18 | Mediating Change: Translation and Mediation in the Context of Bricolage |
| **Helsinki, Finland – 1998** | | |
| Schultze (1998) | 79 | Investigating the Contradictions in Knowledge Management |
| Gasson (1998) | 28 | A Social Action Model of Situated Information Systems Design |
| **Bnaff, Canada – 2001** | | |
| Lyytinen & Damsgaard (2001) | 58 | What's Wrong with the Diffusion of Innovation Theory? |
| Pries-Heje & Tyrde (2001) | 14 | Diffusion and Adoption of IT Products and Processes in a Danish Bank |
| **Sydney, Australia – 2002** | | |
| Themistocleous & Irani (2002) | 10 | A Model for Adopting Enterprise Application Integration Technology |
| Serour & Henderson-Sellers (2002) | 8 | Organizational Culture on the Adoption and Diffusion of Software Engineering Process: an Empirical |
| **Copenhagen, Denmark – 2003** | | |
| Boving & Bodker (2003) | 5 | Where Is the Innovation? The Adoption of Virtual Work Spaces |
| Heikkila et al. (2003) | 5 | Taking Organizational Implementation Seriously: The Case of IOS Implementation |

**Table 10.** (*continued*)

| Atlanta, USA – 2005 | | |
|---|---|---|
| Abrahamsson et al. (2005) | 4 | Improving Business Agility Through Technical Solutions: A Case Study on Test-Driven Development in Mobile Software Development |
| Dove (2005) | 4 | Agile Enterprise Cornerstones: Knowledge, Values, and Response Ability |
| Levine (2005) | 4 | Reflections on Software Agility and Agile Methods: Challenges, Dilemmas, and the Way Ahead |
| **Galway, Ireland – 2006** | | |
| Helfert & Duncan (2006) | 4 | Aspects on Information Systems Curriculum: A Study Program in Business Informatics |
| **Manchester, UK – 2007** | | |
| Parsons et al. (2007) | 4 | The Impact of Methods and Techniques on Outcomes from Agile Software Development Projects |
| No citations for papers from the 2008 (Madrid, Spain) proceedings | | |

**Table 11.** Total Citation Counts for Most Active Authors from IFIP WG8.6 Conferences (Retrieved form Google Scholar on May 1, 2009)

| Author | Citation # | Avg Citation | Author | Citation # | Avg Citation |
|---|---|---|---|---|---|
| Zmud, R. W. | 128 | 32.0 | Swanson, E. B. | 8 | 2.0 |
| McMaster, T. | 92 | 9.2 | Henriksen, H. Z. | 7 | 1.8 |
| Damsgaard, J. | 85 | 12.1 | Ginn, M. L. | 5 | 1.7 |
| Lyytinen, K. | 82 | 11.7 | Sambamurthy, V. | 4 | 1.3 |
| Wastell, D. G. | 74 | 8.2 | Sauer, C. | 4 | 1.3 |
| Vidgen, R. T. | 71 | 23.7 | Costello, G. J. | 3 | 1.0 |
| Pries-Heje, J. | 43 | 4.3 | Donnellan, B. | 3 | 1.0 |
| Kautz, K. | 35 | 2.3 | Fowler, P. | 3 | 1.0 |
| Fichman, R. G. | 30 | 10.0 | Borjesson, A. | 2 | 0.7 |
| Baskerville, R. L. | 21 | 7.0 | Chiasson, M. W. | 2 | 0.7 |
| Levine, L. | 18 | 2.3 | Dwivedi, Y. K. | 2 | 0.5 |
| Fitzgerald, B. | 16 | 2.3 | Nielsen, P. A. | 2 | 0.5 |
| Larsen, T. J. | 11 | 1.8 | Bunker, D. | 1 | 0.2 |
| Mathiassen, L. | 11 | 1.8 | Finnegan, P. | 0 | 0.0 |
| Leon, G. | 9 | 2.3 | Feller, J. | 0 | 0.0 |

Citation data (citation count and article frequency) from Google Scholar was retrieved on May 1, 2009, for all 271 articles appearing in IFIP 8.6 proceedings between the years 1993 and 2008. A total of 19 studies with larger values of citation counts from

**Table 12.** Most Frequently Utilized Keywords (Approach Adapted from Dwivedi, Lal et al. 2008; Dwivedi et al. 2009)

| Conference | # of KW | Most Frequently Used KW |
|---|---|---|
| All | 959 | Organizational Impacts (15); Technology Transfer (14); Diffusion (14); Software Engineering (13); Adoption (12); Information Systems (11); Actor-Network Theory (11); Diffusion of Innovation(s) (10); Implementation (10); Management of Computing and Information Systems (10); Open Innovation (9); Innovation (9); Software Process (9); Case Study (8); Project and People Management (8); Action Research (7); Computer and Society (7); Agility (6); Information Technology (6); ICT (5); Institutional Theory (5); Design (4); Organizational Change (4); Technology Adoption (4); Tools and Techniques (4); Translation (4); Software Development (4); Organizational Resilience (4); Knowledge Management (4); SMEs (4); Installation Management (3); Diffusion Theory (3); ERP (3); IT Diffusion (3); Interorganizational Systems (3); E-Business (3); Information Infrastructure (3); Grounded Theory (3); EDI (3); Electronic Data Interchange (3); Resilience (3); Management (3); Organization (3); Change Management (3) |
| Pittsburgh, USA | 107 | Organizational Impacts (15); Management of Computing and Information Systems (10); Project and People Management (8); Software Engineering (8); Computer and Society (7); Information Systems (5); Technology Transfer (4); Tools and Techniques (4); Installation Management (3) |
| Oslo, Norway | 54 | Implementation (3); Technology Transfer (3); Adoption (2) |
| Ambleside, UK | 111 | Implementation (4); Innovation (4); Technology Transfer (4); Diffusion (3); Actor-Network Theory (2); Case Study (2); Diffusion Theory (2); Translation (2) |
| Helsinki, Finland | 124 | Action Research (2); Information Systems (2); IS Development (2); Lotus Notes (2); Software Process Improvement (2); Technological Determinism (2); Technology Transfer (2) |
| Banff, Canada | 21 | Diffusion and its Variations Diffusion and Adoption; Diffusion and Adoption of IT; Diffusion of Innovation Theory; Diffusionism |
| Sydney, Australia | 47 | Case Study (2); Diffusion (2); E-Business (2); Interorganizational Systems (2) |
| Copenhagen, Denmark | 50 | Adoption (3); Health care (2) |

**Table 12.** (*continued*)

| Atlanta, USA | 62 | Agility (6); Software Process Improvement (3) |
|---|---|---|
| Galway, Ireland | 97 | Organizational Resilience (4); Resilience (3); Action Research (2); Diffusion of Innovation (2) |
| Manchester, UK | 139 | Software Development (4); Actor–Network Theory (2); Diffusion of Innovation (4); Case Study (3); Software Process Improvement (2); SMEs (2); ICT (2); Work Practices (2); Information Systems (2); RFID (2); Agile Method (2) |
| Madrid, Spain | 147 | Open Innovation (9); Diffusion (4); Adoption (3); Value Creation (2); ERP (2); Telecommunication (2); ICT (2); Innovation (2); Institutional Theory (2) |

each year are listed in Table 10, which includes the study with the largest count—Saga and Zmud (1993)—with a citation count of 103, followed by Moore and Benbasat (1995), which has received 83 citations (see Table 10).

In terms of impact of researchers, with 128 citations Zmud emerged as a most-cited contributor to IFIP 8.6 conferences, followed by McMaster with 92 total citations. Damsgaard, Lyytinen, Wastell, and Vidgen have also received significant citation counts for their publications appearing in the IFIP 8.6 proceedings. Total citation counts and average citation counts (Total Citation Counts/Total Number of Papers) for most active authors are presented in Table 11. When average citation was considered, impact of the listed authors slightly differs. For example, McMaster was the second most-cited according to total citations but placed at seventh position if we consider average citation according to author.

### 4.9  Keyword Analysis:  Popular Keywords

In order to assess the most frequently utilized (employed) keywords, all keywords were collected from 271 studies published in the IFIP 8.6 proceedings.  These keywords were then sorted into alphabetical order to explore the most frequently utilized keywords. Table 12 presents the breakdown of the number of keywords from different conferences. A total of 959 keywords were extracted from the 271 articles, including 45 keywords that were used three or more times.  These 45 keywords, along with their frequency, are listed in Table 12. *Organizational impact* was the most frequently used keyword, with 15 papers utilizing it, followed by *technology transfer* and *diffusion*, each represented by 14 articles. *Software engineering* emerged as the third most utilized keyword, with 13 studies using this keyword. This was closely followed by *adoption* (12), *information systems* (11), *actor–network theory* (11), and *diffusion of innovation(s)* (10). Table 12 summarizes the frequency of usage of the 45 most frequently utilized keywords. The table also presents the most frequently utilized keywords and their frequency from each conference. The trend of keyword utilization suggests that IFIP 8.6 is the leading forum for presentation and publication of timely and relevant research in the domain of adoption and diffusion of IT/IS as a large number of topics were investigated in the previous IFIP 8.6 conferences

(Table 12). The keyword list presented in the table shows that research published in IFIP 8.6 has evolved from basic issues (such as examining the organizational impacts, tools, and techniques) to issues pertaining to contemporary themes such as open innovation. The keyword list also shows that the dominant theoretical perspectives popular among the researchers in this community include diffusion of innovation, actor– network theory, and institutional theory, while the most popular methods include case study and action research.

## 5  Conclusions

The aim of this paper was to contribute to a greater understanding of the evolution of the activities of the IFIP WG 8.6 research community by presenting the results of an analysis of the 271 articles that appeared in the conference proceedings between the years 1993 and 2008. The paper presented the results of an investigation along a series of demographic dimensions including most active authors, research impact of most active authors, authors' backgrounds, universities, country, region, and most frequently used keywords. The following are the summary key points that have emerged from the analysis presented in the paper:

- In terms of most active authors, one author was a clear distance ahead of the rest with 15 publications in total.
- Authors were predominantly male.
- A large proportion of IFIP WG 8.6 authors hold professorships, followed by practitioners and lecturers.
- Although IFIP WG 8.6 authorship includes a large proportion of industry experts, their numbers are significantly lower than academic contributors. This suggests that there is further scope for involving contributors from industry in order to make the conference more relevant and interesting.
- IFIP 8.6 articles illustrated a high level of collaborative work, both among academic authors and between academic and industry experts.
- The university with the largest number of contributors (31) is the Copenhagen Business School in Denmark. The top 30 list also includes a number of universities from the United States, the United Kingdom, Singapore, Hong Kong, and Australia, and number of European countries.
- It is also interesting to note that a commercial Organization (Ericsson AB) appeared within the list of most active institutions.
- The United States closely followed by the United Kingdom are the largest contributors of IFIP 8.6 authors and institutions. Consequently, a portion of AIS Region 2 (Europe and the United Kingdom) emerged as the most dominant region, followed by a portion of AIS Region 1 (United States and Canada).
- The highest research impact is reported for the paper by Saga and Zmud (1993), followed by Moore and Benbasat (1993), determined by citations obtained from Google Scholar for all articles published in IFIP 8.6 proceedings.
- In terms of individual author, the highest research impact is reported for Zmud, followed by McMaster, again determined by citations obtained from Google Scholar for all articles by a particular author published in IFIP 8.6 proceedings.

- A keywords analysis indicated that organizational impact, technology transfer, diffusion, software engineering, and adoption were the most utilized keywords, or in other words, the most investigated research issues.
- Actor–network theory, diffusion of innovation, and institutional theory are the most frequently utilized keywords that relate to theoretical perspectives in IFIP 8.6 publications. Action research and case study form examples of the most frequently utilized methodological keywords.

### 5.1  Future Research Implications

The results obtained can be utilized as input to a number of further analyses along different lines. For instance, the authors intend to conduct additional content analysis of IFIP WG 8.6 proceedings in order to examine variables such as units of analysis, research methods, and analysis techniques employed, and hence contribute to an understanding of past and current methodological and theoretical practices within the research community. This will reveal the level of diversity, and provide an indication to whether there is a need to promote and encourage greater diversity in IFIP WG 8.6 research. Second, the authors intend to carry out an analysis along the lines of social network analysis in order to illustrate the evolution of the IFIP WG 8.6 research community. Finally, more extensive work on keywords analysis would be valuable. This would potentially illustrate the changing perspectives and trends in the focus of IFIP WG 8.6, and could also involve the creation of a classification scheme to group existing keywords in different categories so that future archival analysis would be able to identify topics that have become less relevant over time, and those that have emerged since the establishment of the classification scheme.

## References

Avison, D., Dwivedi, Y.K., Fitzgerald, G., Powell, P.: The Beginnings of a New Era: Time to Reflect on 17 Years of the ISJ. Information Systems Journal 18(1), 5–21 (2008)

Dwivedi, Y.K., Kiang, M., Lal, B., Williams, M.D.: Profiling Research Published in the Journal of Electronic Commerce Research. Journal of Electronic Commerce Research 9(2), 77–91 (2008)

Dwivedi, Y.K., Kuljis, J.: Profile of IS Research Published in the European Journal of Information Systems. European Journal of Information Systems 17(6), 678–693 (2008)

Dwivedi, Y.K., Lal, B., Mustafi, N., Williams, M.D.: Profiling IS Research Published in the Information Systems Frontiers. Information Systems Frontiers 11(1), 87–102 (2009)

Dwivedi, Y.K., Williams, M.D., Lal, B.: The Diffusion of Research on the Adoption & Diffusion of Information Technology. In: León, G., Bernardos, A., Casar, J., Kautz, K., DeGross, J.I. (eds.) Open IT-Based Innovation: Moving Towards Cooperative IT Transfer and Knowledge Diffusion, pp. 3–22. Springer, Boston (2008)

Levine, L. (ed.): Diffusion, Transfer, & Implementation of Information Technology. North-Holland, Amsterdam (1994)

Moore, G.C., Benbasat, I.: Integrating Diffusion of Innovations and Theory of Reasoned Action Models to Predict Utilization of Information Technology by End-Users. In: Pries-Heje, J., Kautz, K. (eds.) Business Agility and Information Technology Diffusion, pp. 132–146. Chapman & Hall, London (1995)

Palvia, P., Pinjani, P., Sibley, E.H.: A Profile of Information Systems Research Published in the Information & Management. Information & Management 44, 1–11 (2007)

Saga, V.L., Zmud, R.W.: The Nature and Determinants of IT Acceptance, Routinization, and Infusion. In: Levine, L. (ed.) Diffusion, Transfer and Implementation of Information Technology, pp. 67–86. North-Holland, Amsterdam (1993)

Whitley, E.A., Galliers, R.D.: An Alternative Perspective on Citation Classics: Evidence from the First 10 Years of the European Conference on Information Systems. Information & Management 44(5), 441–455 (2007)

Williams, M.D., Dwivedi, Y.K., Lal, B., Schwarz, A.: Contemporary Trends and Issues in IT Adoption and Diffusion Research. Journal of Information Technology 24(1), 1–10 (2009)

## About the Authors

**Yogesh K. Dwivedi** is a senior lecturer in Information Systems at the School of Business and Economics, Swansea University, Wales, UK. He obtained his Ph.D. and M.Sc. in Information Systems from Brunel University, UK. He has coauthored several papers which have appeared in international referred journals such as *Communications of the ACM, DATA BASE, European Journal of Information Systems, Information Systems Journal, Information Systems Frontiers, Journal of Computer Information Systems, Journal of Information Technology, Journal of the Operational Research Society,* and *Industrial Management & Data Systems.* He is a senior editor of *DATA BASE,* an assistant editor of *Transforming Government: People, Process and Policy,* and managing editor of *Journal of Electronic Commerce Research,* and a member of the editorial and review boards of several journals. He is also a member of the Association for Information Systems and IFIP WG8.6. He can be reached at ykdwivedi@gmail.com.

**Linda Levine** is a senior member of the technical staff at Carnegie Mellon University's Software Engineering Institute. Her research focuses on acquisition of software intensive systems, agile software development, system of systems interoperability, diffusion of innovations, and knowledge integration and transfer. She holds a Ph.D. in Rhetoric from Carnegie Mellon University. She is a member of the Association for Information Systems, IEEE Computer Society, National Communication Association, and is a cofounder and chair of IFIP Working Group 8.6 on Diffusion, Transfer and Implementation of Information Technology. Contact her at ll@sei.cmu.edu.

**Michael D. Williams** is a professor in the School of Business and Economics at Swansea University in the UK. He holds a B.Sc. from the CNAA, an M.Ed. from the University of Cambridge, and a Ph.D. from the University of Sheffield. He is a member of the British Computer Society and is registered as a Chartered Engineer. Prior to entering academia, Professor Williams spent 12 years developing and implementing ICT systems in both public and private sectors in a variety of domains including finance, telecommunications, manufacturing, and local government, and since entering academia, has acted as a consultant for both public and private organizations. He is the author of numerous fully refereed and invited papers within the ICT domain, has editorial board membership with a number of academic journals, and has obtained external research funding from sources including the European Union, the Nuffield Foundation, and the Welsh Assembly Government. He can be reached at m.d.williams@swansea.ac.uk.

**Mohini Singh** is a professor of Information Systems at the School of Business Information Technology at RMIT University in Australia. She earned her Ph.D. from Monash University and has published widely in the areas of e-business and new technology and innovation management. Her publications comprise books, book chapters, journal articles, and conference papers. She serves as a member on the editorial boards of a number of journals and co-chairs tracks on e-government and IT diffusion at a number of international conferences. The focus of her current research is on the diffusion of Web 2.0 technologies in business organizations, mobile technologies, and e-government. She can be contacted at mohini.singh@rmit.edu.au.

**David Wastell** is a professor of Information Systems at Nottingham University Business School. He began his research career as a psycho-physiologist before moving into information systems. His research interests are in public sector reform, innovation and design, management epistemology, and cognitive ergonomics. He has co-organized two previous IFIP WG8.6 conferences (1997 and 2007) and was research co-chair for the IFIP WG8.2 conference in Manchester in 2004. David may be contacted at david.wastell@nottingham.ac.uk.

**Deborah Bunker** is a senior lecturer in the Business Information Systems discipline at the University of Sydney having previously held senior academic and administrative positions at the University of New South Wales and University of Wollongong. Her research interests are in IS philosophy, IS management, IS diffusion, and e-commerce/e-business. She is also president of the Australasian Association of IS and vice chair of IFIP WG 8.6, Diffusion, Transfer, and Implementation of Information Technology. Deborah can be reached at D.Bunker@econ.usyd.edu.au.

# Part 5

# Design Science

# Functional Service Domain Architecture Management: Building the Foundation for Situational Method Engineering

Daniel Stock, Robert Winter, and Jörg H. Mayer

Institute of Information Management,
University of St. Gallen,
St. Gallen, Switzerland

**Abstract.** Functional service domains are logical design artifacts that are intended to achieve better business/IT alignment. Their widespread utilization clearly indicates their perceived usefulness in managing the complexity of aligning business structures with IT structures. However, a common understanding of functional service domains and the associated principles that govern their design and evolution is still missing. So far, the literature provides only little guidance in closing this gap. This article contributes to the foundations that allow for the design of a situational method for functional service domain architecture management. Reviewing current literature, a framework is proposed that supports the identification of functional service domain architecture management patterns. Based on a better understanding of functional domain architecture management approaches, situational method engineering for functional domains can be applied by identifying context types and goal vectors, designing fragments, and associating successfully adopted method fragments with specific situations. The validity of the proposed framework is tested by five case studies.

**Keywords:** Functional service domain, enterprise architecture management, situational method engineering.

## 1 Introduction

### 1.1 Motivation

In large enterprises, the complexity of the information system landscape has grown constantly. This does not only concern the number of information systems, but also their interdependencies and connecting information flows. Functional service domains (for the sake of simplicity herein after referred to as *domains*) are clusters of linkages between business structures and IT structures on a maximum level of aggregation. Domains are a widespread concept that is intended to reduce the complexity of modeling and managing the information system landscape. Despite their perceived importance by practitioners, domains are rarely actively managed in enterprises to unfold their full potential. The literature provides only little guidance in closing this

J. Pries-Heje et al. (Eds.): IS Design Science Research, IFIP AICT 318, pp. 245–262, 2010.

gap, discussing only very specific aspects of domain architecture such as domain modeling (Kurpjuweit 2009) or decoupling of domains (Schlamann 2004). A comprehensive approach to domain architecture management that allows for situational (e.g., context and/or goal specific) adaptations is missing. This article contributes to a situational design of domain architecture management by proposing a model that allows identifying patterns in domain architecture. The model is based on an analysis of five practice cases.

## 1.2  Functional Service Domain Architecture

While the definitions of *domain* vary by context, most authors agree that a domain represents a view on the information system landscape that is characterized by a high congruence from a business (not technical) point of view (Aier 2007; Engels et al. 2008; Schlamann 2004; Schwinn 2006). In order to differentiate domains from applications, Schelp and Winter (2008) point out that the main difference is the level of aggregation, which is in line with several authors that use the term *sub-domains* to specify a different level of aggregation (Dodd 2005; Engels et al. 2008; Richter et al. 2005). In addition it should be noted that domain is not a fully established term and that many synonyms are in use. Domains are, for example, designated as building blocks (Jung 2004), application clusters (Lankes et al. 2005), or service segments (FEA PMO 2007; Open Group 2009).

Architecture in general is defined by ANSI/IEEE 1471-2000 as "the fundamental organization of a system, embodied in its components, their relationships to each other and the environment, and the principles governing its design and evolution" (IEEE 2000). Therefore, architecture serves a specific purpose (IEEE 2000; Lankhorst 2005; Rohloff 2008). In reference to this understanding, domain architecture can be defined as the fundamental organization of an enterprise's information system landscape, embodied in domains, the relationship between domains and to other enterprise architecture artifacts, as well as the principles governing their design and evolution.

This definition comprises two core elements that are subsumed under the term architecture: an aggregate model that constitutes the relations of a complex system, and guidelines for the design and evolution of the modeled system (Sinz 1999). According to this definition, domain architecture has method character since it consists of activity specifications (domain architecture specification guidelines/activities) and respective result specifications (domain architecture model) (Winter et al. 2009). The application of domain architecture to achieve a specific purpose (in this case, business/IT alignment) is designated as domain architecture management.

## 1.3  Objectives

Domains are predominantly discussed in two contexts: enterprise architecture (EA) in general (e.g., FEA PMO 2007; Open Group 2009), and enterprise application integration/service-oriented architecture (EAI/SOA) in particular (e.g., Engels et al. 2008; Heutschi 2007; Josuttis 2008; Schlamann 2004).

In EA, domains are very generically understood as an artifact type that aligns business and IT structures, but without further guidelines for identification, specification, and evolution of domains. In EAI/SOA, the scope of domain architecture is limited to the decoupling of application clusters through services. This narrow, mostly IT-oriented focus tends to disregard further application scenarios of domain architecture such as the increase of transparency or flexibility from a business perspective. In summary, a comprehensive proposal for domain architecture management that can be tailored to specific goals is missing so far.

Situational method engineering (Harmsen 1997; Kumar and Welke 1992; van Slooten and Hodes 1996) aims at constructing methods that can be adapted to different design problem classes (situations). In general, two modification techniques can be differentiated: configuration and aggregation (vom Brocke 2003). The configuration technique follows the so-called adaptive principle: subsequent changes are explicitly allowed for and planned at the moment of the initial construction of the artifact. On the other hand, the aggregation technique follows the compositional principle, permitting subsequent changeability that is, at least to a certain degree, almost unrestricted.

Both techniques require the identification of situation characteristics that a certain base-method is tailored to (in the configuration case) or that serve as the basis for the combination and aggregation of method fragments (in the aggregation case) (Bucher et al. 2007). In order to specify situation characteristics, Bucher et al. differentiate between so-called project-type and context-type characteristics. Project-type characteristics are factors that influence the project and are under the control of the project (e.g., goals), while context-type characteristics are factors that influence the project but are beyond its control (e.g., company size, industry specifics). In order to apply situational method engineering for constructing domain architecture management artifacts, the different goals (or goal vectors) and their implications for the results and activities of domain architecture management need to be understood. Therefore, this article proposes a model that allows identifying patterns of domain architecture management in practice, which is needed for constructing a method that takes situational characteristics into account.

## 1.4  Research Methodology

Information systems research is mainly characterized by two paradigms: behavioral research and design research. While behavioral research concentrates on the development and verification of explanatory, descriptive theories, design research focuses on the development of innovative, generic solutions for practical problems and, thereby, on accomplishing utility (Hevner et al. 2004; March and Smith 1995). According to Hevner et al. and March and Smith, the outcomes of a construction process under the design research paradigm can be classified as constructs, models, methods, and instantiations. The goal of this article is to contribute to the design of a situational method for domain architecture management by providing a morphological model (designated in the following as *morphology*) which can be used to identify and document patterns in practice as a starting base.

In order to develop the artifacts mentioned earlier, several reference models for the construction process have been proposed (Hevner et al. 2004; March and Smith 1995; Peffers et al. 2006; Rossi and Sein 2003). The process of March and Smith that specifies *build* and *evaluate* activities is predominant in literature (Hevner et al. 2004). This article focuses on the build part of the morphology through a review of current literature and uses a two-stage explorative validation with five practice cases.

In step one, four cases are used for an indicative assessment of the differentiating potential of the proposed morphology. In step two, the artifact is evaluated with regard to completeness, clearness, and relevance through an in-depth analysis of one further practice case. In contrast to the four cases used for assessing the differentiating potential of the proposed morphology that has already been documented in the literature, the evaluation case is described here for the first time.

It should be noted that the explorative evaluation presented here is part of an iterative design approach, which seems the most promising in identifying and justifying adaptations to the morphology. Therefore, further evaluation of the artifact as well as the subsequent design of a situational method for domain architecture management is subject to further research.

This article is structured as follows. Section 2 derives a morphology for domain architecture in order to differentiate practice approaches along certain constituent dimensions. In section 3, the proposed morphology is used to analyze four practice cases from the literature in order to provide an indicative validation of its differentiating potential. Section 4 introduces a new case in detail in order to provide a first validation of the morphology's information value. The article closes with a discussion of the results and a proposal for further research in section 5.

## 2  Derivation of Dimensions for Functional Service Domain Architecture Specification

In order to present a compact overview of different approaches to domain architecture, this section derives a morphology from current literature as a basic structure to present practice cases. In a first step the dimensions of the morphology are identified by decomposing domain architecture into its components and assigning respective degrees of freedom. In a second step each dimension is detailed through potential values that an instantiation might realize. The descriptive value of the resulting morphology is then evaluated against a first explorative set of cases in the next section.

As discussed earlier, domain architecture in general constitutes results and activities that are tailored to a specific target state (goal orientation). This definition of domain architecture comprises three high-level components (*target, results,* and *activities*) that are subject to further detailing:

- Derived from general EA goals, the target of domain architecture can be specified by its *application scenarios* (Winter et al. 2007) and its *stakeholders* (Niemi 2007; Op't Land et al. 2009; Ylimäki 2006).
- The result of domain architecture is the domain model, which is specified by the *domain definition/separation* and the included artifacts and relationships (Aier et al. 2009). The selection of the latter is defined by the *viewpoints* that are needed to satisfy the concerns of the respective stakeholders.
- According to the constituent elements of a method (Gutzwiller 1994; Heym 1993), the activities category can be decomposed into *design and evolution principles* (what is done), *implementation approach* (how is it done), and *organization* (who does it).

This results in seven dimensions that fall into the three above categories. For each of these dimensions, potential values need to be defined:

- According to the literature review of Heutschi (2007), domain architecture is used in three application scenarios: (1) *Increasing transparency* (for business/IT alignment), for example, by providing a map/inventory of available enterprise services within each domain. (2) *Reducing complexity/interdependencies* (Schlamann 2004) by decoupling interdomain linkages, for example, using some bus technology. (3) *Decentralization of responsibilities* (see FEA PMO 2007; Josuttis 2008; Open Group 2009), for example, by allocating domain overarching and domain specific responsibilities.
- According to the literature review of Winter and Fischer (2006), domains are elements of the architectural alignment layer that is positioned between the business and IT layers of enterprise architecture. Therefore, the generic stakeholders of a domain model can be specified as *business*, *IT*, or *business and IT*.
- Domain definition/separation is structured along *business processes* (of business units or product lines), *business entities*, or *business dimensions* (e.g., channels, products, customer segments) (see Cherbakov et al. 2005; Engels et al. 2008; Pohland 2000). It should be noted that pure forms of these concepts can be rarely found in practice, even if they tend to demonstrate a dominant approach.
- Kurpjuweit (2009) identifies two basic viewpoints: *inventory* and *landscape*. The former presents a list of applications within a domain, while the latter specifies the information flows between applications. These two viewpoints may have varying levels of detail. On the one hand, the inventory viewpoint can either constitute a simple listing (*application inventory*), or on top specify the functionality of and business entities maintained by the respective applications (*functions inventory*). On the other hand, the landscape viewpoint might specify interdomain information flows only (*domain landscape*) or both inter- and intradomain information flows (*application landscape*).
- Design and evolution principles operationalize the strategic targets (application scenarios): *consistency* in modeling artifacts and relationships to increase transparency, *reuse* to increase business/IT alignment, and *loose coupling* (through services) for reducing complexity and installing autonomy (see Heutschi 2007).
- Hafner and Winter (2008) present several distinct approaches to implement the design and evolution principles that range from a purely passive to a purely active mandate: *architecture communication*, *architecture lobbying*, and *architecture enforcement*. Within an architecture communication approach, the organizational reach-through is limited to the publication of information material. In contrast, an architecture enforcement approach implies a respective governance structure in order to actively push architecture guidelines into the organization. Architecture lobbying constitutes a compromise of these two, where the architecture unit is consulted to promote their design and evolution principles, but the right of decision remains out of their scope.
- Niemann (2006) identifies four different models to organize architecture management according to whether strategic and/or operational architecture management are implemented in a centralized or decentralized form: *centralized* architecture

management (strategic and operational architecture management within one central functional unit), *diversified* organization (strategic and operational architecture separated in two central functional units), *distributed* architecture management (operational architecture management decentralized), and *decentralized* architecture management (strategic and operational architecture management decentralized).

According to the remarks above, each dimension is associated with three to four potential values. It should be noted that, in some cases, the values are not mutually exclusive. This is due to the fact that some dimensions imply a kind of maturity logic. For example, it can be assumed that architecture communication is a prerequisite for architecture lobbying and in the same course a prerequisite to architecture enforcement. Similar argumentation holds true for the dimensions application scenario, viewpoints, and design and evolution principles. In these cases, the different values are lined up from left to right in order of increasing maturity. This results in the morphology that is illustrated by Table 1.

**Table 1.** Proposed Morphology for Functional Service Domains

| Category | Dimension | Potential values | | | |
|---|---|---|---|---|---|
| Target | Application scenarios | Increasing transparency | Reducing complexity | Decentralization of responsibilities | |
| | Stakeholder | Business | IT | Business and IT | |
| Results | Domain definition | Business processes | Business entities | Business dimensions | |
| | Viewpoints | Application inventory | Functions inventory | Domain landscape | Application landscape |
| Activities | Design and evolution | Consistency | Reuse | Loose coupling | |
| | Implementation approach | Architecture communication | Architecture lobbying | Architecture enforcement | |
| | Organization | Centralized | Diversified | Distributed | Decentralized |

## 3 Assessment of the Differentiating Potential of the Proposed Morphology

This section presents four practice cases for domain architecture: Credit Suisse (Hafner and Winter 2008; Hagen 2003; Schlamann 2004), Swisscom IT Services AG (Schwinn 2006), Axpo Informatik (Schwinn 2006), and PostFinance (Dietzsch 2008). By structuring each case along the findings of the previous section, a first explorative validation of the proposed morphology and its potential to identify patterns for later construction of a situational method are provided.

## 3.1 Practice Cases

### 3.1.1 Domains in Credit Suisse Architecture Management

Credit Suisse is one of the largest banks in Switzerland and operates globally. Domain architecture at Credit Suisse[1] primarily aims at the reduction of complexity that arises from interdependencies between applications. This is addressed by grouping applications along the core business entities into domains, while information flows across domain boundaries are loosely coupled through services. A domain is detailed through its applications and each application through its public interfaces, which offer functionality and access to data across domain boundaries. The domain architecture is enforced by the central Integration Architecture Group. Within Credit Suisse, the domain architecture is primarily targeted for the use within IT. An overview of this approach to domain architecture is given by Table 2. The respective values are highlighted, while dimensions without information are marked unavailable.

### 3.1.2 Domains in Swisscom IT Services Architecture Management

Swisscom IT Services is not only the IT service provider of the largest Swiss tele-communications company, but also a large provider of IT services to other companies, primarily in Switzerland. Domain architecture at Swisscom IT Services[2] primarily aims at the identification of interdependencies in order to undertake integration efforts in development projects. Therefore, domains are structured across the core business processes and the information flows between domains are modeled in a consistent manner to specify interdomain interdependencies. Information about the implementation approach and organization of the dimensions is not available. An overview is provided by Table 3.

**Table 2.** Credit Suisse Approach Specified Using the Proposed Methodology

| Category | Dimension | Potential values | | | |
|---|---|---|---|---|---|
| **Target** | Application scenarios | Increasing transparency | Reducing complexity | | Decentralization of responsibilities |
| | Stakeholder | Business | IT | | Business and IT |
| **Results** | Domain definition | Business processes | Business entities | | Business dimensions |
| | Viewpoints | Application inventory | Functions inventory | Domain landscape | Application landscape |
| **Activities** | Design and evolution principles | Consistency | Reuse | | Loose coupling |
| | Implementation approach | Architecture communication | Architecture lobbying | | Architecture enforcement |
| | Organization | Centralized | Diversified | Distributed | Decentralized |

---

[1] https://www.credit-suisse.com/ch/en/index.jsp (Credit Suisse Private Banking).
[2] http://www.swisscom.com/IT/content/home.htm?lang=en

**Table 3.** Swisscom IT Services Approach Specified Using the Proposed Morphology

| Category | Dimension | Potential values | | | |
|---|---|---|---|---|---|
| **Target** | Application scenarios | Increasing transparency | Reducing complexity | Decentralization of responsibilities | |
| | Stakeholder | Business | IT | Business and IT | |
| **Results** | Domain definition | Business processes | Business entities | Business dimensions | |
| | Viewpoints | Application inventory | Functions inventory | Domain landscape | Application landscape |
| **Activities** | Design and evolution principles | Consistency | Reuse | Loose coupling | |
| | Implementation approach | Not available | | | |
| | Organization | Not available | | | |

**Table 4.** Axpo Informatik Approach Specified Using the Proposed Morphology

| Category | Dimension | Potential values | | | |
|---|---|---|---|---|---|
| **Target** | Application scenarios | Increasing transparency | Reducing complexity | Decentralization of responsibilities | |
| | Stakeholder | Business | IT | Business and IT | |
| **Results** | Domain definition | Business processes | Business entities | Business dimensions | |
| | Viewpoints | Application inventory | Functions inventory | Domain landscape | Application landscape |
| **Activities** | Design and evolution principles | Consistency | Reuse | Loose coupling | |
| | Implementation approach | Not available | | | |
| | Organization | Not available | | | |

### 3.1.3 Domains in Axpo Informatik Architecture Management

Axpo Informatik is the IT service provider of a large network of power utility companies in Switzerland. Domain architecture at Axpo Informatik[3] is primarily targeted at facilitating the communication between business and IT. At an aggregate level, interdomain information flows are modeled in a consistent manner to make the necessary integration efforts during development processes quantifiable. Information

---

[3] http://www.axpo.ch/internet/axpo/en/ueberuns/gruppe/informatik.html

about the implementation approach and organization of the dimensions is not available. An overview is provided by Table 4.

### 3.1.4  Domains in PostFinance Architecture Management

PostFinance is the financial services business unit of the Swiss Postal Service. PostFinance is the largest payment processor in Switzerland and is offering an increasing number of other financial service. Domain architecture at PostFinance[4] is positioned as a passive instrument that makes interdependencies transparent. Domains are primarily structured according to products and channels. Domain architecture is managed by a central body outside IT. Information about the stakeholder and viewpoints of the dimensions is not available. An overview is provided by Table 5.

## 3.2  Learnings from Practice Cases

This first assessment of the resulting distribution of characteristics along the dimensions and values of the proposed morphology (see Table 6) indicates improvement potentials especially in the *target* category. It could be the case that *decentralization of responsibilities* is not a discrete application scenario and that *increasing transparency* is a too general scenario that needs further detailing. The same might hold true for the dimension *design and evolution principles* in the *activities* category where the validity of the potential value *reuse* and the granularity of the value *consistency* need further investigation. Finally, within the *stakeholder* dimension, *business* does not seem to be a discrete value, which might be attributed to the generic IT affinity of artifacts such as applications, services, and information flows.

**Table 5.** PostFinance Approach Specified Using the Proposed Morphology

| Category | Dimension | Potential values | | | |
|---|---|---|---|---|---|
| **Target** | Application scenarios | Increasing transparency | Reducing complexity | Decentralization of responsibilities | |
| | Stakeholder | Not available | | | |
| **Results** | Domain definition | Business processes | Business entities | Business dimensions | |
| | Viewpoints | Not available | | | |
| **Activities** | Design and evolution principles | Consistency | Reuse | Loose coupling | |
| | Implementation approach | Architecture communication | Architecture lobbying | Architecture enforcement | |
| | Organization | Centralized | Diversified | Distributed | Decentralized |

---

[4] http://www.postfinance.ch/pf/content/en.html

**Table 6.** Overview Occurrences of Potential Values in Practice Cases

| Category | Dimension | Potential values | | | |
|---|---|---|---|---|---|
| **Target** | Application scenarios | Increasing transparency | Reducing complexity | Decentralization of responsibilities | |
| | Stakeholder | Business | IT | Business and IT | |
| **Results** | Domain definition | Business processes | Business entities | Business dimensions | |
| | Viewpoints | Application inventory | Functions inventory | Domain landscape | Application landscape |
| **Activities** | Design and evolution principles | Consistency | Reuse | Loose coupling | |
| | Implementation approach | Architecture communication | Architecture lobbying | Architecture enforcement | |
| | Organization | Centralized | Diversified | Distributed | Decentralized |

Zero occurrences     Four occurrences

In contrast, the dimension *domain definition* is the only dimension whose potential values are all reflected in the sample, indicating a good differentiating potential of the morphology in this regard. Due to the small sample size and some missing values, no general assessment should be made for the remaining dimensions *viewpoints*, *implementation approach*, and *organization*. However, these preliminary findings will be further investigated in the following section.

# 4   Explorative Evaluation of the Proposed Morphology

This section presents the domain architecture management approach of Suva,[5] a Swiss insurance company. By structuring this case along the findings of the previous section, a first explorative validation of the proposed morphology and its potential to identify patterns for later construction of a situational method for domain architecture management is provided. For the analysis of the Suva case, presentations and process documentation were analyzed and an interview with one of the lead architects of Suva was conducted. The results that are presented herein were reviewed thoroughly and approved by Suva's architecture team and communications department.

## 4.1   Company Profile

Formed in 1918, Suva has a total workforce of around 2,900 employees who are based at its head office in Lucerne, at its two rehabilitation clinics in Bellikon and Sion, and at its 19 agencies throughout Switzerland. A financially independent body incorporated under public law, Suva insures around 110,000 companies and 2 million

---

[5] http://www.suva.ch/en/home_en

employees (as well as unemployed people) against the consequences of accidents and occupational diseases. It is also responsible for military insurance by government mandate. Its range of services encompasses prevention, insurance, and rehabilitation. Suva communicates this wide range of services under the following brands: SuvaPro (occupational safety), SuvaLiv (leisure time safety), SuvaRisk (premiums and capital investment), and SuvaCare (claims management and rehabilitation). Table 7 provides a short overview on Suva in general and its financial performance in 2008.

**Table 7.** Company Profile of Suva

| Suva (2008) | |
|---|---|
| Head office | Lucerne |
| Industry sector | Insurance |
| Business segments | Prevention, insurance, and rehabilitation |
| Turnover (in m CHF) | 7,919 |
| Profit (in m CHF) | -149 |
| Companies insured | 114,882 |
| Insurees | 2,008,000 |
| Employees (average) | 2,904 |
| Contact | http://www.suva.ch |

### 4.2  Domains in Suva Architecture Management

The domain architecture is one strategic aspect of Suva's service-oriented architecture management (SOAM) program that was started in the first half of 2007. The domain architecture is targeted to serve three consecutive purposes. In step one, transparency is created on (the most relevant) business services that are needed to support Suva's operations. In step two, the potential for reusing existing business functionality is identified and responsibilities for consolidation efforts are delegated. Finally, in step three, the flexibility is increased by decoupling domains through an enterprise service bus. So far, step one is implemented in full, while the process of consolidation and decoupling is still in progress.

The Suva domain model is clustered into four domain types and the domain definition/separation is predominantly structured along business processes (see Figure 1). A suitable set of functional service domains was identified through a joint business-IT project. This approach accounted, on one hand, for the existing interdependencies in the actual application system landscape (bottom-up analysis of IT) and, on the other hand, incorporated a business perspective on the target state (top-down analysis of business).

Dependent on the individual complexity, a domain can comprise several sub-domains. Each domain/sub-domain is then characterized by (unambiguous) associated business services (e.g., claim elicitation) and respective business entities. Each business service is implemented by an application system that provides access to the functionality of the business service through one or more dedicated interfaces (see Figure 2).

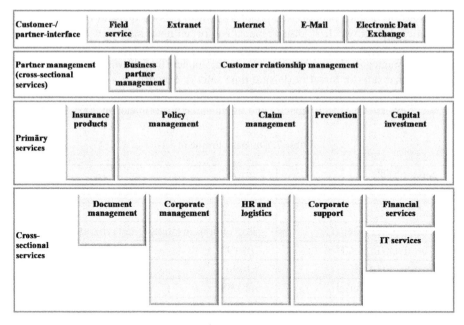

**Fig. 1.** Suva's Functional Service Domain Model

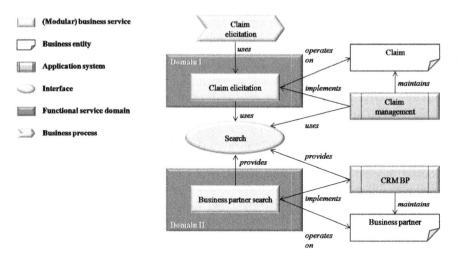

**Fig. 2.** Elements of a Functional Service Domain at Suva

In order to reduce interdomain dependencies, Suva is about to implement several design and evolution principles. The most relevant principles to ensure loose coupling of domains are (so far)

- An application system needs to be unambiguously assigned to one single functional service domain/sub-domain.

- The access of business functionality in a different domain must occur through centrally managed interfaces.
- One business service needs to be implemented through a single application system. One application system can implement one or several business services.

Every development project is enforced to comply with these and other design and evolution principles. If a project is assessed to have architectural relevance during its specification phase, the solutions design needs approval by a central architecture board (AB). The AB bases its decision on the assessment/recommendations of the domain center of excellence (DCE) and the architecture center of excellence (ACE). The DCE is comprised of the responsible domain architect and the responsible business analyst. It assesses the functional architecture concept. The ACE is comprised of the responsible application systems architect and the responsible integration architect. It assesses the technical architecture design. Even though the involvement of central architects is mandatory, they are not entitled to strictly enforce the above specified design and evolution principles. Currently the respective governance is revised, but it remains unclear if this will result in a strengthening of the role of the central architects. In summary, the domain architecture management approach of Suva can be structured along the proposed morphology as specified in Table 8.

**Table 8.** Suva Domain Architecture Specified Using the Proposed Morphology

| Category | Dimension | Potential values | | | |
|---|---|---|---|---|---|
| **Target** | Application scenarios | Increasing transparency | Reducing complexity | Decentralization of responsibilities | |
| | Stakeholder | Business | IT | Business and IT | |
| **Results** | Domain definition | Business processes | Business entities | Business dimensions | |
| | Viewpoints | Application inventory | Functions inventory | Domain landscape | Application landscape |
| **Activities** | Design and evolution principles | Consistency | Reuse | Loose coupling | |
| | Implementation approach | Architecture communication | Architecture lobbying | Architecture enforcement | |
| | Organization | Centralized | Diversified | Distributed | Decentralized |

### 4.3  Learnings from Suva Case

In order to identify improvement potential for the proposed morphology, its information value was collaboratively assessed with one of the leading architects of Suva in a semi-structured interview. The following five questions framed the discussion:

1. Are the dimensions and potential values complete (with respect to the findings of the previous section)?
2. Is each dimension/potential value relevant for the identification of patterns in practice?

3.  Is the Suva case unambiguously classifiable along the morphology?
4.  Do the dimensions and potential values yield the appropriate level of detail, differentiating enough on one hand, but still abstract enough to identify patterns (with respect to the findings of the previous section)?
5.  Is the assumed maturity logic in the dimensions *application scenario*, *viewpoints*, *design and evolution principles*, and *implementation approach* compelling?

**Table 9.** Adapted Morphology After Explorative Evaluation

| Category | Dimension | Potential values | | | |
|---|---|---|---|---|---|
| **Target** | Application scenarios | Increasing transparency | Consolidating | Increasing flexibility | Decentralization of responsibilities |
| | Stakeholder | IT | | Business and IT | |
| **Results** | Domain definition | Business processes | Business entities | | Business dimensions |
| | Domain definition approach | Top-down | Bottom-up | | Meet-in-the-middle |
| | Viewpoints | Application inventory | Functions inventory | Domain landscape | Application landscape |
| **Activities** | Design and evolution principles | Consistency | Reuse | | Loose coupling |
| | Implementation approach | Architecture communication | Architecture lobbying | | Architecture enforcement |
| | Organization | Centralized | Diversified | Distributed | Decentralized |

| x | New | x | Adapted | *x* | Deprecated |
|---|---|---|---|---|---|

| *Target* | *Application scenarios* | *Increasing transparency* | *Reducing complexity* | *Decentralization of responsibilities* |
|---|---|---|---|---|
| | *Stakeholder* | *Business* | *IT* | *Business and IT* |

While the derived morphology was assessed to fulfill the requirements stated in question 2, the interviewee challenged the morphology regarding questions 1, 3, 4, and 5. Regarding question 1, the interviewee suggested adding a further dimension in category *results*. In addition to the dimension *domain definition*, a dimension *domain definition approach* should be added to assess whether the domain landscape was structured from a functional perspective (*top-down*), from an IT perspective (*bottom-up*), or a combination of both (*meet-in-the-middle*). This dimension could reveal interesting relations to the targeted audience and the design and evolution principles applied. Regarding question 3 (in combination with question 5), the Suva case was not unambiguously classifiable in the dimension *design and evolution principles* since the assumed maturity logic does not hold true for this dimension. The intention for reuse is not a prerequisite for the loose coupling of an application landscape. Therefore, the interviewee suggested either concentrating on the predominant design and evolution principle of a company (comparably to the dimension *domain definition*) or allowing in this particular case for multiple answers. Regarding question

4, the potential values of the dimension *application scenarios* were not capable of reflecting the three-level approach of Suva (first, install transparency; second, consolidate; third, increase flexibility). In order to increase the differentiating potential of the morphology, the potential value *reducing complexity* could be broken down into the two components *consolidating* (reduce data and function redundancy) and *increasing flexibility* (while on top reducing the interface complexity by means of bus technologies). The adapted morphology that results from these lessons from of the Suva case is illustrated in Table 9.

# 5 Conclusions

This article proposes a morphology to classify domain architecture management approaches in practice. The dimensions and respective values of the model were initially derived from literature and validated/amended in a two-stage approach. In step one, a first assessment of four cases from the literature resulted in a couple of open questions regarding the differentiating potential of the proposed morphology. In step two, a single case was analyzed in-depth in order to answer the open questions of step one and to validate the completeness, clearness, and relevance of the proposed model. Following the ideas of iterative artifact construction in design research, the lessons from this case resulted in various adaptations to the proposed morphology. While the resulting artifact has undergone first validations and evaluations, it does certainly lack representativeness. Therefore, further cases need to be analyzed to allow for a thorough validation.

In the cause of further research, three successive steps are necessary. First, as mentioned above, further evaluation of the proposed morphology is required to validate its utility and strengthen its recommendation character. The necessary, thorough evaluation can be achieved through applying the proposed morphology in a field experiment with additional practice cases. An ongoing iterative approach for conducting these case studies seems most promising in order to identify and justify possible adaptations to the morphology. Second, a representative survey should be conducted in order to identify patterns along the refined morphology. Cluster analysis could be used to reveal a limited number of relevant use cases for domain architecture management and common associations between certain values in different dimensions. Based on the findings of the cluster analysis, the third and final step would be the design of a situational approach to domain architecture management. By the means of either method configuration or method fragment aggregation, activities as well as roles, result specifications, and techniques will then be constructed in a way that allows them to be adapted to a particular positioning of domain architecture management in a company or a government agency.

# References

Aier, S.: Integrationstechnologien als Basis einer nachhaltigen Unternehmensarchitektur - Abhängigkeiten zwischen Organisation und Informationstechnologie. Gito, Berlin (2007)

Aier, S., Kurpjuweit, S., Saat, J., Winter, R.: Enterprise Architecture Design as an Engineering Discipline. AIS Transactions on Enterprise Systems 1(1), 36–43 (2009)

Bucher, T., Klesse, M., Kurpjuweit, S., Winter, R.: Situational Method Engineering: On the Differentiation of 'Context' and 'Project Type'. In: Brinkkemper, S., Henderson-Sellers, B., Ralyte, J. (eds.) ' Situational Method Engineering: Fundamentals and Experiences, pp. 33–48. Springer, Boston (2007)

Cherbakov, L., Galambos, G., Harishankar, R., Kalyana, S., Rackham, G.: Impact of Service Orientation at the Business Level. IBM Systems Journal 44(4), 653–668 (2005)

Dietzsch, A.: Enterprise Architecture als Teil der strategischen Unternehmensentwicklung, St.Galler Anwenderforum, St. Gallen, Switzerland (2008)

Dodd, J.: Practical Service Specification and Design Part 1: Planning the Services. CBDi Journal, 22–29 (March 2005)

Engels, G., Hess, A., Humm, B., Juwig, O., Lohmann, M., Richter, J., Voss, M., Willkomm, J.: Quasar Enterprise - Anwendungslandschaften serviceorientiert gestalten. Dpunkt.verlag, Heidelberg (2008)

FEA PMO. FEA Practice Guidance, Federal Enterprise Architecture Program Management Office (2007), http://www.whitehouse.gov/omb/assets/fea_docs/ FEA_Practice_Guidance_Nov_2007.pdf

Gutzwiller, T.A.: Das CC RIM-Referenzmodell für den Entwurf von betrieblichen, transaktionsorientierten Informationssystemen. Physica, Heidelberg (1994)

Hafner, M., Winter, R.: Processes for Enterprise Application Architecture Management. In: Proceedings of the 41st Annual Hawaii International Conference on System Sciences, pp. 396–405. IEEE Computer Society Press, Los Alamitos (2008)

Hagen, C.: EAI@CS - Credit Suisse Integration Architecture. In: Proceedings des EAI Tag Berlin, Berlin: Lehrstuhl für Systemanalyse und EDV der Technischen Universität Berlin, pp. 1–26 (2003)

Harmsen, A.F.: Situational Method Engineering, dissertation. University of Twente, Twente (1997)

Heutschi, R.: Serviceorientierte Architektur, dissertation, Universität St. Gallen, St. Gallen, Switzerland (2007)

Hevner, A.R., March, S.T., Park, J., Ram, S.: Design Science in Information Systems Research. MIS Quarterly 28(1), 75–105 (2004)

Heym, M.: Methoden-Engineering - Spezifikation und Integration von Entwicklungsmethoden für Informationssysteme, dissertation, Universität St. Gallen, St. Gallen, Switzerland (1993)

IEEE. IEEE Recommended Practice for Architectural Description of Software Intensive Systems, IEEE Std 1471-2000, Software Engineering Standards Committee of the IEEE Computer Society, New York (2000), http://www.dia.uniroma3.it/~cabibbo/ ids/altrui/ieee1471.pdf

Josuttis, N.: SOA in der Praxis - System-Design für verteilte Geschäftsprozesse. Dpunkt.verlag, Heidelberg (2008)

Jung, E.: Ein unternehmensweites IT-Architekturmodell als erfolgreiches Bindeglied zwischen der Unternehmensstrategie und dem operativen Bankgeschäft. Wirtschaftsinformatik 46(4), 313–314 (2004)

Kumar, K., Welke, R.J.: Methodology Engineering: A Proposal for Situation-Specific Methodology Construction. In: Cotterman, W.W., Senn, J.A. (eds.) Challenges and Strategies for Research in Systems Development, pp. 257–269. John Wiley & Sons, New York (1992)

Kurpjuweit, S.: Stakeholder-orientierte Modellierung und Analyse der Unternehmensarchitektur, dissertation, Universität St. Gallen, St. Gallen, Switzerland (2009)

Lankes, J., Matthes, F., Wittenburg, A.: Softwarekartographie: Systematische Darstellung von Anwendungslandschaften. In: Internationale Tagung Wirtschaftsinformatik, pp. 1443–1462. Physica Verlag, Heidelberg (2005)

Lankhorst, M.: Enterprise Architecture at Work: Modelling, Communication and Analysis. Springer, Berlin (2005)

March, S.T., Smith, G.F.: Design and Natural Science Research on Information Technology. Decision Support Systems 15(4), 251–266 (1995)

Niemann, K.D.: From Enterprise Architecture to IT Governance: Elements of Effective IT Management. Vieweg, Wiesbaden (2006)

Niemi, E.: Enterprise Architecture Stakeholders: A Holistic View. In: Proceedings of the 13th Americas Conference on Information Systems, Keystone, Colorado, August 9-12 (2007)

Open Group. The Open Group Architecture Framework (TOGAF), Version 9, Enterprise Edition, Document No. G091, The Open Group, Reading, Berkshire, United Kingdom (2009)

Op't Land, M., Proper, E., Waage, M., Cloo, J., Steghuis, C.: Enterprise Architecture: Creating Value by Informed Governance. Springer, Berlin (2009)

Peffers, K., Tuunanen, T., Gengler, C.E., Rossi, M., Hui, W., Virtanen, V., Bragge, J.: The Design Science Research Process: A Model for Producing and Presenting Information Systems Research. In: Proceedings of the First International Conference on Design Science Research in Information Systems and Technology, Claremont, CA, February 24-25, pp. 83–106 (2006)

Pohland, S.: Globale Unternehmensarchitekturen – Methode zur Verteilung von Informationssystemen. Weißensee-Verlag, Berlin (2000)

Richter, J.P., Haller, H., Schrey, P.: Serviceorientierte Architektur. Informatik Spektrum 28(5), 413–416 (2005)

Rohloff, M.: Framework and Reference for Architecture Design. In: Proceedings of the 14th Americas Conference on Information Systems, Toronto, Canada, August 14-17, pp. 1–14 (2008)

Rossi, M., Sein, M.K.: Design Research Workshop: A Proactive Research Approach. Presentation to the 26th International Systems Research in Scandinavia (IRIS) Conference, Porvoo, Finland, August 9-12 (2003), http://www.cis.gsu.edu/~emonod/epistemology/Sein%20and%20Rossi%20-%20design%20research%20-%20IRIS.pdf (23.04.2009)

Schelp, J., Winter, R.: Entwurf von Anwendungssystemen und Entwurf von Enterprise Services – Ähnlichkeiten und Unterschiede. Wirtschaftsinformatik 50(1), 6–15 (2008)

Schlamann, H.: Service Orientation: An Evolutionary Approach. Cutter IT Journal 17(5), 5–13 (2004)

Schwinn, A.: Entwicklung einer Methode zur Gestaltung von Integrationsarchitekturen für Informationssysteme, dissertation, Difo-Druck, Bamberg, Germany (2006)

Sinz, E.J.: Architektur von Informationssystemen. In: Rechenberg, P., Pomberger, G. (eds.) Informatik-Handbuch, pp. 1035–1046. Hanser Fachbuch, Munich (1999)

van Slooten, K., Hodes, B.: Characterizing IS Development Projects. In: Brinkkemper, S., Lyytinen, K., Welke, R. (eds.) Method Engineering: Principles of Method Construction and Tool Support, pp. 29–44. Chapman & Hall, London (1996)

vom Brocke, J.: Referenzmodellierung - Gestaltung und Verteilung von Konstruktionsprozessen. Logos Verlag, Berlin (2003)

Winter, R., Bucher, T., Fischer, R., Kurpjuweit, S.: Analysis and Application Scenarios of Enterprise Architecture: An Exploratory Study (Reprint). Journal of Enterprise Architecture 3(3), 33–43 (2007)

Winter, R., Fischer, R.: Essential Layers, Artifacts, and Dependencies of Enterprise Architecture. In: Proceedings of the EDOC Workshop on Trends in Enterprise Architecture Research (TEAR 2006), pp. 30–37. IEEE Computer Society Press, Los Alamitos (2006)

Winter, R., Gericke, A., Bucher, T.: Method Versus Model – Two Sides of the Same Coin? In: Albani, A., Barijis, J., Dietz, J.L.G. (eds.) Advances in Enterprise Engineering III, pp. 1–15. Springer, Berlin (2009)

Ylimäki, T.: Potential Critical Success Factors for Enterprise Architecture. Journal of Enterprise Architecture 2(4), 29–40 (2006)

## About the Authors

**Daniel Stock** is a research assistant at the Institute of Information Management, University of St. Gallen (HSG), Switzerland. He received a Diploma (Master equivalent) in Business Engineering (2007) from University Karlsruhe, Germany. Daniel can be reached by e-mail at daniel.stock@unisg.ch.

**Robert Winter** is a full professor of business and information systems engineering at University of St. Gallen (HSG), director of HSG's Institute of Information Management, and academic director of HSG's Executive Master of Business Engineering programme. After master studies in business administration and business education at Goethe University, Frankfurt (Germany), he joined Frankfurt's institute of information systems for 10 years before being tenured in St. Gallen in 1996. Dr. Winter's research interests are information logistics management (since 1999), enterprise architecture management (since 2000), integration management (since 2002), healthcare networking (since 2005), and corporate controlling systems (since 2006). He is department editor of *Business & Information Systems Engineering* (formerly *Wirtschaftsinformatik*) and member of the editorial boards of *Information Systems and e-Business Management*, *Enterprise Modelling and Information Systems Architectures*, *AIS Transactions on Enterprise Systems*, and *International Journal of Organizational Design and Engineering*. Dr. Winter can be reached by e-mail at robert.winter@unisg.ch.

**Jörg H. Mayer** is a project manager at the Institute of Information Management, University of St. Gallen (HSG), Switzerland. He received a Diploma (Master equivalent) in Business Administration and Industrial Engineering (1994) from University Darmstadt, Germany. As a research assistant with University Darmstadt, he received a doctorate in social sciences for his work in the field of executive information systems (1999). Dr. Mayer can be reached by e-mail at joerg.mayer unisg.ch.

# Management Design Theories

Jan Pries-Heje and Richard L. Baskerville

[1] Roskilde University,
4000 Roskilde, Denmark
[2] Georgia State University,
Atlanta, Georgia, USA

**Abstract.** This paper elaborates a design science approach for management planning anchored to the concept of a management design theory. Unlike the notions of design theories arising from information systems, management design theories can appear as a system of technological rules, much as a system of hypotheses or propositions can embody scientific theories. The paper illustrates this form of management design theories with three grounded cases. These grounded cases include a software process improvement study, a user involvement study, and an organizational change study. Collectively these studies demonstrate how design theories founded on technological rules can not only improve the design of information systems, but that these concepts have great practical value for improving the framing of strategic organizational design decisions about such systems. Each case is either grounded in an empirical sense, that is to say, actual practice, or it is grounded to practices described extensively in the practical literature. Such design theories will help managers more easily approach complex, strategic decisions.

**Keywords:** Design science research, management design, decision design, technological rules, design theory.

## 1 Introduction

This paper proposes a design science research approach to management planning. Design science research (March and Smith 1995) is a *generative* mode of research.

Generative research means that scientific discoveries proceed from the design and creation of artefacts, and from evaluation of such artefacts in use. Design scientists create knowledge by generating designs, generating artefacts from these designs, and studying these artefacts in practical usage. Design science operates with prescriptive rather than descriptive theories because the nature of designs is action oriented. This action orientation arises because designs show how we "do things." Design theories fundamentally relate a general class of design problems with a general class of design solutions.

Design science research has great potential value for management and information systems. It offers a possible improvement in the usefulness of research for management, which is regarded by some authorities as a problem: "academic management

J. Pries-Heje et al. (Eds.): IS Design Science Research, IFIP AICT 318, pp. 263–281, 2010.

research has a serious utilization problem" (van Aken 2004, p. 219). From this perspective, management research results are too descriptive and historical. For reflective studies for managers facing current problems, the direct usefulness of such histories is questionable. Post mortem analyses of last year's decisions are less relevant than help and advice for the issues managers face. If management research became less descriptive and more prescriptive, and less historical and more design-oriented, the utility of management research could be increased dramatically. Management research could lead to a new form of theory, a design theory consisting of "field-tested and grounded technological rules" (van Aken 2004, 2005b). This notion constitutes a design science research approach to management.

Designing involves developing prescriptive, not descriptive, knowledge. In van Aken's design rules, there are two possible outputs (artefacts or interventions) and three kinds of designs in a professional episode (object-design, realization-design, or process-design). An object-design defines the artefact or intervention. A realization-design defines a plan for implementing the object-design. A process-design defines how the design process itself is carried out.

Van Aken expresses a design in the form of technological rules. "A technological rule follows the logic of 'if you want to achieve Y in situation Z, then perform action X'. The core of the rule is this X, a general solution concept for a type of field problem" (van Aken 2005a, p. 23).

Technological rules must be grounded. "Without grounding, the use of technological rules degenerates to mere 'instrumentalism,' i.e., to a working with theoretically ungrounded rules of thumb (Archer 1995, p. 153).

> In engineering and in medicine, grounding of technological rules can be done with the laws of nature and other insights from the natural and the life sciences (as well as from insights developed by these design sciences themselves). In management, grounding can be done with insights from the social sciences (van Aken 2005a, p. 25).

Just identifying technological rules per se is insufficient, regardless of how helpful they may be to managers. The rules must be properly grounded from a social science perspective.

In discussing technological rules, Pawson and Tilley (1997) raised the issue of causality. Which of the generative mechanism(s) that are used in an intervention actually produces the outcome in a given context? This question leads to the formulation of the CIMO-logic that can be formulated in the following way: "In this class of problematic Contexts, use this Intervention type to invoke these generative Mechanism (s), to deliver these Outcome(s)" (Denyer et al. 2008, p. 395).

Besides detailing the formulation of technological rules by virtue of the CIMO-logic, Denyer et al. (2008) suggest the term *design proposition* instead of *technological rule* arguing that "the latter term suggests—contrary to our intentions—a rather mechanistic, precise instruction."

The empirical cases we are reporting below used the technological rules rather than the CIMO-logic. While perhaps less logically comprehensive, the technological rules were simpler and more accessible for our cases.

The remainder of the paper is organized as follows. We first discuss in general how design science could improve management. Then we discuss design science research in management and demonstrate it through three grounded cases. Finally, we conclude that it is possible to help managers approach complex, strategic decisions by using the concept of technological rules.

## 2 Design Science in Management

Simon (1996) defines the science of design as the study of the artificial: "the way in which that adaptation of means to environments is brought about" (p. 113). Vaishnavi and Kuechler (2004) define design science research in information systems as "the analysis of the use and performance of designed artefacts to understand, explain and very frequently to improve on the behavior of aspects of Information Systems." The key concept is the design of an artefact that is meant to be somehow present in reality. While the artefact must be real, is could be a construct, a model, a method, or a material instantiation (March and Smith 1995).

Science and design are related in ways that are complex and contentious. Design is a generative production arising when the faculties of reason align in a way that is different from the analytical productions that are prized in science (see Kant 1908). Conflating science with design will frame the act of designing at a higher level of abstraction. At this level, designs are more universal and address a more general class of problems. We can contrast design science from design itself, which addresses a single, unique design problem. Generality demands theory, and in design science, a design theory is a special form of theory. Design theories share particular characteristics such as principles of form or function, principles of implementation, etc. (Gregor and Jones 2007; Walls et al. 1992).

Design science can be found in a variety of professional disciplines such as architecture, information systems, computer science, and engineering. In management, it arises mostly in decision science. As described earlier, van Aken (2004, 2005a, 2005b) argues that the utility of management research would increase if management research becomes prescriptive and design-oriented. Where van Aken proposed technological rules for designing decisions, these can also be used to express a design theory. This opens the possibility for a design science research approach to management.

We have chosen three cases to demonstrate that it is in fact possible to increase utility and help managers in a way that makes it possible and plausible to make better decisions in complex and/or strategic decision situations. The three cases we use are organizational change management, user involvement, and process improvement. For each case, we show how a new design theory appears using "technological rules" as suggested by van Aken. At the end of each case, we also discuss the grounding in social science as well as the (potential) application by managers and the practical implication(s).

## 3 Case 1: Process Improvement

Improving organizational processes and managing product and process quality is a particular area where advice for managers is urgently needed. The basic assumption made in this arena is that the quality of products and services is a direct result of the quality of organizational processes. The principle is simple and proven: Improve the organization's processes, and the goods and services it produces will also improve. Here design theories could prove highly practical as well as academically novel. The "big three" approaches to process improvement are the general International Standards Organization (ISO) standards for quality management systems (ISO 9000), the more technical and product-development oriented Capability Maturity Model (CMM), and the more specific ISO standards for process improvement and capability determination (ISO 15504/SPICE) (Hunter and Thayer 2001).

There are also many variations, enhancements, and proprietary alternatives, as well as opportunities to adapt general quality management models directly for software quality improvement (e.g., Six Sigma and Juran). Like the more general quality improvement approaches, there is little work that provides helpful guidance about which of these approaches to choose for which kinds of software organizations.

Management not only involves administering process improvement efforts, but also deciding which of these myriad approaches should be used to frame the effort within the product development organization at hand.    This approach selection process can be viewed as a design problem because it is concerned with the adaptation of available means to an environment (Simon 1996).    However, it is a managerial design problem.

We analyzed seven normative models for software process improvement (can be understood as process improvement in software developing organizations): Balanced Scorecard, Bootstrap, Business Excellence, CMM, ISO 9000, Juran, and Six Sigma. We identified common elements that could be used to distinguish and characterize different type of models. The major common element identified we called *agenda*, and it was characteristic that agenda differed among the models. We defined the agenda as the perspective on outcomes (of improving the organization) that drives the entire process improvement effort. Second, normative process improvement models share knowledge generating activities similar to those of research methods viz., observation, analysis, and synthesis. These three are also a kind of common element, but they follow after (or pertain to) agenda (see Figure 1).

In Figure 1, we have shown agenda with the three subsequent common elements underlying the agenda. Together, the four elements define a process theory that delineates what kind of recommendations can be derived for a specific organization. It is, therefore, a working classification system that could be restated as a simple hypotheses. In this way, it is equivalent to the set of research questions (the system of hypotheses) that drive a research project.

Agendas are set according to the process improvement goal and the general management viewpoint on organizations. Goals vary. Some managers seek to achieve a balance in the organizational activities and resources for an optimum performance. Other managers seek to provide a direction for the organization, a path to a future, desirable state. Organizational viewpoints also vary. Some managers see software organizations as quite similar and believe a set of universal solutions can be applied in most organizations. Others see organizations as highly unique instances, intersections of very particular resources and people (see Figure 2).

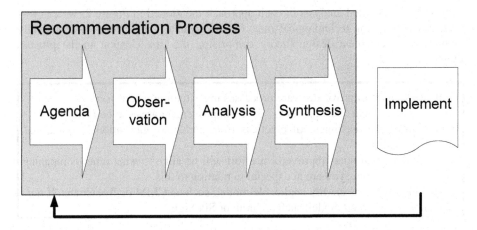

**Fig. 1.** Overview of the General Improvement Recommendation Process

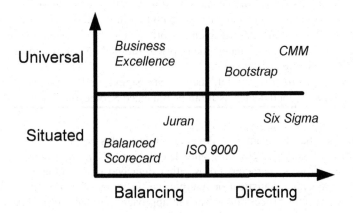

**Fig. 2.** Agenda Examples (from Pries-Heje and Baskerville 2003)

ISO 9000 has a very simple agenda: OK or not-OK. The organization is measured against a standard. The agenda in CMM is to improve processes by moving up to the next step on a five-step scale. The agenda in Bootstrap is partly the same as for CMM; the organization is measured against a number of processes. But Bootstrap focuses more on business goals. The Six Sigma agenda is focused on five sets of deliverables that correspond to each of the five steps in the six sigma roadmap. The agenda in EFQM is a press toward Business Excellence following nine specific criteria. In BSC, the agenda embraces a pronounced vision, mission, and strategy for the organization and sets concerted objectives, measures, targets, and initiatives in each of four perspectives: learning and growth, business process, customer, and financial. Finally, the agenda in Juran is to bring processes under statistical control. There is no specific direction, and it is contingent on what processes are selected for control.

Based on a detailed analysis of each approach mentioned in Figure 2, we can formulate the following technological rules for the agenda. These rules systematically embody a management design theory comprising the first element in the process theory of Figure 1.

---

If you want to improve software processes in a situation where you
- believe that "best practices" for an improvement area can be identified,
- trust the usefulness of practices from another organizational or national setting,
- agree that your improvement effort will be alike to what other companies have done; you are not special in relation to this,

then choose a *universally* applicable model, such as CMM or Bootstrap. If not, then choose a *situated* model, such as Juran or Six Sigma.

---

If you want to improve software processes in a situation where you
- need a vision to motivate and give direction to your improvement effort,
- believe there is one and only one path to a future desirable state,
- agree that your improvement effort should be directed by one single vision—and *not* balance many organizational activities and resources as to optimize performance,

then choose a *directing* model, such as Six Sigma, or ISO 9000. If not, then choose a *balancing* model such as Juran or Balanced Scorecard.

---

Our analysis has been able to develop similar rules for the remaining process elements of the theory depicted in Figure 1: observation, analysis, and synthesis processes. Observation is characterized as either detached or participatory. Analysis is characterized as either statistical or interpretive. In terms of modes of synthesis, we found that the various process improvement approaches either confined developers to a finite recommendation set, or allowed an open-ended, generative style for recommendations. Some approaches used a synthesis approach that involved a distinct model for synthesis. Other approaches had less-defined synthesis stages that were dependent on the tacit knowledge or know-how of the developers.

### 3.1  Grounding the Process Improvement Case in Social Science

In terms of social science research methodology, this paper reports work that is conceptual in nature; it is design theorizing for the purpose of improving management of process improvement. The theorizing is grounded in an analysis of the published process improvement models, and the theoretical results are expressed as models and technological rules.

The analysis (Pries-Heje and Baskerville 2003) of the published models was done following grounded theory coding techniques (Glaser and Strauss 1967; Strauss and Corbin 1998). In the concrete, grounded theory is a qualitative social science research methodology that takes its name from the practice of discovering theory that is grounded in data. Grounded theory is best used in research where one has relatively uncharted territory, as was the case with the identification of technological rules implicit and embedded in process improvement models. Grounded theories are inductively discovered by careful collection and analysis of qualitative empirical data. That is, this method does not begin with a theory, and then seek proof. Instead, it begins with an area of study and allows the relevant theory to emerge from that area through a three-step process called open, axial, and selective coding (Strauss and Corbin 1998). Figure 1 is a pictorial representation of what emerged in this first case.

### 3.2 Practical Implications of the Process Improvement Case

The set of matrices, technological rules, and underlying principles form a *framework* that can help organizations make sense of different normative models, and link them to their organizational and improvement goals. Our framework distinguishes between four significant dimensions: agenda, observation, analysis, and synthesis. These dimensions can be used to examine an organization's needs and then select an appropriate improvement model in an informed and systematic way.

In practice, a manager should try to place his own organization, its values, and its beliefs within the framework. Let us take agenda as an example. A *universal perspective* embeds trust in maturity models such as CMM and Bootstrap. More generally, the universal perspective focuses on models of best practices and, consequently, models of general process problems. A *situated perspective*, on the other hand, focuses on what software practitioners and their managers perceive as problems in the process.

Furthermore, the manager should consider their end goal. Is CMM level 5 regarded as an attractive state-of-the-practice in the organization? In general, models having a *cosmopolitan vision* provide an organizational direction toward better and better development. Such models assume that the organization is in a development "state" and has the opportunity to change to an improved state. Usually, this goal also assumes that there will be further opportunities to improve so the improvement process is seen as progressive. On the other hand, *harmonious standard models* have a clear aim toward building a value system for quality among other important organizational values. A balancing strategy assumes that something is missing in the development organization: some activity, value, or element that must be added or restored in order to improve the software process.

## 4   Case 2: User Involvement

User participation can be defined as "participation in the system development process by potential users or their representatives" (Barki and Hartwick 1989, p. 53). Many have identified lack of fulfilment of user needs in information technology projects as a major problem. Clavadetcher (1998, p. 30) summarized the problem:

> Quite simply, the software we build does not meet our customers' needs. Those of us who build large software programs fail miserably—90 percent of the time—to deliver what customers want, when they want it, at the agreed-upon price. We fail to adequately manage the software development process.

> User– developer communication breaks down; the requirements control process breaks down; we have runaway requirements, budgets, schedules, and "death march" projects.

Traditionally, user participation has been found to be a major factor in systems' success. This finding builds on theories of participative decision making (Barki and Hartwick 1994) and the user role in organizational change (Baroudi et al. 1986). There is not total agreement on the benefits of user participation. For example, Ives and Olson (1984), in a review of IS research, found mixed results on user participation. Likewise, Cavaye (1995) studied the relationship between user participation and success and found that the relationship was more complex than just more user participation leading to more success.

As with organizational change there are also many different fundamental theories for user participation. Bødker (2004) provides an excellent overview of a number of these techniques for user participation. For certain specific techniques, such as paper prototypes, Bødker recommends user participation early in the development process in order to elicit requirements from the users. Saleem (1996) recommends user participation when task uncertainty is high. However, the combination where one involves users early in projects with high task uncertainty cannot be found in the literature.

The process by which an IT project—typically by the project manager—selects the appropriate approach and time for user participation is often *ad hoc*. Each approach has its advocates and adherents, and there is little comparative research for choosing among such approaches. Thus we set out to develop a framework of technological rules that could be useful in this situation.

The combined findings from a literature study and a field study (see section 4.4 on grounding) describe a management design theory about user participation that comprises three major influences on user participation: complexity, resources, and user identity. For shorthand, we will call this the CRU management design theory for user participation. Below we systematically elaborate each element of the CRU management design theory and formulate technological rules for each of these three elements.

## 4.1 Complexity

The complexity issue is characterized by six major factors that give rise to complexity. These include domain knowledge, task complexity, size, technical knowledge, perceived change, and the type of system.

The first factor leading to complexity is the degree of knowledge held by the developers in the domain in which the users work. Developers need knowledge about the existing working styles in order to develop the right system for future work. Lack of domain knowledge among developers is one of the three key problems of systems development when the system is large (Curtis et al. 1988). Where developers lack knowledge of the users' work, they need to observe and experience the users while they do their work (Kensing and Munk-Madsen 1993). Where the users' work is well-known to the developers, then reviews are needed to ensure the knowledge is still accurate. A high degree of user participation is needed where developers lack domain knowledge (Saleem 1996), and this participation is less urgent where developers have strong domain knowledge. Cavaye (1995) notes that user participation is less urgent if user requirements are well known.

The second factor is task complexity. Where tasks are structured at the operational level, the demand for user participation is minimal. Where tasks are unstructured and only described at the strategic level, then the need for user participation is urgent (Cavaye 1995). This determination is complicated by the presence of both operational and strategic tasks. For example, cases where the users involved are not knowledgeable enough about certain tasks to determine if these were operational or strategic may lead to partial failures in the inevitable system (Wilson et al. 1997). When task uncertainty is high, then a high degree of user participation is recommended (Saleem 1996). On the other hand, if a system is well structured and well defined, then it is not necessary to involve users for purposes of system quality (Ives and Olson 1984) but perhaps for system acceptance.

Size is the third factor we found that influences complexity. Size is one of the main influences both on system risk (Applegate et al. 1999) and complexity (Cavaye 1995). User participation is common where the system is perceived as large, such that participation may be impractical if the system is perceived as small (Cavaye 1995). The distinction between large and small will, of course, vary from setting to setting. For our purposes, we asked participants in our field study how they would distinguish large from small systems. For this setting, the users indicated that projects longer than 36 man months (or 24 calendar months) are large, while a project of less than 12 man months or 12 calendar months was perceived as a small system.

The fourth influence factor on complexity was knowledge of the technology. Lack of technological knowledge (i.e., on hardware, operating system, database management, programming language, etc.) increases complexity. This factor is a known area that increases risk (Applegate et al. 1999), and we know that there is a need for a balance between the complexity of the application and the complexity of the technology (Nicholas 1985). User participation may be unsuitable when considerable technical expertise is needed (Ives and Olson 1984).

The fifth influence factor is perceived change for stakeholders. If change is perceived to be considerable, then there is an advantage in involving users (Cavaye 1995). In addition, a larger the number of stakeholders is more likely to have a wider variety of goals for the system.

Finally, the sixth influence factor is the type of system. For transaction based systems the traditional way of involving users is through information given from users to developers. Based on this information, the developers then formulate user needs and requirements. While this may be sufficient for transaction systems, decision support systems involve more complex work flows and a higher degree of user participation may be needed (Hawk and Dos Santos 1991). This finding is consistent with work showing that when developing standard applications, such as a payroll system, a small degree of user participation may suffice (Saleem 1996). One useful way of determining the type of system in this regard is to relate complexity to the number of different kinds of interfaces involved.

A management decision on what to do with user involvement in reaction to complexity could be "designed" through the development of the following technological rule:

> If the
> - degree of domain knowledge by developers is low, or
> - task complexity is high, or
>   - size of system to be build is large, or
>   - technical knowledge is low, or
>   - perceived change is great, or
> - the type of system is decision support (as opposed to transaction based),
>
> then a **higher** degree of user participation is needed.

## 4.2  Resources

The literature review developed three major influence factors regarding resources.

The first factor was management support. This support will increase the prospect of user participation (Cavaye 1995). Where senior managers are only moderately positive, or worse still, resistant, then risk increases considerably (Applegate et al. 1999). Management must support user participation in both word and deed, along with commanding results from the participation of users.

The second factor involves resources in the form of adequate budget and staff for the project (Cavaye 1995). When a project has limited resources, then users will be less involved simply because user participation is expensive. For example, a workshop with 12 users for two days may involve three or four developers in preparation and follow-up. The total cost of such a workshop may be more than two man months.

The third factor is time, especially with regard to whether the project has a hard or a soft deadline. If a project has a hard deadline, it may be more difficult to find the calendar time for user participation. User participation techniques often require planning well in advance. For example, finding a day for a workshop involving 12 busy people is impossible with short notice. Projects with hard deadlines can exclude effective engagement for user participation (Wilson et al. 1997).

The technological rule that we designed based on these findings (Pries-Heje and Baskerville 2008) was

> If the
> - management support is high, and/or
> - the budget and staff allocated for project is adequate, and/or
> - time pressure is insignificant,
>
> then a **higher** degree of user participation can be advantageous.

## 4.3  User Identity

The degree to which the users are personally known to the developers depends on the type of development. User identity is classified as "named" or "nameless" users. For example, Grudin (1991) distinguishes between in-house development, custom development, competitively bid and contract development, and product development. For in-house and custom development, the developers know the users from the very beginning. The most practical measure of this identity is whether the developers can name the users, or at least to obtain the names of the users in advance. In product development, developers do not know their users until the users buy the product. It is possible to identify potential users such as representative users of the last version of a product, but the complete set of users necessarily remain nameless until they acquire the product.

This leads to the simple technological rule:

> If the
> * users are nameless,
> then traditional user participation should be avoided.

Collectively, these three technological rules systematically define the CRU management design theory much as a system of hypotheses might define an explanatory scientific theory.

### 4.4  Grounding the User Involvement Case in Social Science

To develop a useful framework of technological rules for deciding when to have users participate in an IT project, we carried out a study involving three researchers: one tenured professor (one author of this paper) and two students writing a dissertation on user participation. In order to solve the how and when problem of user participation, we researched methods and techniques for user participation. As step one, we identified and reviewed hundreds of research papers and books on the subject. From this review, we developed a set of popular but alternative methods and techniques for user participation. Based on this set of techniques, we then conducted a field study in ten companies. We call this field study phase 1. In the concrete, we conducted exploratory interviews focusing on how user participation in practice took place. These were followed by semi-structured interviews, using a think-aloud test. After the field study (phase 1) we initiated phase 2, analyzing the alternative approaches discovered in the first phase. This lead to the technological rules presented above.

### 4.5  Practical Implications of the User Involvement Case

There seems to be widespread agreement that user participation is positive, is of high utility, and can be extremely valuable. However, many IT project managers don't know how and when to do what. They cannot implement user participation in practice in their project. The result being, in many cases, that user participation in practice is just something that is talked about and not practiced.

To solve that problem, we have developed the user participation technological rules that can help IT project managers decide when and how to have users participate. The technological rules were developed based on an extensive literature survey, an interview study, as well as a field study.

The technological rules approach is meant to be used at a workshop in the early phases of an IT project. We rigorously tested the technological rules in practice with project managers from ten companies. The project managers found that we had designed one possible and (to them) useful answer to the user participation problem (Pries-Heje and Baskerville 2008).

## 5  Case 3: Organizational Change

How can an organization select the best change strategy from the abundance of different foundational theories for organizational change? Each theory has its advocates and adherents, and there is little comparative research to aid the selection. The theories are so varied that comparisons are usually drawn between only a few alternatives (Tingey 1997). Our next case focuses on this selection issue, the lack of formulated tools to help organizational change managers to select from these change theories. Our intention is to improve the ability for organizational change managers to rationally select the most appropriate change strategies by designing technological rules to guide the decision making.

In connection with our survey of the organizational change literature, we conducted a number of search conferences involving participants from the Danish companies in order to assemble a catalogue of change approaches, which have been used successfully in practice. From the search conferences, we identified a number of high-level overall approaches. We analyzed them to determine their distinguishing characteristics and related them to the theories in the literature. We focused on the essential attributes of the organizational setting and the particular way of approaching change strategy. These are refined into ten prominent change strategies that can be represented as technological rules.

Each of these approaches was founded on the presence of highly specific conditions in the organizational setting, specific goals for the organizational change, and particular reasons for implementing change in the context of the organizational setting. These foundations embody a management design theory based on conditions, goals, and reasons. For shorthand, we will call this the CGR management design theory.

Following this analysis, we set out to elaborate the CGR management design theory to create technological rules to guide change managers in choosing which of the 10 change strategies would be most appropriate in an actual organizational setting. For example, for the change strategy called "commanding," we formulated the following assertions:

- Right now, we need change to happen fast
- It is primarily organizational structures that need to be changed
- In the past, we have had successes in requiring or dictating change

And for the change approach called "optionality," we formulated the assertions:

- Our employees are self-aware and always have an opinion
- We have very knowledgeable employees that know their areas well
- There are vast differences between the tasks of different employees

A management decision to adopt one of these two approaches to organizational change could be "designed" through the development of the following two technological rules. The references indicate examples of the approach recommended in the rule.

> If you want to initiate organizational change in a situation where you believe
> - that formal structures needs change, and
> - change is needed fast,
>
> then choose a *commanding* approach where change is driven and dictated by (top) management; one where management takes on the roles as owner, sponsor, and change agents (Huy 2001).

> If you want to initiate organizational change in a situation where you believe
> - that target group is very diverse and has large individual differences, and
> - the target group are experts,
>
> then choose an *optionality* approach where change is driven by the motivation and need of the individual; it is to a large degree optional (Rogers 2003).

Following similar developments, we defined eight further technological rules.

> If you want to initiate organizational change in a situation where you believe
> - that the need for change arises among the employees,
> - that there is no need for a standardized approach, that the result is more important than the process, and
> - an open management style will allow change to arise from the bottom,
>
> then choose an *employee driven* approach where change is driven from the bottom of the organizational hierarchy when needs for change arise among employees (Andersen et al. 2001; Kensing 2003; Kensing and Blomberg 1998).

> If you want to initiate organizational change in a situation where you believe
> - that dynamic and complex surroundings make it important to explore an open management style that will allow change to arise from the bottom,
>
> then choose an *exploration* approach where change is driven by the need for flexibility, agility, or a need to explore new markets, technology or customer groups (Benner and Tushman 2003; Mintzberg 1983).

> If you want to initiate organizational change in a situation where you believe
> - there is a need for change in attitudes and/or behavior,
> - the organization is talented in learning, and
> - relationships between means and goals are unclear,
>
> then choose a *learning driven* approach where change is driven by a focus on organizational learning, individual learning, and what creates new attitudes and behavior (Huy 2001).

If you want to initiate organizational change in a situation where you believe
- there are relatively stable surroundings so measurements from the past can be used to decide the future,

then choose a *metrics driven* approach where change is driven by metrics and measurements (Oakland 2003; Pande and Holpp 2000).

If you want to initiate organizational change in a situation where you believe
- there are relatively stable surroundings, and
- there are many homogeneous resources and work flows,

then choose a *production organized* approach where change is driven by the need for optimization and/or cost reduction (Benner and Tushman 2003; Huy 2001).

If you want to initiate organizational change in a situation where you believe
- a need exists for major change (for example, when organization has ground to a halt),
- nothing new happens,
- decisions are made but not carried out, and
- a crisis is eminent,

the choose a *reengineering* approach where change is driven by fundamentally rethinking and redesigning business processes to achieve dramatic improvements in critical, contemporary measures of performance, such as cost, quality, service, and speed (Bashein et al. 1994; Boudreau and Robey 1996; Davenport 1993; Hammer 1990; Hammer and Champy 1993; King 1994; Malhotra 1998; Willcocks et al. 1997).

If you want to initiate organizational change in a situation where you believe
- organizational skills and capabilities need to be developed,
- no unhealthy power struggles occur (so people can talk), and
- employees that can be exemplars are available,

then choose a *socializing* approach where change in organizational capabilities is driven by working with social relationships and diffusion of innovations happens through personal contacts rather than through plans and dictates (Huy 2001).

If you want to initiate organizational change in a situation where you believe
- work has vast complexity and variety so there really is a need for special knowledge, and
- there is access to necessary specialists, eventually by in-sourcing them,

then choose a *specialist driven* approach where change is driven by specialists, either with professional, technical, or domain knowledge (Ciborra 2000; Mintzberg 1983; Simon 1973, 1983; Woods 1988; Woods and Hollnagel 1987).

All of these technological rules represent systematic expressions of the CGR theory, conditions in the organizational setting, a stated goal of organizational change, and the reason for implementing change in the context of the organizational setting.

## 5.1  Grounding the Organizational Change Case in Social Science

We exercised these technological rules in two organizations, using them to design organizational change initiatives in each organization (Pries-Heje and Baskerville 2008). The rules took the form of a query form where managers expressed their degree of agreement or disagreement with the conditions underlying the rule connoted by statements. The degree to which the conditions for change in that organization can be compared to the conditions for each of the 10 rules is presented in Table 1. The fit of each is indicated by the percentage (0 to 100 percent) to which the rule's conditions are present in the particular organization. Take, for example, socializing. Here the rule is three-fold, consisting of answers to the following three statements: (1) we have situations where we believe organizational skills and capabilities need to be developed; (2) we have no unhealthy power struggles occuring (so people can talk); and (3) employees that can be exemplars are available. If the group of managers fully agree (equals 100 percent) with statement (1), partly agree (67 percent) with statement (2), and partly disagree (33 percent) with statement (3). Then the combined fit is calculated as (100 + 67 + 33 / 3).

A fit calculated above 67 percent means that the corresponding change strategy fits the organization well (will be successful). This application led us to change design recommendations in each company to achieve the best-fitting change strategies.

In both companies, the management of the IT division found the results quite positive and considered them very useful. In Company A, the CIO called the results a major "Aha!" experience. The recommendations at Company B led to a hybrid design using the "optionality" strategy on those change initiatives driven by the individual's or group's need and motivation and using the "commanding" strategy for designing change initiatives where they really needed to drive change fast.

**Table 1.** The Degree of Fit for Each of the 10 Change Strategies in the Evaluations

| Company A | Company B |
|---|---|
| 60%  Socializing | 71 %  Optionality |
| 60%  Learning driven | 65 %  Commanding |
| 56%  Production organized | 59 %  Socializing |
| 55%  Employee driven | 58 %  Production organized |
| 54%  Optionality | 56 %  Specialist driven |
| 42%  Metrics driven | 40 %  Metrics driven |
| 37.5%    Specialist driven | 34 %  Learning driven |
| 35%  Exploration | 29 %  Exploration |
| 34,5%    Commanding | 28 %  Reengineering |
| 31%  Reengineering | 18 %  Employee driven |

## 5.2   Practical Implications of the Organizational Change Case

We designed and implemented the organizational change technological rules as a coherent artifact and evaluated it within a research project involving three participating companies. The IT organization in two of these companies was particularly involved in evaluating through an action research field study. In one of the evaluated organizations, the management group committed to the prescribed change strategy—not in detail, but in principle. This result is nearly ideal in relation to the prescriptions from the nexus. In the other organization evaluated, the results were also quite positive and the framework of technological rules was evaluated as very useful.

Whether the visions for strategic change in the two organizations will be achieved will take another two to three years to develop. At the moment, however, the organizational change framework of technological rules clearly leads to operational management decisions about change strategy.

# 6   Conclusion

This paper contributes a fresh perspective on how management planning based on design science operates through expressions of a particular type of design theory called management design theory. These types of theories can be expressed through systems of technological rules. By applying design science research as a guide for designing general frameworks for decision making (that is to say, heuristics), we help managers (in their own perception) more easily approach complex, strategic decisions. The approach is built on the concept of simple design theories and technological rules, a simple expression of the design theory that relates a general organizational situation to a general course of action. Three grounded cases—process improvement, user involvement, and organizational change management—illustrate and validate the concepts.

Our three cases provide practical contributions. However, in general, this design science approach to designing management decisions demonstrates that design concepts have great worth for improving management activities, a field of work that is not usually associated with design. This strategic framing of organizational design decisions contributes to the general core of design research by demonstrating that technological rules are an operational form of managerial design theory.

## References

Andersen, C.V., Krath, F., Krukow, L., Mathiassen, L., Pries-Heje, J.: The Grass Root Effort. In: Mathiassen, L., Pries-Heje, J., Ngwenyama, O. (eds.) Improving Software Organizations: From Principles to Practice. Addison-Wesley, Upper Saddle River (2001)

Applegate, L., McFarlan, F.W., McKenney, J.L.: Corporate Information Systems Management: Text and Cases. Irwin–McGraw Hill, New York (1999)

Archer, M.S.: Realist Social Theory: The Morphogenetic Approach. Cambridge University Press, Cambridge (1995)

Barki, H., Hartwick, J.: Rethinking the Concept of User Involvement. MIS Quarterly 13(1), 55–63 (1989)

Barki, H., Hartwick, J.: Rethinking the Concept of User Involvement and User Attitude. MIS Quarterly 18(1), 59–79 (1994)

Baroudi, J.J., Olson, M.H., Ives, B.: An Empirical Study of the Impact of User Involvement on System Usage and Information Satisfaction. Communications of the ACM 29(3), 232–238 (1986)

Bashein, B.J., Markus, M.L., Riley, P.: Preconditions for BPR Success: And How to Prevent Failures. Information Systems Management 11(2), 7–13 (1994)

Benner, M., Tushman, M.: Exploitation, Exploration, and Process Management: The Productivity Dilemma Revisited. Academy of Management Review 28(2), 238–256 (2003)

Bødker, K., Simonsen, J., Kensing, F.: Participatory IT Design: Designing for Business and Workplace Realities. The MIT Press, Boston (2004)

Boudreau, M.-C., Robey, D.: Coping with Contradictions in Business Process Reengineering. Information Technology and People 9(4), 40–57 (1996)

Cavaye, A.L.M.: User Participation in System Development Revisited. Information Management 29, 311–323 (1995)

Ciborra, C.U.: From Control to Drift: The Dynamics of Corporate Information Infrastructures. Oxford University Press, Oxford (2000)

Clavadetscher, C.: User Involvement: Key to Success. IEEE Software 15(2), 30–32 (1998)

Curtis, B., Krasner, H., Iscoe, N.: A Field Study of the Software Design Process for Large Systems. Communications of the ACM 31(11), 1268–1287 (1988)

Davenport, T.H.: Process Innovation: Re-engineering Work through Information Technology. Harvard Business School Press, Boston (1993)

Denyer, D., Tranfield, D., van Aken, J.: Developing Design Propositions through Research Synthesis. Organization Studies 29(3), 393–413 (2008)

Glaser, B.G., Strauss, A.L.: The Discovery of Grounded Theory, Strategies for Qualitative Research. Aldine Publishers, Chicago (1967)

Gregor, S., Jones, D.: The Anatomy of a Design Theory. Journal of the Association for Information Systems 8(5), 312–335 (2007)

Grudin, J.: Interactive Systems: Bridging the Gaps Between Developers and Users. IEEE Computer 24(4), 59–69 (1991)

Hammer, M.: Reengineering Work: Don't Automate, Obliterate. Harvard Business Review, 104–112 (July-August 1990)

Hammer, M., Champy, J.: Reengineering the Corporation: A Manifesto for Business Revolution. Harper Business, New York (1993)

Hawk, S., Dos Santos, B.L.: Successful System Development: The Effect of Situational Factors on Alternate User Roles. IEEE Transactions on Engineering Management 38(4), 316–327 (1991)

Hunter, R.B., Thayer, R.H.: Introduction. In: Hunter, R.B., Thayer, R.H. (eds.) Software Process Improvement, pp. 1–4. IEEE Computer Society Press, Los Alamitos (2001)

Huy, Q.N.: Time, Temporal Capability, and Planned Change. Academy of Management Review 26(4), 601–623 (2001)

Ives, B., Olson, M.H.: User Involvement in MIS Success: A Review of Research. Management Science 30(5), 586–603 (1984)

Kant, I.: The Critique of Pure Reason (1781); J. Watson, trans., In: Rand, B. (ed.) Modern Classical Philosophers, pp. 370–456. Houghton Mifflin, Cambridge (1908)

Kensing, F.: Methods and Practices in Participatory Design. ITU Press, Copenhagen (2003)

Kensing, F., Blomberg, J.: Participatory Design: Issues and Concerns. Computer Supported Cooperative Work 7(3/4), 167–185 (1998)

Kensing, F., Munk-Madsen, A.: PD: Structure in the Toolbox. Communications of the ACM 36(6), 78–85 (1993)

King, W.R.: Process Reengineering: The Strategic Dimensions. Information Systems Management 11(2), 71–73 (1994)

Malhotra, Y.: Business Process Redesign: An Overview. IEEE Engineering Management Review 26(3), 27–31 (1998)

March, S.T., Smith, G.: Design and Natural Science Research on Information Technology. Decision Support Systems 15(4), 251–266 (1995)

Mintzberg, H.: Structure in Fives: Designing Effective Organizations. Prentice-Hall, Upper Saddle River (1983)

Nicholas, J.M.: User Involvement: What Kind, How much and When? Journal of Systems Management 36, 23–37 (1985)

Oakland, J.S.: TQM—Text with Cases, 3rd edn. Butterworth-Heinemann, Burlington (2003)

Pande, P.S., Holpp, L.: What Is Six Sigma? McGraw-Hill, New York (2000)

Pawson, R., Tilley, N.: Realistic Evaluation. Sage Publications, London (1997)

Pries-Heje, J., Baskerville, R.: Improving Software Organizations: An Analysis of Diverse Normative Models. Paper presented at the EuroSPI, Graz, Austria (2003)

Pries-Heje, J., Baskerville, R.: The Design Theory Nexus. MIS Quarterly 32(4), 731–755 (2008)

Rogers, E.M.: Diffusion of Innovations, 5th edn. Free Press, New York (2003)

Saleem, N.: An Empirical Test of the Contingency Approach to User Participation in Information Systems Development. Journal of Management Information Systems 13, 145–166 (1996)

Simon, H.A.: The Structure of Ill Structured Problems. Artificial Intelligence 4, 181–201 (1973)

Simon, H.A.: Search and Reasoning in Problem Solving. Artificial Intelligence 21, 7–29 (1983)

Simon, H.A.: The Science of the Artificial, 3rd edn. MIT Press, Cambridge (1996)

Strauss, A., Corbin, J.: Basics of Qualitative Research: Techniques and Procedures for Developing Grounded Theory, 2nd edn. Sage Publications, Thousand Oaks (1998)

Tingey, M.O.: Comparing ISO 9000, Malcolm Baldrige, and the SEI CMM for Software: A Reference and Selection Guide. Prentice, Upper Saddle River (1997)

Vaishnavi, V., Kuechler, W.: Design Research in Information Systems. Association for Information Systems (2004), http://www.isworld.org/Researchdesign/drisISworld.htm (retrieved October 2, 2004)

van Aken, J.E.: Management Research Based on the Paradigm of the Design Sciences: The Quest for Field-Tested and Grounded Technological Rules. The Journal of Management Studies 4(2), 219–246 (2004)

van Aken, J.E.: Management Research as a Design Science: Articulating the Research Products of Mode 2 Knowledge Production in Management. British Journal of Management 16(1), 19–36 (2005a)

van Aken, J.E.: Valid Knowledge for the Professional Design of Large and Complex Design Processes. Design Studies 26(4), 379–404 (2005b)

Walls, J.G., Widmeyer, G.R., El Sawy, O.A.: Building an Information System Design Theory for Vigilant EIS. Information Systems Research 3(1), 36–59 (1992)

Willcocks, L., Feeny, D., Islei, G.: Managing IT as a Strategic Resource. McGraw-Hill, New York (1997)

Wilson, S., Bekker, M., Johnson, P., Johnson, H.: Helping and Hindering User Involvement: A Tale of Everyday Design. Paper presented at the CHI 1997, Atlanta, Georgia (1997)

Woods, D.D.: Coping with Complexity: The Psychology of Human Behavior in Complex Systems. In: Goodstein, L.P., Andersen, H.B., Olsen, S.E. (eds.) Tasks, Errors and Mental Models, pp. 128–148. Taylor and Francis, London (1988)

Woods, D.D., Hollnagel, E.: Mapping Cognitive Demands in Complex Problem-Solving Worlds. International Journal of Man-Machine Studies 26, 257–275 (1987)

# About the Authors

**Jan Pries Heje** is Professor in Information Systems, Department of Communication, Business and Information Technologies, Roskilde University, and head of the User Driven IT-Innovation Research Group. His research focuses on designing and building innovative solutions to managerial and organizational IT problems. Previous and current projects explore process improvement as design, the ability for an organization to improve, and how one can design a process for making better sourcing decisions. Dr. Pries-Heje is co-chair of the joint IFIP 8.2/8.6 working conference on "Human Benefit through the Diffusion of IS Design Science," and, from January 2010, chair of IFIP TC 8 Working Group 8.2 on Information Systems. He can be reached by e-mail at janph@ruc.dk.

**Richard L. Baskerville** is a Board of Advisors Professor of Information Systems at Georgia State University. His research and authored works regard security of information systems, methods of information systems design and development, and the interaction of information systems and organizations. Dr. Baskerville currently serves as editor-in-chief of the *European Journal of Information Systems*. He is a Chartered Engineer, holds a B.S. (summa cum laude) from the the University of Maryland, and M.Sc. and Ph.D. degrees from the London School of Economics, University of London. He can be reached by e-mail at baskerville@acm.org.

# Modeling Forensic Evidence Systems Using Design Science

Colin Armstrong and Helen Armstrong

School of Information Systems,
Curtin University of Technology,
Bentley, WA, Australia

**Abstract.** This paper presents an overview of the application of design science research to the tactical management of forensic evidence processing. The opening discussion addresses the application of design science techniques to specific socio-technical information systems research in regard to processing forensic evidence. The discussion then presents the current problems faced by those dealing with evidence and a conceptual meta-model for a unified approach to forensic evidence is developed. Any practical application of the suggested model would be predominantly law enforcement driven; evaluation of sections of the model has been carried out by law enforcement participants in several international jurisdictions.

**Keywords:** Design science research, socio-technology, forensic evidence.

## 1 Introduction

Design science is not just a methodology for devising solutions utilizing technology. It is an approach that offers the researcher the ability to investigate problem spaces and devise theories and designs that could address such problem spaces. Most problem spaces encompass various stakeholders, each with a particular perspective on that problem. The field of forensic evidence is no different, with three main stakeholder groups: law enforcement, the first responders to a crime situation; forensic scientists, who take physical items (DNA, weapons, disk drives, mobile phone, etc.) and, using scientific standards and methodologies, form opinions and interpretations of the evidence; and the judiciary, who employ information about the evidence derived from law enforcement and forensic science to present arguments for either the prosecution or defense.

Electronic devices are increasingly appearing as important items of evidence in criminal investigations, due to the spread of technology and society's dependence upon that technology in everyday life. Although digital forensics is a frequent topic in information systems security research, the focus in this area is broadening to consider the links between all types of forensic evidence (digital and otherwise) for many types of traditional crime, not just computer crime. This is due to the increasing amount of potential evidence stored electronically on devices such as computers,

J. Pries-Heje et al. (Eds.): IS Design Science Research, IFIP AICT 318, pp. 282–300, 2010.

Internet and ISP servers, mobile phones, portable storage devices, and other electronic devices and media for traditional and digital crimes.

Investigation of the area of evidence illustrates a number of problems emerging as technology becomes more pervasive. Using design science as the chosen research approach, this paper describes a study of the forensic evidence problem space through the perspectives of the three main stakeholder groups and the design of a meta-model for the effective management of forensic evidence at the tactical level. The meta-model presented provides an opportunity to employ a number of different technological solutions, depending upon the perspective and needs of the interested party. As law enforcers are the stakeholders with the majority of exposure to, and interaction with, evidence, the evaluation of the suggested processes and models has been undertaken by a focus group of experienced law enforcement officers.

## 2  Why Design Science?

Evidence takes the form of both physical objects and information about those objects. Evidence can be comprised of fragments of disparate data that combine to produce something larger and more meaningful in the context of the investigation. So why design science? In design science research, "knowledge and understanding of a problem domain and its solution are achieved in the building and application of the designed artifact" (Hevner et al. 2004, p. 75). Furthermore, design science attempts to create things that serve human needs (March and Smith 1995) and benefits those affected by the problem situation. With the focus on designing solutions Design Science is an ideal approach for the analysis of the forensic evidence problem space and the design of a model to eliminate or reduce that problem domain.

## 3  Design Science and Soft Approaches

Much of the literature in support of design science focuses on the engineering or "hard" side involving scientific rigor pertaining to the physical artifact and technology (together with the associated systems development). However, the "soft" side of information systems recognizing the social and organizational aspects is also emerging. Baskerville et al. (2007) highlight the need for a soft design science research approach to accommodate IT/IS artifacts in natural organizational settings. Information systems encompass both social, human, and organizational aspects, as well as tools and technology, and all of these aspects need to be considered in problem studies and the associated solution design. Checkland and Scholes (1990) discuss the need to recognize that problems are seen through the world view of an individual, which they refer to as the *weltanschauung*. Human beings "interpret what they perceive. Moreover, the interpretation may, in principle, be unique to a particular observer. This means that multiple perspectives are always available" (Checkland and Scholes 1990, p. 25). In the context of this research the authors propose that world views can be either individual or group perspectives, depending upon the nature and scope of the problem domain under consideration.   A full understanding of the problem situation incorporating the perspectives of the different stakeholders provides a holistic view for those attempting to design solutions. Softer approaches also permit the consideration of social and political issues that form an integral part of problem situations. The consideration of human and organizational issues is crucial for the design and implementation of effective solutions.

March and Smith (1995) and March and Storey (2008) propose the two cornerstones of design science as building and evaluating artifacts. In order to design, build, and evaluate artifacts, it is necessary to understand the problem causes and impact to ensure that the artifact does actually address the problem.

# 4  The Problem Space

A problem exists when a stakeholder in a given situation perceives there is a difference between the desired state and the current state (Checkland and Scholes 1990; Jayaratna 1999; Jonassen 2000). Key to the recognition of a problem is that a stakeholder group affected by the situation perceives a gap between the two states. The same problem can be perceived differently by each stakeholder group within the problem situation based upon their perspective of the world. In order to fully understand a problem situation, the perspectives of different stakeholder groups must be considered. To be of value and significance, design science should address a class of problem (faced by a collection rather than by one individual), be nontrivial in nature (significant), as well as relevant (germane and useful).

A clear understanding of the problem and its causes is needed in order to develop a theory relating to the design of a solution and also before an in-depth design of a solution is embarked upon. As the aim is to reduce or eliminate the problem space, interaction with theory conceptualization and development, the solution design process, plus the solution evaluation is essential.

# 5  The Solution Space

Inextricably linking the problem and solution spaces is the theory space. Walls et al. (1992) differentiated design theory from scientific theory by considering the overall objectives of each. While scientific theory seeks to understand and predict natural phenomenon, the aim of design theory is to guide artifact creation. March and Smith (1995) and later also Venable (2006) note the interchangeable nature of models and theories as forms for representing knowledge.

Venable highlights the importance and inclusion of theory building as a specific component of the design science research process, claiming that theorizing and theory building actually occur before, during, throughout, at the end, and as a result of design science research. Venable proposes a cyclic approach that recognizes the central role played by theory and theorizing.

The theory realm holds value as the theory or hypothesis is expressed in a design with particular application to the given problem space. The theory realm also is dependent on the stakeholder's perspective. Where particular stakeholder groups are removed from consideration, there will be no debate or understanding of the holistic situation. A holistic viewpoint facilitates and promotes a successful solution design and ownership of the artifact.

The design is a conceptualization of a specified solution that is one of many potential solutions envisaged to reduce or eliminate the problem. Each potential solution is an instantiation of a conceptualization and, in information systems terms, a solution design could be a detailed physical model illustrating application in a specific *in situ* or a logical model that could be applied in a number of physical modes.

A project to investigate the problem space in forensic evidence management and the design of a socio-technological solution space has been undertaken. With a strong socio-political element, the solution design devised took the form of a meta-model enveloping, a number of lower-level interactive models to shape a management system. An iterative approach was employed in this research using three main stages of data collection and analyses (see Figure 1). The stakeholders were interviewed in three groups over a period of two years, with participants in the judiciary, forensic practitioners, and law enforcement stakeholder groups interviewed in each period. This enabled a gradual development of the model together with solutions on a progressive basis. The data gathered in stages 2 and 3 was used to confirm the findings from the interviews in earlier stages and further develop the new model and solutions.

## 6  Forensic Evidence Problem Space

The essence of the forensic evidence problem space is the disparate conceptualization of the usage and tactical management of evidence. Exposure and association with forensic evidence by the three primary perspective groups is sequential in nature and the three groups do not enjoy forensic evidence associations equally. A simplistic observation would describe law enforcement as the first responders, forensic scientists as the experts, and the judiciary as that highly respected independent determinator of an accused's fate. The problem space of the forensic evidence management project is illustrated in the rich picture presented in Figure 2. The nature, purpose, and importance of forensic evidence is viewed differently by each of the stakeholder groups and, with no common understanding or standards to underpin the realm, misunderstandings commonly arise.

Once a perceived wrong has been brought to the attention of the enforcers of law, an enquiry may commence and, to discover the facts behind the perceived wrong, evidence is sought. To better interpret and understand the meaning of evidence, we rely on scientific expertise. Finally, when sufficient information is gathered, it is presented in order to persuade the finder of fact in determining an accused's guilt. The association between evidence and each of these three perspectives reflects very different relationships, as can be seen in Figure 2.

The law enforcement community has the greatest exposure to forensic evidence. It identifies and collects the evidence at the scene of a violation; it manages the safe handling of the evidence in order for it to be admissible to a court of law; it directs the appointment of forensic scientists for evidence analysis and collates forensic results; and finally, it presents evidence in court predominantly representing the prosecution. Forensic scientists carry out testing and analyses specific to the inquiry, and the judiciary presents evidence to support an argument of guilt or non-guilt.

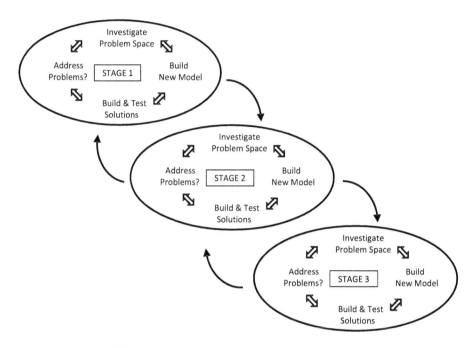

**Fig. 1.** Iterative Approach Employed in the Research

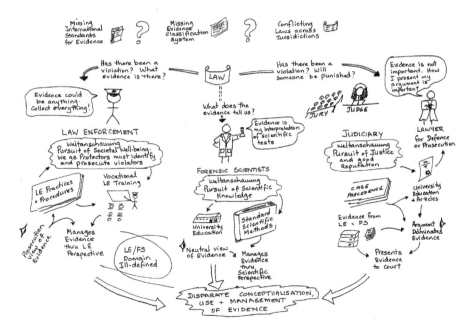

**Fig. 2.** Forensic Evidence Management Problem Space

The lack of standard procedures, underlying classifications, and international standards relating to evidence, as well as differing laws, has a major effect upon law enforcers, in comparison to the minor influence it plays for the judiciary and forensic scientists.

## 6.1 Law Enforcement

Law enforcers are held responsible, not only as first responders to secure evidence locations; in most situations, they are solely responsible for the collection and management of forensic evidence. Law enforcers are considered less-educated blue collar workers and, therefore, not as well qualified to assess issues as forensic scientists or the judiciary. They tend to be faced with the chaotic frontier of humanity at its worst and tasked with responsibility for forensic evidence management while being required to preserve peace and security in our communities. This situation results in little or no time for law enforcers to contemplate the intricacies of an incident and, because anything could be evidence, adopt the practice of collecting everything.

Law enforcers do not have internationally agreed standards ensuring unified best practices for forensic evidence processes, relying on jurisdictional policies and procedures. This does not suggest that law enforcers do a poor job. It does suggest, however, that even though there is a great deal of international cooperation and that enforcement agencies and personnel strive to provide the best service, there is little national or global agreement as to what constitutes best practice and service.

## 6.2 Forensic Scientists

Unless working alongside law enforcers, forensic scientists are not first responders, do not secure evidence locations, do not collect evidence, and are only responsible for the management of forensic evidence while it is in their care for analysis. Forensic scientists often become involved only after law enforcers have collected potential evidence. As forensic scientists usually have university education in a scientific field, they are perceived to be educated and professional experts in their particular domain of research. This group is perceived to be experts without a bias toward either prosecution or defense because they pursue discovery of facts based on dispassionate scientific methods. Hence, forensic scientists are perceived to be divorced from determinations of guilt or otherwise.

Forensic experts are regularly afforded the luxury of retiring to a secured laboratory far from the influences of a chaotic world and, therefore, have more time and an environment more conducive to contemplating the meaning of evidence items. Forensic experts are often excluded from the rest of an enquiry and only called upon for specialized expert opinion. When granted access to complete case file information, forensic experts do have time to contemplate the intricacies of an incident. Generally, forensic scientists are only associated with particular items of case evidence and not with every collected item.

As scientists, forensic scientists are members of organizations that are international and that establish and maintain agreed standard practices for conducting scientific processes. Many fields within forensic science have their own classification systems or methods of categorizing objects; however, these are isolates and form well-defined boundaries resulting is discrete, unintegrated systems.

## 6.3  Judiciary

Although the judiciary group members fall into three separate subgroups—prosecution, defense, and finder of fact—they have yet another point of view relating to evidence. Judiciary group members tend to focus most strongly on interpretations of evidence that support their particular objective: either proving guilt, defending and disputing evidence interpretations, or passing culpability judgement. The judiciary are rarely first responders; they are not responsible for securing evidence locations or collecting evidence, but they are responsible for the management of forensic evidence if it is given into their care.

In contrast to the law enforcement and the forensic science stakeholders, the judiciary believe the evidence itself is not the key factor, but their presentation of the argument pertaining to that evidence in a court of law, or in other words their ability to persuade the finders of fact of guilt or innocence. The judiciary is perceived by society as being highly educated as well as respected, independent determiners of an accused's fate. The judiciary often deals with the worst results from the chaotic frontier of humanity, but does so in the comfort of a secured environment. The judiciary is not perceived as being expert in scientific matters but do have access to specialized publications relating scientific matters to the law and legal precedents. This group specializes in contemplation of evidence, its meanings, and the case in question before the courts and, by ensuring decisions are not hasty, engenders the perception that evidence matters are well and carefully contemplated. However, the judiciary only deals with a small but essential selection of the total collected case evidence and features only that evidence supporting the prosecution or defense case.

The judiciary maintains a deep abidance to rigorously established rules and procedures relating to evidence that are accepted internationally even though the same set of rules are not applied in the same manner in every jurisdiction.

## 6.4  Global and Local Problems

The resulting operational situation presents law enforcers with having to resolve a problem situation because it has greater impact on their operations than the other two perspective groups. The forensic scientists are, for the most part, isolated from the entire case under investigation and limited to providing an expert opinion of the evidence based on scientific principles. Finally, the judiciary determine justice based on only that small amount of evidence essential to argue their case.

The problems emerging from this consideration are both global and local, and include

- a lack of international standards, policies, and procedures for the identification, collection, analysis and presentation of evidence
- no classification systems for evidence, only classifications and categorization for certain types of objects that may be used as evidence
- the lack of tools and techniques to provide a big picture in the consideration of criminal cases, resulting in a piecemeal rather than informed, holistic approach to decision making about evidence

- the bias of perspective and the different perspectives of the stakeholders, resulting in the value of evidence being viewed differently by each of the stakeholder groups

## 7 Forensic Evidence Theory and Model Design

An extensive archival search was conducted to identify prior work done to address the above problems and any standards or models already developed in the area. The findings were that the work has been piecemeal with no interdisciplinary solutions proposed. In all, 52 professionals across the three domains were interviewed and data collected regarding the nature of evidence, the problems they faced, and a desired state. A set of models was then developed based on analyses of that data.

The models, designed to reflect perspectives in forensic evidence tactical management, draw upon established theories and modeling approaches. The journey along the evidence path from raw data to courtroom-presented evidence is at times complex and chaotic. No single theory adequately addresses the modeling of forensic evidence. There are two main streams of theory providing the elements underpinning such modeling. The first approach addresses the organization of evidence, which draws on theories associated with systems. The second approach accommodates the nature of evidence, which includes legal perspectives.

General systems theory is the overriding approach to the organization of evidence and associated information. To this are incorporated elements from a number of interconnected theoretical bases including chaos theory, complexity theory, network theory, social–network theory, and actor–network theory.

The overriding theories addressing the legal perspective are legal theory and evidence theory, which are strongly linked with justice and policing theories. As burdens of proof are not absolute they are dealt with as probability values. Probability theory is in turn accompanied by Bayesian statistical theory and Dempster-Shafer theory. In addition to theories, principles such as Locard's exchange principle are applied to the analysis of crime scenes.

Other theories contributing to the design of these models include elements from Heisenberg's uncertainty principle, information theory, scientific theory, model theory, and stakeholder theory. The development of the designed models draws on elements from these theory foundations.

The aim was to design a high-level conceptual model that provided an interdisciplinary view of tactical management of forensic evidence. Such an approach offers a broad opportunity to satisfactorily address the challenges presented in the forensic evidence problem space. A unifying holistic forensic evidence model necessarily consists of components specifically designed to address both global and local problems. There are six components considered desirable for inclusion in a model for the tactical management of forensic evidence processing.

1. A method for understanding the transitional information flow as raw data related to forensic evidence changes to become evidence due to the information that practitioners extract from the raw collected data and convert into knowledge.
2. A method for determining the particular relationship between the enquirer and the evidence.

3. A system for examining the interrelatedness of forensic evidence in a network of case evidence.
4. A method of visualizing forensic evidence networks.
5. A repository for forensic evidence information.
6. A system to accommodate classification of forensic evidence, and provide standards and best practices.

The Armstrong forensic evidence meta-model (see Figure 3) brings together the six components identified as desirable for the tactical management of forensic evidence processing. Modeling the six components reveals that four components are processes and two are frameworks. Modeling also reveals that two components address sociological aspects and four components address technological aspects of forensic evidence. The six models forming the meta-model are

- evidence data to knowledge conversion
- evidence stakeholder perspective
- evidence relationships network
- evidence resource library
- evidence network analysis
- evidence classification scheme

The *evidence data to knowledge conversion* process (see Figure 4) models an entry point into the inquiry-related data and provides the mechanism for determining the status of evidence entering an inquiry. Some data is self evident in nature and less disputable than other data. During the processes inculcated in this model, initial statistical data collection commences and practitioners form conclusions based on the accumulation of data. The major contribution of this process is in the modeling of data integrity entering an inquiry.

During the inquiry process, all incoming evidence arrives, initially, as data, and in a spasmodic manner. Then, as reasoning and analysis commences, the data undergoes

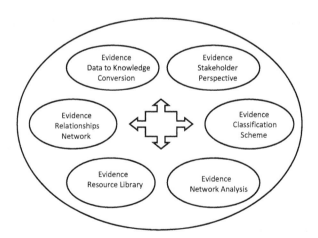

**Fig. 3.** The Armstrong Forensic Evidence Meta-Model

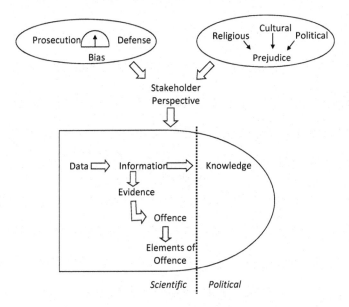

**Fig. 4.** Evidence Data to Knowledge Conversion

a transitional process that sees some data progress to become knowledge based on information processing while other data items may be held awaiting further clarification, discounted, or discarded.

Evidence can only exist in the human mind and it is that information that per-suades. Forensic evidence is that information that persuades to a level determined by the court within a jurisdiction's legal system. Commonly in matters of civil dispute the burden of proof is "in all likelihood," and in criminal matters the burden of proof is "beyond a reasonable doubt."

This process models the data transition by requiring the inquirer to recognize the bias and prejudices they will be perceived to possess. Recognition of the inquirer's perceived associations to the evidence is essential in determining the meanings attributed to evidence interpretations. The purpose of establishing the inquirer's association to evidence is not to change the meanings attributed to evidence analysis but rather to better understand the reasoning processes that have lead to conclusions based on the analysis of evidence.

The purpose of modeling the transitional nature of data into evidence is to under-stand better how the evidence explains what occurred.

The *evidence stakeholder perspective* (illustrated in Figure 5) provides the mech-anism for assessing the justification of a practitioner entering the enquiry and illustrates the practitioner's relationship to evidence. This facilitates a mechanism for determining bias and defines the extent of the practitioner's engagement in the enquiry process. The major contribution of this process is the explicit statement of association between enquirer and evidence.

As an inquirer may enter the inquiry process at any time during the process, their entry should be justifiable, having a legitimate reason for being granted access to the

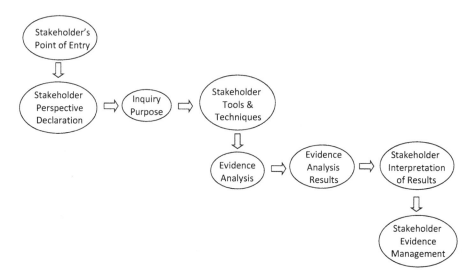

**Fig. 5.** Evidence Stakeholder Perspective

case evidence. Without a clear purpose for entering the inquiry process, access should be denied. Each entrant to the inquiry process will possess attributes deemed desirable that will contribute to drawing the case to a satisfactory conclusion.

Having been granted entry to an inquiry, the next step requires an explicit recognition of the bias and prejudices the entrant may be perceived to possess. The entrant will possess skills, knowledge, and qualifications considered worthy in furthering the progress of the inquiry but others may maintain an opinion as to how the entrant may conduct evidence analysis. As evidence may be defined as information possessing an ability to persuade, it is important to also understand the persuasive nature of the inquirer. The persuasive nature of the inquirer is directly associated with how others perceive them.

The next step in the inquiry process requires determining the purpose for which the entrant has been granted access to case evidence. The reason for entering the inquiry process designates the scope of conduct permitted to the inquirer. There are many reasons one may seek access to evidence, including: crime scene reconstruction based on forensic evidence, determining appropriate storage of evidence items, developing an evidence matrix for determining commonalities between witness statements, filing inquiry information, and determining appropriate methods of evidence analysis. The reason for limiting the scope of inquirer activity with the evidence is to assist in ensuring that the integrity of the evidence is not damaged during the progress of the investigation, and that the entrant only conducts those activities deemed necessary by their role.

Based on the entrant's skills, knowledge, and qualifications, together with a defined purpose, the inquirer may choose certain tools and techniques to apply to the evidence. It is important that the choice of tools and techniques are appropriate to the entrant's reason for accessing the evidence.

Once the preceding steps have been achieved to a level commensurate with the nature of the inquiry, the entrant may access the evidence. It is at this stage of the process that the inquirer shall conduct whatever examination of the evidence meets the specific needs of the inquiry. Following the examination and analyses of evidence, the results are produced, with such results varying dependent upon the nature of the examination process. Having obtained sets of analysis results, the inquirer sets about interpreting meanings to explain those particular aspects of the case being examined.

The final step in the inquiry process refers to evidence management. During a complex inquiry, there may be many subordinate inquiry processes, some conducted sequentially, others concurrent to the overall inquiry. Evidence management in this step relates only to the inquirer at hand and their management of the materials passing into their realm of responsibility. Most inquirers will only have access to small selections of the complete set of case related evidence. Having conducted their specific tasks with the evidence, the evidence continues along the inquiry process journey. Depending on the nature of the tasks conducted, the evidence may continue its journey, may have been subjected to destructive testing, or may transition into a case report.

The *evidence relationships network* (see Figure 6) process provides explanations for the linking relationships of categorized enquiry evidence discovered by practitioners when adopting a link perspective of evidence. As we tend to focus on what we can directly see, the major contribution of this process is directing the enquirer to examine the intangible links.

The purpose of this process is to understand the relationships between evidence, the inquiry domain, and other sets of information affecting evidence.

Within the inquiry domain, certain common elements tend to be associated with an inquiry. The common elements are attributes associated with the incident, its location, the associated actors, and an offence. Evidence tends to be directly or indirectly linked to one or more of these four elements. This process draws the inquirer to identify the intangible links that exist between these four elements. The intangible links may exist between what, when, where, who, why, and how with incident, location, actor, and offence. The intangible links may relate to actions, inactions, ownership, possession, and knowledge of, or assist in explaining causes and effects.

The *evidence network analysis* (see Figure 7) process provides a network science perspective of an inquiry, thereby permitting visualizing the inquiry as an interrelated web and additionally providing a mathematical method for describing the relationships between evidence items. The major contribution of this process is the statistical analyses and visualizations of links and the absence of links that are enabled by adopting network science techniques.

The network science approach models objects in a defined situation as nodes, joined by links or relationships. A network consists of nodes linked to other nodes. Network science provides the underlying theory, tools, and techniques for determining the strength of nodes and links, and analyzes the changes in network structure and linkages in a dynamic situation. The importance of a node is measured according to a few simple rules. Determining the importance of networked nodes is achieved by examining centrality measures of degree, closeness, betweenness, and path length, in addition to overall network density. These measures indicate the strength of a node based on how well it is connected to the rest of the network.

As the scientific and legal efforts supporting forensic evidence continue to progress and develop, consolidation of resources enhances forensic evidence practitioner capabilities. To date much of the work conducted has been restricted to silos of expertise. The resource library models an approach to facilitate interactive multidisciplinary progress of evidence processes. It comprises both social and technological elements, presenting an extensive repository of data in the form of the evidence information system (EIS). The overall motivations of the stakeholders are represented by the top block above the EIS and forms the objectives. Data is contributed by the three stakeholder groups shown on the left-hand side of the EIS, with the action represented by the right-hand block, the project and process management. The technologies applied are shown in the lower block.

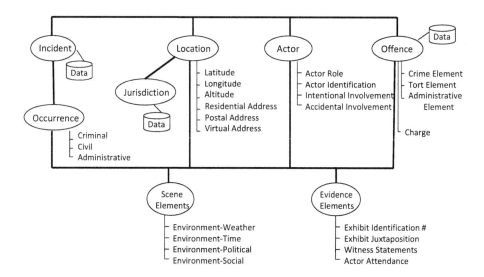

**Fig. 6.** Evidence Relationships Network

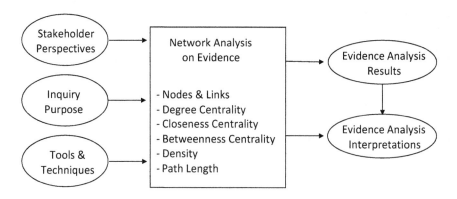

**Fig. 7.** Evidence Network Analysis

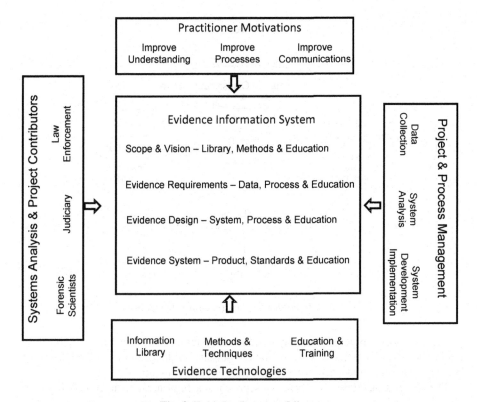

**Fig. 8.** Evidence Resource Library

The participants interviewed across the three domains agreed that the evidence resource library was the most important component as well as the most difficult to develop as all stakeholder groups need to agree upon the foundation theories, standards, and ontologies. However, the development of such an integrated resource for evidence practitioners is considered an integral component to a holistic model for the tactical management of forensic evidence.

The *evidence classification scheme* (see Figure 9) facilitates the various procedural practices for classifying physical evidence items and, more particularly, classifying forensic evidence relationships. The major contribution of this process is providing a basic foundation for the identification, organization, and categorization of evidence at a global level, for application in law enforcement, forensic science and judicial domains.

A complex inquiry is made up of diverse components. Apart from evidence associated with the case, there are people from different perspectives charged with undertaking different tasks. Each evidence practitioner, charged with different objectives to achieve, addresses evidence in a different manner. There is confusion arising from variations in terminologies and phrases applied to the same evidence. Legal requirements of evidence also vary between jurisdictions. This process presents a holistic approach to managing these diverse components.

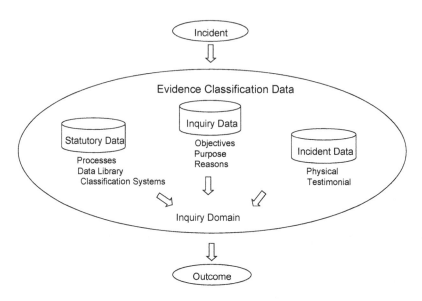

**Fig. 9.** Evidence Classification Scheme

Each evidence practitioner may require a system to organize the evidence set before them. Hence processes are defined to classify evidence items, and relationships between evidence items, according to the purpose of the inquiry.

The integration of the six processes presents a high-level meta-model for more effective handling of forensic evidence and its management across the three stakeholder domains. The meta-model exists only as a conceptual model as further analysis of component processes requires further detailed design before any prototype can be developed and tested in practice.

## 8   Forensic Evidence Model Evaluation

The building of the meta-model took place while interviews with the participants from the three stakeholder groups were in progress. This enabled a progressive development of processes to address problems and suggest potential solutions, moving between design of the new model, the underlying theories and considerations as to how it could be applied in practice. As the law enforcers were the drivers of the change, a focus group of law enforcement officers reviewed the meta-model and applied specific lower-level solutions to actual cases under investigation. A law enforcement focus group was chosen for the initial evaluation before progressing to the other two stakeholder groups. If the conceptual model cannot be applied in law enforcement, then no progression to the other stakeholder realms is justified. The focus group consisted of 10 law enforcement officers, each specializing in a different area and at varying levels of responsibility.

Earlier discussion in the forensic evidence problem space identified four broadly based local and global problems. Over one year, numerous situations were evaluated by the law enforcement focus group members; however, only a small portion of these implementations is reported in this discussion. Evaluation of the model by law enforcers has lead to many instances being suitable examples. These examples are taken from multiple international locations, but are considered to be representative of a local problem space.

## 8.1  Evaluation Example One

The identified problem was that there was no apparent formalized method or system for determining what the existence or nonexistence of evidence means to an investigation. A implementation of network science was applied to a cold case review instance. Instigating network science techniques raised a line of case-related questions regarding the existence of different evidence items, particularly in regard to information pertaining to bank account, cell phone, and family member contact activity currently as compared to previous periods, and that at the time of the initial investigation. Analysis of the dynamic network over time was necessary for an informed analysis of the evidence.

Practitioner responses included

- This approach, when compared with our traditional methods, has resulted in significant differences in understanding about the whole case and lead to renewed enthusiasm because of the new lines of enquiry offered.
- The linking of evidence items and the absence of links provided direction for further investigation.

## 8.2  Evaluation Example Two

The identified problem was that investigators find that sorting and arranging forensic evidence in a meaningful manner is necessary yet impractical. A consideration of different stakeholder perspectives was needed. The model implemented showed that the researcher's association with the case evidence was different than that of investigating officers and that the detective has a different perspective than the police chief and other assisting officers. This implementation also highlighted that the purpose was to conduct a cold case review, examining the collected evidence, and asking questions about the evidence. The evidence had previously been collected and was assembled in one location and available for immediate examination and analysis. Those conducting the investigation were subject to limitations in that the evidence came to them in a piecemeal fashion, not in a sequential manner, and over different time periods. This caused the investigator to see the case evidence in small snapshots spread over a period of time in contrast to a situation where the evidence was available in its totality and sequentially arranged, offering a more holistic perspective.

This implementation facilitated assessment of a solution based on a specific rather than a general evidence classification.

Practitioner responses included

- Until exposed to this concept, evidence was just evidence and we had not thought about the character of evidence.

- Evidence was always associated to a case and that was the end of the story.
- It was not that we did not do some of this stuff, it was just that we did not think about it nor fully understand our associations with the evidence.

## 8.3  Evaluation Example Three

The identified problem was that there is no apparent agreed method or system for describing or grouping types of relationships between evidence items. The network science process was undertaken, resulting in raising a line of case-related questions regarding evidence relationships. The problem relating to relationships pertained to current and previous activities of an actor in the investigation, highlighting the different types of relationships that could exist between things, between people, and between people and things bought new perspectives to the investigators. This process brought about an appreciation regarding evidence connectedness. The relationships between evidence can be mutual (that is, in both directions), asymmetrical (either inward to an evidence node or outward away from an evidence node), or null (signifying no relationship exists), leading investigators to realize another perspective regarding evidence interrelatedness.  Another informal trial confirmed results of a previous evaluation (example one above), which illustrated the differences in approach between investigating officers.

Practitioner responses included

- The difference in approach results in significant differences in understanding the whole case.
- The building of relationships between evidence items and between people and evidence items was improved and holistic views of the case were now possible.

## 8.4  Evaluation Example Four

The identified problem was that law enforcement officers were unaware of technology capacities because lack of financial support had lead to lack of technology- related training. The solution related to a specific and challenging instance. Use of a resource library system (limited in nature as compared to the theoretical model) showed that suitably arranged repositories of forensic evidence information can assist officers in resolving operational challenges. The demonstration assisted case resolution by taking paper-based GPS records and converting them into a digital format for storage and analysis in a database before plotting the recorded GPS coordinates onto a map, showing when and where a particular vehicle and person had traveled. This data was then able to be digitally compared with other information regarding mobile motor vehicle registration numbers stored in a computerized system.

Practitioner responses include

- This enabled us to visualize and link items of evidence from disparate sources.
- This shows interrelationships between different items of evidence not previously considered important.

The progressive nature of the movement between the problem space, theorizing about the design, and consolidating the design and application in a restricted event environment offered by design science provided a flexible approach for the research not available through other research methods.

# 9  Limitations

A major restriction in providing practicable solutions to the defined forensic evidence problem space is that the three stakeholder groups are not governed by an overarching body, so there is no direct enticement to view evidence holistically. With such a large space under consideration, it is difficult to employ and evaluate solutions in order to address the global problems identified.

Although design science provided a suitable mechanism for the research process, this method does not provide a formalized set of steps for conducting the work. New researchers applying design science may have difficulty estimating how far through the process they have progressed. In addition, design science has not yet addressed the handling of different perspectives, a necessity when dealing with domains involving complex human interactions.

# 10  Conclusion

The research at hand involved designing a model for the management of forensic evidence. Design science was used as the research method with mixed results. It allowed the researcher to get down and dirty at the operational level and readily move between theorizing and building. Although the iterative nature of design science provides the opportunity to immerse into the problem and solution spaces at the same time, at times it can be too flexible.

The models developed by the researcher in conjunction with the participants from the three stakeholder groups provide a holistic framework for effective management of forensic evidence. The implementation of such a high-level model across three domains is fraught with difficulty. Initial evaluation carried out by law enforcers provided positive feedback for specific models. Further research is needed for the detailed design of the component models and their implementation across the three domains. With regard to design science, research is also needed in complex human activity systems in order to provide guidance in the accommodation of different stakeholder perspectives.

# References

Baskerville, R., Pries-Heje, J., Venable, J.: Soft Design Science Research: Extending the Boundaries of Evaluation in Design Science Research. In: Proceedings of the 2nd International Conference on Design Science Research in Information Systems and Technology, Pasadena, CA, May 13-15 (2007)

Checkland, P., Scholes, J.: Soft Systems Methodology in Action. John Wiley & Sons, Chichester (1990)

Hevner, A.R., March, S.T., Park, J., Ram, S.: Design Science in Information Systems Research. MIS Quarterly 28(1), 75–105 (2004)

Jayaratna, N.: Understanding and Evaluating Methodologies. McGraw-Hill, London (1999)

Jonassen, D.H.: Toward a Design Theory of Problem Solving. Educational Technology, Research and Development 48(4), 63–85 (2000)

March, S.T., Smith, G.F.: Design Science and Natural Science Research on Information Technology. Decision Support Systems 15, 251–266 (1995)

March, S., Storey, V.: Design Science in the Information Systems Discipline: An Introduction to the Special Issue on Design Science Research. MIS Quarterly 32(4), 725–730 (2008)

Venable, J.: The Role of Theory and Theorising in Design Science Research. In: Proceedings of DESRIST, Claremont Graduate University, Claremont, CA, February 24-25 (2006)

Walls, J.G., Widmeyer, G.W., El Sawy, O.A.: Building an Information Systems Design Theory for Vigilant EIS. Information Systems Research 3(1), 36–59 (1992)

## About the Authors

**Colin Armstrong** lectures in security subjects in the School of Information Systems at Curtin University. He works closely with law enforcement, government, and industry in consulting, teaching, and research in cyber-security and digital forensics. Colin can be contacted at colin.armstrong@cbs.curtin.edu.au.

**Helen Armstrong** coordinates higher degrees by research in the School of Information Systems at Curtin University in Perth, Western Australia. Helen's areas of interest in teaching and research include cyber-security and network science. Helen can be contacted at h.armstrong@ curtin.eu.au.

# Part 6
# Participation in Design

# Participatory Design Activities and Agile Software Development

Karlheinz Kautz

Department of Informatics,
Copenhagen Business School,
DK-2000 Frederiksberg, Denmark

**Abstract.** This paper contributes to the studies of design activities in information systems development. It provides a case study of a large agile development
project and focusses on how customers and users participated in agile development and design activities in practice. The investigated project utilized the agile
method eXtreme Programming. Planning games, user stories and story cards,
working software, and acceptance tests structured the customer and user involvement. We found genuine customer and user involvement in the design
activities in the form of both direct and indirect participation in the agile development project. The involved customer representatives played informative,
consultative, and participative roles in the project. This led to their functional
empowerment— the users were enabled to carry out their work to their own
satisfaction and in an effective, efficient, and economical manner.

**Keywords:** Participatory design, agile software development eXtreme
programming, customer and user involvement, case study research.

## 1 Introduction

A central tenet of participatory design (PD) is the direct involvement of people in the
co-design of things and technologies they use. Although not that different from approaches already discussed in the 1980s under the label *prototyping* (Merisalo-
Rantanen et al. 2005), agile (software) development (ASD) has recently gained
immense popularity. In agile development—based on intensive direct communication and a few, short specification documents—interface, functional, and technical
design, and the more technical development activities such as coding and testing are
much more intertwined than in traditional information systems development (ISD)
(Gross et al. 2008). In an agile manifesto, the advocates of agile development state
their now well-known four pairs of values, namely (1) individuals and interactions
over processes and tools; (2) working software over comprehensive documentation;
(3) customer collaboration over contract negotiation; and (4) responding to change
over following a plan (see www.agilemanifesto.org).

Agile development practices and principles insist on the customer taking control
and being constantly involved and stress a collaborative partnership based on daily
interaction between the developers and the customer (Highsmith 2002). Studies of

J. Pries-Heje et al. (Eds.): IS Design Science Research, IFIP AICT 318, pp. 303–316, 2010.
© IFIP International Federation for Information Processing 2010

agile practice have, however, shown that customer representatives might have decision power, but only a limited understanding of the users' needs; they might not be the actual users of the software to be developed, who in turn might have the necessary knowledge, but not the authority to decide on system features (Robinson and Sharp 2005). Users rarely take the role of the customers (Martin et al. 2004). The customer role might even have been carried out by substitutes from the development organization such as product managers or marketing staff (Robinson and Sharp 2003).

It is surprising that agile software development and its relation to user involvement and participatory design has hardly been a topic in the ISD community in general, and in the PD community in particular. This is even more astonishing in light of the fact that Cockburn (2002), a prominent member of the agile movement and author of one agile method, has described how much his approach is indebted to Ehn's work, himself one of the prominent proponents of PD by explicitly relating to Ehn's (1992) article, "Scandinavian Design: On Participation and Skill," as a major source of inspiration.

Investigating user involvement and participation very much follows a request from Markus and Mao (2004), who argue for a need to revisit the concept and to study it in novel, exciting environments such as agile development. In addition, Bratteteig (2007) calls for studying design practice and emphasizes the need for practice studies with regard to user involvement and participatory design. This is in line with Dybå and Dingsøyr (2008), who in a comprehensive study surveyed nearly 2,000 ASD related articles published prior to 2006 and who only found 33 scientifically sound, empirical studies of the phenomenon. They conclude that more such studies are needed.

On this background, in the following we will report from our research, which attempts to answer the question how customers and users participate in agile development and design activities in practice. In the next section, we will provide a literature review of related research publications and describe the theoretical background for the study. We then introduce our research method and the setting of our study, present our analysis, and discuss our findings; we finish with some conclusions.

## 2  Related Work and Theoretical Background

Some research originating in the area of agile development, such as the previously mentioned work by Robinson and Sharp (2003, 2005) and by Martin et al. (2004), studies the task of the customer and the relationship of the customer and user roles, but less the actual participation of customers and users in the design and development activities of projects that use an agile development approach.

As we were interested in the relation between participatory design activities and agile software development, our literature search concentrated on studies that focused on both areas. Our literature search of the participatory design literature, however, only led to a few contributions related to the question of user involvement in agile design and development activities.

In the only explicit PD paper we found on the topic Rittenbruch et al. (2002) provide a conceptual comparison of an agile development method, in their case eXtreme Programming (XP; for more information on XP, see section 4, "The Case Setting"), and PD. On this basis, they developed their own approach, which integrates techniques from both agile development and PD. They tested their method in a research project, where the customers were fellow IT-literate researchers, to provide a proof of their concept. Their research provides a number of practical recommendations to deal with the (from their perspective) limited conception of user participation in XP. However, their work does not provide any insights about user involvement in practice.

Hansson et al. (2006) present a practice study of how to include users in the development of off-the-shelf software and claim theirs is a case of complementing PD with agile development. However, the organization under investigation neither explicitly uses an agile method nor participatory design. The authors map the practices they find, namely the users' feedback on the product through meetings, support sessions, and courses onto the two concepts. But they also admit that the users never actually participated in any design activities and that the developers totally controlled the process of selecting any of the proposals for design and development. Thus, while this is an interesting account of practice and a valuable description of user involvement in the further development of packaged software, the work does not investigate user involvement in agile practice.

In another study of possible interest in this context, Ferreira et al. (2007) investigated the relation between agile development and user interface and interaction design. They report about the cooperation of software developers and interaction designers from two cases in practice. Their descriptive account, based on a grounded theory inspired research method, surfaces a number of important themes such as up-front interaction design, continuous designer involvement, designer–developer interaction, and the valued role of interaction designers, but the work does not study user involvement at all.

Chamberlain et al. (2006) set out to develop a framework for integrating agile development and user-centered design. Analyzing the similarities and differences between the two approaches, they conclude that these are compatible. However, in a practice study, which investigated the use of agile methods and user-centered design, they identified a clear distinction between designers, who were responsible for user-centered activities, and developers, who produced code. They also found little, if any, customer and user involvement in the form of users being interviewed and asked for their opinion in limited tests sessions. On this basis they propose five principles for successful integration of the approaches including an explicit demand for user involvement. Unfortunately, the study does not provide a proof of concept based on empirical data to verify the viability of the framework.

There definitely seems to be a lack of empirical studies of participatory design activities in agile software development. We attempt to contribute to filling this gap and provide a case study, which we analyze based on the following theoretical backdrop.

To study participatory design, and within the design activities—more precisely, customer and user involvement—in agile software development, we will apply the concept of user focus. Iivari and Iivari (2006) distinguish between individual, average, and fictive user focus: With an individual focus the designer tries to satisfy each actual user and emphasizes each individual's capabilities and needs. With a focus on an average user, interaction designers typically apply some heuristics or general human factor principles. Focusing on a fictive user, HCI specialists or interaction designers base their design (proposals) on, for example, personas, which are descriptions of hypothetical archetypes of actual users.

Our further analysis will then be based on the following important concepts of user participation: (1) forms of involvement and participation, (2) user roles in user involvement and participation, and (3) the purpose of user involvement and participation as introduced by Mumford (1983), Damodaran (1996), and Clement (1994), respectively.

Clement argues that the purpose of user participation is user empowerment and he distinguishes between functional empowerment and democratic empowerment. The former means that the users should be able to carry out their work to their own satisfaction and in an effective, efficient, and economical manner. Their participation in the design process supports reaching this objective. Democratic empowerment means that they should have the mandate to participate in decision-making in their workplace including the design and development of software and IT-based systems.

Damodaran differentiates three user roles in the design and development process. The user can play an informative, consultative, or participative role. As informants, users merely provide information about their work and might be the objects of some observation. In a consultative role, they are asked to comment on preset design solutions. In a participative role, they actively participate in the design process and have decision-making power regarding the solution.

Mumford, who provided the first distinction of user roles, further classifies two different forms of involvement, namely direct user participation and indirect user participation, where the user is represented by some kind of intermediary. Direct and indirect participation are defined through the users' direct participation in the project (team) or their direct or indirect contact with project staff from the development organization.

## 3   Research Method

Our research follows the approach of engaged scholarship (Van de Ven 2007), which is a participative form of research for seeking advice and perspectives of key stakeholders to understand and theorize about a complicated problem. Given the limited literature concerning our research topic, understanding the participatory design activities, and customer and user involvement, our investigation is based on an exploratory, qualitative, single case study (Creswell 2003) of an ASD project. While it is often stated that it is not possible to generalize and certainly not to theorize from a single case study, Walsham (1995) suggests that it is possible to generalize case study findings among others in the form of a contribution of rich insight. So inspired, we have used our theoretical backdrop, which consists of important concepts that make up user participation, as one background for our data analysis.

The research presented is part of a larger project that aims at understanding agile development in practice and at contributing to sustainable theories of ISD in general and agile development in particular (Kautz and Zumpe 2008; Matook and Kautz 2008). In the context of this paper, we focus on the role of the customers and users and how they are involved in the design and development process. Our research is based on an empirical case study of a commercial agile development project in a large

German public sector organization, called WaterWorks, performed by a German software company, called AgDev, which specializes in agile development.

The empirical data for the case study was collected in semi-structured, open-ended interviews that were conducted by a team of two researchers in a three-day period at the development site. The research team performed 12 interviews with 11 individuals (the AgDev project manager was interviewed twice). This included nearly a third of the development team and a representative sample of key players and future users in the customer organization. The interviews were tape-recorded and subsequently transcribed. For the qualitative data analysis, a software tool (NVIVO7) was used. The interview data was supplemented with company and project documents such as method, requirements, and release descriptions, as well as project plans.

The data collection, the coding of the data, and the data analysis have been guided by the four pairs of values underlying agile development previously introduced in this paper. As stated earlier, for the research presented here, the data was in particular analyzed with regard to participatory design and customer and user involvement. As a prerequisite for the analysis, we produced an account of our case setting, which focuses on the structural profile of the investigated project. It consists of descriptions of the information system under development, of the formalized method (Fitzgerald et al. 2002) to be used—as opposed to the method-in-use—of the project's structural context, and of the structural characteristics of the involved development team, its members, and associated staff such as customers and end users. This is presented in the next section.

## 4  The Case Setting: The OMS Project

The project under investigation was concerned with the development of an operations management system (OMS) for the WaterWorks of a large German city. Founded 150 years ago, the organization is now partially privatized with the city council holding 50.1 percent of the ownership. The system was developed with a web-based graphical user interface and a backend to interface the technical infrastructure as defined by an underlying ERP system.

The project was organized in four subprojects to provide IT support ranging from customer management to the maintenance of the sewer and duct system. After several attempts of traditional ISD based on a standard ERP system that had not led to the desired results, the organization opened a tendering process. It was won by a small software company, AgDev.

At the time of the project, AgDev consisted of about 25 employees 20 of them being developers, and based its development approach on the agile method XP (Beck and Andres 2004). The formalized method includes planning techniques for releases and iterations called planning games, user stories and story cards to specify user requirements (in XP formally the customer writes the stories onto simple index cards), onsite customers to support customer–developer communication, daily stand-up meetings of the whole project team to support team communication, pair program-ming, re-factoring, collective ownership, continuous integration and testing of code to develop the software proper, and regular tuning workshops to improve the development processes. The company extended the method with some project management processes to cater for larger projects such as an elaborate overall project plan, formal reporting mechanisms, and a formal contract based on a requirements specification called a realization concept, which had been produced by the customer.

The project was organized in two phases. In a first 12-month exploration phase, prototype catching requirements and possible solutions were developed. This led to the development of the realization concept by the customer organization and their decision to contract AgDev also for the development of the OMS proper.

In this main development phase, a team of about 12 development staff with multiple roles such as project manager, subproject manager, analyst, customer contact, and developer worked onsite in a building owned by WaterWorks. A sophisticated management structure with one subproject manager acting as contact person from AgDev and one subproject manager acting as onsite customer from WaterWorks for each of the four subprojects was established, in addition to two overall project managers, one from each company. The WaterWorks subproject managers and onsite customers were managers and team leaders in the operational divisions of the application areas and as such also actual users of the OMS. These customers were, by and large, not onsite the entire time. The project also comprised a varying number of other users, representing operational staff, from the different divisions. These users were, for the most part, actively involved in feedback and testing activities, as will be described and discussed in more detail in the next section.

When this study was performed, phase one had been successfully closed and, after a break of over a year due to internal politics at WaterWorks, phase two had been going on for four months. Responding to an inquiry call during our analysis, the AgDev project manager stated that the project ended 10 months later, on time and budget, with all parts of the OMS being operational. The collected data is mostly related to phase two.

With this structural profile in mind, we will now analyze the project in more detail with regard to participatory design and user involvement.

## 5   An Analysis of the OMS Project

The OMS project was described by both the customer and the supplier as a success. The emerging information system afforded, in the words of one of the WaterWorks subproject managers, the ability to identify synergies among the various departments; in particular, in the duct department it enabled improved planning that resulted in the possibility to dispose cleaning vehicles and reduce related staff. With regard to the focus of this paper, one of the WaterWorks subproject managers explicated that their end users had been very satisfied.

However, various comments were made about reaching the right balance of customer collaboration and user involvement. AgDev's project manager commented on onsite customer behavior: *"Yesterday he said something and today he says something else. Requirements have to be clear at the beginning of an iteration and cannot change right in the middle of it. We are agile, but not on a daily or hourly change request rate."*

Customer and user involvement took place on an ongoing basis and the planning games and story cards, the presentation of working software, as well as the acceptance tests structured the continuous day-to-day-contacts, communication, and collaboration. In addition, the project showed one very particular instance of user involvement. One AgDev subproject manager reported on one user, who—based on his background and experience—had become a full member of the development team.

In the following we will use the planning games and story cards, the presentation of the working software, and the acceptance tests to arrange our description and analysis of the user involvement in the project's development and design activities.

## 5.1 Planning Games, User Stories, and Story Cards

At the start of phase two, a number of different documents existed, which were all comparable short and concise. From a customer perspective, these were related as follows: An overall realization concept built the basis for the development contract with the customer. The realization concept was refined into requirements lists. These lists governed what should be the outcome of an iteration and what should be the basis for the acceptance tests. Individual requirements or groups of requirements were then described as a story and each story was written down on a story card. The story cards represented the final detailed plans and specifications for the developers' work tasks and processes.

The planning games at the beginning of each iteration were based on the overall realization concept and the requirements lists. These were largely produced by AgDev's project manager and some of the subproject managers. They developed these documents with input from the onsite customers. The story cards were solemnly produced and estimated by the developers in developer team work sessions, because the subproject managers as well as other possible end users at WorkWorks were mostly operational staff, which had some impact on their abstraction capabilities and their ability to write texts. Yet, the developers and the customers together prioritized the cards.

In this context, WaterWorks' subproject managers saw their role as facilitators and communicators. To back up the development of the operations management system based on an agreement with the staff council and with management, some of them had been assigned full-time to the project to be available and involved in the project whenever necessary.

The subproject managers did not develop the requirements at their own discretion, but had significant contact with the employees in their divisions and carried the requirements from their divisions into the project. They also prepared the prioritization of the requirements according to their importance and the available budget.

An AgDev subproject manager talked about the difficulties of converting the requirements into design and declared that design was the task of the developers: *"It nearly becomes our design task as contact partners...it's not easy to find out from the WaterWorks people what they want; when I say 'do you want it this way,' they say 'yes,' and when I ask 'do you rather want it that way,' they also say 'yes'... .and they say 'we have this and this problem, but to design an interface out of this information is our problem."*

However, the design was always developed with close participation of the WaterWorks subproject managers and other users and always under the mandate of the WaterWorks subproject managers. While the AgDev subproject managers had the liberty to make proposals, the customers could always say no, and with really important issues, AgDev would always get back to the users before they would go forward. This also included direct contact between those developers, who did not act as contact persons or subproject managers, and the onsite customers.

Some AgDev subproject managers even felt that, through the WaterWorks involvement, the project participants from the WaterWorks somehow developed the OMS themselves. One of them thus explained that AgDev had not developed something, which they had invented themselves without communication with WaterWorks. This form of customer collaboration provided some structure to cope with the complexities of a comparatively large ASD project, while leaving room for less structured, but necessary, collaboration as well.

That is to say, when implementing the story cards, it became obvious that some additional collaboration was needed. One WaterWorks subproject manager stated that contact with the onsite customer was necessary for nearly every story card. He put forward that maybe two thirds of a card's contents were clear, but that the other 40 percent had to be directly coordinated—20 percent in the middle of an iteration and 20 percent in the end when the customers and users looked at the working software and found that their requirements weren't understood the way they meant them. This illustrates the importance of the working software for the development and design process, which we will discuss in more detail in the next subsection.

## 5.2 Working Software

The presentations of working software were identified as another basis for customer and user involvement. In the OMS project, a first software release was provided after three months with the others to be delivered every three to six months. Each release was organized in iterations of three to six weeks duration, meaning that at the time of our investigation each subproject had at least gone through two iterations.

Feedback about and change requests for the software design were brought forward by the onsite customers in weekly feedback loops, which were built into an iteration, based on presentations and demonstrations of working software. This always led to smaller changes.

The AgDev project manager described how the working software, which was produced by story card, attracted the WaterWorks subproject managers and how they seamlessly participated in the development process. He confirmed that beyond the scheduled weekly meetings for all subproject managers, some of the WaterWorks subproject managers turned up at the project nearly on a daily basis while others came at least on a regular basis and looked over the shoulders of the developers. This allowed for fixing problems and providing working software before an iteration was officially released. This was very important for the WaterWorks subproject managers, as they continuously could see progress. The developers, however, had to get acquainted with this close involvement as they were not that used to sitting at the customer site and having customers pass by every day, which they sometimes considered as quite disturbing.

Beyond these contacts with the onsite customers, the working software was also presented to larger groups of prospective users (presentations to one onsite customer were not considered sufficient). Thus the set up, with at least four subproject managers, who also acted as onsite customers, was supplemented with other user representatives. The AgDev project manager summarized the situation: *"Well, at the latest when an iteration is finished, sometimes already in the middle of it, or whenever, presentations are run for users. Well, not always in front of many users, but the customer subproject manager gets some people together and says: 'Here, look, do we develop in the right direction?'"*

In addition, using a similar format, the onsite customer representatives regularly performed "road shows" with the working software in the user departments to collect feedback and ideas and proposals for improvements.

The AgDev subproject managers also sought direct contact with the users and one of them reported that he had seated himself for two weeks in the duct operation station with the objective to extensively test onsite and to look at how well the software actually fitted the operation. This resulted in the direct involvement of those employees onsite, who arranged or actually performed cleaning the ducts. Another AgDev subproject manager had chosen the same strategy and even involved some of his developers in the process. After installing a release at one division, they went there for several days, discussed the release with the users, registered bugs, and then rebuilt the software accordingly.

The frequent feedback loops were taken very serious and immediately responded to with action. This had the effect that minor misunderstandings were caught and dealt with as changes early before they could grow into larger problems. As a consequence, the users developed trust and a feeling that they had an impact on the development of the system and even the employees in the divisions, who were not directly involved, were quickly integrated into the project.

But the working software also brought to light some initial problems related to the distribution of roles in the project. The WaterWorks subproject managers expected that AgDev's developers would bring more of their own ideas into the project and that they would come up with smart technical solutions. They were frustrated that the AgDev developers always just did what the customers told them to do, because they saw this as a sign that the developers were not good enough to develop their own proposals. After a clarification of the roles in an agile development project, the cooperation between the different groups of project participants continued without further problems.

### 5.3  Acceptance Tests

The AgDev project manager also explained that, between two iterations, there was always a test phase that was a "post" activity of the preceding iteration and that there was a concept phase that was the preceding activity of the next phase. He confirmed that the acceptance tests were run by the customer, meaning that the customer had the responsibility and decision power for and in these tests. The tests were similar to the formal presentations of the working software, but they were performed according to a protocol and they always comprised end users. Thus, customer and user involvement also took place during and in the form of the acceptance tests. The requests for changing the software design that came up during the scheduled acceptance test sessions were dealt with in the next iteration.

Before an acceptance test was performed, less formal preparations took place, often triggered by a WaterWorks subproject manager, who would try out the new functionalities as described on the story cards. As valid feedback was considered important, end users—not just the customer as represented by the subproject leaders—were performing the tests. An acceptance test was then always led by a responsible Water-Works subproject leader, who also approved or rejected the new version of the system. A typical acceptance test lasted just one day with four to six people participating. Two or three divisional managers and other employees, who owned the task and who had to work with it, were present and tested. There was an official test protocol where the requirements for the iteration were listed. The responsible WaterWorks subproject manager's approval, conditional approval, or rejection as a test leader was documented, together with what was missing, and where, to achieve a full approval.

The AgDev subproject managers were always present during the tests, which otherwise were the responsibility of WaterWorks. The AgDev subproject managers also monitored the acceptance test and recorded the errors and bugs on "private" bug lists. The developers usually did not participate. There were, however, exceptions from this rule as we learned from an AgDev subproject manager: *"In the end, we participated in the test, me, our project manager, and the respective WaterWorks subproject manager, and in this case another developer as well."*

One AgDev subproject manager described that this way many mistakes were found and that encouraging feedback was provided. The employees involved in the tests stated that they could imagine working with the system and that they liked it better than the ERP-based solution that had been proposed earlier.

The WaterWorks subproject managers declared that this approach, with the acceptance tests before an iteration was approved and the iterations as such, helped them to quickly and regularly get something tangible and to get in touch with the end users. They confirmed that in this context the test sessions, which were also coordinated with the staff council, were decisive. By and large, WaterWorks' subproject managers were content with this form of participation and considered themselves as part of the development. They also reported on content end users and based this appraisal on the feedback they had received from the end users after the tests. The acceptance tests had a significant influence on the further design of the system components, as requests for changes and new requirements always came up as a result of a test.

However, despite the general positive reception of the acceptance tests, still more involvement and more tests were also demanded, as can be seen by the following final statement made by one WaterWorks subproject manager: *"The tests were good, but there were too few."*

## 6  Discussion

Prior research into user participation in agile development has shown that end users rarely take the role of the customers, and sometimes the customer is even represented by a development organization's own staff (Martin et al. 2004; Robinson and Sharp 2003, 2005). In contrast, in our case we found genuine customer and user participation in an agile development project.

We can to some degree empirically confirm Chamberlain et al.'s (2006) conceptual work that agile development and user-centered design are compatible; user participation and agile development go well together. But user participation in our case was an integral part of the chosen methodology and thus no special attempt to integrate the two approaches, as Chamberlain et al. demand it, was necessary. There were not two approaches, nor was there a distinction between designers and developers, which others (Chamberlain et al. 2006; Robinson and Sharp 2003, 2005) have found in practice.

This might have been the case in the OMS project, because of its user focus. In the OMS project the focus was not on any average user nor was it on a fictive user. It was on the actual individual customers and users. Our empirical data show that they— even if they were not always content with the fact that they had to take that role— through their continuous feedback acted as designers themselves.

Our case also illustrates how, in agile development, design and development are intertwined. This confirms earlier work on agile development (see Gross et al. 2008), but has also been known for other ISD and software development approaches for many years (see Swartout and Balzer 1982).

Returning to participatory design, customer and user involvement and participation, we base the further discussion of our findings on the concepts introduced in our theoretical background.

In terms of Mumford (1983), we found, in the OMS project, both direct and indirect participation: the onsite customers were WaterWorks staff, who themselves would work with the future system to a certain extent. As such, they exerted direct participation. They were also intermediaries for other users, for example, operative staff in the customer division and the duct net division. These employees indirectly participated when they commented during presentations or when they provided their viewpoints or descriptions of their work processes to the onsite customers. However, they also participated directly when they tested the results of the iterations or when they were observed or conferred the developers, who were in contact with them directly in the divisions, such as the developer, who visited and stayed in the duct net division while the result of an iteration was in operation.

Although one of the WaterWorks subproject managers went so far as to report to management that only things that the employees wanted were done, a more differentiated picture appears when we analyze the various user roles (Damodaran 1996). Those users in the divisions, who were not also onsite customers, had the role of informative or consultative users. They provided both the onsite customers and the development staff at AgDev with information about their work, their needs, and their preferences. Some of them were observed during their work by some developers and they provided their comments during presentations and tests. Although this information and the comments were taken into account and much of it was realized, it goes too far to consider this a participative role as it was primarily the onsite customers, who had a decision-making mandate. Thus, in so far as their positions as (a minority among the) future users were concerned, they were clearly in a participative role, although they did not themselves write the user stories and the story cards. However, no design decision could be taken without their agreement. Beyond their participative role, the onsite customers also had informative and consultative roles.

Finally, with regard to empowerment (Clement 1994), we can determine that functional empowerment has been achieved. All stakeholder groups reported that they were content with the outcome of the project. We have, however, no evidence for any democratic empowerment other than the staff council's peripheral involvement and the onsite customers' authority to take decisions concerning their staff's and their own workplaces. This leads us to a concluding statement.

The PD movement has traditionally advocated workplace democracy, a participative role for the users, and direct involvement (Bjerknes and Bratteteig 1995), while in large parts of the mainstream IS literature, functional empowerment with users in informative or consultative roles, directly or indirectly involved, has been the focus of research (Kujala 2003). Given the results for our analysis, it could be argued that our research does not really show a case of participatory design in agile development. It can, however, be counter-argued whether this is relevant given that all involved stakeholders in the case were satisfied with the outcome of the OMS project.

Furthermore, in 1995, Bjerknes and Bratteteig had already shown how the focus on workplace democracy had shifted to a cooperative design approach, at least in the Scandinavian PD community. On this basis, they then put forward the challenge for future PD research to contribute to democracy in a changing environment for working lives and workplaces. They claimed that other kinds of actions and institutions, different from traditional PD approaches, might be necessary to reintroduce the democratic dimension in PD and ISD research. It may thus be that agile development, with its local focus on constant cooperation, reviews, and feedback, and with direct communication as its preferred development method, is, after all, one possible way to tackle this challenge.

# 7 Conclusion

In this paper, we investigated the question of how customers and users participate in agile development and design activities in practice.

Our work demonstrates the applicability of concepts developed to understand participatory design to analyze customer and user involvement in ISD projects that apply an agile approach. As such, it follows Markus and Mao's (2004) call and revisits the concepts and shows that they are still useful.

We also contribute with a practice study of a design process as requested by Bratteteig (2007) to broaden the perspective on design science research, and we provide a sound, empirical study of agile development as demanded by Dybå and Dingsøyr (2008).

Our research contributes to the body of knowledge in information systems development with rich insight (Walsham 1995) and provides a link between the otherwise often-disconnected research areas and research communities of participatory design, agile development, and design science. Further research is necessary to allow for more theorizing about the relation of the three fields.

## Acknowledgments

I would like to thank the participants of the OMS project for their time and insights in agile development practice. I am also indebted to Ralf Klischewski, who was a member of the original interview team, and Sabine Matook (neé Zumpe), who performed parts of the data analysis with me, as well as to Helen Sharp, who directed our attention to the body of knowledge and provided literature, which documents empirical studies of user involvement in agile development.

# References

Beck, K., Andres, C.: Extreme Programming Explained: Embrace Change, 2nd edn. Addison-Wesley Professional, Boston (2004)

Bjerknes, G., Bratteteig, T.: User Participation and Democracy: A Discussion of Scandinavian Research on System Development. Scandinavian Journal of Information Systems 7(1), 73–98 (1995)

Bratteteig, T.: Design Research in Informatics: A Response to Iivari. Scandinavian Journal of Information Systems 19(2), 65–73 (2007)

Clement, A.: Computing at Work: Empowering Action By 'Low-level Users. Communications of the ACM 37(1), 52–63 (1994)

Chamberlain, S., Sharp, H., Maiden, N.A.M.: Towards a Framework for Integrating Agile Development and User-Centred Design. In: Abrahamsson, P., Marchesi, M., Succi, G. (eds.) XP 2006. LNCS, vol. 4044, pp. 143–153. Springer, Heidelberg (2006)

Cockburn, A.: Agile Software Development. Addison-Wesley, Boston (2002)

Creswell, J.W.: Research Design – Qualitative, Quantitative and Mixed Methods Approaches. Sage Publications, Thousand Oaks (2003)

Damodaran, L.: User Involvement in the Systems Design Process: A Practical Guide for Users. Behaviour and Information Technology 15(6), 363–377 (1996)

Dybå, T., Dingsøyr, T.: Empirical Studies of Agile Software Development: A Systematic Review. Information and Software Technology 50(9/10), 833–859 (2008)

Ehn, P.: Scandinavian Design: On Participation and Skill. In: Adler, P.S., Winograd, T.A. (eds.) Usability: Turning Technologies into Tools, pp. 96–132. Oxford University Press, New York (1992)

Ferreira, J., Noble, J., Biddle, R.: Interaction Designers on eXtreme Programming Teams: Two Case Studies from the Real World. In: Proceedings of the Fifth New Zealand Computer Science Research Student Conference, Hamilton, New Zealand (2007)

Fitzgerald, B., Russo, N.L., Stolterman, E.: Information Systems Development, Methods in Action. McGraw Hill, London (2002)

Gross, J.B., Daughtry III, J.M., Lee, J.C.: Heurists of the World Unite! Merging Agile Methods in Software and Interaction Design. Agile Journal 3(2) (2008)

Hansson, C., Dittrich, Y., Randell, D.: How to Include Users in the Development of Off-the-Shelf Software: A Case for Complementing Participatory Design with Agile Development. In: Proceedings of the 39th Hawaiian International Conference on System Science. IEEE Computer Society Press, Los Alamitos (2006)

Highsmith, J.: Agile Software Development Ecosystems. Addison-Wesley, Boston (2002)

Iivari, J., Iivari, N.: Varieties of User-Centeredness. In: Proceedings of the 39th Annual Hawaii International Conference on System Sciences. IEEE Computer Society Press, Los Alamitos (2006)

Kautz, K., Zumpe, S.: Just Enough Structure at the Edge of Chaos: Agile Information Systems Development in Practice. In: Abrahamsson, P., Baskerville, R., Conboy, K., Fitzgerald, B., Morgan, L., Wang, X. (eds.) Agile Processes in Software Engineering and Extreme Programming—Proceedings of the International Conference XP 2008, pp. 137–146. Springer, Berlin (2008)

Kujala, S.: User Involvement: A Review of the Benefits and Challenges. Behaviour and Information Technology 22(1), 1–16 (2003)

Markus, M., Mao, Y.: User Participation in Development and Implementation: Updating an Old Tired Concept for Today's IS Contexts. Journal of the Association for Information Systems 5(11-12), 514–544 (2004)

Martin, A., Biddle, R., Noble, J.: The XP Customer Role in Practice: Three Studies. In: Proceedings of the Second Agile Development Conference, June 22-26, pp. 42–54. IEEE Computer Society, Washington (2004)

Matook, S., Kautz, K.: Mindfulness and Agile Software Development. In: Cragg, P., Mills, A. (eds.) Proceedings of the 19th Australasian Conference on Information Systems (ACIS): Creating the Future: Transforming Research into Practice, Christchurch, New Zealand, pp. 638–647 (2008)

Merisalo-Rantanen, H., Tuunanen, T., Rossi, M.: Is Extreme Programming Just Old Wine in New Bottles: A Comparison of Two Cases. Journal of Database Management 16(4), 41–61 (2005)

Mumford, E.: Designing Human Systems for New Technology: The ETHICS Method. Manchester Business School, Manchester (1983)

Rittenbruch, M., McEwan, G., Ward, N., Mansfield, T., Bertenstein, D.: Extreme Participation: Moving Extreme Programming Towards Participatory Design. In: Proceedings of the Participatory Design Conference (PDC), Malmo, Sweden, June 23-25, pp. 29–41 (2002)

Robinson, H., Sharp, H.: XP Culture: Why the Twelve Practices Both Are and Are Not the Most Significant Thing. In: Proceedings of the Conference on Agile Development, June 25-28. IEEE Computer Society, Washington (2003)

Robinson, R., Sharp, H.: The Social Side of Technical Practices. In: Baumeister, H., Marchesi, M., Holcombe, M. (eds.) XP 2005. LNCS, vol. 3556, pp. 100–108. Springer, Heidelberg (2005)

Swartout, W.R., Balzer, R.: On the Inevitable Intertwining of Specification and Implementation. Communications of the ACM 25(7), 438–440 (1982)

Van de Ven, A.H.: Engaged Scholarship: A Guide for Organizational and Social Research. Oxford University Press, New York (2007)

Walsham, G.: Interpretive Case Studies in IS Research: Nature and Method. European Journal of Information System 4, 74–81 (1995)

## About the Author

**Karlheinz Kautz** is a professor in Systems Development and Software Engineering in the Department of Informatics at the Copenhagen Business School, Denmark. His primary research interests are in information systems development, knowledge management, software quality and process improvement in the IT industry, and the diffusion and adoption of information technology innovations. Karl is a founding member and former chair of IFIP TC8 WG 86 on Diffusion, Transfer, and Implementation of Information Technology. Karl's e-mail address is Karl.Kautz@cbs.dk.

# Participation in Living Lab: Designing Systems with Users

Birgitta Bergvall-Kåreborn[1], Debra Howcroft[2], Anna Ståhlbröst[1]
and Anita Melander Wikman[3]

[1] Social Informatics,
Luleå University of Technology,
Luleå, Sweden
[2] Manchester Business School,
The University of Manchester,
Manchester, United Kingdom
[3] Health and Rehabilitation
Luleå University of Technology
Luleå, Sweden

**Abstract.** Drawing on a case study of a living lab, this paper considers the process of participation during the design stages of a health care project for the elderly in Sweden. While participation has an established history, more recently it has been described as an "old, tired concept" that is in need of revitalization in order to cater for changing IS practices. In this paper, we reflect on how participation materializes in a context that is quite dissimilar from more traditional development settings and report on the kinds of practices that may be used to assist design with users.

**Keywords:** Living lab, design with users, participatory design, e-health, formIT.

## 1 Introduction

This paper focuses on living labs and the process of participation that took place during the design of a health project for the elderly. Living labs are an emerging phenomena and largely function as public–private partnerships whereby firms, academics, public sector authorities, and citizens work together for the creation, development, and adoption of new services and technologies in multi-contextual real-life environments (Bergvall-Kåreborn and Ståhlbröst 2009). The purpose of a living lab is to create a shared arena in which digital services, processes, and new ways of working can be developed and tested with users who can stimulate and challenge both research and development. Part of the rationale driving these innovations is the desire to open up company boundaries in order to harvest creative ideas from different stakeholder groups. Most living lab projects are practically focused and are largely neglected in the wider academic literature.

J. Pries-Heje et al. (Eds.): IS Design Science Research, IFIP AICT 318, pp. 317–326, 2010.

In this paper, we report on the early stages of a living lab project and link it to the broader field of participatory design (PD). A shared understanding within living lab projects is that users should not be viewed merely as passive information providers: *"One thing is common for all of us; the human-centric involvement and its potential for development of new ICT-based services and products"* (Open Living Labs, http://www.openlivinglabs.eu/concept.html). We intend to revisit participation in the context of a living lab project, which differs substantially from what is often considered a more traditional IS development project— one with clear organizational boundaries, where the users are often full-time employees using systems in an operational capacity, and where the systems developers guide the direction of the project. The case study illustrates how participation is invoked in real-life situations and aims to show that there is much scope for injecting a more radical element of co-design into these projects, based on the principles and foundations of PD.

## 2   Participatory Design

Involving users in the design and development of information systems has long been a core concept with a distinction between North American and European traditions (Lamb and Kling 2003). The Scandinavian countries have been at the forefront of participatory design that is based on the foundational principle of democracy (Iivari and Lyytinen 1998), which practically translates into people participating in the design process as co-designers (Ehn 2008). Therefore, a key concern is the need to understand how collaborative design processes can be steered by people that are affected by that design. Although the Scandinavia approach is by no means the only driver of participatory approaches, nevertheless it has a radical history with a number of early projects committed to promoting industrial democracy and quality of working life. However, over time this approach has lost much of its critical edge (Iivari and Lyytinen 1998) and, in practice, the notion of joint decision-making and worker influence has virtually disappeared (Kyng 1998).

Indeed, there has been limited attention paid to PD over the last decade, which has been described as an "an old, tired concept" (Markus and Mao 2004) that is desperately in need of revitalization to accommodate more contemporary environments. Yet looking beyond the IS discipline, user participation is advocated within areas like innovation and product development, using concepts such as open innovation, lead users, user-driven design, crowd sourcing, and living lab, although many of these approaches take a managerial as opposed to a user perspective. These technological developments attract limited attention from PD researchers, yet the living lab environment could benefit from drawing on PD principles that are well-established within the Information Systems field. In this paper, it is our intention to draw upon the history of PD to provide broader insights for living lab since this approach differs substantially from what is often considered a more traditional, IS development project. Before turning our attention to the empirical part of the paper, we draw on the well-founded history of PD to outline three types of participatory processes. The terminology originates from the Riva del Sol conference in 1982 (Briefs et al. 1983) and offers a useful frame for distinguishing between participatory processes.

- *Design for users.* With this approach, products and services are designed on behalf of users. While users are consulted, they do not actively participate in the design process, nor do they have influence in the decision-making process, and there is a clear split between what is perceived as technical and nontechnical expertise. The developers have the controlling role, initiating, and running the process and shaping "the solution space" (von Hippel 2001). The objective is to increase developers' understanding of the actual use context by gaining access to users' tacit knowledge, skills, and expertise. One of the main motivations is to improve system quality while gaining commitment and buy-in from users and diffusing tensions and conflicts.

  The users play a relatively passive role and are designated *consumers* of technical expertise (Beath and Orlikowski 1994), providing feedback on items such as requirements specifications and working prototypes. The task of the user is to provide feedback on design rather than to significantly influence or change it. While users are always constrained by the bounds of their knowledge and skills in relation to technical expertise, nevertheless their understanding of their situated context is often undervalued. They are seldom viewed as competent practitioners; they are often perceived as naïve at best (Bannon 1991).

- *Design with users.* According to this approach, products and services are co-designed by developers and users. The approach is based on the assumption that people have the right to influence the systems that they will use and that, to achieve this, they should have influence and a "voice" throughout the process. The sharp distinction between users and developers is less prominent than design for users, but there are still notable differences in their roles. The process is one of continual iteration between the developers and the users with a focus on knowledge sharing. The developers continue to initiate and run the process, operating as change agents, supporting users in their endeavors and ensuring opportunities are provided for them to take decisions in an informed manner. The developers still predominate with regard to technical activities whereas the users provide direction with the provision of a detailed understanding of the use environment and the appropriateness of ICTs to that particular context. According to this perspective, users are not seen as mere informants: "For us, user participation does not mean interviewing a sample of potential users or getting them to rubber stamp a set of system specifications. It is, rather, the active involvement of users in the creative process we call design" (Greenbaum and Kyng 1991, p. 3).

- *Design by users.* This approach involves the design of products and services by users with developers providing assistance throughout the process. The users initiate and steer the project while the developers both facilitate and comprise the supporting infrastructure, which can be drawn upon to enhance the users' potential in the design space when needed. In this type of context, the users are "evoked" (Kanstrup and Christiansen 2006), as they draw on their situated knowledge to design and develop product or service innovations that can be supported by the developers. While this approach has the potential to create a radical shift in technological development and open up the design space to a broader constituency (for example, open source software; see Levina 2005), equally it could be sabotaged by firms looking to exploit open innovation for profit maximization.

We now turn to our case study, which will be used to illuminate some of the issues discussed above.

# 3 MyHealth@Age

## 3.1 Background

The case is based on MyHealth@Age, which is intended to contribute to the health and well being of the aging population in peripheral and remote communities (specifically Sweden, Norway, and Northern Ireland). MyHealth@Age aims to provide its client population with mobile ICT products and services that help facilitate a more active role in healthcare rehabilitation, sustain autonomous living, and become fully active participants in healthcare and medical treatment programs in cooperation with relevant organizations. Drawing on Nolan's (2006) work on "relationship-centered care," three areas were identified for the project: safety, prescribed healthcare, and social networking. The focus on developing ICTs for elderly persons to manage their own health is somewhat unique, since the majority of IT-based health systems are directed at health organizations as users, rather than having a primary focus on the patients or public. Therefore, it was imperative that the development process would allow for the elderly to take an active role, should they wish to do so. For the purpose of this paper, we will focus on the first part of the development process—understanding user needs—and we concentrate on the process and findings in Sweden.

## 3.2 FormIT

The development methodology that has guided the project—FormIT (full details of FormIT can be found in Bergvall-Kåreborn and Ståhlbröst 2009)—is a human-centered approach to developing IT-based artifacts and services. It aims to facilitate the development of innovative services that are based on a holistic understanding of people's needs, paying due consideration to issues of equity, autonomy, and control in relation to actual use situations. FormIT is grounded in the theoretical streams of soft systems thinking (Checkland 1981; Checkland and Scholes 1990), appreciative inquiry (Cooperrider and Avital 2004; Norum 2001), and NeedFinding (Patnaik and Becker 1999). The process consists of three cycles: concept design, prototype design, and final system design. The focus of this paper is the first phase of the first cycle: appreciate opportunities.

## 3.3 The Planning Process

The planning began by writing the research funding application with partners from the three countries together with three elderly people representing potential users. This provided the elderly with an opportunity to have an impact on the scope of the project, rather than be enrolled at a later stage when project objectives had been

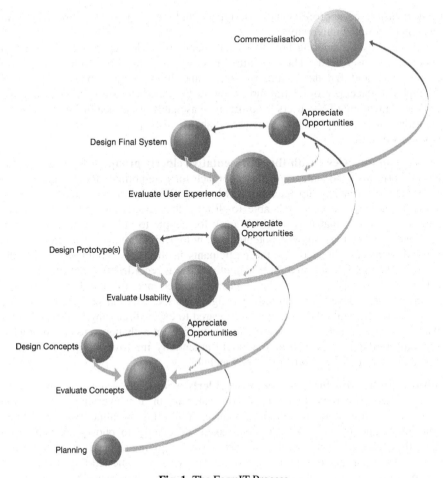

**Fig. 1.** The FormIT Process

agreed and defined. Effort was made to construct user groups that represent people with different experiences and expertise. The following became involved throughout the process:

- *The elderly reference group*, who participated in writing the application.
- *The elderly organization group*, which involved people representing elderly organizations, who are often elderly themselves.
- *The elderly representative group*, who were recruited to represent the target group of the proposed system.

### 3.4   Phase 1: Appreciate Opportunities

The participants in Sweden consist of the project leader, the reference group (three people), the elderly organizations (five people), the representative group (six to seven people), health care professionals, designers and developers from industry, and researchers from the university.

We began by considering how to recruit members of the representative group to denote diverse user needs. Thus we aimed to cover users aged between 55 and 85; a mix of male and female; a mix of single and living with a partner; a varied geographical placement of central, urban and rural; users who are ICT-proficient and familiar with mobile/PCs; users who are in reasonably good health but with some conditions such as high blood pressure, diabetes, osteoporosis, heart problem, or respiratory disease.

**Focus group interviews with the representative elderly group:** A focus group was held because of the advantages of this approach for assembling data on experiences, beliefs, attitudes, and group interaction (Morgan 1997). It was intended to create a situation whereby the users felt able to discuss their needs and difficulties, since research has shown that it is relatively easy for people to talk about their everyday experiences rather than suggest potential technological solutions. The process was informal as it was intended that the participants in the study would also guide the research. The discussion lasted for 90 minutes and was recorded and transcribed.

The focus group proved to be a positive experience for the facilitators (the researcher and a developer), providing insight into the different perspectives of the users. However, while the participants appeared to enjoy discussing health and other related issues with their peers, nevertheless they found it a challenge to envision what they may need for support, how this could potentially improve the quality of their lives, and the role that could be played by technology.

**Cultural probe with the representative elderly group:** We wanted to create ways for the elderly to express themselves more naturally in their everyday context, free from the constraints of facilitator guidance. With this in mind, we distributed disposable cameras and notebooks and asked the elderly to photograph situations where they felt secure or insecure; when they were enjoying a social occasion, or felt hindered from participation in a social occasion. We also requested they write a few lines of narrative to accompany each picture, describing how it made them feel. If taking photographs was inappropriate, note-taking would suffice. This was to be carried out for two weeks, the aim being to gain an understanding of the feelings and experiences of potential users in their everyday situations. From the designers' perspective, the data offers real insight into understanding "a day in the life" of elderly people at a fairly intimate level.

**Analyzing and tracing user needs:** Next, a number of needs were interpreted by the researchers from the statements and stories provided by the elderly. While this activity could have been carried out in conjunction with the elderly, we felt that the task was too time-consuming and that it would be worthwhile for the researchers to interpret their stories and ask for feedback.

Aware of the need to move toward a more thematic approach, we were concerned that our interpretations should be transparent and could be traced back to user statements and so this information was linked together graphically. This allowed the elderly representative group to provide feedback on areas of misunderstanding. A common problem when generating user requirements is that the process is often opaque and users are expected to make the mental leap from translating their practical needs into abstract diagrammatical representations.

**Ranking the needs:** After the needs had been agreed in project meetings by the three elderly groups, we still lacked understanding regarding how representative the needs were and the levels of importance that were attached to each need. We, therefore, developed a questionnaire that was distributed to the representative group. This was designed to avoid leading respondents into particular answers and care was taken to vary the format of questions to allow positive and negative responses. For each need, they were asked to indicate if this applied to their own circumstances and indicate its level of importance using a Likert scale. All of the participants completed the questionnaire and the findings were summarized and discussed at a multi-stakeholder meeting.

The next stage involved clustering needs. Initially, a meeting of multiple stakeholders took place whereby participants formed five smaller groups (of two to four people) to carry out the clustering of needs into categories and then provide a concept/heading that represented the cluster overall. This resulted in common themes (such as social networks, safety, and medical care), as well as unique categories (such as personal decision-making and self-care) from particular groups. This illustrates the importance of open discussion of both the meaning of the need statements as well as the headings for the clusters.

Additional meetings occurred where the elderly, health professionals, designers, developers, and researchers together discussed how the identified needs may be supported by ICTs. At this phase the project leader, developers, and researcher adopted a more dominant role with the elderly participating in assessment and evaluation, rather than idea generation. Scenarios were developed to depict a "typical user" and their range of needs in order to provide the developers with a broader understanding of the users, their context, and important situations in their life. The aim was to create a bridge between the people carrying out the fieldwork and the system developers, while maintaining close contact with the users. Direct quotations from the users were added in order to give the developers a more diverse picture, adding richness to the scenarios and generating further debate. During this phase, we also identified the needs that fell within the boundary of the project and constituted the base for the conceptual models and requirements. This was done during multi-stakeholder meetings, which are continuing to take place every six weeks to discuss issues concerning needs, design concepts, and emerging requirements from different perspectives.

## 4   Summary and Conclusion

In this paper, it has been our intention to reflect on participatory practices in the context of a living lab, a contemporary phenomenon that is reflective of changing IS environments. MyHealth@Age offers an illustration of how contexts may differ from more traditional development settings and the kinds of practices that may be used for co-design. Working on a project that was focused on wider societal concerns with users that were co-opted on a voluntary basis, meant that the traditional structures of manager– developer–user no longer held and their background and experiences are quite dissimilar from users involved with more traditional in-house development projects. It was deemed important to attract a varied group of participants and so effort was put into enrolling the support of users with different experiences. While it can often be challenging to get users to participate in workplace settings, the elderly users appeared keen to be involved and seemed to enjoy the discussions and meetings with the project group.

A recurring challenge within PD concerns how to communicate the needs of users in such a way that developers can understand them while developers need to be able to feed back their understanding of system requirements in a manner such that the users can make sense of it. The project offers an example of how nontechnical participation activities can take place, using primarily paper-based techniques and open debate rather than technical prototypes. It was hoped that this would shift the locus of control to the users, rather than placing them in a position of merely endorsing design decisions that had already been made. The process involved various types of engagement, including focus groups, a questionnaire, diaries, and picture-taking in order to collect different types of data and also to allow for different formats for user contributions, recognizing that some users enjoy open discussion while others who are less vocal may prefer an opportunity to construct a narrative about their experiences or take photographs of significant events. Referring back to the three categories of participation, the project illustrates that it is not the quantity of user involvement that determines the categorization, but rather the influence that is wielded by the users.

Therefore, the quality of interaction among all of the parties has consequences for the project. Building a strong, ongoing relationship with users was crucial, since their involvement required a considerable time commitment on their part as well as psychological involvement. From the outset, the elderly were involved in the research application so that they contributed to scoping the project before the terms of reference had been agreed. From then on, the users took charge of generating needs with the researchers organizing meetings, drawing their attention to different techniques for needs expression, and providing opportunities for them to make decisions and suggestions. In this respect, the design stages can be described as "design with users." This could potentially take on a much more radical element of co-design, should we wish to progress living lab by drawing on the historical roots of PD.

From the perspective of the researchers, this phase has been successful so far, but we acknowledge that it cannot then be assumed that the project from here on will be just as successful, since the link between successful design and successful implementation may be weak, nonexistent, or irrelevant (Markus and Mao 2004). The project is ongoing and future papers will report on how our best intentions to apply the principles of PD to changing IS settings continue to roll out in practice.

## Acknowledgments

This work has been financed by the Swedish Foundation for Strategic Research; Vinnova (Research and Innovation for Sustainable Growth); and the EU through the Northern Peripheral Program.

# References

Bannon, J.L.: From Human Factors to Human Actors: The Role of Psychology and Human-Computer Interaction Studies in System Design. In: Greenbaum, J., Kyng, M. (eds.) Design at Work: Cooperative Design of Computer Systems, pp. 25–44. Lawrence Erlbaum Associates, London (1991)

Beath, C.M., Orlikowski, W.J.: The Contradictory Structure of Systems Development Methodologies: Deconstructing the IS-User Relationship in Information Engineering. Information Systems Research 5(4), 350–377 (1994)

Bergvall-Kåreborn, B., Ståhlbröst, A.: Living Lab: An Open and Citizen-Centric Approach for Innovation. International Journal of Innovation and Regional Development 1(4), 356–370 (2009)

Briefs, U., Ciborra, C., Schneider, L. (eds.): Systems Design For, With and By the User. North-Holland, Amsterdam (1983)

Checkland, P.: Systems Thinking, Systems Practice. John Wiley & Sons, Chichester (1981)

Checkland, P., Scholes, J.: Soft Systems Methodology in Action. John Wiley & Sons, Chichester (1990)

Cooperrider, D.L., Avital, M. (eds.): Advances in Appreciative Inquiry, Constructive Discourse and Human Organization. Elsevier, Oxford (2004)

Ehn, P.: Participation in Design Things. In: Simonsen, J., Robertson, T., Hakken, D. (eds.) Proceedings of the 10th Anniversary Conference on Participatory Design, Bloomington, Indiana, pp. 92–101 (2008)

Greenbaum, J., Kyng, M.: Introduction: Situated Design. In: Greenbaum, J., Kyng, M. (eds.) Design at Work: Cooperative Design of Computer Systems, pp. 1–24. Lawrence Erlbaum Associates, London (1991)

Iivari, J., Lyytinen, K.: Research on Information Systems Development in Scandinavia: Unity in Plurality. Scandinavian Journal of Information Systems 10(1&2), 135–185 (1998)

Kanstrup, A.M., Christiansen, E.: Selecting and Evoking Innovators: Combining Democracy and Creativity. Paper presented at Nordic CHI, Changing Roles, Oslo, Norway, October 14-18 (2006)

Kyng, M.: Users and Computers: A Contextual Approach to Design of Computer Artifacts. Scandinavian Journal of Information Systems 10(12), 7–44 (1998)

Lamb, R., Kling, R.: Reconceptualizing Users as Social Actors in Information Systems Research. MIS Quarterly 27(2), 197–235 (2003)

Levina, N.: Collaborating on Multiparty Information Systems Development Projects: A Collective Reflection-in-Action View. Information Systems Research 16(2), 109–130 (2005)

Markus, L.M., Mao, J.: Participation in Development and Implementation: Updating an Old, Tired Concept for Todays's IS Contexts. Journal of the Association for Information Systems 5(11-12), 514–544 (2004)

Morgan, D.: Focus Groups as Qualitative Research. Sage Publications, Thousand Oaks (1997)

Nolan, M.: The Senses Framework: Improving Care for Older People Through a Relationship-Centered Approach. Paper presented to Getting Research into Practice (GRIP), University of Sheffield (2006)

Norum, K.E.: Appreciative Design. Systems Research and Behavioral Science (18), 323–333 (2001)

Patnaik, D., Becker, R.: Needfinding: The Why and How of Uncovering People's Needs. Design Management Journal 10(2), 37–43 (1999)

von Hippel, E.: Perspective: User Toolkit for Innovation. The Journal of Product Innovation Management 18(4), 247–257 (2001)

# About the Authors

**Birgitta Bergvall-Kåreborn** is a professor in Social Informatics at Luleå University of Technology. Her current research interests concern participatory design in distributed and open environments; human centric and appreciative methodologies for design and learning; as well as he relation between IT-use and IT-design. She can be reached by e-mail at Birgetta.Bergvall-Kareborn@ltu.se.

**Debra Howcroft** is a professor of Technology and Organizations at Manchester Business School and a member of the ESRC-funded Centre for Research on Socio-Cultural Change (CRESC). Broadly, her research interests are concerned with the drivers and consequences of socio-economic restructuring in a global context. She can be reached by e-mail at Debra.Howcroft@mbs.ac.uk.

**Anna Ståhlbröst** is a researcher and project manager at Luleå University of Technology. Her research interest is process-based methods for innovative technology development in living lab environments. These methods specifically focus on generating user needs from different real-world use situations and assessing the users' experience of specific IT artifacts in order to assure that innovative technologies will represent user needs, and thereby give the users an added value. She can be reached by e-mail at Anna.Stahlbrost@ltu.se.

**Anita Melander Wikman** has an M.Sc, a Fil.Lic. and a Ph.D. in Physiotherapy and is working as a senior lecturer at Luleå University of Technology. Her research interests lies within the field of the empowerment of elderly people and rehabilitation. The focus on her research is to explore how elderly people experience self-determination and participation in relation to rehabilitation and how mobile ICT can support them. Anita's intentions is to foreground the client's perspective. She can be reached by e-mail at Anita.Melander-Wikman@ltu.se.

# Manufacturing Accomplices: ICT Use in Securing the Safety State at Airports

Thomas Østerlie, Ole Martin Asak, Ole Georg Pettersen, and Håvard Tronhus

Department of Computer and Information Science,
Norwegian University of Science and Technology,
Trondheim, Norway

**Abstract.** Based on a study of ICT use at an airport security checkpoint, this paper explores a possible explanation to the paradox that travelers find existing airport security measures inadequate while at the same time believing air travel to be sufficiently secure. We pursue this explanation by showing that, for the security checkpoint to function properly in relation to the overall function of the airport, travelers have to be enrolled in a particular program of action. They are then locked into this program through sanctions. Travelers are forced into participating in a system many of them find ethically and morally objectionable. Yet, active participation makes it difficult for them to object to the moral and ethical issues of their actions without damning themselves. Our explanation of the security paradox is, therefore, that while travelers remain critical of airport security, they avoid damning themselves by criticizing the system in terms of its own logic. They have been made accomplices.

**Keywords:** Social implications of ICT, airport security, ICT-enabled risk management, safety state, grounded theory.

## 1 Introduction

Two aircraft rammed into the World Trade Center on the morning of September 11, 2001. Pictures of the exploding aircraft and the subsequent collapse of the buildings were televised time and again in the days and weeks to follow. While in continuous development since the 1970s (Elphinstone 2008), airport security never engaged the public imagination prior to 2001. The September 11 attacks changed this.

Airport security has undergone rapid and profound changes since 2001 (Salter 2008b). Expenditures have risen correspondingly. In 2007, the International Air Transportation Association (IATA) estimated that annual expenditures on airport security had increased by U.S.$5.6 billion worldwide since 2001 (IATA 2007). A significant part of these investments were new ICT-based security technologies. Avinor, Norway's national airport operator, reports that security expenditures have increased by 150 percent during the three-year period from 2005 to 2007 (Avinor 2007).

It is, therefore, puzzling that 7 out of 10 respondents to a recent Norwegian survey believe that existing airport security measures provide inadequate security (Steria

J. Pries-Heje et al. (Eds.): IS Design Science Research, IFIP AICT 318, pp. 327–342, 2010.

2007). A study by the Norwegian Institute of Transport Economics further compounds this puzzle. In this study, 78 percent of respondents state that inadequate security measures do not contribute to less-secure flights (TØI 2007). We refer to the paradox of travelers find existing security measures inadequate while at the same time believing air travel to be sufficiently secure as the *security paradox.*

In this paper, we seek to offer a possible explanation to this paradox. Through a substantive theory of information and communication technology (ICT) use at the airport security checkpoint, we explore this explanation against the background of the emergence of the safety state (Raab 2005). Through the substantive theory, we argue that *manufacturing accomplices* is a core process of the security checkpoint. By this, we mean that travelers are coerced into taking actions that are indispensable for the checkpoint to function properly. With limited latitude of actions, travelers are forced into participating in a system many of them find ethically and morally objectionable. Yet, active participation makes it difficult for them to object to the moral and ethical issues of their actions without damning themselves. Our explanation of the security paradox is, therefore, that while travelers remain critical of airport security, they avoid damning themselves by criticizing the system in terms of its own logic. They have been made accomplices.

The substantive theory and the following discussion is the main contribution of this paper. We believe this should be of use to three audiences. Our explicit goal with studying the social implications of ICT use in airport security is to engage in research and debate on an issue of political and moral value. Avgerou (2005) argues that more research on such issues is required to challenge the predominant managerial agenda within IS research. Our substantive theory is a contribution toward furthering such a non-managerial agenda. The key audience for this paper is, therefore, other IS researchers who are involved with design research, action research, or policy analysis to actively bring about social change. Second, we hope our theory may contribute to reflection among IS researchers in general on the more problematic effects of ICT diffusion. Finally, this research is also a contribution to the broader interdisciplinary debate on social implications of airport security. While research exists on issues such as surveillance and social sorting (Lyon 2006), the ICT perspective of this paper offers an original contribution to this debate.

The remainder of the paper is organized as follows. First, we present key elements of our perspective on airport security, ICTs, and the safety state. We then present the research setting and methods, before progressing with the analysis. We discuss the analysis and conclude by offering a possible explanation to the security paradox.

## 2   Airport Security, ICT Use, and the Safety State

Few sites are more iconographic of the opportunities and vulnerabilities of contemporary globalization than international airports (Salter 2008a). As a central icon of modern culture, the airport has continuously changed in reflection of contemporary society (Gordon 2004). Reflecting the adventurous spirit of the early 1900s, the airport was originally a point of departure for journeys into the unknown. During its golden years in the late 1950s and early 1960s, the airport was a glamorous and futuristic meeting point for jetsetters and globetrotters. Following the increasingly turbulent geopolitical climate of the 1960s, the 1970s exploded in a series of high-profile terror attacks on airports and aircraft. Since then, anti-terror measures have turned airports into an electronically controlled environment, *the fortress airport*, "a place of jaded realism, apathy, and paranoia" (Gordon 2004, p. 229).

It is this electronically controlled environment that interests us. We regard airport security as an *ensemble* (Orlikowski and Iacono 2001) of technologies, organizations, laws, and regulations, as well as airport personnel and travelers. ICTs, understood as computer- and software-based technologies dedicated to collecting and processing information (Lyytinen and King 2006), are embedded as integral and ubiquitous elements of this ensemble. The ICTs in the airport ensemble range from conventional information systems such as passenger booking systems, through computer-assisted passenger screening systems (Bennett 2008), to computer-based security technologies such as x-ray machines, electromagnetic archways, backscatter x-ray machines, and explosives detection systems (Salter 2008b).

Few places apart from airports are equally explicit about creating "a public expectation for absolute security" (Salter 2008b, p. 1). While public perceptions are an important part of the security paradox, airport security also needs to be considered against the broader societal background of the emergence of the *safety state* (Raab 2005). The safety state elevates safety to the preferable condition for situations, institutions, and organizations. Social inequality is no longer the main concern in the safety state. Instead, the safety state is concerned with increasing safety through managing risks. The rise of the safety state is, therefore, closely related to the notion of the *risk society*. Beck (1992) uses this term to argue that the unpredictability of events and the increased number of risks we face are the most prevalent characteristic of contemporary society. Managing risks to increase safety is, therefore, the positive goal of policy in the risk society. However, Giddens (1999) points out that the idea of risk society does not mean that the world has become more hazardous, but rather that a society increasingly occupied with safety generates the notion of risk.

Risk is a problematic term. Different academic disciplines and even authors within the same discipline use the term differently. Within the technical literature, a much used definition of risk is "the potential for realization of unwanted, negative consequences of an event" (Rowe 1977, p. 24). Douglas and Wildavsky (1983), however, observe that there is a difference between knowable and unknowable dangers. Concerned with the impact and probability of risk, the technical literature is concerned with knowable dangers. Unknowable dangers, on the other hand, reside in the realm of speculation. It is these unknowable risks that arise within the risk society and with which the safety state seeks to come to grips. Yet, for these kinds of risks, quantitative assessment is inherently problematic. Zedner (2006) proposes to differentiate between risk assessment and risk management to address this challenge. *Risk assessment* is the technical activity of calculating the probability and cost of unwanted events. This is related to knowable risks. *Risk management*, on the other hand, deals with the ethical, political, and social implications of decision making.

As we acknowledge that unknowable risks often can't be anticipated, Beck (1992) argues that we become more geared to detecting and managing potential risk. Related to safety, such an emphasis on potentiality is an important contributor to what Hornqvist (2004) calls the *security mentality*. The security mentality replaces law with security as the principle from which physical force and other coercive measures proceed. Whereas law emphasizes what a person has done, the security mentality shifts focus to what people may do. It is a shift toward trying to determine if a person constitutes a risk. In the security mentality, the presence of positive indicators is replaced with the absence of negative indicators. The absence of negative indicators, however, is faced with *the problem of sufficiency*: "one can never know whether one is doing enough to prevent a hazard from occurring" (Douglas and Wildavsky 1983, p. 4).

Airport security is based on screening passengers prior to departure. Computer-assisted passenger profiling systems are used to screen travelers against a database of suspected terrorists after booking their tickets (Bennett 2008). At the airport, security technologies such as x-ray machines, electromagnetic archways, backscatter x-ray machines, and explosives detection systems are used to screen passengers moving from the check-in to the boarding area (Salter 2008b). These are all computer-based technologies. Current airport security screening is, therefore, a form of *ICT-enabled risk management* (Scott 2000). Screening as a risk management strategy is a good illustration of the shift from law to security. Passenger screening procedures treat all travelers as possible security threats. It is not until proven otherwise, through the absence of negative indicators, that travelers are considered no threat to security.

# 3 Research Setting and Methods

We substantiate our explanation of the security paradox through a substantive theory of ICT use at the security checkpoint. This substantive theory has been constructed as part of a study of ICT use in airport security. In this section, we first introduce the research setting. We then present the research methods employed in this study.

## 3.1 The Airport

We have studied ICT use at the security checkpoint at one of Norway's largest airports. For confidentiality reasons, we simply call it *the Airport*. The Airport has daily international arrivals and departures. It is also a national hub. This means that many travelers catch connecting flights either abroad or to other parts of the country at the Airport. Approximately 3 million travelers pass through the Airport every year. In comparison, approximately 15 million travelers pass through Norway's national airport every year, while 67 million travelers pass through the world's busiest airport, London Heathrow, every year.

Like most international airports, the Airport is an umbrella organization. Numerous stakeholders are responsible for different functions. These stakeholders include airlines, baggage handling companies, catering companies, security companies, police, and customs. The Airport Operator owns the Airport, and is responsible for implementing airport security in compliance with national and international regulations. The daily operation of airport security, however, is subcontracted to the Security Company. Civil aviation authorities use the term *security* to refer to safeguarding airports and aircraft "from acts of unlawful interference" (Karimbocus 2008).

While airport security encompasses perimeter watch, luggage checking, and general access control to restricted areas of the Airport, we have focused our study on the security checkpoint between the check-in and boarding area, as this is the part of airport security with which travelers interact directly. Figure 1 offers a schematic overview of the security check.

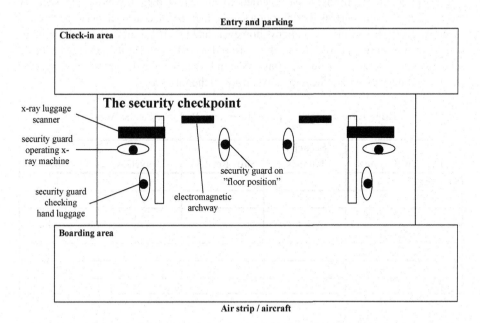

**Fig. 1.** Overview of Security Checkpoint

The security checkpoint is organized in three positions. The security guard on floor position is responsible for doing secondary checks when the electromagnetic archway indicates metal on travelers passing through. This secondary check is a full body search. One security guard mans the x-ray luggage scanner. The security guard in the third position does secondary checks on luggage when the x-ray machine indicates suspicious objects.

### 3.2 Research Methods

This research draws on grounded theory as formulated by Charmaz (2006) to construct a descriptive and explanatory theory of ICT use at the security checkpoint. Whitley and Hosein (2007) argue that we as IS researchers are well positioned for contributing to the public debate with concepts that offer insight into the relationship between ICTs and their wider societal context. As the stated purpose of this research is to engage in research and debate on a social issue, we find grounded theory's emphasis on conceptualization particularly well suited for our purpose.

Grounded theory is commonly used within IS research as a set of analytic techniques for coding qualitative data (Urquhart 2002). Our main concern with using grounded theory, however, has been to systematically conceptualize ICT use at the security checkpoint through a *constant comparative process* (Glaser 2002). We have, therefore, used different coding techniques, extensive memo writing, and the progressive integration of codes into concepts and concepts into categories in support of the constant comparative process.

For comparative purposes, we decided to interview both travelers and security guards. Table 1 summarizes the interviews. We had free access to interview travelers at the Airport. The Security Company, however, had two requirements for allowing us to interview security guards. First, they offered us 30 minutes of interview with 10 security guards over a period of 3 days. Second, the Security Company insisted that we use an interview guide they approved prior to the interviews.

**Table 1.** Number and Types of Interviews Performed at the Airport

| Interview Sessions | Security Guards | Shift Leaders | Travelers | Total |
|---|---|---|---|---|
| October 27, 2008 | - | - | 4 | 4 |
| October 31, 2008 | - | - | 15 | 15 |
| November 17, 2008 | - | - | 10 | 10 |
| November 25, 2008 | 2 | 1 | - | 3 |
| November 26, 2008 | 3 | 1 | - | 4 |
| November 27, 2008 | 2 | 1 | - | 3 |
| Total | 7 | 3 | 29 | 39 |

Collecting data through *theoretical sampling* supports the constant comparative method. In grounded theory, data collection and analysis is iterative. The Security Company agreed that we used the interview guide as the starting point for an open-ended conversation with the security guards. Still, their two requirements by and large prevented us from iteratively collecting and analyzing data from our interviews with security guards. These requirements have limited our ability to fully explore variations in the processes occurring at the security checkpoint.

We sought to compensate for these limitations during analysis. In addition to line-by-line coding of individual interviews and extensive memo writing, we constructed analytical categories through a process of (1) comparing codes within individual interviews, (2) comparing codes between interviews with security guards, (3) comparing codes between interviews with travelers, and (4) comparing codes between interviews with travelers and security guards. We then elaborated on these categories by making comparisons between categories under different conditions such as (1) time of day, (2) travelers' age, gender, and flying frequency, as well as (3) security guards' job experience. Finally, we sought to integrate the categories by putting relevant categories into a coherent argument.

The analysis below refers to quotes from interviews with security guards on the form "G#<number>:<paragraph>" and with travelers on the form "T#<number>:<paragraph>." "<number>" indicates the unique identifier assigned the interview, while "<paragraph>" indicates the paragraph in the transcribed interview where the quote is found.

# 4  Analysis

The security checkpoint is caught in an inherent contradiction between two conflicting functions at the Airport. The overall function of the Airport is to facilitate rapid movement of people between places, both within the Airport as well as to other airports. Yet, the *"security checkpoint is an obstacle"* (G#10:47) to this. Screening travelers and hand luggage disrupts such rapid movement within the Airport and consequently also between airports. This section argues that making the security checkpoint function properly in relation to the overall function of the Airport is a collective achievement of travelers and security guards alike in *interweaving competing temporal rhythms.* In this analysis, we seek to show how travelers as well as security guards play an active role in minimizing disruptions to the rapid movement of travelers between the check-in and boarding areas.

We elaborate on this argument by looking at two major processes of the security checkpoint. Reconciling the conflicting functions requires the active participation of travelers as well as security guards. The first process, *interweaving temporal rhythms,* elaborates this. At the security checkpoint, travelers have to abide by a strict program of action to minimize disruptions to the flow of travelers. Failure to enact this program of action is met by a series of sanctions. The second major process, *disciplining disobedience,* elaborates this.

## 4.1  Interweaving Temporal Rhythms

The Airport is bustling with activity from the time it opens in the morning until it closes for the night. It is constantly filled with people on the move between places. It is never quiet, always buzzing with the background sounds of a multitude of activities. Often unrecognized by the ordinary traveler, the intensity of these background sounds ebbs and flows throughout the day, following deeper patterns as the Airport resonates with the throbbing of *interweaving temporal rhythms.* These rhythms are temporal structures (Orlikowski and Yates 2002) that the Airport's many denizens enact as they go about their activities.

The security checkpoint's temporal rhythm is also intertwined with several of the Airport's other rhythms. The production of security, therefore, has to be conceptualized in the context of the temporal rhythms that run through and intertwine at the security checkpoint. Producing security is not merely about securing the Airport. It is equally concerned with intertwining the temporal rhythms that run through and intersect at the checkpoint. In particular, it is about the activity of *interweaving competing rhythms* to avoid disrupting the flow of people between the check-in and boarding areas.

### 4.1.1  Temporal Rhythms at the Security Checkpoint
The *flight schedule* is the heartbeat of the Airport. Practically all of the Airport's activities resonate with this temporal rhythm. In the morning, Airport staff open the Airport in preparation for the day's first departures and arrivals. Late at night, as the last arrivals drain out the building, Airport staff close the Airport. For the security guards at the checkpoint, the flight schedule is experienced as a *sequence* of peak and off-peak periods.

*The day starts somewhat abruptly [with many flights], when you have a lot of queues and stress... .Then there are off-peak periods of calm where we eat and so on, and then we have a couple more peaks throughout the day.* (G#2:13)

Travelers enact this temporal rhythm in moving through the security checkpoint in time for their flights. They follow the *rhythm of traveling*: arriving at the airport, checking in, passing through the security checkpoint, and boarding. In order for travelers to reach their flights, this sequence of activities needs to follow the flight schedule. Yet, at the security checkpoint, these two rhythms interweave with the checkpoint's own temporal rhythm. The sequence of activities in this rhythm is more erratic than that of the flight schedule and of traveling. Certain activities such as sending objects through the x-ray, passing through the electromagnetic archway, and reclaiming hand luggage are stable. This is followed by the security guards at the checkpoint, who inspect the luggage in the x-ray machine and observe the electromagnetic archway. The sequence is repeated with each traveler passing through the security checkpoint. This is the *cycle* of the checkpoint's rhythm.

The secondary check, however, is a more sporadic part of the checkpoint's rhythm. The guard on floor position performs a secondary check on travelers when the archway sounds the alarm. The guard manning the x-ray machine indicates to his colleague in the luggage check when there is need for a secondary check of the hand luggage.

*The warning bell starts chiming at once when you see something you don't recognize, or when there is so much clutter in the luggage that you cannot see properly through. We simply have to open and take a look inside, it is as simple as that. That is our drill.* (G#6:27)

While the regular sequence in the security check is of limited impact on the overall flow of people through the checkpoint, secondary checks have more impact. We will, therefore, elaborate on the temporal interactions between rhythms.

### 4.1.2 Temporal Interactions
The temporal rhythms enacted by travelers and security guards at the checkpoint interact as their sequences and cycles interweave with each other. Temporal interaction affects the rhythms' *tempo*. Every temporal rhythm has its own tempo. Whereas sequences are often fixed, tempo need not be fixed. While travelers have to check in and pass through the security checkpoint before they can board the aircraft, they can speed up the tempo of the rhythm by running from the security checkpoint to the gate.

Security guards talk of temporal interactions in terms of their experience of the checkpoint as busy or intense. The checkpoint is busy *"in the morning when there are a lot of businesspeople, which we see on the throughput as things move along quickly with businesspeople [because] they travel three or four times a week"* (G#3:45). While there are a lot of travelers passing through the busy security checkpoint, the temporal rhythms are *in harmony*. When temporal rhythms are in harmony, they have limited impact on each other's tempo.

In contrast, when the checkpoint is intense, there is a lot of *"queuing and stress"* (G#2:13). This is not necessarily related to the number of passengers passing through the checkpoint, but rather that the rhythms compete. Rhythms are competing when one rhythm interrupts the tempo of another rhythm. This is the kind of temporal interaction that causes the inherent tension between securing the flow of people through the checkpoint and the secondary check. This leads to *temporal disruptions*.

### 4.1.3 Interweaving Competing Rhythms
The security checkpoint fills up with travelers as temporal rhythms compete for the travelers' and security guards' attention. First, throughput starts dwindling as travelers have to wait before walking through the electromagnetic archway; then, it ceases completely as the security checkpoint fills up, preventing waiting travelers from passing through the archway. In response, the queue grows, tempers flare, and, as a security guard put it, *"It is obvious, you know, that nobody remains unaffected when the queue stretches all the way to the gas station [down the road from the Airport]"* (G#6:15).

Travelers and security guards alike have to simultaneously enact multiple temporal rhythms at the security checkpoint. The ICT-based technologies at the checkpoint, however, have few such concerns. They relentlessly exact their own timetable. When the archway indicates metal objects on a traveler, it cares little about the length of the queue or travelers' departures. It sounds the alarm regardless, and a security guard has to perform a secondary check. Similarly, when the x-ray indicates prohibited objects in the hand luggage, a security guard has to perform a secondary check of the hand luggage. The secondary check follows its own tempo, *disrupting the tempo* of people flowing through the checkpoint.

> *I don't feel I'm affected by stress. I take things in the correct tempo. A secondary check is to take approximately two minutes, regardless [of the queue].* (G#5:91).

Similarly, technologies *disrupt the cycle* of travelers. Once the archway has detected metal, the security guards *"do not give up until [the archway] stops beeping"* (G#4:18). It therefore befalls travelers and security guards to interweave competing rhythms to reduce temporal disruptions at the checkpoint.

Travelers are active participants in interweaving the competing rhythms by abiding by a program of action aimed at not triggering a secondary check by not carrying prohibited items in the hand luggage or on their person. It is the process of enrolling and keeping travelers in this program of action to which we will now turn.

## 4.2 Disciplining Disobedience

Reducing temporal disruptions to ensure rapid movement of people between the check-in and boarding areas is indispensable for the proper functioning of the security checkpoint as part of the Airport as a whole. Interweaving competing rhythms to reduce temporal disruptions is the key to facilitating such rapid movement of people. Without travelers' active participation, temporal disruptions threaten to reduce the movement of travelers between the two areas.

Through its material setup of information signs, queuing lines, tables, and ICTs such as hand luggage x-ray scanners and electromagnetic archways, as well as routines for sorting hand luggage in separate trays and standardized plastic bags, the security checkpoint inscribes a program of action (Latour 1999). This program of action is aimed at reducing the temporal disruptions to the flow of people through the checkpoint. Failure to comply with the inscribed program of action is met with an array of *sanctions*.

The security checkpoint is a total system in that it is enforced as the obligatory passing point (Latour 1999) for anyone wanting to travel by plane. The traveler has to pass through the security check to board the aircraft. As one security guard put it, *"We just have to tell them [travelers] that we can't let them pass if they won't let us control them, and then they won't catch their plane for sure that usually does the trick"* (G#4:42). Travelers have no choice. Not only do they have to pass the security check to board the aircraft, they have to behave in accordance to the program of action to avoid sanctions.

### 4.2.1 Imposing Sanctions

Travelers and hand luggage are subjected to secondary checks when they are found to carry prohibited objects. Secondary checks cause temporal disruptions as they reduce the number of passengers who can pass through the checkpoint. Secondary checks are, from a security point of view, required to prove that travelers pose no threat to security. This follows from the logic of the security mind set, as risk management at the security checkpoint seeks the absence of negative indicators.

Travelers, however, often regard the activities surrounding the secondary check as sanctions aimed at disciplining disobedience to reduce temporal disruptions. From the point of view of the security guards, the travelers are accountable for the temporal disruption of the secondary checks: *"It is their own fault, because they have forgotten to place liquids in the [required] bags, for instance, when they pass through [the checkpoint]"* (G#4:42). They may even use the secondary checks as a way of imposing sanctions on travelers who cause temporal disruptions: *"We have to take quite a lot of crap at the checkpoint, so one also has to hit back. So a slight [secondary] check, there are not many [travelers] who appreciate that"* (G#5:39).

From the point of view of travelers, the activities surrounding the secondary check have both *means* and *effects* as sanctioning mechanisms. The means are threefold: (1) detention, (2) intrusion of personal space, and (3) confiscation of property. Being pulled over for a secondary check is a form of detention. Many travelers find this reduces their position from that of an independent adult to an inferior person. One traveler explained it this way:

> *Yes, and then you are incredibly stressed [emphasizes the last two words] because you are standing there and the plane is about to leave and they [the security guards] are detaining you and, like [paraphrasing the security guards] "This is not up for discussion. You are not leaving until we have cleared this situation. The plane will just have to leave without you."* (T#20:10)

Many find body searches and inspections of their hand luggage an intrusion of their personal space: *"No one wants to have someone feel them up"* (T#2:7). Security guards will confiscate any prohibited items travelers try to bring through the security check. By deprivation of personal autonomy, we mean that travelers are no longer free to control their own behavior. By inscribing rigid programs of behavior, loss of personal autonomy is a central characteristic of the security check. Where the security check seeks to collectively standardize the behavior of travelers, the sanctions for failing to comply with the inscribed program singles out individual travelers for sanctions. For many, being singled out like this amplifies the experience of losing personal autonomy.

Being deprived of personal autonomy is one of the three effects of the sanctions. The other two are *public humiliation,* and *collective punishment.*

When a traveler fails to act according to the inscribed program of behavior, sanctions are invoke that involve public punishment. When the metal detector gate beeps, the attention of other travelers is turned toward the non-complying passenger. Body searches, scanning with handheld metal detectors, and luggage searches are performed on the spot, in full display of the other travelers:

> *They [the security guards] say it is an inconvenience for me to open my suitcase. RUBBISH!!! I find having to put my things on display for everyone to gawk at disagreeable.* (T#14:39)

The effect of such public humiliation, both to the traveler subjected to it, but also to those witnessing it, is to discipline future actions to avoid further sanctions.

Finally, sanctions are collective. When a security guard orders a passenger to take off their shoes or remove a belt before passing through the security gate, those queuing behind him or her have to wait while the traveler does so. While the sanctions themselves are directed at individual travelers, they cause temporal disruptions at the security checkpoint, leading to a longer waiting time for everyone. It is the collective nature of the direct sanctions that lead to the disciplining of the self.

### 4.2.2 The Discipline of the Self

The generative function of the punishments leveled by the security guards' sanctions is that they instill a discipline of the self in travelers. There are two dimensions to this process: (1) regulating personal behavior and (2) personal sanctions.

There is a marked difference in the way experienced and less experienced travelers approach the security checkpoint. While less experienced travelers are unaware of the sanctions at the checkpoint, they tend to show great emotions when the sanctions are imposed upon them. Experienced travelers, on the other hand, have adopted a disciplined approach to the security checkpoint. For them, interweaving temporal rhythms starts while preparing to travel. These travelers embody the security checkpoint's program of action in the way they *regulate their personal behavior* when traveling.

This discipline of the self is motivated by the intent *"to avoid any difficulties at the security checkpoint"* (T#7:16). These are deliberate actions to avoid the sanctions imposed by security guards. At the Airport, prior to entering the security check, individuals also discipline their actions. These are often minor details. One traveler, for instance, said he always makes sure he empties his trouser pockets of all loose change. The loose change is put in his jacket instead. When asked whether loose change will trigger the metal detector accompanied by routines at the airport to avoid secondary check, he responds, *"Yes, I think it does [posed halfway between a question and a statement]. Hell if I know. But to make sure "*(T#8:29).

Other travelers explain how they start preparing for the metal detector by removing belts, taking off shoes, removing wristwatches, and so on while queuing. All of these small gestures are to avoid problems in the security check.

While many travelers speak of the discipline of the self in terms of "avoiding difficulties at the security checkpoint," these troubles are not only related to the sanctions imposed by the security guards. Travelers also impose *personal sanctions* on themselves. Many express indignation when fellow passengers trigger a secondary check. When they themselves trigger a secondary check, they project this indignation onto themselves, saying they can literally feel the other travelers glaring at them when they are checked.

## 5  Manufacturing Accomplices

The analysis above pursues the argument that, for the security checkpoint to function properly in relation to the overall function of the Airport, travelers have to actively participate in intertweaving competing temporal rhythms at the security checkpoint. To this end, a set of sanctions enrolls and retains travelers in a particular program of action aimed at reducing temporal disruptions.

Many travelers find the security checkpoint morally and ethically objectionable. They find it *demeaning* to be *"criminalized in a way"* (T#6:10). Through a shift from the presence of positive indicators to the absence of negative indicators (Hornqvist 2004), they are assumed guilty before proven otherwise. Travelers also find the checkpoint, and in particular the secondary checks, *intrusive*. As all travelers participating in our study believe there is little danger of terror attacks on civil aviation, they think it is pointless to be subjected to such demeaning and intrusive practices.

We were, therefore, not surprised to learn that practically all travelers were critical of the security checkpoint. We were, however, surprised by the nature of the travelers' critique. Practically all travelers, even those who expressed moral and ethical misgivings, criticized the checkpoint in terms of security holes and inconsistencies. We did expect security guards to be concerned with inconsistencies and security holes. It is, after all, their job to secure the Airport. But why do travelers reflect along the same lines?

Several researchers elaborate on how the media, politicians, and corporations prey upon people's basal fearfulness to further their own ends (Stearns 2006). This *culture of fear thesis* sees contemporary society as regressing into a state of irrational fear. Current escalation of airport security could be seen as an expression of such a regression. While the travelers we have interviewed are indeed preoccupied with the shortcomings of existing security measures at the Airport, none of them express any fears of terror attacks on civil aviation. Indeed, most find the terror threat highly exaggerated.

The culture of fear thesis draws upon a long tradition of thinking that considers civilization a thin, fragile veneer on top of primitive human instincts like fear and aggression. Within this tradition, mankind is not only in constant danger of regressing into a primitive state; it does so on a regular basis. The Holocaust is an oft-used example, where Nazi Germany's regression into barbarism gives rise to mass-slaughter.

Bauman (2000), however, argues that the Holocaust is better understood in terms of social regulation through a well-functioning bureaucracy. Similarly, risk management is a form of regulation based on identifying impurities to be regulated and managed. Rather than seeing airport security as an expression of a society gripped in fear, airport security is better understood in terms of ever-expanding regulation and bureaucratization.

Before something can be regulated, however, it needs to be known. ICTs are pivotal for those processes through which objects are rendered amenable to intervention and regulation by being formulated in a particular way (Foucault 1991). Civil aviation authorities consider ICTs critical in securing the safety state at airports. However, the crude screening mechanisms these ICTs implement shape the material arrangements and practices at the security checkpoint.

The ICTs seek to render individual travelers and pieces of hand luggage into knowable objects through screening. The problem in terms of the overall functionality of the Airport, however, is that they implement rather crude screening mechanisms. The electromagnetic archway, for instance, indicates the presence of metal objects on travelers, but is unable to differentiate between a knife and a belt buckle. The effect is numerous false alarms unless travelers remove harmless metal objects before passing through the archway. The activities in interweaving competing temporal rhythms and disciplining disobedience are, therefore, aimed at supporting the ICTs by reducing the number of false alarms.

What we find, then, is that travelers are caught in a double-bind situation: while they find it pointless to be subjected to demeaning and intrusive practices, they also find it in their best interest to actively participate in reducing temporal disruptions to avoid delays and "stay out of trouble." Travelers are not merely made compliant through disciplining mechanisms; they find themselves actively engaged in regulating their personal behavior to minimize temporal disruptions. Moreover, while many travelers find the security checkpoint ethically and morally objectionable, they also find themselves taking an active part in disciplining disobedience through openly expressing discontent when other travelers trigger the secondary check. It may, therefore, seem that travelers assume the systemic viewpoint, and find themselves an integral part of the system many of them find morally and ethically objectionable. Through their own actions, however, they incriminate themselves. They are made accomplices, rendering themselves incapable of objecting without also damning their own actions.

## 6   Conclusions

This leads us back to a possible explanation of the security paradox: To avoid damning themselves, travelers assume the systemic viewpoint when encouraged to reflect critically upon the security checkpoint. In so doing, they become preoccupied with security holes and inconsistencies. As such, while the travelers are not particularly worried about the possibility of a terror attack, through their preoccupation with detecting and managing potential risks (Beck 1992), they find existing security measures inadequate in relation to the ideal of absolute absence of danger (Salter 2008a).

Yet, detecting and managing potential risks with the goal of absolute absence of danger is a never-ending process. While new risks may be discovered, the problem of sufficiency will always loom in the background (Douglas and Wildavsky 1983). One can simply never know whether one is doing enough to prevent hazards from occurring. As such, for as long as absolute absence of danger is the espoused goal, travelers will find airport security inadequate.

We observe similar dynamics at play with legislators and regulating bodies. There is a continued emphasis on introducing new ICTs to secure the safety state at airports. In the process of striving toward the ideal condition of the safety state, however, we stand the chance of losing track of the social costs of securing safety. Our concern is, therefore, that continued emphasis on screening will lead to a continued technological escalation with subsequent expenses and oppressive measures to travelers.

## Acknowledgments

The authors thank the Security Company, its security guards, and travelers at the Airport who have given generously of their time to advance this study. We also thank Charles Raab, colleagues in the Researcher Factory, and three anonymous reviewers for invaluable comments. This work was financed partially through Eric Monteiro and partially through the Research Council of Norway's project 183235.

## References

Avgerou, C.: Doing Critical Research in Information Systems: Some Further Thoughts. Information Systems Journal 15(2), 103–109 (2005)
Avinor, Avinor Annual Report, Avinor, Gardermoen, Norway (2007)
Bauman, Z.: Modernity and the Holocaust. Polity Press, Cambridge (2000)
Beck, U.: Risk Society: Towards a New Modernity. SAGE Publications, London (1992)
Bennett, C.J.: Unsafe at Any Altitude. In: Salter, M. (ed.) Politics at the Airport, pp. 51–76. SAGE Publications, Thousand Oaks (2008)
Charmaz, K.: Constructing Grounded Theory: A Practical Guide Through Qualitative Analysis. SAGE Publications, Thousand Oaks (2006)
Douglas, M., Wildavsky, A.: Risk and Culture: An Essay on the Selection of Technological and Environmental Dangers. University of California Press, Berkeley (1983)
Elphinstone, G.: The Early History of Aviation Security Practice. In: Thomas, A.R. (ed.) Aviation Security Management, pp. 1–8. Praeger Security International, Westport (2008)
Foucault, M.: Governmentality. In: Burchell, G., Gordon, C., Miller, P. (eds.) The Foucault Effect: Studies in Governmentality, pp. 87–104. University of Chicago Press, Chicago (1991)
Giddens, A.: Risk and Responsibility. Modern Law Review 62(1), 1–10 (1999)
Glaser, B.G.: Conceptualization: On Theory and Theorizing Using Grounded Theory. International Journal of Qualitative Methods 1(2), 1–31 (2002)
Gordon, A.: Naked Airport: A Cultural History of the World's Most Revolutionary Structure. Chicago University Press, Chicago (2004)
Hornqvist, M.: The Birth of Public Order Policy. Race Class 46(1), 30–52 (2004)
IATA. The Air Transport Industry Since 11 September 2001, International Air Transport Association, Montreal, Canada (2007)

Karimbocus, M.: The Human Element in Aviation Security. In: Thomas, A.R. (ed.) Aviation Security Management, pp. 65–76. Praeger Security International, Westport (2008)

Latour, B.: Pandora's Hope. Harvard University Press, Cambridge (1999)

Lyon, D.: Airport Screening, Surveillance, and Social Sorting: Canadian Responses to 9/11 in Context. Canadian Journal of Criminology & Criminal Justice 48(3), 397–411 (2006)

Lyytinen, K., King, J.L.: Standard Making: A Critical Research Frontier for Information Systems Research. MIS Quarterly (30:special issue), 405–411 (August 2006)

Orlikowski, W.J., Iacono, C.S.: Research Commentary: Desperately Seeking the 'IT' in IT Research—A Call to Theorizing the IT Artifact. Information Systems Research 12(2), 121–134 (2001)

Orlikowski, W.J., Yates, J.: It's About Time: Temporal Structuring of Organizations. Organization Science 13(6), 684–700 (2002)

Raab, C.D.: Governing the Safety State, inaugural lecture, University of Edinburgh (2005)

Rowe, W.D.: An Anatomy of Risk. John Wiley & Sons, Inc., New York (1977)

Salter, M.: Airport Assemblage. In: Salter, M. (ed.) Politics at the Airport, pp. i–xix. University of Minnesota Press, Minneapolis (2008a)

Salter, M.: The Global Airport: Managing Space, Speed, and Security. In: Salter, M. (ed.) Politics at the Airport, pp. 1–28. University of Minnesota Press, Minneapolis (2008b)

Scott, S.V.: IT-Enabled Credit Risk Modernization: A Revolution Under the Cloak of Normality. Accounting, Management and Information Technologies 10(3), 221–255 (2000)

Stearns, P.N.: Fear and Contemporary History: A Review Essay. Journal of Social History 40(2), 477–484 (2006)

Steria. Positive til biometrisk sikkerhetsteknologi (2007), http://www.steria.no/gloria/id/11003246/subid/0

TØI. Trygt eller truende? Opplevelse av risiko på reisen, Report 913/2007, Norwegian Institute of Transport Economics, Etterstad, Norway (2007)

Urquhart, C.: Regrounding Grounded Theory—Or Reinforcing Old Prejudices? A Brief Reply to Bryant. Journal of Information Technology Theory and Application 4(3), 43–54 (2002)

Whitley, E.A., Hosein, I.R.: Policy Engagement as Rigorous and Relevant Information Systems Research: The Case of the LSE Identity Project. In: Proceedings of the 15th European Conference on Information Systems, St. Galen, Switzerland, June 7-9, pp. 1301–1312 (2007)

Zedner, L.: Neither Safe Nor Sound? The Perils and Possibilities of Risk. Canadian Journal of Criminology & Criminal Justice 48(3), 423–434 (2006)

## About the Authors

**Thomas Østerlie** is a postdoctoral fellow at the Department of Computer and Information Science, Norwegian University of Science and Technology, where he also earned his Ph.D. His research focuses on the dynamic relationship between ICTs and their wider context of development and use. In particular, he is concerned with the relationship between ICT-enabled risk management and social change. Thomas can be reached at thomas.osterlie@idi.ntnu.no.

**Ole Martin Asak** received an M.Sc. in informatics from the Norwegian University of Science and Technology. His research has focused upon how security is produced at airports in the interplay between security guards and ICTs in everyday work. Ole

Martin has a background as a security guard himself. He is currently working as a system developer at Adactus and can be reached at ole_asak2@hotmail.com.

**Ole Georg Pettersen** earned an M.Sc. in informatics from the Norwegian University of Science and Technology. Ole Georg is currently working as a software consultant with SiriusIT, and can be reached at olegeorg@gmail.com.

**Håvard Tronhus** received the M.Sc. in informatics from the Norwegian University of Science and Technology. Together with Ole Georg, he has studied travelers' experience of security and danger in encountering airport security. Håvard can be reached at havard@ tronhus.net.

# Part 7
# Panels

# A Brief History of IFIP WG 8.2 Research: The People, the Places, the Methods, and the Issues

Nancy L. Russo[1] and Michael D. Myers[2]

[1] Northern Illinois University,
DeKalb, Illinois, USA
[2] University of Auckland,
Auckland, New Zealand

This panel will present a high-level examination of the research papers that have appeared in proceedings of the International Federation for Information Processing Working Group 8.2, which addresses the interaction between information systems and the organization. More specifically, Working Group 8.2 is "concerned with the generation and dissemination of descriptive and normative knowledge about the development and use of information technologies in organizational contexts," as described in its statement of scope (www.ifipwg82.org). Both information systems and organizations are viewed broadly within the context of research covered by the Working Group.

The Working Group held its first conference in 1979. A total of 26 conferences have been organized by the Working Group, including four organized jointly with other working groups, prior to the current conference. During these conferences spanning 30 years, approximately 500 research papers have been presented.

Following the approach used by Dwivedi and other colleagues (e.g., Dwivedi and Kuljis 2008; Dwivedi et al. 2009) to study contents of various journals and the research output of IFIP WG 8.6 (published elsewhere in this *Proceedings*), data on a number of variables including author information and keywords were collected from all available proceedings of past conferences of IFIP WG 8.2.

Panel participants will discuss the outcome of the analysis of this data, including changing trends in research approaches and topics, the people and universities most represented, and other factors of interest.

## References

Dwivedi, Y.K., Kuljis, J.: Profile of IS Research Published in the European Journal of Information Systems. European Journal of Information Systems 17(6), 678–693 (2008)

Dwivedi, Y.K., Lal, B., Mustafi, N., Williams, M.D.: Profiling a Decade of Information Systems Frontiers' Research. Information Systems Frontiers 11(1), 87–102 (2009)

J. Pries-Heje et al. (Eds.): IS Design Science Research, IFIP AICT 318, p. 345, 2010.
© IFIP International Federation for Information Processing 2010

# The Role of Public Policy in Enhancing the Design and Diffusion of Information Systems and Technology for Human Benefit

John Venable[1], Peter Newman[2], Nick Letch[3], and Sue Ash[4]

[1] Curtin University of Technology,
Perth, Western Australia
[2] Curtin University Sustainability Policy Institute,
Perth, Western Australia
[3] University of Western Australia,
Perth, Western Australia
[4] Western Australian Council of Social Service Inc.,
West Perth, Western Australia

Technologies for human benefit, such as information systems and information technology, have a key role to play in the realization of quality of life for all citizenry by modern societies. New forms of IS and IT can be developed and used creatively to improve education, health, social equity, environmental conditions, social and environmental sustainability, government and not-for-profit services, participation in government, and enjoyment of life in general.

However, potentially valuable new technologies for human benefit may not be utilized due to barriers inherent in capitalist economies, including barriers to design and development of new technologies and barriers to adoption and diffusion of those new technologies. Some barriers to development stem from the profit motive, including lack of funding where sufficient return (profit) is not expected (or not returned soon enough), competitive forces leading to incompatibilities between different technologies (e.g., through product differentiation and creation of barriers to entry), and potential competition of new technologies for human benefit with established profit-making technologies. Barriers to adoption and diffusion of new technologies for human benefit include the expense and risk of new, possibly untried technologies, issues of organizational and social change, and lack of understanding of the role, purpose, potential benefits, and ways to obtain and use newly developed technologies.

Public policy has a key role to play in the development of new and adoption of new or existing technologies for human benefit. Governments and other policy development organizations may propose and implement public policy that provides funding or other incentives for development and adoption of technologies. Public policy may be used to set key priorities or technical directions or establish appropriate shared infrastructure. Public policy may regulate (or deregulate) how businesses or other organizations develop, deploy, or compete for and use new technologies to achieve improved human benefit.

J. Pries-Heje et al. (Eds.): IS Design Science Research, IFIP AICT 318, pp. 346–347, 2010.
© IFIP International Federation for Information Processing 2010

This panel will examine the role of public policy in encouraging the design, development, and adoption of new technologies, particularly information systems and technologies that have the goal of providing benefit to members of the public and humanity in general. Key areas and priorities for needed or changed public policy will be identified, together with recommendations for useful changes to public policy and how researchers may best engage in influencing public policy for human benefit.

# Opening up the Agile Innovation Process

Kieran Conboy[1], Brian Donnellan[2], Lorraine Morgan[3], and Xiaofeng Wang[4]

[1] National University of Ireland,
Galway, Ireland
[2] National University of Ireland,
Maynooth, Ireland
[3] University of Limerick,
Limerick, Ireland
[4] The Irish Software Engineering Research Center,
Dublin, Ireland

The objective of this panel is to discuss how firms can operate both an open and agile innovation process. In an era of unprecedented changes, companies need to be open and agile in order to adapt rapidly and maximize their innovation processes. Proponents of agile methods claim that one of the main distinctions between agile methods and their traditional bureaucratic counterparts is their drive toward creativity and innovation. However, agile methods are rarely adopted in their textbook, "vanilla" format, and are usually adopted in part or are tailored or modified to suit the organization. While we are aware that this happens, there is still limited understanding of what is actually happening in practice. Using innovation adoption theory, this panel will discuss the issues and challenges surrounding the successful adoption of agile practices. In addition, this panel will report on the obstacles and benefits reported by over 20 industrial partners engaged in a pan-European research project into agile practices between 2006 and 2009.

The panel will also discuss the benefits and implications of a more open agile innovation process. While teamwork and the role of the customer play an essential part in the agile innovation process, which in turn leads to creativity and increased innovativeness, it is useful to consider how the agile innovation process can benefit from becoming more "open," for instance, by networking with other stakeholders besides the customer. For example, it has been found that companies must increasingly work with each other to enhance their agility in adapting to market developments and developing new products and services cheaper and faster. Thus, elements of the open innovation paradigm will be considered in the panel. In this model, firms commercialize both external and internal ideas and use both external and internal resources to generate and maximize value. Innovation occurs across the boundaries of the firm and both value creation and capture processes are spread across a value network, rather than being controlled within the boundaries of a single firm. Networks are viewed as vehicles for producing, synthesizing, and distributing ideas and increasingly the success of a firm is linked to the depth of their ties to other stakeholders (Powell et al. 1998). This open concept challenges the dominant view of closed innovation, where it was assumed that it was the experts *within* the company that invented and designed innovative new products to meet customer needs. However, unprecedented changes such as decreasing product life cycles, industrial

J. Pries-Heje et al. (Eds.): IS Design Science Research, IFIP AICT 318, pp. 348–349, 2010.

research, and the rising costs of development, in addition to a lack of resources, have motivated a change toward a more open approach. As Chesbrough (2006) suggests, ideal businesses now search outside their own companies for the best ideas and knowledge, seeking input from other companies, including competitors, as well as from customers, suppliers, and vendors.

However, a more open and networked approach to agile innovation will present some major challenges for firms. For example, a shift in focus from ownership and control to a more open approach will require firms to rethink their value creation and value capture strategies. Thus, the panel will be beneficial in discussing some of the consequences of embracing a more open agile approach. In addition, it will provide knowledge and expertise in the area of agile adoption and open innovation, while promoting the exchange of information, ideas, and experiences on common issues, challenges, and benefits pertinent to agile and open innovation adoption in various work environments.

# References

Chesbrough, H.: Open Business Models: How to Thrive in the New Innovation Landscape. Harvard Business School Press, Boston (2006)

Powell, W.W., Koput, K.W., Smith-Doerr, L.: Interorganizational Collaboration and the Locus of Innovation: Networks of Learning in Biotechnology. Administrative Science Quarterly 41(1), 116–145 (1998)

# Author Index

Aaen, Ivan   73
Al-Debei, Mutaz M.   28
Armstrong, Colin   282
Armstrong, Helen   282
Asak, Ole Martin   327
Ash, Sue   346

Baskerville, Richard L.   263
Bergvall-Kåreborn, Birgitta   317
Bunker, Deborah   1, 225

Conboy, Kieran   348

Donnellan, Brian   348
Dwivedi, Yogesh K.   192, 225

Ferneley, Elaine   125
Fitzgerald, Guy   28

Hicks, Michael   89
Hossain, Mohammad Alamgir   179
Hovorka, Dirk S.   13
Howcroft, Debra   317

Jarulaitis, Gasparas   209

Kautz, Karlheinz   303
Khan, Imran   125

Lal, Banita   192
Lawrence, Carl   108
Letch, Nick   346
Levine, Linda   225
Lind, Mikael   159

Mathiassen, Lars   52
Mayer, Jörg H.   245

Morgan, Lorraine   348
Mustafee, Navonil   192
Myers, Michael D.   108, 345

Newman, Peter   346

Østerlie, Thomas   327

Perrin, Brian   89
Pervan, Graham   89
Pettersen, Ole Georg   327
Pries-Heje, Jan   1, 263

Quaddus, Mohammed   179

Rudmark, Daniel   159
Russo, Nancy L.   1, 345

Seigerroth, Ulf   159
Singh, Mohini   225
Singh, Ramanjit   143
Ståhlbröst, Anna   317
Stock, Daniel   245

Tronhus, Håvard   327
Tscherning, Heidi   52
Tuunanen, Tuure   108

Venable, John R.   1, 346

Wang, Xiaofeng   348
Wastell, David G.   225
Wikman, Anita Melander   317
Williams, Michael D.   192, 225
Winter, Robert   245
Wood-Harper, Trevor   143